A Concise Introduction to Logic

Patrick J. Hurley

W9-APU-806

CENGAGE
Learning

Australia • Brazil • Japan • Korea • Mexico • Singapore • Spain • United Kingdom • United States

CENGAGE
Learning™

A Concise Introduction to Logic

Patrick J. Hurley

Executive Editors:
Michele Baird
Maureen Staudt
Michael Stranz

Project Development Manager:
Linda deStefano

Senior Marketing Coordinators:
Sara Mercurio
Lindsay Shapiro

Senior Production / Manufacturing Manager:
Donna M. Brown

PreMedia Services Supervisor:
Rebecca A. Walker

Rights & Permissions Specialist:
Kalina Hintz

Cover Image:
Getty Images*

For product information and technology assistance, contact us at
Cengage Learning Customer & Sales Support, 1-800-354-9706

For permission to use material from this text or product,
submit all requests online at **cengage.com/permissions**
Further permissions questions can be emailed to
permissionrequest@cengage.com

ISBN-13: 978-0-495-63214-6

ISBN-10: 0-495-63214-7

Cengage Learning
5191 Natorp Boulevard
Mason, Ohio 45040
USA

Cengage Learning is a leading provider of customized learning solutions with office locations around the globe, including Singapore, the United Kingdom, Australia, Mexico, Brazil, and Japan. Locate your local office at:
international.cengage.com/region

Cengage Learning products are represented in Canada by Nelson Education, Ltd.

For your lifelong learning solutions, visit **custom.cengage.com**

Visit our corporate website at **cengage.com**

Printed in the United States of America

1

Basic Concepts

1.1 Arguments, Premises, and Conclusions

Logic may be defined as the organized body of knowledge, or science, that evaluates arguments. All of us encounter arguments in our day-to-day experience. We read them in books and newspapers, hear them on television, and formulate them when communicating with friends and associates. The aim of logic is to develop a system of methods and principles that we may use as criteria for evaluating the arguments of others and as guides in constructing arguments of our own. Among the benefits to be expected from the study of logic is an increase in confidence that we are making sense when we criticize the arguments of others and when we advance arguments of our own.

An **argument,** in its most basic form, is a group of statements, one or more of which (the premises) are claimed to provide support for, or reasons to believe, one of the others (the conclusion). All arguments may be placed in one of two basic groups: those in which the premises really do support the conclusion and those in which they do not, even though they are claimed to. The former are said to be good arguments (at least to that extent), the latter bad arguments. The purpose of logic, as the science that evaluates arguments, is thus to develop methods and techniques that allow us to distinguish good arguments from bad.

As is apparent from the given definition, the term *argument* has a very specific meaning in logic. It does not mean, for example, a mere verbal fight, as one might have with one's parent, spouse, or friend. Let us examine the features of this definition in greater detail. First of all, an argument is a group of statements. A **statement** is a sentence that is either true or false—in other words, typically a declarative sentence or a sentence component that could stand as a declarative sentence. The following sentences are statements:

> Chocolate truffles are loaded with calories.
> Melatonin helps relieve jet lag.
> Political candidates always tell the complete truth.
> No wives ever cheat on their husbands.
> Tiger Woods plays golf and Maria Sharapova plays tennis.

The first two statements are true, the second two false. The last one expresses two statements, both of which are true. Truth and falsity are called the two possible **truth values** of a statement. Thus, the truth value of the first two statements is true, the truth value of the second two is false, and the truth value of the last statement, as well as that of its components, is true.

Unlike statements, many sentences cannot be said to be either true or false. Questions, proposals, suggestions, commands, and exclamations usually cannot, and so are not usually classified as statements. The following sentences are not statements:

Where is Khartoum?	(question)
Let's go to a movie tonight.	(proposal)
I suggest you get contact lenses.	(suggestion)
Turn off the TV right now.	(command)
Fantastic!	(exclamation)

The statements that make up an argument are divided into one or more premises and one and only one conclusion. The **premises** are the statements that set forth the reasons or evidence, and the **conclusion** is the statement that the evidence is claimed to support or imply. In other words, the conclusion is the statement that is claimed to follow from the premises. Here is an example of an argument:

All film stars are celebrities.
Halle Berry is a film star.
Therefore, Halle Berry is a celebrity.

The first two statements are the premises; the third is the conclusion. (The claim that the premises support or imply the conclusion is indicated by the word "therefore.") In this argument the premises really do support the conclusion, and so the argument is a good one. But consider this argument:

Some film stars are men.
Cameron Diaz is a film star.
Therefore, Cameron Diaz is a man.

In this argument the premises do not support the conclusion, even though they are claimed to, and so the argument is not a good one.

One of the most important tasks in the analysis of arguments is being able to distinguish premises from conclusions. If what is thought to be a conclusion is really a premise, and vice versa, the subsequent analysis cannot possibly be correct. Many arguments contain indicator words that provide clues in identifying premises and conclusion. Some typical **conclusion indicators** are

therefore	accordingly	entails that
wherefore	we may conclude	hence
thus	it must be that	it follows that
consequently	for this reason	implies that
we may infer	so	as a result

Whenever a statement follows one of these indicators, it can usually be identified as the conclusion. By process of elimination the other statements in the argument are the premises. Example:

Tortured prisoners will say anything just to relieve the pain. Consequently, torture is
not a reliable method of interrogation.

The conclusion of this argument is "Torture is not a reliable method of interrogation,"
and the premise is "Tortured prisoners will say anything just to relieve the pain."

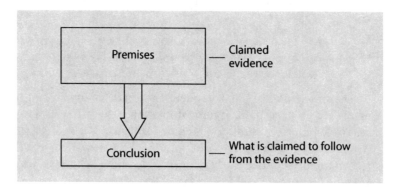

If an argument does not contain a conclusion indicator, it may contain a premise
indicator. Some typical **premise indicators** are

since	in that	seeing that
as indicated by	may be inferred from	for the reason that
because	as	inasmuch as
for	given that	owing to

Any statement following one of these indicators can usually be identified as a premise.
Example:

Expectant mothers should never use recreational drugs, since the use of these drugs
can jeopardize the development of the fetus.

The premise of this argument is "The use of these drugs can jeopardize the development of the fetus," and the conclusion is "Expectant mothers should never use recreational drugs."

In reviewing the list of indicators, note that "for this reason" is a conclusion indicator, whereas "for the reason that" is a premise indicator. "For this reason" (except when
followed by a colon) means for the reason (premise) that was just given, so what follows is the conclusion. On the other hand, "for the reason that" announces that a
premise is about to be stated.

Sometimes a single indicator can be used to identify more than one premise. Consider the following argument:

It is vitally important that wilderness areas be preserved, for wilderness provides essential habitat for wildlife, including endangered species, and it is a natural retreat
from the stress of daily life.

The premise indicator "for" goes with both "Wilderness provides essential habitat for
wildlife, including endangered species," and "It is a natural retreat from the stress of

daily life." These are the premises. By method of elimination, "It is vitally important that wilderness areas be preserved" is the conclusion.

Some arguments contain no indicators. With these, the reader/listener must ask such questions as: What single statement is claimed (implicitly) to follow from the others? What is the arguer trying to prove? What is the main point in the passage? The answers to these questions should point to the conclusion. Example:

> The space program deserves increased expenditures in the years ahead. Not only does the national defense depend on it, but the program will more than pay for itself in terms of technological spinoffs. Furthermore, at current funding levels the program cannot fulfill its anticipated potential.

The conclusion of this argument is the first statement, and all of the other statements are premises. The argument illustrates the pattern found in most arguments that lack indicator words: the intended conclusion is stated first, and the remaining statements are then offered in support of this first statement. When the argument is restructured according to logical principles, however, the conclusion is always listed *after* the premises:

> P_1: The national defense is dependent on the space program.
> P_2: The space program will more than pay for itself in terms of technological spinoffs.
> P_3: At current funding levels the space program cannot fulfill its anticipated potential.
> C: The space program deserves increased expenditures in the years ahead.

When restructuring arguments such as this, one should remain as close as possible to the original version, while at the same time attending to the requirement that premises and conclusion be complete sentences that are meaningful in the order in which they are listed.

Note that the first two premises are included within the scope of a single sentence in the original argument. For the purposes of this chapter, compound arrangements of statements in which the various components are all claimed to be true will be considered as separate statements.

Passages that contain arguments sometimes contain statements that are neither premises nor conclusions. Only statements that are actually intended to support the conclusion should be included in the list of premises. If, for example, a statement serves merely to introduce the general topic, or merely makes a passing comment, it should not be taken as part of the argument. Examples:

> The claim is often made that malpractice lawsuits drive up the cost of health care. But if such suits were outlawed or severely restricted, then patients would have no means of recovery for injuries caused by negligent doctors. Hence, the availability of malpractice litigation should be maintained intact.

> Currently 47 million Americans are without health insurance. When these people go to a hospital, they are routinely charged two to three times the normal cost for treatment. This practice, which covers the cost of treating indigent patients, is clearly unfair. For these reasons, a national health insurance program should be adopted. Politicians who oppose this change should be ashamed of themselves.

In the first argument, the opening statement serves merely to introduce the topic, so it is not part of the argument. The premise is the second statement, and the conclusion is the last statement. In the second argument, the final statement merely makes a passing comment, so it is not part of the argument. The premises are the first three statements, and the statement following "for these reasons" is the conclusion.

Closely related to the concepts of argument and statement are those of inference and proposition. An **inference,** in the narrow sense of the term, is the reasoning process expressed by an argument. In the broad sense of the term, "inference" is used interchangeably with "argument." Analogously, a **proposition,** in the narrow sense, is the meaning or information content of a statement. For the purposes of this book, however, "proposition" and "statement" are used interchangeably.

Note on the History of Logic

The person who is generally credited as the father of logic is the ancient Greek philosopher Aristotle (384–322 B.C.). Aristotle's predecessors had been interested in the art of constructing persuasive arguments and in techniques for refuting the arguments of others, but it was Aristotle who first devised systematic criteria for analyzing and evaluating arguments.

Aristotle's chief accomplishment is called **syllogistic logic,** a kind of logic in which the fundamental elements are *terms,* and arguments are evaluated as good or bad depending on how the terms are arranged in the argument. Chapters 4 and 5 of this textbook are devoted mainly to syllogistic logic. But Aristotle also deserves credit for originating **modal logic,** a kind of logic that involves such concepts as possibility, necessity, belief, and doubt. In addition, Aristotle catalogued several informal fallacies, a topic treated in Chapter 3 of this book.

After Aristotle's death, another Greek philosopher, Chrysippus (280–206 B.C.), one of the founders of the Stoic school, developed a logic in which the fundamental elements were *whole propositions.* Chrysippus treated every proposition as either true or false and developed rules for determining the truth or falsity of compound propositions from the truth or falsity of their components. In the course of doing so, he laid the foundation for the truth functional interpretation of the logical connectives presented in Chapter 6 of this book and introduced the notion of natural deduction, treated in Chapter 7.

For thirteen hundred years after the death of Chrysippus, relatively little creative work was done in logic. The physician Galen (A.D. 129–ca. 199) developed the theory of the compound categorical syllogism, but for the most part philosophers confined themselves to writing commentaries on the works of Aristotle and Chrysippus. Boethius (ca. 480–524) is a noteworthy example.

The first major logician of the Middle Ages was Peter Abelard (1079–1142). Abelard reconstructed and refined the logic of Aristotle and Chrysippus as communicated by Boethius, and he originated a theory of universals that traced the universal character of general terms to concepts in the mind rather than to "natures" existing outside the mind, as Aristotle had held. In addition, Abelard distinguished arguments that are valid because of their form from those that are valid because of their content, but he

■ EMINENT LOGICIANS

Aristotle 384–322 B.C.

Aristotle was born in Stagira, a small Greek town situated on the northern coast of the Aegean sea. His father was a physician in the court of King Amyntas II of Macedonia, and the young Aristotle was a friend of the King's son Philip, who was later to become king himself and the father of Alexander the Great. When he was about seventeen, Aristotle was sent to Athens to further his education in Plato's Academy, the finest institution of higher learning in the Greek world. After Plato's death Aristotle left for Assos, a small town on the coast of Asia Minor, where he married the niece of the local ruler.

Six years later Aristotle accepted an invitation to return to Macedonia to serve as tutor of the young Alexander. When Alexander ascended the throne following his father's assassination, Aristotle's tutorial job was finished, and he departed for Athens where he set up a school near the temple of Apollo Lyceus. The school came to be known as the Lyceum, and Alexander supported it with contributions of money and specimens of flora and fauna derived from his far-flung conquests. After Alexander's death, an anti-Macedonian rebellion forced Aristotle to leave Athens for Chalcis, about thirty miles to the north, where he died one year later at the age of sixty-two.

Aristotle is universally recognized as the originator of logic. He defined *logic* as the study of the process by which a statement follows by necessity from one or more other statements. The most fundamental kind of statement, he thought, is the categorical proposition, and he classified the four kinds of categorical propositions in terms of their being universal, particular, affirmative, and negative. He also developed the square of opposition, which shows how one such proposition implies the truth or falsity of another, and he identified the relations of conversion, obversion, and contraposition, which provide the basis for various immediate inferences.

His crowning achievement is the theory of the categorical syllogism, a kind of argument consisting of three categorical propositions. He showed how categorical syllogisms can be catalogued in terms of mood and figure, and he developed a set of rules for determining the validity of categorical syllogisms. Also, he showed how the modal concepts of possibility and necessity apply to categorical propositions. In addition to the theory of the syllogism, Aristotle advanced the theory of definition by genus and difference, and he showed how arguments could be defective in terms of thirteen forms of informal fallacy.

Aristotle made profound contributions to many areas of human learning including biology, physics, metaphysics, epistemology, psychology, aesthetics, ethics, and politics. However, his accomplishments in logic were so extensive and enduring that two thousand years after his death, the great philosopher Immanuel Kant said that Aristotle had discovered everything that could be known about logic. His logic was not superseded until the end of the nineteenth century when Frege, Whitehead, and Russell developed modern mathematical logic.

held that only formal validity is the "perfect" or conclusive variety. The present text follows Abelard on this point.

After Abelard, the study of logic during the Middle Ages flourished through the work of numerous philosophers. A logical treatise by William of Sherwood (ca. 1200–1271) contains the first expression of the "Barbara, Celarent . . ." poem quoted in Section 5.1 of this book, and the *Summulae Logicales* of Peter of Spain (ca. 1205–1277) became the standard textbook in logic for three hundred years. However, the most original contributions from this period were made by William of Ockham (ca. 1285–1347). Ockham extended the theory of modal logic, conducted an exhaustive study of the forms of valid and invalid syllogisms, and further developed the idea of a metalanguage, a higher-level language used to discuss linguistic entities such as words, terms, and propositions.

Toward the middle of the fifteenth century, a reaction set in against the logic of the Middle Ages. Rhetoric largely displaced logic as the primary focus of attention; the logic of Chrysippus, which had already begun to lose its unique identity in the Middle Ages, was ignored altogether, and the logic of Aristotle was studied only in highly simplistic presentations. A reawakening did not occur until two hundred years later through the work of Gottfried Wilhelm Leibniz (1646–1716).

Leibniz, a genius in numerous fields, attempted to develop a symbolic language or "calculus" that could be used to settle all forms of disputes, whether in theology, philosophy, or international relations. As a result of this work, Leibniz is sometimes credited with being the father of symbolic logic. Leibniz's efforts to symbolize logic were carried into the nineteenth century by Bernard Bolzano (1781–1848).

In the middle of the nineteenth century, logic commenced an extremely rapid period of development that has continued to this day. Work in symbolic logic was done by many philosophers and mathematicians, including Augustus De Morgan (1806–1871), George Boole (1815–1864), William Stanley Jevons (1835–1882), and John Venn (1834–1923). The rule bearing De Morgan's name is used in Chapter 7 of this book. Boole's interpretation of categorical propositions and Venn's method for diagramming them are covered in Chapters 4 and 5. At the same time a revival in inductive logic was initiated by the British philosopher John Stuart Mill (1806–1873), whose methods of induction are presented in Chapter 10.

Across the Atlantic, the American philosopher Charles Sanders Peirce (1839–1914) developed a logic of relations, invented symbolic quantifiers, and suggested the truth-table method for formulas in propositional logic. These topics are covered in Chapters 6 and 8 of this book. The truth-table method was completed independently by Emile Post (1897–1954) and Ludwig Wittgenstein (1889–1951).

Toward the end of the nineteenth century, the foundations of modern mathematical logic were laid by Gottlob Frege (1848–1925). His *Begriffsschrift* sets forth the theory of quantification presented in Chapter 8 of this text. Frege's work was continued into the twentieth century by Alfred North Whitehead (1861–1947) and Bertrand Russell (1872–1970), whose monumental *Principia Mathematica* attempted to reduce the whole of pure mathematics to logic. The *Principia* is the source of much of the symbolism that appears in Chapters 6, 7, and 8 of this text.

During the twentieth century, much of the work in logic has focused on the formalization of logical systems and on questions dealing with the completeness and

consistency of such systems. A now-famous theorem proved by Kurt Gödel (1906–1978) states that in any formal system adequate for number theory there exists an undecidable formula—that is, a formula such that neither it nor its negation is derivable from the axioms of the system. Other developments include multivalued logics and the formalization of modal logic. Most recently, logic has made a major contribution to technology by providing the conceptual foundation for the electronic circuitry of digital computers.

EXERCISE 1.1

I. Each of the following passages contains a single argument. Using the letters "P" and "C," identify the premises and conclusion of each argument, writing premises first and conclusion last. List the premises in the order in which they make the most sense (usually the order in which they occur), and write both premises and conclusion in the form of separate declarative sentences. Indicator words may be eliminated once premises and conclusion have been appropriately labeled. The exercises marked with a star are answered in the back of the book.

★1. Titanium combines readily with oxygen, nitrogen, and hydrogen, all of which have an adverse effect on its mechanical properties. As a result, titanium must be processed in their absence.

(Illustrated World of Science Encyclopedia)

2. Since the good, according to Plato, is that which furthers a person's real interests, it follows that in any given case when the good is known, men will seek it.

(Avrum Stroll and Richard Popkin, Philosophy and the Human Spirit)

3. As the denial or perversion of justice by the sentences of courts, as well as in any other manner, is with reason classed among the just causes of war, it will follow that the federal judiciary ought to have cognizance of all causes in which the citizens of other countries are concerned.

(Alexander Hamilton, Federalist Papers, No. 80)

★4. When individuals voluntarily abandon property, they forfeit any expectation of privacy in it that they might have had. Therefore, a warrantless search or seizure of abandoned property is not unreasonable under the Fourth Amendment.

(Judge Stephanie Kulp Seymour, United States v. Jones)

5. Artists and poets look at the world and seek relationships and order. But they translate their ideas to canvas, or to marble, or into poetic images. Scientists try to find relationships between different objects and events. To express the order they find, they create hypotheses and theories. Thus the great scientific theories are easily compared to great art and great literature.

(Douglas C. Giancoli, The Ideas of Physics, 3rd ed.)

6. The fact that there was never a land bridge between Australia and mainland Asia is evidenced by the fact that the animal species in the two areas are very different. Asian placental mammals and Australian marsupial mammals have not been in contact in the last several million years.

(T. Douglas Price and Gary M. Feinman, Images of the Past)

★7. Cuba's record on disaster prevention is impressive. After October 1963, when Hurricane Flora devastated the island and killed more than a thousand people, the Cuban government overhauled its civil defense system. It was so successful that when six powerful hurricanes thumped Cuba between1996 and 2002 only 16 people died. And when Hurricane Ivan struck Cuba in 2004 there was not a single casualty, but the same storm killed at least 70 people in other Caribbean countries.

(Newspaper clipping)

8. The classroom teacher is crucial to the development and academic success of the average student, and administrators simply are ancillary to this effort. For this reason, classroom teachers ought to be paid at least the equivalent of administrators at all levels, including the superintendent.

(Peter F. Falstrup, letter to the editor)

9. An agreement cannot bind unless both parties to the agreement know what they are doing and freely choose to do it. This implies that the seller who intends to enter a contract with a customer has a duty to disclose exactly what the customer is buying and what the terms of the sale are.

(Manuel G. Velasquez, "The Ethics of Consumer Production")

★10. Punishment, when speedy and specific, may suppress undesirable behavior, but it cannot teach or encourage desirable alternatives. Therefore, it is crucial to use positive techniques to model and reinforce appropriate behavior that the person can use in place of the unacceptable response that has to be suppressed.

(Walter Mischel and Harriet Mischel, *Essentials of Psychology*)

11. Profit serves a very crucial function in a free enterprise economy, such as our own. High profits are the signal that consumers want more of the output of the industry. High profits provide the incentive for firms to expand output and for more firms to enter the industry in the long run. For a firm of above-average efficiency, profits represent the reward for greater efficiency.

(Dominic Salvatore, *Managerial Economics,* 3rd ed.)

12. Cats can think circles around dogs! My cat regularly used to close and lock the door to my neighbor's doghouse, trapping their sleeping Doberman inside. Try telling a cat what to do, or putting a leash on him—he'll glare at you and say, "I don't think so. You should have gotten a dog."

(Kevin Purkiser, letter to the editor)

★13. Since private property helps people define themselves, since it frees people from mundane cares of daily subsistence, and since it is finite, no individual should accumulate so much property that others are prevented from accumulating the necessities of life.

(Leon P. Baradat, *Political Ideologies, Their Origins and Impact*)

14. To every existing thing God wills some good. Hence, since to love any thing is nothing else than to will good to that thing, it is manifest that God loves everything that exists.

(Thomas Aquinas, *Summa Theologica*)

15. Women of the working class, especially wage workers, should not have more than two children at most. The average working man can support no more and the average working woman can take care of no more in decent fashion.

(Margaret Sanger, *Family Limitations*)

★16. Radioactive fallout isn't the only concern in the aftermath of nuclear explosions. The nations of planet Earth have acquired nuclear weapons with an explosive power equal to more than a million Hiroshima bombs. Studies suggest that explosion of only half these weapons would produce enough soot, smoke, and dust to blanket the Earth, block out the sun, and bring on a nuclear winter that would threaten the survival of the human race.

(John W. Hill and Doris K. Kolb, *Chemistry for Changing Times*, 7th ed.)

17. An ant releases a chemical when it dies, and its fellows then carry it away to the compost heap. Apparently the communication is highly effective; a healthy ant painted with the death chemical will be dragged to the funeral heap again and again.

(Carol R. Ember and Melvin Ember, *Cultural Anthropology*, 7th ed.)

18. Every art and every inquiry, and similarly every action and pursuit, is thought to aim at some good; and for this reason the good has rightly been declared to be that at which all things aim.

(Aristotle, *Nicomachean Ethics*)

★19. Poverty offers numerous benefits to the nonpoor. Antipoverty programs provide jobs for middle-class professionals in social work, penology, and public health. Such workers' future advancement is tied to the continued growth of bureaucracies dependent on the existence of poverty.

(J. John Palen, *Social Problems*)

20. Corn is an annual crop. Butcher's meat, a crop which requires four or five years to grow. As an acre of land, therefore, will produce a much smaller quantity of the one species of food than the other, the inferiority of the quantity must be compensated by the superiority of the price.

(Adam Smith, *The Wealth of Nations*)

21. Neither a borrower nor lender be
For loan oft loses both itself and friend,
And borrowing dulls the edge of husbandry.

(William Shakespeare, *Hamlet* I, 3)

★22. The stakes in whistleblowing are high. Take the nurse who alleges that physicians enrich themselves in her hospital through unnecessary surgery; the engineer who discloses safety defects in the braking systems of a fleet of new rapid-transit vehicles; the Defense Department official who alerts Congress to military graft and overspending: all know that they pose a threat to those whom they denounce and that their own careers may be at risk.

(Sissela Bok, "Whistleblowing and Professional Responsibility")

23. If a piece of information is not "job relevant," then the employer is not entitled qua employer to know it. Consequently, since sexual practices, political beliefs, associational activities, etc., are not part of the description of most jobs, that is, since they do not directly affect one's job performance, they are not legitimate information for an employer to know in the determination of the hiring of a job applicant.

(George G. Brenkert," Privacy, Polygraphs, and Work")

24. Many people believe that a dark tan is attractive and a sign of good health, but mounting evidence indicates that too much sun can lead to health problems. One of the most noticeable effects is premature aging of the skin. The sun also contributes to certain types of cataracts, and, what is most worrisome, it plays a role in skin cancer.

(Joseph M. Moran and Michael D. Morgan, *Meteorology,* 4th ed.)

★25. Contrary to the tales of some scuba divers, the toothy, gaping grin on the mouth of an approaching shark is not necessarily anticipatory. It is generally accepted that by constantly swimming with its mouth open, the shark is simply avoiding suffocation. This assures a continuous flow of oxygen-laden water into their mouths, over their gills, and out through the gill slits.

(Robert A. Wallace et al., *Biology: The Science of Life*)

26. Not only is the sky blue [as a result of scattering], but light coming from it is also partially polarized. You can readily observe this by placing a piece of Polaroid (for example, one lens of a pair of Polaroid sunglasses) in front of your eye and rotating it as you look at the sky on a clear day. You will notice a change in light intensity with the orientation of the Polaroid.

(Frank J. Blatt, *Principles of Physics,* 2nd ed.)

27. Since the secondary light [from the moon] does not inherently belong to the moon and is not received from any star or from the sun, and since in the whole universe there is no other body left but the earth, what must we conclude? What is to be proposed? Surely we must assert that the lunar body (or any other dark and sunless orb) is illuminated by the earth.

(Galileo Galilei, *The Starry Messenger*)

★28. Anyone familiar with our prison system knows that there are some inmates who behave little better than brute beasts. But the very fact that these prisoners exist is a telling argument against the efficacy of capital punishment as a deterrent. If the death penalty had been truly effective as a deterrent, such prisoners would long ago have vanished.

("The Injustice of the Death Penalty," *America*)

29. Though it is possible that REM sleep and dreaming are not necessary in the adult, REM deprivation studies seem to suggest otherwise. Why would REM pressure increase with deprivation if the system is unimportant in the adult?

(Herbert L. Petri, *Motivation: Theory and Research,* 2nd ed.)

30. World government and the balance of power are in many ways opposites. World government means one central authority, a permanent standing world police force, and clearly defined conditions under which this force will go into action. A balance of power system has many sovereign authorities, each controlling its own army, combining only when they feel like it to control aggression. To most people world government now seems unattainable.

(David W. Ziegler, *War, Peace, and International Politics,* 4th ed.)

II. The following arguments were taken from magazine and newspaper editorials and letters to the editor. In most instances the main conclusion must be rephrased to capture the full intent of the author. Write out what you interpret the main conclusion to be.

★1. University administrators know well the benefits that follow notable success in college sports: increased applications for admissions, increased income from licensed logo merchandise, more lucrative television deals, post-season game revenue and more successful alumni fund drives. The idea that there is something ideal and pure about the amateur athlete is self-serving bunk.

(Michael McDonnell, letter to the editor)

2. In a nation of immigrants, people of diverse ethnic backgrounds must have a common bond through which to exchange ideas. How can this bond be accomplished if there is no common language? It is those who shelter the immigrant from learning English by encouraging the development of a multilingual society who are creating a xenophobic atmosphere. They allow the immigrant to surround himself with a cocoon of language from which he cannot escape and which others cannot penetrate.

(Rita Toften, letter to the editor)

3. The health and fitness of our children has become a problem partly because of our attitude toward athletics. The purpose of sports, especially for children, should be to make healthy people healthier. The concept of team sports has failed to do this. Rather than learning to interact and cooperate with others, youngsters are taught to compete. Team sports have only reinforced the notion that the team on top is the winner, and all others are losers. This approach does not make sports appealing to many children, and some, especially among the less fit, burn out by the time they are twelve.

(Mark I. Pitman, "Young Jocks")

★4. College is the time in which a young mind is supposed to mature and acquire wisdom, and one can only do this by experiencing as much diverse intellectual stimuli as possible. A business student may be a whiz at accounting, but has he or she ever experienced the beauty of a Shakespearean sonnet or the boundless events composing Hebrew history? Most likely not. While many of these neoconservatives will probably go on to be financially successful, they

are robbing themselves of the true purpose of collegiate academics, a sacrifice that outweighs the future salary checks.

(Robert S. Griffith, "Conservative College Press")

5. History has shown repeatedly that you cannot legislate morality, nor does anyone have a right to. The real problem is the people who have a vested interest in sustaining the multibillion-dollar drug industry created by the laws against drugs. The legalization of drugs would remove the thrill of breaking the law; it would end the suffering caused by unmetered doses, impurities, and substandard paraphernalia. A huge segment of the underground and extralegal economy would move into a legitimate economy, taking money away from criminals, eliminating crime and violence, and restoring many talented people to useful endeavor.

(Thomas L. Wayburn, letter to the editor)

6. Infectious disease is no longer the leading cause of death in this country, thanks to antibiotics, but there are new strains of bacteria that are resistant to—and others that grow only in the presence of—antibiotics. Yet Congress wants to cut the National Institutes of Health budget. Further cuts would leave us woefully unprepared to cope with the new microbes Mother Nature has cooking in her kitchen.

(Valina L. Dawson, letter to the editor)

★7. At a time when our religious impulses might help heal the pains and strains in our society, today's television pulpiteers preach intolerance, censure, and discrimination. They package a "believer life-style," and rail against everyone who doesn't fit it—homosexuals, communists, Jews and other non-Christians, sex educators, and so on. Such intolerance threatens to undermine the pluralism that marks our heritage. The packaging of that intolerance in slick Hollywood programming or under the guise of patriotic fervor is skillfully accomplished on many fronts. That, however, does not make it right.

(Peter G. Kreitler, "TV Preachers' Religious Intolerance")

8. Ideally, decisions about health care should be based on the doctor's clinical judgment, patient preference, and scientific evidence. Patients should always be presented with options in their care. Elective cesarean section, however, is not used to treat a problem but to avoid a natural process. An elective surgery like this puts the patient at unnecessary risk, increases the risk for complications in future deliveries, and increases health care costs.

(Anne Foster-Rosales, M.D., letter to the editor)

9. Parents who feel guilty for the little time they can (or choose to) spend with their children "pick up" after them—so the children don't learn to face the consequences of their own choices and actions. Parents who allow their children to fail are showing them greater love and respect.

(Susan J. Peters, letter to the editor)

★10. Most of the environmental problems facing us stem, at least in part, from the sheer number of Americans. The average American produces three quarters of a ton of garbage every year, consumes hundreds of gallons of gasoline, and uses large amounts of electricity (often from a nuclear power plant, coal burning, or a dam). The least painful way to protect the environment is to limit population growth.

(Craig M. Bradley, letter to the editor)

III. Define the following terms:

logic	conclusion	inference
argument	conclusion indicator	proposition
statement	premise indicator	truth value
premise		

IV. Answer "true" or "false" to the following statements:

1. The purpose of the premise or premises is to set forth the reasons or evidence given in support of the conclusion.

2. Some arguments have more than one conclusion.

3. All arguments must have more than one premise.

4. The words "therefore," "hence," "so," "since," and "thus" are all conclusion indicators.

5. The words "for," "because," "as," and "for the reason that" are all premise indicators.

6. In the strict sense of the terms, *inference* and *argument* have exactly the same meaning.

7. In most (but not all) arguments that lack indicator words, the conclusion is the first statement.

8. Any sentence that is either true or false is a statement.

9. Every statement has a truth value.

10. The person usually credited with being the father of logic is Aristotle.

1.2 **Recognizing Arguments**

Not all passages contain arguments. Because logic deals with arguments, it is important to be able to distinguish passages that contain arguments from those that do not. In general, a passage contains an argument if it purports to prove something; if it does not do so, it does not contain an argument. Two conditions must be fulfilled for a passage to purport to prove something:

1. At least one of the statements must claim to present evidence or reasons.

2. There must be a claim that the alleged evidence supports or implies something—that is, a claim that something follows from the alleged evidence or reasons.

As we have seen, the statements that claim to present the evidence or reasons are the premises, and the statement that the evidence is claimed to support or imply is the

Acknowledgements

The content of this text has been adapted from the following product(s):

A Concise Introduction to Logic (with ThomsonNOW™ Printed Access Card)
Hurley ISBN-10: (0-495-50383-5)
ISBN-13: (978-0-495-50383-5)

Table Of Contents

conclusion. It is not necessary that the premises present actual evidence or true reasons nor that the premises actually support the conclusion. But at least the premises must *claim* to present evidence or reasons, and there must be a *claim* that the evidence or reasons support or imply something.

The first condition expresses a **factual claim,** and deciding whether it is fulfilled often falls outside the domain of logic. Thus, most of our attention will be concentrated on whether the second condition is fulfilled. This second condition expresses what is called an **inferential claim.** The inferential claim is simply the claim that the passage expresses a certain kind of reasoning process—that something supports or implies something or that something follows from something. Also, you should recognize that this claim is not equatable with the intentions of the arguer. Intentions are subjective and, as such, are usually not accessible to the evaluator. Rather, the inferential claim is an objective feature of an argument grounded in its language or structure.

An inferential claim can be either explicit or implicit. An *explicit* inferential claim is usually asserted by premise or conclusion indicator words ("thus," "since," "because," "hence," "therefore," and so on). Example:

> Mad cow disease is spread by feeding parts of infected animals to cows, and this practice has yet to be completely eradicated. Thus, mad cow disease continues to pose a threat to people who eat beef.

The word "thus" expresses the claim that something is being inferred, so the passage is an argument.

An *implicit* inferential claim exists if there is an inferential relationship between the statements in a passage, but the passage contains no indicator words. Example:

> The genetic modification of food is risky business. Genetic engineering can introduce unintended changes into the DNA of the food-producing organism, and these changes can be toxic to the consumer.

The inferential relationship between the first statement and the other two constitutes an implicit claim that evidence supports something, so we are justified in calling the passage an argument. The first statement is the conclusion, and the other two are the premises.

In deciding whether there is a claim that evidence supports or implies something, keep an eye out for (1) indicator words and (2) the presence of an inferential relationship between the statements. In connection with these points, however, a word of caution is in order. First, the mere occurrence of an indicator word by no means guarantees the presence of an argument. For example, consider the following passages:

> Since Edison invented the phonograph, there have been many technological developments.

> Since Edison invented the phonograph, he deserves credit for a major technological development.

In the first passage the word "since" is used in a *temporal* sense. It means "from the time that." Thus, the first passage is not an argument. In the second passage "since" is used in a *logical* sense, and so the passage *is* an argument.

The second cautionary point is that it is not always easy to detect the occurrence of an inferential relationship between the statements in a passage, and one may have to review a passage several times before making a decision. In reaching such a decision, one may find it helpful to mentally insert the word "therefore" before the various statements to see whether it makes sense to interpret one of them as following from the others. Even with this mental aid, however, the decision whether a passage contains an inferential relationship (as well as the decision about indicator words) often involves a heavy dose of interpretation. As a result, not everyone will agree about every passage. Sometimes the only answer possible is a conditional one: "*If* this passage contains an argument, then these are the premises and that is the conclusion."

To assist in distinguishing passages that contain arguments from those that do not, let us now investigate some typical kinds of nonarguments. These include simple noninferential passages, expository passages, illustrations, explanations, and conditional statements.

Simple Noninferential Passages

Simple noninferential passages are unproblematic passages that lack a claim that anything is being proved. Such passages contain statements that could be premises or conclusions (or both), but what is missing is a claim that any potential premise supports a conclusion or that any potential conclusion is supported by premises. Passages of this sort include warnings, pieces of advice, statements of belief or opinion, loosely associated statements, and reports.

A **warning** is a form of expression that is intended to put someone on guard against a dangerous or detrimental situation. Examples:

> Watch out that you don't slip on the ice.
> Whatever you do, never confide personal secrets to Blabbermouth Bob.

If no evidence is given to prove that such statements are true, then there is no argument.

A **piece of advice** is a form of expression that makes a recommendation about some future decision or course of conduct. Examples:

> You should keep a few things in mind before buying a used car. Test drive the car at varying speeds and conditions, examine the oil in the crankcase, ask to see service records, and, if possible, have the engine and power train checked by a mechanic.

> Before accepting a job after class hours, I would suggest that you give careful consideration to your course load. Will you have sufficient time to prepare for classes and tests, and will the job produce an excessive drain on your energies?

As with warnings, if there is no evidence that is intended to prove anything, then there is no argument.

A **statement of belief** or **opinion** is an expression about what someone happens to believe or think about something. Examples:

> We believe that our company must develop and produce outstanding products that will perform a great service or fulfill a need for our customers. We believe that our

business must be run at an adequate profit and that the services and products we offer must be better than those offered by competitors.

> (Robert D. Hay and Edmund R. Gray, "Introduction to Social Responsibility")

> When I can read the latte menu through the hole in my server's earlobe, something is seriously out of whack. What happened to an earring, maybe two, in each lobe? Now any surface is game. Brow, lip, tongue, cheek, nose. I've adjusted to untied shoelaces and pants that make mooning irrelevant. But when it comes to piercings, I just can't budge.

> (Debra Darvick, "Service with a Smile, and Plenty of Metal")

Because neither of these authors makes any claim that his or her belief or opinion is supported by evidence, or that it supports some conclusion, there is no argument.

Loosely associated statements may be about the same general subject, but they lack a claim that one of them is proved by the others. Example:

> Not to honor men of worth will keep the people from contention; not to value goods that are hard to come by will keep them from theft; not to display what is desirable will keep them from being unsettled of mind.

> (Lao-Tzu, *Thoughts from the Tao Te Ching*)

Because there is no claim that any of these statements provides evidence or reasons for believing another, there is no argument.

A **report** consists of a group of statements that convey information about some topic or event. Example:

> Even though more of the world is immunized than ever before, many old diseases have proven quite resilient in the face of changing population and environmental conditions, especially in the developing world. New diseases, such as AIDS, have taken their toll in both the North and the South.

> (Steven L. Spiegel, *World Politics in a New Era*)

These statements could serve as the premises of an argument, but because the author makes no claim that they support or imply anything, there is no argument. Another type of report is the news report:

> Witnesses said they heard a loud crack before a balcony gave way at a popular nightspot, dropping dozens of screaming people fourteen feet. At least eighty people were injured at the Diamond Horseshoe casino when they fell onto broken glass and splintered wood. Investigators are waiting for an engineer's report on the deck's occupancy load.

> (Newspaper clipping)

Again, because the reporter makes no claim that these statements imply anything, there is no argument.

One must be careful, though, with reports *about* arguments:

"The Air Force faces a serious shortage of experienced pilots in the years ahead, because repeated overseas tours and the allure of high paying jobs with commercial
airlines are winning out over lucrative bonuses to stay in the service," says a
prominent Air Force official.

(Newspaper clipping)

Properly speaking, this passage is not an argument, because the author of the passage
does not claim that anything is supported by evidence. Rather, the author reports the
claim by the Air Force official that something is supported by evidence. If such passages
are interpreted as "containing" arguments, it must be made clear that the argument is
not the author's but one made by someone about whom the author is reporting.

Expository Passages

An **expository passage** is a kind of discourse that begins with a topic sentence followed by one or more sentences that develop the topic sentence. If the objective is not
to prove the topic sentence but only to expand it or elaborate it, then there is no argument. Examples:

There are three familiar states of matter: solid, liquid, and gas. Solid objects ordinarily
maintain their shape and volume regardless of their location. A liquid occupies a
definite volume, but assumes the shape of the occupied portion of its container.
A gas maintains neither shape nor volume. It expands to fill completely whatever
container it is in.

(John W. Hill and Doris K. Kolb, *Chemistry for Changing Times,* 7th ed.)

There is a stylized relation of artist to mass audience in the sports, especially in baseball. Each player develops a style of his own—the swagger as he steps to the plate,
the unique windup a pitcher has, the clean-swinging and hard-driving hits, the
precision quickness and grace of infield and outfield, the sense of surplus power
behind whatever is done.

(Max Lerner, *America as a Civilization*)

In each passage the topic sentence is stated first, and the remaining sentences merely develop and flesh out this topic sentence. These passages are not arguments, because they
lack an inferential claim. However, expository passages differ from simple noninferential
passages (such as warnings and pieces of advice) in that many of them can also be taken
as arguments. If the purpose of the subsequent sentences in the passage is not only to
flesh out the topic sentence but also to prove it, then the passage is an argument. Example:

Skin and the mucous membrane lining the respiratory and digestive tracts serve as
mechanical barriers to entry by microbes. Oil gland secretions contain chemicals
that weaken or kill bacteria on skin. The respiratory tract is lined by cells that sweep
mucus and trapped particles up into the throat, where they can be swallowed. The
stomach has an acidic pH, which inhibits the growth of many types of bacteria.

(Sylvia S. Mader, *Human Biology,* 4th ed.)

In this passage the topic sentence is stated first, and the purpose of the remaining
sentences is not only to *show how* the skin and mucous membranes serve as barriers to

microbes but also to *prove* that they do this. Thus, the passage can be taken as both an expository passage and an argument.

In deciding whether an expository passage should be interpreted as an argument, try to determine whether the purpose of the subsequent sentences in the passage is merely to develop the topic sentence or also to prove that it is true. In borderline cases, ask yourself whether the topic sentence makes a claim that everyone accepts or agrees with. If it does, the passage is probably not an argument. In real-life situations authors rarely try to prove something is true when everyone already accepts it. However, if the topic sentence makes a claim that many people do not accept or have never thought about, then the purpose of the remaining sentences may be both to prove the topic sentence is true as well as to develop it. If this be so, the passage is an argument.

Finally, if even this procedure yields no definite answer, the only alternative may be to say that *if* the passage is taken as an argument, then the first statement is the conclusion and the others are the premises.

Illustrations

An **illustration** is an expression involving one or more examples that is intended to show what something means or how it is done. Illustrations are often confused with arguments because many illustrations contain indicator words such as "thus." Examples:

> Chemical elements, as well as compounds, can be represented by molecular formulas. Thus, oxygen is represented by "O_2," water by "H_2O," and sodium chloride by "NaCl."

> A deciduous tree is any tree that loses its leaves during the winter. For example, maples are deciduous. And so are elms, poplars, hawthorns, and alders.

These selections are not arguments, because they make no claim that anything is being proved. In the first selection, the word "thus" indicates how something is done—namely, how chemical elements and compounds can be represented by formulas. In the second, the examples cited are intended to illustrate the meaning of the word "deciduous." It pins down the meaning by providing concrete instances.

However, as with expository passages, many illustrations can be taken as arguments. Such arguments are often called **arguments from example.** Here is an instance of one:

> Although most forms of cancer, if untreated, can cause death, not all cancers are life-threatening. For example, basal cell carcinoma, the most common of all skin cancers, can produce disfigurement, but it almost never results in death.

In this passage the example given is intended to prove the truth of "Not all cancers are life-threatening." Thus, the passage is best interpreted as an argument.

In deciding whether an illustration should be interpreted as an argument, determine whether the passage merely shows how something is done or what something means, or whether it also purports to prove something. In borderline cases it helps to note whether the claim being illustrated is one that practically everyone accepts or agrees with. If it is, the passage is probably not an argument. As already noted, in real-life situations authors rarely attempt to prove what everyone already accepts. But if the claim being illustrated is one that many people do not accept or have never thought about, then the passage may be interpreted as an argument.

Thus, in reference to the first two examples we considered, most people are aware that elements and compounds can be expressed by formulas—practically everyone knows that water is H_2O—and most people have at least a vague idea of what a deciduous tree is. But they may not have ever considered whether some forms of cancer are not life-threatening. This is one of the reasons for evaluating the first two examples as mere illustrations and the last one as an argument.

Explanations

One of the most important kinds of nonargument is the explanation. An **explanation** is an expression that purports to shed light on some event or phenomenon. The event or phenomenon in question is usually accepted as a matter of fact. Examples:

> The sky appears blue from the earth's surface because light rays from the sun are scattered by particles in the atmosphere.

> The AIDS virus causes sickness and death because it infects certain white blood cells called T cells, and these cells are essential to the body's immune system.

> Naval oranges are called by that name because they have a growth that resembles a human naval on the end opposite the stem.

Every explanation is composed of two distinct components: the explanandum and explanans. The **explanandum** is the statement that describes the event or phenomenon to be explained, and the **explanans** is the statement or group of statements that purports to do the explaining. In the first example above, the explanandum is the statement "The sky appears blue from the earth's surface" and the explanans is "Light rays from the sun are scattered by particles in the atmosphere."

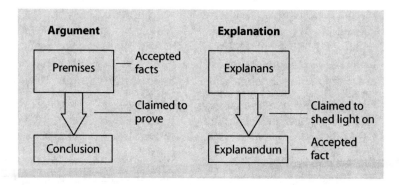

Explanations are sometimes mistaken for arguments because they often contain the indicator word "because." Yet explanations are not arguments, because in an explanation the purpose of the explanans is to shed light on, or to make sense of, the explanandum event—not to prove that it occurred. In other words, the purpose of the explanans is to show *why* something is the case, whereas in an argument, the purpose of the premises is to prove *that* something is the case.

In the first example given, the fact that the sky is blue is readily apparent to everyone. The statement that light rays from the sun are scattered by particles in the atmosphere is not intended to prove *that* the sky is blue, but rather to show *why* it is blue. In the second example, practically everyone knows that the AIDS virus causes sickness and death. The purpose of the passage is to explain *why* this happens—not to prove *that* it happens. Similarly, in the third example, it is obvious that naval oranges are called naval oranges. The purpose of the passage is to shed light on why they have this name.

Thus, to distinguish explanations from arguments, identify the statement that is either the explanandum or the conclusion (usually this is the statement that precedes the word "because"). If this statement describes an accepted matter of fact, and if the remaining statements purport to shed light on this statement, then the passage is an explanation.

This method usually works to distinguish arguments from explanations. However, some passages can be interpreted as both explanations and arguments. Example:

> Women become intoxicated by drinking a smaller amount of alcohol than men because men metabolize part of the alcohol before it reaches the bloodstream, whereas women do not.

The purpose of this passage could be to prove the first statement to those people who do not accept it as fact, and to shed light on that fact to those people who do accept it. Alternately, the passage could be intended to prove the first statement to a single person who accepts its truth on blind faith or incomplete experience, and simultaneously to shed light on this truth. Thus, the passage can be correctly interpreted as both an explanation and an argument.

Perhaps the greatest problem confronting the effort to distinguish explanations from arguments lies in determining whether something is an accepted matter of fact. Obviously, what is accepted by one person may not be accepted by another. Thus, the effort often involves determining which person or group of people the passage is directed to—the intended audience. Sometimes the source of the passage (textbook, newspaper, technical journal, etc.) will decide the issue. But when the passage is taken totally out of context, ascertaining the source may prove impossible. In those circumstances the only possible answer may be to say that *if* the passage is an argument, then such-and-such is the conclusion and such-and-such are the premises.

Conditional Statements

A **conditional statement** is an "if . . . then . . ." statement; for example:

> If professional football games incite violence in the home, then the widespread approval given to this sport should be reconsidered.

> If Lance Armstrong has won the Tour de France seven consecutive times, then he ranks as king of the hill in the world's most famous bicycle race.

Every conditional statement is made up of two component statements. The component statement immediately following the "if" is called the **antecedent,** and the one following the "then" is called the **consequent.** (Occasionally, the word "then" is left out, and occasionally the order of antecedent and consequent is reversed.) In the first example, the antecedent is "Professional football games incite violence in the home," and the consequent is "The widespread approval given to this sport should be reconsidered." In both of these examples, there is a meaningful relationship between antecedent and consequent. However, such a relationship need not exist for a statement to count as conditional. The statement "If Janet Jackson is a singer, then Denver is in Colorado" is just as much a conditional statement as those about professional football and Lance Armstrong.

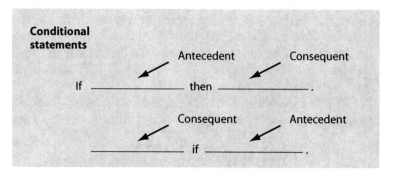

Conditional statements are not arguments, because they fail to meet the criteria given earlier. In an argument, at least one statement must claim to present evidence, and there must be a claim that this evidence implies something. In a conditional statement, there is no claim that either the antecedent or the consequent presents evidence. In other words, there is no assertion that either the antecedent or the consequent is true. Rather, there is only the assertion that *if* the antecedent is true, then so is the consequent. Of course, a conditional statement as a whole may present evidence because it asserts a relationship between statements. Yet when conditional statements are taken in this sense, there is still no argument, because there is then no separate claim that this evidence implies anything.

Some conditional statements are similar to arguments, however, in that they express the outcome of a reasoning process. As such, they may be said to have a certain inferential content. Consider the following:

> If Arnold Schwarzenegger was born a citizen of Austria, then he cannot be elected president of the United States.

> If Jennifer Lopez is Marc Anthony's wife, then Marc Anthony is Jennifer Lopez's husband.

The link between the antecedent and consequent of these conditional statements resembles the inferential link between the premises and conclusion of an argument. Yet there is a difference because the premises of an argument are claimed to be true, whereas no such claim is made for the antecedent of a conditional statement. Accordingly, these conditional statements are not arguments.* Yet their inferential content may be reexpressed to form arguments:

---

*In saying this we are temporarily ignoring the possibility of these statements being enthymemes. As we shall see in Chapter 5, an *enthymeme* is an argument in which a premise or conclusion (or both) is implied but not stated. If, to the second example, we add the premise "Jennifer Lopez is Marc Anthony's wife" and the conclusion "Therefore, Marc Anthony is Jennifer Lopez's husband," we have a complete argument. To decide whether a conditional statement is an enthymeme, we must be familiar with the context in which it occurs.

Arnold Schwarzenegger was born a citizen of Austria.
Therefore, he cannot be elected president of the United States.

Jennifer Lopez is Marc Anthony's wife.
Therefore, Marc Anthony is Jennifer Lopez's husband.

Finally, while no single conditional statement is an argument, a conditional statement may serve as either the premise or the conclusion (or both) of an argument, as the following examples illustrate:

If Iran is developing nuclear weapons, then Iran is a threat to world peace.
Iran is developing nuclear weapons.
Therefore, Iran is a threat to world peace.

If borders are secure, then terrorists cannot enter the country.
If terrorists cannot enter the country, then acts of terrorism will be reduced.
Therefore, if borders are secure, then acts of terrorism will be reduced.

The relation between conditional statements and arguments may now be summarized as follows:

1. A single conditional statement is not an argument.
2. A conditional statement may serve as either the premise or the conclusion (or both) of an argument.
3. The inferential content of a conditional statement may be reexpressed to form an argument.

The first two rules are especially pertinent to the recognition of arguments. According to the first rule, if a passage consists of a single conditional statement, it is not an argument. But if it consists of a conditional statement together with some other statement, then, by the second rule, it *may* be an argument, depending on such factors as the presence of indicator words and an inferential relationship between the statements.

Conditional statements are especially important in logic because they express the relationship between necessary and sufficient conditions. A is said to be a **sufficient condition** for B whenever the occurrence of A is all that is needed for the occurrence of B. For example, being a dog is a sufficient condition for being an animal. On the other hand, B is said to be a **necessary condition** for A whenever A cannot occur without the occurrence of B. Thus, being an animal is a necessary condition for being a dog. These relationships are expressed in the following conditional statements:

If X is a dog, then X is an animal.
If X is not an animal, then X is not a dog.

The first statement says that being a dog is a sufficient condition for being an animal, and the second that being an animal is a necessary condition for being a dog. However, a little reflection reveals that these two statements say exactly the same thing. Thus, each expresses in one way a necessary condition and in another way a sufficient condition. The terminology of sufficient and necessary conditions will be used in later chapters to express definitions and causal connections.

Summary

In deciding whether a passage contains an argument, you should look for three things: (1) indicator words such as "therefore," "since," "because," and so on; (2) an inferential relationship between the statements; and (3) typical kinds of nonarguments. But remember that the mere occurrence of an indicator word does not guarantee the presence of an argument. You must check to see that the statement identified as the conclusion is claimed to be supported by one or more of the other statements. Also keep in mind that in many arguments that lack indicator words, the conclusion is the first statement. Furthermore, it helps to mentally insert the word "therefore" before the various statements before deciding that a statement should be interpreted as a conclusion. The typical kinds of nonarguments that we have surveyed are as follows:

warnings	reports
pieces of advice	expository passages
statements of belief	illustrations
statements of opinion	explanations
loosely associated statements	conditional statements

Keep in mind that these kinds of nonargument are not mutually exclusive, and that, for example, one and the same passage can sometimes be interpreted as both a report and a statement of opinion, or as both an expository passage and an illustration. The precise kind of nonargument a passage might be is nowhere near as important as correctly deciding whether or not it is an argument.

After working the exercises in this section, you may, if you wish, proceed directly to Section 1.6 ("Extended Arguments").

EXERCISE 1.2

I. Determine which of the following passages are arguments. For those that are, identify the conclusion. For those that are not, determine the kind of nonargument.

★1. The turkey vulture is called by that name because its red featherless head resembles the head of a wild turkey.

2. If public education fails to improve the quality of instruction in both primary and secondary schools, then it is likely that it will lose additional students to the private sector in the years ahead.

3. Freedom of the press is the most important of our constitutionally guaranteed freedoms. Without it, our other freedoms would be immediately threatened. Furthermore, it provides the fulcrum for the advancement of new freedoms.

★4. A mammal is a vertebrate animal that nurses its offspring. Thus, cats and dogs are mammals, as are sheep, monkeys, rabbits, and bears.

5. It is strongly recommended that you have your house inspected for termite damage at the earliest possible opportunity.

6. Mosquito bites are not always the harmless little irritations most of us take them to be. For example, some mosquitoes carry West Nile virus, and people who are infected can become very sick or even die.

★7. If stem-cell research is restricted, then future cures will not materialize. If future cures do not materialize, then people will die prematurely. Therefore, if stem-cell research is restricted, then people will die prematurely.

8. Fictional characters behave according to the same psychological probabilities as real people. But the characters of fiction are found in exotic dilemmas that real people hardly encounter. Consequently, fiction provides us with the opportunity to ponder how people react in uncommon situations, and to deduce moral lessons, psychological principles, and philosophical insights from their behavior.

(J. R. McCuen and A. C. Winkler, *Readings for Writers,* 4th ed.)

9. I believe that it must be the policy of the United States to support free peoples who are resisting attempted subjugation by armed minorities or by outside pressures. I believe that we must assist free peoples to work out their own destinies in their own way. I believe that our help should be primarily through economic and financial aid, which is essential to economic stability and orderly political processes.

(President Truman, Address to Congress, 1947)

★10. Five college students who were accused of sneaking into the Cincinnati Zoo and trying to ride the camels pleaded no contest to criminal trespass yesterday. The students scaled a fence to get into the zoo and then climbed another fence to get into the camel pit before security officials caught them, zoo officials said.

(Newspaper clipping)

11. Mortality rates for women undergoing early abortions, where the procedure is legal, appear to be as low as or lower than the rates for normal childbirth. Consequently, any interest of the state in protecting the woman from an inherently hazardous procedure, except when it would be equally dangerous for her to forgo it, has largely disappeared.

(Justice Blackmun, *Roe v. Wade*)

12. The pace of reading, clearly, depends entirely upon the reader. He may read as slowly or as rapidly as he can or wishes to read. If he does not understand something, he may stop and reread it, or go in search of elucidation before continuing. The reader can accelerate his pace when the material is easy or less than interesting, and can slow down when it is difficult or enthralling. If what he reads is moving he can put down the book for a few moments and cope with his emotions without fear of losing anything.

(Marie Winn, *The Plug-In Drug*)

★13. I'm sick and tired of living in fear. I'm tired of plastic bags and duct tape. I'm tired of alerts telling me whether or not I can walk outside. America should be a bastion of hope. Jobs, affordable health care and respect from the world. These will bring hope, and hope is what prevents terrorism.

(Steve Mavros, letter to the editor)

14. Lions at Kruger National Park in South Africa are dying of tuberculosis. "All of the lions in the park may be dead within ten years because the disease is incurable, and the lions have no natural resistance," said the deputy director of the Department of Agriculture.

(Newspaper clipping)

15. Economics is of practical value in business. An understanding of the overall operation of the economic system puts the business executive in a better position to formulate policies. The executive who understands the causes and consequences of inflation is better equipped during inflationary periods to make more intelligent decisions than otherwise.

(Campbell R. McConnell, *Economics,* 8th ed.)

★16. Bear one thing in mind before you begin to write your paper: Famous literary works, especially works regarded as classics, have been thoroughly studied to the point where prevailing opinion on them has assumed the character of orthodoxy.

(J. R. McCuen and A. C. Winkler, *Readings for Writers,* 4th ed.)

17. Young people at universities study to achieve knowledge and not to learn a trade. We must all learn how to support ourselves, but we must also learn how to live. We need a lot of engineers in the modern world, but we do not want a world of modern engineers.

(Winston Churchill, *A Churchill Reader,* ed. Colin R. Coote)

18. No business concern wants to sell on credit to a customer who will prove unable or unwilling to pay his or her account. Consequently, most business organizations include a credit department which must reach a decision on the credit worthiness of each prospective customer.

(Walter B. Meigs and Robert F. Meigs, *Accounting*)

★19. For organisms at the sea surface, sinking into deep water usually means death. Plant cells cannot photosynthesize in the dark depths. Fishes and other animals that descend lose contact with the main surface food supply and themselves become food for strange deep-living predators.

(David H. Milne, *Marine Life and the Sea*)

20. Since the 1950s a malady called whirling disease has invaded U.S. fishing streams, frequently attacking rainbow trout. A parasite deforms young fish, which often chase their tails before dying, hence the name.

("Trout Disease—A Turn for the Worse," *National Geographic*)

21. Dachshunds are ideal dogs for small children, as they are already stretched and pulled to such a length that the child cannot do much harm one way or the other.

(Robert Benchley, quoted in *Cold Noses and Warm Hearts*)

★22. Atoms are the basic building blocks of all matter. They can combine to form molecules, whose properties are generally very different from those of the constituent atoms. Table salt, for example, a simple chemical compound formed from chlorine and sodium, resembles neither the poisonous gas nor the highly reactive metal.

(Frank J. Blatt, *Principles of Physics,* 2nd ed.)

23. The coarsest type of humor is the *practical joke:* pulling away the chair from the dignitary's lowered bottom. The victim is perceived first as a person of conse- quence, then suddenly as an inert body subject to the laws of physics: authority is debunked by gravity, mind by matter; man is degraded to a mechanism.

(Arthur Koestler, *Janus: A Summing Up*)

24. If a man holding a belief which he was taught in childhood or persuaded of afterwards keeps down and pushes away any doubts which arise about it in his mind, purposely avoids the reading of books and the company of men that call in question or discuss it, and regards as impious those questions which cannot easily be asked without disturbing it—the life of that man is one long sin against mankind.

(W. K. Clifford, "The Ethics of Belief")

★25. It is usually easy to decide whether or not something is alive. This is because living things share many common attributes, such as the capacity to extract energy from nutrients to drive their various functions, the power to actively respond to changes in their environment, and the ability to grow, to differen- tiate, and to reproduce.

(Donald Voet and Judith G. Voet, *Biochemistry*, 2nd ed.)

26. Words are slippery customers. The full meaning of a word does not appear until it is placed in its context. . . . And even then the meaning will depend upon the listener, upon the speaker, upon their entire experience of the lan- guage, upon their knowledge of one another, and upon the whole situation.

(C. Cherry, *On Human Communication*)

27. Haydn developed the string quartet from the eighteenth century *diverti- mento,* giving more substance to the light, popular form and scoring it for two violins, a viola, and a cello. His eighty-three quartets, written over the course of his creative lifetime, evolved slowly into a sophisticated form. To- gether they constitute one of the most important bodies of chamber music literature.

(Robert Hickok, *Exploring Music*)

★28. A person never becomes truly self-reliant. Even though he deals effectively with things, he is necessarily dependent upon those who have taught him to do so. They have selected the things he is dependent upon and determined the kinds and degrees of dependencies.

(B. F. Skinner, *Beyond Freedom and Dignity*)

29. There is no doubt that some businessmen conspire to shorten the useful life of their products in order to guarantee replacement sales. There is, similarly, no

doubt that many of the annual model changes with which American (and other) consumers are increasingly familiar are not technologically substantive.

(Alvin Toffler, *Future Shock*)

30. Water is a good solvent for many different substances, and it picks them up as it moves through the environment. For example, rain water flowing over and under the ground dissolves minerals such as limestone.

(Gilbert Castellan et al., *The World of Chemistry*)

★31. In areas where rats are a problem, it is very difficult to exterminate them with bait poison. That's because some rats eat enough poison to die but others eat only enough to become sick and then learn to avoid that particular poison taste in the future.

(Rod Plotnik, *Introduction to Psychology*, 4th ed.)

32. Men are less likely to develop osteoporosis until later in life than women and seldom suffer as severely because they have 30 percent more bone mass on the average and don't undergo the sudden drop in estrogen that occurs with menopause.

(Matt Clark, "The Calcium Craze," *Newsweek*)

33. Newspapers, radio, and television are essential for a democracy. They are the critical link between the people and their government. They provide information and analysis about policy issues, and they also sensitize policymakers to public opinion—which enables them to respond to the needs and desires of the population. Finally, the media play a critical role in reporting and evaluating the decisions of government.

(Stephen J. Wayne et al., *The Politics of American Government*)

★34. Nations are made in two ways, by the slow working of history or the galvanic force of ideas. Most nations are made the former way, emerging slowly from the mist of the past, gradually coalescing within concentric circles of shared sympathies, with an accretion of consensual institutions. But a few nations are formed and defined by the citizens' assent to a shared philosophy.

(George Will, "Lithuania and South Carolina")

35. Although the plane mirror is perhaps the oldest optical instrument known to man, it remains an important element in the modern arsenal of sophisticated optical devices. For example, the earth-moon laser-ranging experiments, initiated in 1969, rely on high-quality reflectors.

(Frank J. Blatt, *Principles of Physics,* 2nd ed.)

II. The following selections were originally submitted as letters to the editor of newspapers and magazines. Determine which of them can, with good reason, be considered arguments. In those that can, identify the conclusion.

★1. What this country needs is a return to the concept of swift and certain justice. If we need more courts, judges and prisons, then so be it. And as for capital punishment, I say let the punishment fit the crime. When criminals behave more like humans, then we can start to treat them more humanely. In the meantime, I would like to see the Night Stalkers of our society swiftly executed rather than coddled by our courts and prisons.

(John Pearson)

2. The big problem with computers in elementary schools isn't their minimal educational value but the fact that they often replace science in the budget and curriculum. Our local Parent Teachers Association is throwing away science equipment as fervently as it raises money for more computers. I use computers extensively in the college physics classes I teach, so I appreciate their value in communications and advanced computation. But in elementary schools, too much is being sacrificed so that children can have all those pricey beige boxes.

(Roger G. Tobin)

3. Is there any country in the world that worries more about its kids having fun in school, making lessons exciting and relevant, and then is more disappointed with the result than the United States? We think learning is like buying a car or smoking a cigarette. Just get into the thing or draw a breath and you will be effortlessly transported to lands of pleasure and excitement.

(Charles M. Breinin)

★4. After reading your cover story, I find that cable TV has simply flooded our airwaves with more sex, violence, and teen-age punk junk. Now our children can spend even less time studying and we can spend more time in blank-space stares at the idiot box. Cable would be fine with more educational channels—and fewer cheap thrills aimed at narrow-minded bubble brains.

(Jacqueline Murray)

5. In opposing obligatory prayer in the public schools, I am not deserting my god (and I would like to think of myself as a Christian). On the contrary, it is perfectly possible that I am thus serving my god, who I believe wants his children to pray to him of their own free will and not because some legislator, who may or may not be motivated by truly religious considerations, forces them to.

(Philip D. Walker)

6. My own son returned from his public elementary school with a book on dinosaurs loaned to him by his first-grade "science" teacher. It depicted the beasts as fire-breathing dragons and said the Bible informs us they were this way. God help us to achieve an educated and scientifically literate society, because these narrow-minded cretins won't.

(Bruce Strathdee)

★7. The poor quality of parenting and the lack in continuity of adult care provided to many U.S. children contribute to a passivity and a sense of helplessness that hobbles individuals for the remainder of their lives. Their subsequent unemployment, lack of education, and inability to make necessary life-style changes such as quitting an addiction can be attributed, in large part, to the helplessness they learned from childhood.

(William J. McCarthy)

8. Forty-one million Americans cannot afford health insurance in this time of global capitalism. At the same time, nine insurance executives earned more than $10 million last year, according to a recent study. If this is the celebrated triumph of capitalism over other forms of economic organization, what exactly did we win? Have we gained the world at the cost of our souls?

(Jason Reynolds)

9. The suggestion by sociobiologists that stepparent child abuse has evolutionary advantages is superficial. If there were evolutionary advantages to harming one's mate's offspring of a different parent, then by now there probably wouldn't be loving and generous stepparents around—and there are plenty. I know. I have a loving stepparent and am one.

(Ronald Cohen)

★10. The voting public is as full of bull as the politicians. As a result, we get the kind of officeholders we ask for. Show me a politician who will stand up and tell Americans the truth, and I'll show you a person who will never be elected.

(Huie Dixon)

III. The following statements represent conclusions for arguments. Each is expressed in the form of two alternatives. Select one of the alternatives for each conclusion, and then jot down several reasons that support it. Finally, incorporate your reasons into a written argument of at least 100 words that supports the conclusion. Include premise and conclusion indicators in some of your arguments, but not in all of them.

1. A constitutional amendment that outlaws flag burning should/should not be adopted.
2. Street drugs should/should not be legalized.
3. The death penalty should/should not be abolished.
4. Sanctions should/should not be imposed on students for using speech that is offensive to minorities.
5. Free health care should/should not be guaranteed to all citizens.
6. Same-sex marriages should/should not be recognized by the state.
7. The possession, ownership, and sale of handguns should/should not be outlawed.
8. Cigarettes should/should not be regulated as an addictive drug.
9. Affirmative action programs should/should not be abolished.
10. Doctors should/should not be allowed to assist terminally ill patients in committing suicide.

IV. Define the following terms:

argument from example   explanation
conditional statement   explanandum
antecedent   explanans
consequent   illustration
sufficient condition   expository passage
necessary condition

V. Answer "true" or "false" to the following statements:

1. Any passage that contains an argument must contain a claim that something is supported by evidence or reasons.

2. In an argument, the claim that something is supported by evidence or reasons is always explicit.

3. Passages that contain indicator words such as "thus," "since," and "because" are always arguments.

4. In deciding whether a passage contains an argument, we should always keep an eye out for indicator words and the presence of an inferential relationship between the statements.

5. Some expository passages can be correctly interpreted as arguments.

6. Some passages containing "for example" can be correctly interpreted as arguments.

7. In deciding whether an expository passage or an illustration should be interpreted as an argument, it helps to note whether the claim being developed or illustrated is one that is accepted by everyone.

8. Some conditional statements can be reexpressed to form arguments.

9. In an explanation, the explanandum usually describes an accepted matter of fact.

10. In an explanation, the explanans is the statement or group of statements that does the explaining.

VI. Fill in the blanks with "necessary" or "sufficient" to make the following statements true. After the blanks have been filled in, express the result in terms of conditional statements.

★1. Being a tiger is a _____ condition for being an animal.

2. Being an animal is a _____ condition for being a tiger.

3. Drinking water is a _____ condition for quenching one's thirst.

★4. Having a racket is a _____ condition for playing tennis.

5. Pulling the cork is a _____ condition for drinking an expensive bottle of wine.

6. Stepping on a cat's tail is a _____ condition for making the cat yowl.

★7. Burning leaves is a _____ condition for producing smoke.

8. Paying attention is a _____ condition for understanding a lecture.

9. Taking a swim in the North Sea is a _____ condition for cooling off.

★10. Opening a door is a _____ condition for crossing the threshold.

VII. Page through a book, magazine, or newspaper and find two arguments, one with indicator words, the other without. Copy the arguments as written, giving the appropriate reference. Then identify the premises and conclusion of each.

1.3   **Deduction and Induction**

In the previous section we saw that every argument involves an inferential claim—the claim that the conclusion is supposed to follow from the premises. The question we now address has to do with the strength of this claim. Just how strongly is the conclusion claimed to follow from the premises? If the conclusion is claimed to follow with strict certainty or necessity, the argument is said to be deductive; but if it is claimed to follow only probably, the argument is inductive.

Stated more precisely, a **deductive argument** is an argument incorporating the claim that it is *impossible* for the conclusion to be false given that the premises are true. Deductive arguments are those that involve necessary reasoning. On the other hand, an **inductive argument** is an argument incorporating the claim that it is *improbable* that the conclusion be false given that the premises are true. Inductive arguments involve probabilistic reasoning. Here are two examples:

> The meerkat is closely related to the suricat.
> The suricat thrives on beetle larvae.
> Therefore, probably the meerkat thrives on beetle larvae.

> The meerkat is a member of the mongoose family.
> All members of the mongoose family are carnivores.
> Therefore, it necessarily follows that the meerkat is a carnivore.

The first of these arguments is inductive, the second deductive.

In deciding whether an argument is inductive or deductive, we look to certain objective features of the argument. These features include (1) the occurrence of special indicator words, (2) the *actual* strength of the inferential link between premises and conclusion, and (3) the form or style of argumentation. However, we must acknowledge at the outset that many arguments in ordinary language are incomplete, and because of this, deciding whether the argument should best be interpreted as deductive or inductive may be impossible.

The occurrence of special indicator words is illustrated in the examples we just considered. The word "probably" in the conclusion of the first argument suggests that the argument should be taken as inductive, and the word "necessarily" in the conclusion of the second suggests that the second argument be taken as deductive. Additional inductive indicators are "improbable," "plausible," "implausible," "likely," "unlikely," and "reasonable to conclude." Additional deductive indicators are "certainly," "absolutely," and "definitely." (Note that the phrase "it must be the case that" is simply a conclusion indicator that can occur in either deductive or inductive argments.)

Inductive and deductive indicator words often suggest the correct interpretation. However, if they conflict with one of the other criteria (discussed shortly), we should probably ignore them. Arguers often use phrases such as "it certainly follows that" for rhetorical purposes to add impact to their conclusion and not to suggest that the argument be taken as deductive. Similarly, some arguers, not knowing the distinction between inductive and deductive, will claim to "deduce" a conclusion when their argument is more correctly interpreted as inductive.

The second factor that bears on our interpretation of an argument as inductive or deductive is the *actual* strength of the inferential link between premises and conclusion. If the conclusion actually does follow with strict necessity from the premises, the argument is clearly deductive. In such an argument it is impossible for the premises to be true and the conclusion false. On the other hand, if the conclusion does not follow with strict necessity but does follow probably, it is often best to consider the argument inductive. Examples:

> All entertainers are extroverts.
> David Letterman is an entertainer.
> Therefore, David Letterman is an extrovert.

> The vast majority of entertainers are extroverts.
> David Letterman is an entertainer.
> Therefore, David Letterman is an extrovert.

In the first example, the conclusion follows with strict necessity from the premises. If we assume that all entertainers are extroverts and that David Letterman is an entertainer, then it is impossible that David Letterman not be an extrovert. Thus, we should interpret this argument as deductive. In the second example, the conclusion does not follow from the premises with strict necessity, but it does follow with some degree of probability. If we assume that the premises are true, then based on that assumption it is probable that the conclusion is true. Thus, it is best to interpret the second argument as inductive.

Occasionally, an argument contains no special indicator words, and the conclusion does not follow either necessarily or probably from the premises; in other words, it does not follow at all. This situation points up the need for the third factor to be taken into account, which is the character or form of argumentation the arguer uses.

Deductive Argument Forms

Many arguments have a distinctive character or form that indicates that the premises are supposed to provide absolute support for the conclusion. Five examples of such forms or kinds of argumentation are arguments based on mathematics, arguments from definition, and categorical, hypothetical, and disjunctive syllogisms.

An **argument based on mathematics** is an argument in which the conclusion depends on some purely arithmetic or geometric computation or measurement. For example, a shopper might place two apples and three oranges into a paper bag and then conclude that the bag contains five pieces of fruit. Or a surveyor might measure a square piece of land and, after determining that it is 100 feet on each side, conclude that it contains 10,000 square feet. Since all arguments in pure mathematics are deductive, we can usually consider arguments that depend on mathematics to be deductive as well. A noteworthy exception, however, is arguments that depend on statistics. As we will see shortly, such arguments are usually best interpreted as inductive.

An **argument from definition** is an argument in which the conclusion is claimed to depend merely on the definition of some word or phrase used in the premise or conclusion. For example, someone might argue that because Claudia is mendacious, it follows that she tells lies, or that because a certain paragraph is prolix, it follows that it is excessively wordy. These arguments are deductive because their conclusions follow with necessity from the definitions of "mendacious" and "prolix."

A *syllogism*, in general, is an argument consisting of exactly two premises and one conclusion. Categorical syllogisms will be treated in greater depth in Chapter 5, but for now we will say that a **categorical syllogism** is a syllogism in which each statement begins with one of the words "all," "no," or "some." Example:

> All ancient forests are sources of wonder.
> Some ancient forests are targets of the timber industry.
> Therefore, some sources of wonder are targets of the timber industry.

Arguments such as these are nearly always best treated as deductive.

A **hypothetical syllogism** is a syllogism having a conditional statement for one or both of its premises. Examples:

> If estate taxes are abolished, then wealth will accumulate disproportionately.
> If wealth accumulates disproportionately, then democracy will be threatened.
> Therefore, if estate taxes are abolished, then democracy will be threatened.

> If Fox News is a propaganda machine, then it misleads its viewers.
> Fox News is a propaganda machine.
> Therefore, Fox News misleads its viewers.

Although certain forms of such arguments can sometimes be interpreted inductively, the deductive interpretation is usually the most appropriate.

A **disjunctive syllogism** is a syllogism having a disjunctive statement (i.e., an "either . . . or . . ." statement) for one of its premises. Example:

> Either global warming will be arrested, or hurricanes will become more intense.
> Global warming will not be arrested.
> Therefore, hurricanes will become more intense.

As with hypothetical syllogisms, such arguments are usually best taken as deductive. Hypothetical and disjunctive syllogisms will be treated in greater depth in Chapter 6.

Inductive Argument Forms

In general, inductive arguments are such that the content of the conclusion is in some way intended to "go beyond" the content of the premises. The premises of such an argument typically deal with some subject that is relatively familiar, and the conclusion then moves beyond this to a subject that is less familiar or that little is known about. Such an argument may take any of several forms: predictions about the future, arguments from analogy, inductive generalizations, arguments from authority, arguments based on signs, and causal inferences, to name just a few.

A **prediction** is an argument that proceeds from our knowledge of the past to a claim about the future. For example, someone might argue that because certain meteorological phenomena have been observed to develop over a certain region of central Missouri, a storm will occur there in six hours. Or again, one might argue that because certain fluctuations occurred in the prime interest rate on Friday, the value of the dollar will decrease against foreign currencies on Monday. Nearly everyone realizes that the future cannot be known with certainty; thus, whenever an argument makes a prediction about the future, one is usually justified in considering the argument inductive.

An **argument from analogy** is an argument that depends on the existence of an analogy, or similarity, between two things or states of affairs. Because of the existence of this analogy, a certain condition that affects the better-known thing or situation is concluded to affect the similar, lesser-known thing or situation. For example, someone might argue that because Christina's Porsche is a great handling car, it follows that Angela's Porsche must also be a great handling car. The argument depends on the existence of a similarity, or analogy, between the two cars. The certitude attending such an inference is probabilistic at best.

A **generalization** is an argument that proceeds from the knowledge of a selected sample to some claim about the whole group. Because the members of the sample have a certain characteristic, it is argued that all the members of the group have that same characteristic. For example, one might argue that because three oranges selected from a certain crate were especially tasty and juicy, all the oranges from that crate are especially tasty and juicy. Or again, one might argue that because six out of a total of nine members sampled from a certain labor union intend to vote for Johnson for union president, two-thirds of the entire membership intend to vote for Johnson. These examples illustrate the use of statistics in inductive argumentation.

An **argument from authority** is an argument that concludes something is true because a presumed expert or witness has said that it is. For example, a person might argue that earnings for Hewlett-Packard Corporation will be up in the coming quarter because of a statement to that effect by an investment counselor. Or a lawyer might argue that Mack the Knife committed the murder because an eyewitness testified to that effect under oath. Because the investment counselor and the eyewitness could be either mistaken or lying, such arguments are essentially probabilistic.

An **argument based on signs** is an argument that proceeds from the knowledge of a sign to a claim about the thing or situation that the sign symbolizes. The word "sign," as it is used here, means any kind of message (usually visual) produced by an intelligent being. For example, when driving on an unfamiliar highway one might see a sign indicating that the road makes several sharp turns one mile ahead. Based on this information, one might argue that the road does indeed make several sharp turns one mile ahead. Because the sign might be misplaced or in error about the turns, the conclusion is only probable.

A **causal inference** is an argument that proceeds from knowledge of a cause to a claim about an effect, or, conversely, from knowledge of an effect to a claim about a cause. For example, from the knowledge that a bottle of wine had been accidentally left in the freezer overnight, someone might conclude that it had frozen (cause to effect). Conversely, after tasting a piece of chicken and finding it dry and tough, one might conclude that it had been overcooked (effect to cause). Because specific instances of cause and effect can never be known with absolute certainty, one may usually interpret such arguments as inductive.

Further Considerations

It should be noted that the various subspecies of inductive arguments listed here are not intended to be mutually exclusive. Overlaps can and do occur. For example, many causal inferences that proceed from cause to effect also qualify as predictions. The purpose of this survey is not to demarcate in precise terms the various forms of induction but rather to provide guidelines for distinguishing induction from deduction.

Keeping this in mind, we should take care not to confuse arguments in geometry, which are always deductive, with arguments from analogy or inductive generalizations. For example, an argument concluding that a triangle has a certain attribute (such as a right angle) because another triangle, with which it is congruent, also has that attribute might be mistaken for an argument from analogy. Similarly, an argument that concludes that all triangles have a certain attribute (such as angles totaling two right angles) because any particular triangle has that attribute might be mistaken for an inductive generalization. Arguments such as these, however, are always deductive, because the conclusion follows necessarily and with complete certainty from the premises.

One broad classification of arguments not listed in this survey is scientific arguments. Arguments that occur in science can be either inductive or deductive, depending on the circumstances. In general, arguments aimed at the *discovery* of a law of nature are usually considered inductive. Suppose, for example, that we want to discover a law that governs the time required for a falling body to strike the earth. We drop bodies of various weights from various heights and measure the time it takes them to fall. Comparing our measurements, we notice that the time is approximately proportional to the square root of the distance. From this we conclude that the time required for any body to fall is proportional to the square root of the distance through which it falls. Such an argument is best interpreted as an inductive generalization.

Another type of argument that occurs in science has to do with the *application* of known laws to specific circumstances. Arguments of this sort are often considered to be deductive—but only with certain reservations. Suppose, for example, that we want to apply Boyle's law for ideal gases to a container of gas in our laboratory. Boyle's law states that the pressure exerted by a gas on the walls of its container is inversely proportional to the volume. Applying this law, we conclude that when we reduce the volume of our laboratory sample by half, the pressure will double. Considered purely as a mathematical computation, this argument is deductive. But if we acknowledge the fact that the conclusion pertains to the future and the possibility that Boyle's law may not work in the future, then the argument is best considered inductive.

A final point needs to be made about the distinction between inductive and deductive arguments. There is a tradition extending back to the time of Aristotle that holds that inductive arguments are those that proceed from the particular to the general, while deductive arguments are those that proceed from the general to the particular. (A **particular statement** is one that makes a claim about one or more particular members of a class, while a **general statement** makes a claim about *all* the members of a class.) It is true, of course, that many inductive and deductive arguments do work in this way; but this fact should not be used as a criterion for distinguishing induction from deduction. As a matter of fact, there are deductive arguments that proceed from the general to the general, from the particular to the particular, and from the particular to the general, as well as from the general to the particular; and there are inductive arguments that do the same. For example, here is a deductive argument that proceeds from the particular to the general:

> Three is a prime number.
> Five is a prime number.
> Seven is a prime number.
> Therefore, all odd numbers between two and eight are prime numbers.

And here is one that proceeds from the particular to the particular:

> Gabriel is a wolf.
> Gabriel has a tail.
> Therefore, Gabriel's tail is the tail of a wolf.

Here is an inductive argument that proceeds from the general to the particular:

> All emeralds previously found have been green.
> Therefore, the next emerald to be found will be green.

The other varieties are easy to construct. Thus, the progression from particular to general, and vice versa, cannot be used as a criterion for distinguishing induction and deduction.

Summary

To distinguish deductive arguments from inductive arguments, we attempt to evaluate the strength of the argument's inferential claim—how strongly the conclusion is claimed to follow from the premises. This claim is an objective feature of an argument, and it may or may not be related to the subjective intentions of the arguer.

To interpret an argument's inferential claim we look at three factors: special indicator words, the actual strength of the inferential link between premises and conclusion, and the character or form of argumentation. Given that we have more than one factor to look at, it is possible in a single argument for the occurrence of two of these factors to conflict with each other, leading to opposite interpretations. For example, in drawing a conclusion to a categorical syllogism (which is clearly deductive), an arguer might say "It probably follows that . . ." (which suggests induction). To help alleviate this conflict we can list the factors in order of importance:

1. Arguments in which the premises provide absolute support for the conclusion. Such arguments are always deductive.

2. Arguments having a specific deductive character or form (e.g., categorical syllogism). This factor is often of equal importance to the first, and, when present, it provides a clear-cut indication that the argument is deductive.

3. Arguments having a specific inductive character or form (e.g., a prediction). Arguments of this sort are nearly always best interpreted as inductive.

4. Arguments containing inductive indicator language (e.g., "It probably follows that . . .). Since arguers rarely try to make their argument appear weaker than it really is, such language can usually be trusted. But if this language conflicts with one of the first two factors, it should be ignored.

5. Arguments containing deductive indicator language (e.g., "It necessarily follows that . . .). Arguers occasionally use such language for rhetorical purposes, to make their argument appear stronger than it really is, so such language should be evaluated carefully.

6. Arguments in which the premises provide only probable support for the conclusion. This is the least important factor, and if it conflicts with any of the earlier ones, it should probably be ignored.

Unfortunately, many arguments in ordinary language are incomplete, so it often happens that none of these factors are clearly present. Determining the inductive or deductive character of such arguments may be impossible.

EXERCISE 1.3

I. Determine whether the following arguments are best interpreted as being inductive or deductive. Also state the criteria you use in reaching your decision (i.e., the presence of indicator words, the nature of the inferential link between premises and conclusion, or the character or form of argumentation).

★1. Because triangle A is congruent with triangle B, and triangle A is isosceles, it follows that triangle B is isosceles.

2. The plaque on the leaning tower of Pisa says that Galileo performed experiments there with falling objects. It must be the case that Galileo did indeed perform those experiments there.

3. The rainfall in Seattle has been more than 15 inches every year for the past thirty years. Therefore, the rainfall next year will probably be more than 15 inches.

★4. No e-mail messages are eloquent creations. Some love letters are eloquent creations. Therefore, some love letters are not e-mail messages.

5. Amoco, Exxon, and Texaco are all listed on the New York Stock Exchange. It must be the case that all major American oil companies are listed on the New York Stock Exchange.

6. The longer a pendulum is, the longer it takes to swing. Therefore, when the pendulum of a clock is lengthened, the clock slows down.

★7. Paying off terrorists in exchange for hostages is not a wise policy, since such action will only lead them to take more hostages in the future.

8. The Matterhorn is higher than Mount Whitney, and Mount Whitney is higher than Mount Rainier. The obvious conclusion is that the Matterhorn is higher than Mount Rainier.

9. Although both front and rear doors were found open after the burglary, there were pry marks around the lock on the rear door and deposits of mud near the threshold. It must be the case that the thief entered through the rear door and left through the front.

★10. The *Encylopaedia Britannica* has an article on symbiosis. The *Encyclopedia Americana*, like the *Britannica*, is an excellent reference work. Therefore, the *Americana* probably also has an article on symbiosis.

11. Cholesterol is endogenous with humans. Therefore, it is manufactured inside the human body.

12. Either classical culture originated in Greece, or it originated in Egypt. Classical culture did not originate in Egypt. Therefore, classical culture originated in Greece.

★13. World-renowned physicist Stephen Hawking says that the condition of the universe at the instant of the Big Bang was more highly ordered than it is today. In view of Hawking's stature in the scientific community, we should conclude that this description of the universe is correct.

14. If Alexander the Great died from typhoid fever, then he became infected in India. Alexander the Great did die from typhoid fever. Therefore, he became infected in India.

15. Crater Lake, the deepest lake in the United States, was caused by a huge volcanic eruption 7700 years ago. Since human beings have lived around the mountain for more than 10,000 years, it is likely that people witnessed that eruption.

(National Park Service, "Crater Lake—Its History")

★16. Each element, such as hydrogen and iron, has a set of gaps—wavelengths that it absorbs rather than radiates. So if those wavelengths are missing from the spectrum, you know that that element is present in the star you are observing.

(Rick Gore, "Eyes of Science")

17. Because the apparent daily movement which is common to both the planets and the fixed stars is seen to travel from the east to the west, but the far slower single movements of the single planets travel in the opposite direction from west to east, it is therefore certain that these movements cannot depend on the common movement of the world but should be assigned to the planets themselves.

(Johannes Kepler, *Epitomy of Copernican Astronomy*)

18. Reserves of coal in the United States have an energy equivalent 33 times that of oil and natural gas. On a worldwide basis the multiple is about 10. By shifting to a coal-based economy, we could satisfy our energy requirements for at least a century, probably longer.

(William L. Masterson and Emil J. Slowinski, *Principles of Chemistry*)

★19. When the Romans occupied England, coal was burned. Since coal produces quite a bit of soot and sulfur dioxide, there must have been days almost 2000 years ago when the air in the larger towns was badly polluted.

(Stanley Gedzelman, *The Science and Wonders of the Atmosphere*)

20. The graphical method for solving a system of equations is an approximation, since reading the point of intersection depends on the accuracy with which the lines are drawn and on the ability to interpret the coordinates of the point.

(Karl J. Smith and Patrick J. Boyle, *Intermediate Algebra for College Students*)

21. That [the moons of Jupiter] revolve in unequal circles is manifestly deduced from the fact that at the longest elongation from Jupiter it is never possible to see two of these moons in conjunction, whereas in the vicinity of Jupiter they are found united two, three, and sometimes all four together.

(Galileo Galilei, *The Starry Messenger*)

★22. Lenses function by refracting light at their surfaces. Consequently, their action depends not only on the shape of the lens surfaces, but also on the indices of refraction of the lens material and the surrounding medium.

(Frank J. Blatt, *Principles of Physics*, 2nd ed.)

23. Given present growth rates in underdeveloped countries, the limited practice of birth control, and the difficulty of slowing the current growth momentum, it can be said with virtual certainty that none of the people now reading this book will ever live in a world where the population is not growing.

(J. John Palen, *Social Problems*)

24. The interpretation of the laws is the proper and peculiar province of the courts. A constitution is, in fact, and must be regarded by the judges, as a fundamental law. It therefore belongs to them to ascertain its meaning, as well as the meaning of any particular act proceeding from the legislative body.

(Alexander Hamilton, *Federalist Papers*, No. 78)

★25. The Simpson incident had shown me that a dog was kept in the stables, and yet, though someone had been in and had fetched out a horse, he had not barked enough to arouse the two lads in the loft. Obviously the midnight visitor was someone whom the dog knew well.

(A. Conan Doyle, *Memoirs of Sherlock Holmes*)

26. Eternity is simultaneously whole. But time has a before and an after. Therefore time and eternity are not the same thing.

(Thomas Aquinas, *Summa Theologica*)

27. Ordinary things that we encounter every day are electrically neutral. Therefore, since negatively charged electrons are a part of everything, positively charged particles must also exist in all matter.

(James E. Brady and Gerard E. Humiston, *General Chemistry*)

★28. Animals that live on plant foods must eat large quantities of vegetation, and this consumes much of their time. Meat eaters, by contrast, have no need to eat so much or so often. Consequently, meat-eating hominines [early humans] may have had more leisure time available to explore and manipulate their environment; like lions and leopards, they would have time to spend lying around and playing.

(William A. Haviland, *Cultural Anthropology,* 8th ed.)

29. [Psychologists] Wirtshafter and Davis noted that the glycerol content of the blood is related to the size of the fat cells [in the body]. Since the size of the fat cells would indicate something about the amount of stored fats, increases in blood glycerol should indicate increases in body weight.

(Herbert L. Petri, *Motivation: Theory and Research,* 2nd ed.)

30. Because the moon moves relative to the earth so that it returns to the same position overhead after about 25 hours, there are two high and two low tides at any point every 25 hours.

(Douglas C. Giancoli, *The Ideas of Physics,* 3rd ed.)

II. Define the following terms:

deductive argument	argument from analogy
inductive argument	generalization
argument based on mathematics	prediction
argument from definition	argument from authority
categorical syllogism	argument based on signs
hypothetical syllogism	causal inference
disjunctive syllogism	particular statement
	general statement

III. Answer "true" or "false" to the following statements:

1. In an inductive argument, it is intended that the conclusion contain more information than the premises.

2. In a deductive argument, the conclusion is not supposed to contain more information than the premises.

3. The form of argumentation the arguer uses may allow one to determine whether an argument is inductive or deductive.

4. The actual strength of the link between premises and conclusion may allow one to determine whether an argument is inductive or deductive.

5. A geometrical proof is an example of an inductive argument.

6. Most arguments based on statistical reasoning are deductive.

7. If the conclusion of an argument follows merely from the definition of a word used in a premise, the argument is deductive.

8. An argument that draws a conclusion about a thing based on that thing's similarity to something else is a deductive argument.

9. An argument that draws a conclusion that something is true because some-one has said that it is, is a deductive argument.

10. An argument that presents two alternatives and eliminates one, leaving the other as the conclusion, is an inductive argument.

11. An argument that proceeds from knowledge of a cause to knowledge of an effect is an inductive argument.

12. If an argument contains the phrase "it definitely follows that," then we know for certain that the argument is deductive.

13. An argument that predicts what will happen in the future, based on what has happened in the past, is an inductive argument.

14. Inductive arguments always proceed from the particular to the general.

15. Deductive arguments always proceed from the general to the particular.

IV. Page through a book, magazine, or newspaper and find two arguments, one inductive and the other deductive. Copy the arguments as written, giving the appropriate reference. Then identify the premises and conclusion of each.

1.4   Validity, Truth, Soundness, Strength, Cogency

This section introduces the central ideas and terminology required to evaluate arguments. We have seen that every argument makes two basic claims: a claim that evidence or reasons exist and a claim that the alleged evidence or reasons support something (or that something follows from the alleged evidence or reasons). The first is a factual claim, the second an inferential claim. The evaluation of every argument centers on the evaluation of these two claims. The more important of the two is the inferential claim, because if the premises fail to support the conclusion (that is, if the reasoning is bad), an argument is worthless. Thus we will always test the inferential claim first, and only if the premises do support the conclusion will we test the factual claim (that is, the claim that the premises present genuine evidence, or are true). The material that follows considers first deductive arguments and then inductive.

Deductive Arguments

The previous section defined a deductive argument as one incorporating the claim that it is impossible for the conclusion to be false given that the premises are true. If this claim is true, the argument is said to be valid. Thus, a **valid deductive argument** is an argument in which it is impossible for the conclusion to be false given that the premises are true. In these arguments the conclusion follows with strict necessity from the premises. Conversely, an **invalid deductive argument** is a deductive argument in which it *is* possible for the conclusion to be false given that the premises are true. In these arguments the conclusion does not follow with strict necessity from the premises, even though it is claimed to.

An immediate consequence of these definitions is that there is no middle ground between valid and invalid. There are no arguments that are "almost" valid and "almost" invalid. If the conclusion follows with strict necessity from the premises, the argument is valid; if not, it is invalid.

To test an argument for validity we begin by assuming that all the premises are true, and then we determine if it is possible, in light of that assumption, for the conclusion to be false. Here is an example:

> All television networks are media companies.
> NBC is a television network.
> Therefore, NBC is a media company.

In this argument both premises are actually true, so it is easy to *assume* that they are true. Next we determine, in light of this assumption, if it is possible for the conclusion to be false. Clearly this is not possible. If NBC is included in the group of television networks (second premise) and if the group of television networks is included in the group of media companies (first premise), it necessarily follows that NBC is included in the group of media companies (conclusion). In other words, assuming the premises to be true and the conclusion false entails a strict *contradiction*. Thus, the argument is valid.

Here is another example:

> All automakers are computer manufacturers.
> United Airlines is an automaker.
> Therefore, United Airlines is a computer manufacturer.

In this argument, both premises are actually false, but it is easy to assume that they are true. Every automaker could have a corporate division that manufactures computers. Also, in addition to flying airplanes, United Airlines could make cars. Next, in light of these assumptions, we determine if it is possible for the conclusion to be false. Again, we see that this is not possible, by the same reasoning as the previous example. Assuming the premises to be true and the conclusion false entails a contradiction. Thus, the argument is valid.

Another example:

> All banks are financial institutions.
> Wells Fargo is a financial institution.
> Therefore, Wells Fargo is a bank.

As in the first example, both premises of this argument are true, so it is easy to assume they are true. Next we determine, in light of this assumption, if it is possible for the conclusion to be false. In this case it *is* possible. If banks were included in one part of the group of financial institutions and Wells Fargo were included in another part, then Wells Fargo would *not* be a bank. In other words, assuming the premises to be true and the conclusion false does not involve any contradiction, and so the argument is invalid.

In addition to illustrating the basic idea of validity, these examples suggest an important point about validity and truth. In general, validity is not something that is uniformly determined by the actual truth or falsity of the premises and conclusion. Both the NBC example and the Wells Fargo example have actually true premises and an actually true conclusion, yet one is valid and the other invalid. The United Airlines example has actually false premises and an actually false conclusion, yet the argument is

Table 1.1 Deductive Arguments

	Valid	**Invalid**
True premises **True** conclusion	All wines are beverages. Chardonnay is a wine. Therefore, chardonnay is a beverage. [sound]	All wines are beverages. Chardonnay is a beverage. Therefore, chardonnay is a wine. [unsound]
True premises **False** conclusion	None exist.	All wines are beverages. Ginger ale is a beverage. Therefore, ginger ale is a wine. [unsound]
False premises **True** conclusion	All wines are soft drinks. Ginger ale is a wine. Therefore, ginger ale is a soft drink. [unsound]	All wines are whiskeys. Chardonnay is a whiskey. Therefore, chardonnay is a wine. [unsound]
False premises **False** conclusion	All wines are whiskeys. Ginger ale is a wine. Therefore, ginger ale is a whiskey. [unsound]	All wines are whiskeys. Ginger ale is a whiskey. Therefore, ginger ale is a wine. [unsound]

valid. Rather, validity is something that is determined by the *relationship* between premises and conclusion. The question is not whether the premises and conclusion are true or false, but whether the premises *support* the conclusion. In the examples of valid arguments the premises do support the conclusion, and in the invalid case they do not.

Nevertheless, there is *one* arrangement of truth and falsity in the premises and conclusion that does determine the issue of validity. Any deductive argument having actually true premises and an actually false conclusion is invalid. The reasoning behind this fact is fairly obvious. If the premises are actually true and the conclusion is actually false, then it certainly is *possible* for the premises to be true and the conclusion false. Thus, by the definition of invalidity, the argument is invalid.

The idea that any deductive argument having actually true premises and a false conclusion is invalid may be the most important point in all of deductive logic. The entire system of deductive logic would be quite useless if it accepted as valid any inferential process by which a person could start with truth in the premises and arrive at falsity in the conclusion.

Table 1.1 presents examples of deductive arguments that illustrate the various combinations of truth and falsity in the premises and conclusion. In the examples having false premises, both premises are false, but it is easy to construct other examples having only one false premise. When examining this table, note that the only combination of truth and falsity that does not allow for *both* valid and invalid arguments is true premises and false conclusion. As we have just seen, any argument having this combination is necessarily invalid.

The relationship between the validity of a deductive argument and the truth or falsity of its premises and conclusion, as illustrated in Table 1.1, is summarized as follows:

Premises	Conclusion	Validity
T	T	?
T	F	Invalid
F	T	?
F	F	?

A **sound argument** is a deductive argument that is *valid* and has *all true premises.* Both conditions must be met for an argument to be sound; if either is missing the argument is unsound. Thus, an **unsound argument** is a deductive argument that is invalid, has one or more false premises, or both. Because a valid argument is one such that it is impossible for the premises to be true and the conclusion false, and because a sound argument does in fact have true premises, it follows that every sound argument, by definition, will have a true conclusion as well. A sound argument, therefore, is what is meant by a "good" deductive argument in the fullest sense of the term.

In connection with this definition of soundness, a single proviso is required: For an argument to be unsound, the false premise or premises must actually be needed to support the conclusion. An argument with a conclusion that is validly supported by true premises but with a superfluous false premise would still be sound. By similar reasoning, no addition of a false premise to an originally sound argument can make the argument unsound. Such a premise would be superfluous and should not be considered part of the argument. Analogous remarks, incidentally, extend to induction.

Inductive Arguments

Section 1.3 defined an inductive argument as one incorporating the claim that it is improbable that the conclusion be false given that the premises are true. If this claim is true, the argument is said to be strong. Thus, a **strong inductive argument** is an inductive argument in which it is improbable that the conclusion be false given that the premises are true. In such arguments, the conclusion does in fact follow probably from the premises. Conversely, a **weak inductive argument** is an argument in which the conclusion does not follow probably from the premises, even though it is claimed to.

The procedure for testing the strength of inductive arguments runs parallel to the procedure for deduction. First we assume the premises are true, and then we determine whether, based on that assumption, the conclusion is probably true. Example:

> All dinosaur bones discovered to this day have been at least 50 million years old. Therefore, probably the next dinosaur bone to be found will be at least 50 million years old.

In this argument the premise is actually true, so it is easy to assume that it is true. Based on that assumption, the conclusion is probably true, so the argument is strong. Here is another example:

> All meteorites found to this day have contained sugar. Therefore, probably the next meteorite to be found will contain sugar.

The premise of this argument is obviously false. But if we assume the premise is true, then based on that assumption, the conclusion would probably be true. Thus, the argument is strong.

The next example is an argument from analogy:

> When a lighted match is slowly dunked into water, the flame is snuffed out. But gasoline is a liquid, just like water. Therefore, when a lighted match is slowly dunked into gasoline, the flame will be snuffed out.

In this argument the premises are actually true and the conclusion is probably false. Thus, if we assume the premises are true, then, based on that assumption, it is not probable that the conclusion is true. Thus, the argument is weak.

Another example:

> During the past fifty years, inflation has consistently reduced the value of the American dollar. Therefore, industrial productivity will probably increase in the years ahead.

In this argument, the premise is actually true and the conclusion is probably true in the actual world, but the probability of the conclusion is in no way based on the assumption that the premise is true. Because there is no direct connection between inflation and increased industrial productivity, the premise is irrelevant to the conclusion and it provides no probabilistic support for it. The conclusion is probably true independently of the premise. As a result, the argument is weak.

This last example illustrates an important distinction between strong inductive arguments and valid deductive arguments. As we will see in later chapters, if the conclusion of a deductive argument is necessarily true independently of the premises, the argument is still considered valid. But if the conclusion of an inductive argument is probably true independently of the premises, the argument is weak.

These four examples show that in general the strength or weakness of an inductive argument results not from the actual truth or falsity of the premises and conclusion, but from the probabilistic support the premises give to the conclusion. The dinosaur argument has a true premise and a probably true conclusion, and the meteorite argument has a false premise and a probably false conclusion; yet both are strong because the premise of each provides probabilistic support for the conclusion. The industrial productivity argument has a true premise and a probably true conclusion, but the argument is weak because the premise provides no probabilistic support for the conclusion. As in the evaluation of deductive arguments, the only arrangement of truth and

Table 1.2 Inductive Arguments

	Strong	**Weak**
True premise **Probably true conclusion**	All previous U.S. presidents were older than 40. Therefore, probably the next U.S. president will be older than 40. [cogent]	A few U.S. presidents were lawyers. Therefore, probably the next U.S. president will be older than 40. [uncogent]
True premise **Probably false conclusion**	None exist	A few U.S. presidents were unmarried. Therefore, probably the next U.S. president will be unmarried [uncogent]
False premise **Probably true conclusion**	All previous U.S. presidents were TV debaters. Therefore, probably the next U.S. president will be a TV debater. [uncogent]	A few U.S. presidents were dentists. Therefore, probably the next U.S. president will be a TV debater. [uncogent]
False premise **Probably false conclusion**	All previous U.S. presidents died in office. Therefore, probably the next U.S. president will die in office. [uncogent]	A few U.S. presidents were dentists. Therefore, probably the next U.S. president will be a dentist. [uncogent]

falsity that establishes anything is true premises and probably false conclusion (as in the lighted match argument). Any inductive argument having true premises and a probably false conclusion is weak.

Table 1.2 presents the various possibilities of truth and falsity in the premises and conclusion of inductive arguments. Note that the only arrangement of truth and falsity that is missing for strong arguments is true premises and probably false conclusion.

The relationship between the strength of an inductive argument and the truth or falsity of its premises and conclusion, as illustrated in Table 1.2, is summarized as follows:

Premises	Conclusion	Strength
T	prob. T	?
T	prob. F	Weak
F	prob. T	?
F	prob. F	?

Unlike the validity and invalidity of deductive arguments, the strength and weakness of inductive arguments admit of degrees. To be considered strong, an inductive argument must have a conclusion that is more probable than improbable. In other words, given that the premises are true, the likelihood that the conclusion is true must be more than 50 percent, and as the probability increases, the argument becomes stronger. For this purpose, consider the following pair of arguments:

> This barrel contains 100 apples.
> Three apples selected at random were found to be ripe.
> Therefore, probably all 100 apples are ripe.

> This barrel contains 100 apples.
> Eighty apples selected at random were found to be ripe.
> Therefore, probably all 100 apples are ripe.

The first argument is weak and the second is strong. However, the first is not absolutely weak nor the second absolutely strong. Both arguments would be strengthened or weakened by the random selection of a larger or smaller sample. For example, if the size of the sample in the second argument were reduced to seventy apples, the argument would be weakened. The incorporation of additional premises into an inductive argument will also generally tend to strengthen or weaken it. For example, if the premise "One unripe apple that had been found earlier was removed" were added to either argument, the argument would be weakened.

A **cogent argument** is an inductive argument that is *strong* and has *all true premises;* if either condition is missing, the argument is uncogent. Thus, an **uncogent argument** is an inductive argument that is weak, has one or more false premises, or both. A cogent argument is the inductive analogue of a sound deductive argument and is what is meant by a "good" inductive argument without qualification. Because the conclusion of a cogent argument is genuinely supported by true premises, it follows that the conclusion of every cogent argument is probably true.

There is a difference, however, between sound and cogent arguments in regard to the true premise requirement. In a sound argument it is necessary only that the premises be true and nothing more. Given such premises and good reasoning, a true conclusion is guaranteed. In a cogent argument, on the other hand, the premises must not only be true, but they must also not ignore some important piece of evidence that entails a quite different conclusion. This is called the *total evidence requirement.* As an illustration of the need for it, consider the following argument:

> Swimming in the Caribbean is usually lots of fun. Today the water is warm, the surf is gentle, and on this beach there are no dangerous currents. Therefore, it would be fun to go swimming here now.

If the premises reflect all the important factors, then the argument is cogent. But if they ignore the fact that several large dorsal fins are cutting through the water (suggesting sharks), then obviously the argument is not cogent. Thus, for cogency the premises must not only be true but also not overlook some important fact that requires a different conclusion.

Summary

For both deductive and inductive arguments, two separate questions need to be answered: (1) Do the premises support the conclusion? (2) Are all the premises true?

To answer the first question we begin by *assuming* the premises to be true. Then, for deductive arguments we determine whether, in light of this assumption, it *necessarily* follows that the conclusion is true. If it does, the argument is valid; if not, it is invalid. For inductive arguments we determine whether it *probably* follows that the conclusion is true. If it does, the argument is strong; if not, it is weak. For inductive arguments we keep in mind the requirements that the premises actually support the conclusion and that they not ignore important evidence. Finally, if the argument is either valid or strong, we turn to the second question and determine whether the premises are actually true. If all the premises are true, the argument is sound (in the case of deduction) or cogent (in the case of induction). All invalid deductive arguments are unsound, and all weak inductive arguments are uncogent.

The various alternatives open to statements and arguments may be diagrammed as follows. Note that in logic one never speaks of an argument as being "true" or "false," and one never speaks of a statement as being "valid," "invalid," "strong," or "weak."

■ EMINENT LOGICIANS

© Araldo de Luca/CORBIS

Chrysippus 280–206 B.C.

Chrysippus was born in Soli, a city located in the south east coast of Asia Minor. Early in life he moved to Athens, where he studied under the Stoic philosopher Cleanthes, who in turn was a student of Zeno of Citium, the founder of Stoicism. Upon Cleanthes' death in 232 B.C., Chrysippus took over as leader of the school, and he produced over 700 treatises that systematized Stoic teaching. All of these works have been lost, but fragments survive in the writings of Cicero, Seneca, and others. Because of his extraordinary contribution, Chrysippus is considered to be the second founder of Stoicism.

Stoicism derives its name from the Greek word *stoa*, which means porch; stoic philosophers used to gather on a porch in the Agora (marketplace) in Athens to discuss their views. The stoics prized the virtue of self-sufficiency, and they emphasized the importance of not allowing oneself to be carried away by emotions or passions such as fear or love. Emotions are considered to be false judgments about the goodness or badness of something . The proper therapy for those victimized by emotions is to persuade them that these judgments are indeed false because they constitute obstacles to true happiness.

Chrysippus is often considered to be the originator of propositional logic. Unlike Aristotelian logic, where the fundamental components are terms, in propositional logic the fundamental components are whole propositions or statements. Aristotle had overlooked this kind of logic, but his close friend and successor Theophrastus worked out some of the logic of the pure hypothetical syllogism (If *A* then *B*, if *B* then *C*; therefore if *A* then *C*). Also, Philo of Megara introduced the truth functional interpretation of the material conditional (If *A*, then *B*). Beginning at this point, Chrysippus advanced propositional logic to a high level of development.

Chrysippus divided propositions into simple and compound, and he introduced a set of connectives that were used to produce compound propositions from one or more simple propositions. The compound propositions included negation, conjunction, exclusive disjunction, and implication, and Chrysippus showed how the truth value of a compound statement is a function of the truth values of its simple components. Chrysippus also introduced a set of rules of inference including what is today called *modus ponens, modus tollens,* disjunctive syllogism, and a rule similar to De Morgan's rule. Finally, he introduced the theory of natural deduction by which the conclusion of an argument can be derived from its premises through a series of discrete steps.

The broader philosophy of Chrysippus is characterized by monism and determinism. While most of us think that the universe is made up of millions of discrete entities, Chrysippus argued that in fact only one substance exists, and what appear to be individual substances are really parts of this one primary substance. Furthermore, everything that occurs is strictly governed by fate. Yet, in the face of this rigid causal determinism Chrysippus held that humans are responsible for their actions, and he tried in many ways to prove that the two viewpoints are in fact compatible with each other.

EXERCISE 1.4

I. The following arguments are deductive. Determine whether each is valid or invalid, and note the relationship between your answer and the truth or falsity of the premises and conclusion. Finally, determine whether the argument is sound or unsound.

★1. Since *Moby Dick* was written by Shakespeare, and *Moby Dick* is a science fiction novel, it follows that Shakespeare wrote a science fiction novel.

2. Since London is north of Paris and south of Edinburgh, it follows that Paris is south of Edinburgh.

3. If George Washington was beheaded, then George Washington died. George Washington died. Therefore, George Washington was beheaded.

★4. The longest river in South America is the Amazon, and the Amazon flows through Brazil. Therefore, the longest river in South America flows through Brazil.

5. Since the Spanish-American War occurred before the U.S. Civil War, and the U.S. Civil War occurred after the Korean War, it follows that the Spanish-American War occurred before the Korean War.

6. The Empire State Building is taller than the Statue of Liberty, and the Statue of Liberty is taller than the Eiffel Tower. Therefore, the Empire State Building is taller than the Eiffel Tower.

★7. All leopards with lungs are carnivores. Therefore, all leopards are carnivores.

8. Chicago is a city in Michigan and Michigan is part of the United States. Therefore, Chicago is a city in the United States.

9. If Senator Hillary Clinton represents California, then she represents a western state. Hillary Clinton does not represent a western state. Therefore, she does not represent California.

★10. Every province in Canada has exactly one city as its capital. Therefore, since there are thirty provinces in Canada, there are thirty provincial capitals.

11. Since the Department of Defense Building outside Washington, D.C., has the shape of a hexagon, it follows that it has seven sides.

12. Since Winston Churchill was English, and Winston Churchill was a famous statesman, we may conclude that at least one Englishman was a famous statesman.

★13. Since some fruits are green, and some fruits are apples, it follows that some fruits are green apples.

14. All physicians are individuals who have earned degrees in political science, and some lawyers are physicians. Therefore, some lawyers are persons who have earned degrees in political science.

15. The United States Congress has more members than there are days in the year. Therefore, at least two members of Congress have the same birthday.

II. The following arguments are inductive. Determine whether each is strong or weak, and note the relationship between your answer and the truth or falsity of the premise(s) and conclusion. Then determine whether each argument is cogent or uncogent.

★1. The grave marker at Arlington National Cemetery says that John F. Kennedy is buried there. It must be the case that Kennedy really is buried in that cemetery.

2. The ebb and flow of the tides has been occurring every day for millions of years. But nothing lasts forever. Therefore, probably the motion of the tides will die out within a few years.

3. The vast majority of Rose Bowl games (in Pasadena, California) have been played in freezing cold weather. Therefore, probably the next Rose Bowl game will be played in freezing cold weather.

★4. Franklin Delano Roosevelt said that we have nothing to fear but fear itself. Therefore, women have no reason to fear serial rapists.

5. Most popular film stars are millionaires. Lindsay Lohan is a popular film star. Therefore, probably Lindsay Lohan is a millionaire.

6. Constructing the great pyramid at Giza required lifting massive stone blocks to great heights. Probably the ancient Egyptians had some antigravity device to accomplish this feat.

★7. People have been listening to rock and roll music for over a hundred years. Probably people will still be listening to it a year from now.

8. Paleontologists have unearthed the fossilized bones of huge reptiles, which we have named dinosaurs. Tests indicate that these bones are more than 50 million years old. Therefore, probably dinosaurs really did roam the earth 50 million years ago.

9. The Declaration of Independence says that all men are endowed by their creator with certain unalienable rights. Therefore it probably follows that a creator exists.

★10. Coca-Cola is an extremely popular soft drink. Therefore, probably someone, somewhere, is drinking a Coke right this minute.

11. Every map of the United States shows that Alabama is situated on the Pacific coast. Therefore, Alabama must be a western state.

12. When Neil Armstrong landed on the moon, he left behind a gold-plated Schwinn bicycle, which he used to ride around on the moon's surface. Probably that bicycle is still up there on the moon.

★13. The African American athlete LaDainian Tomlinson is able to withstand tremendous impacts on the football field. However, Serena Williams, like LaDainian Tomlinson, is a great African American athlete. Therefore, Serena Williams should be able to withstand tremendous impacts on the football field.

14. Unlike monkeys, today's humans have feet that are not suited for grasping objects. Therefore, a thousand years from now, probably humans will still have feet that are not suited for grasping objects.

15. A random sample of twenty-five famous country and western singers, including Garth Brooks and Dolly Parton, revealed that every single one of them

studied music in Tasmania. Therefore, probably the majority of famous country and western singers studied music in Tasmania.

III. Determine whether the following arguments are inductive or deductive. If an argument is inductive, determine whether it is strong or weak. If it is deductive, determine whether it is valid or invalid.

★1. Since Agatha is the mother of Raquel and the sister of Tom, it follows that Tom is the uncle of Raquel.

2. When a cook cannot recall the ingredients in a recipe, it is appropriate that she refresh her memory by consulting the recipe book. Similarly, when a student cannot recall the answers during a final exam, it is appropriate that she refresh her memory by consulting the textbook.

3. The sign on the highway leading into Denver, Colorado, says that the city's elevation is 5280 feet. It must be the case that Denver is 1 mile high.

★4. Since Christmas is always on a Thursday, it follows that the day after Christmas is always a Friday.

5. This figure is a Euclidean triangle. Therefore, the sum of its angles is equal to two right angles.

6. By accident Karen baked her brownies two hours longer than she should have. Therefore, they have probably been ruined.

★7. After taking LSD, Alice said she saw a flying saucer land in the shopping center parking lot. Since Alice has a reputation for always telling the truth, we must conclude that a flying saucer really did land there.

8. Since Phyllis is the cousin of Denise, and Denise is the cousin of Harriet, it follows necessarily that Harriet is the cousin of Phyllis.

9. The picnic scheduled in the park for tomorrow will most likely be cancelled. It's been snowing for six days straight.

★10. Circle A has exactly twice the diameter of circle B. From this we may conclude that circle A has exactly twice the area of circle B.

11. Robert has lost consistently at blackjack every day for the past several days. Therefore, it is very likely that he will win today.

12. Since John loves Nancy and Nancy loves Peter, it follows necessarily that John loves Peter.

★13. This cash register drawer contains over 100 coins. Three coins selected at random were found to have dates earlier than 1945. Therefore, probably all of the coins in the drawer have dates earlier than 1945.

14. The Japanese attack on Pearl Harbor happened in either 1941 or 1951. But it didn't happen in 1941. Therefore, it happened in 1951.

15. Harry will never be able to solve that difficult problem in advanced calculus in the limited time allowed. He has never studied anything beyond algebra, and in that he earned only a C−.

★16. Since $x + y = 10$, and $x = 7$, it follows that $y = 4$.

17. If acupuncture is hocus pocus, then acupuncture cannot relieve chronic pain. But acupuncture can relieve chronic pain. Therefore, acupuncture is not hocus pocus.

18. If inflation heats up, then interest rates will rise. If interest rates rise, then bond prices will decline. Therefore, if inflation heats up, then bond prices will decline.

★19. Statistics reveal that 86 percent of those who receive flu shots do not get the flu. Jack received a flu shot one month ago. Therefore, he should be immune, even though the flu is going around now.

20. Since Michael is a Pisces, it necessarily follows that he was born in March.

IV. Define the following terms:

valid argument	strong argument
invalid argument	weak argument
sound argument	cogent argument
unsound argument	uncogent argument

V. Answer "true" or "false" to the following statements:

1. Some arguments, while not completely valid, are almost valid.

2. Inductive arguments admit of varying degrees of strength and weakness.

3. Invalid deductive arguments are basically the same as inductive arguments.

4. If a deductive argument has true premises and a false conclusion, it is necessarily invalid.

5. A valid argument may have a false premise and a false conclusion.

6. A valid argument may have a false premise and a true conclusion.

7. A sound argument may be invalid.

8. A sound argument may have a false conclusion.

9. A strong argument may have false premises and a probably false conclusion.

10. A strong argument may have true premises and a probably false conclusion.

11. A cogent argument may have a probably false conclusion.

12. A cogent argument must be inductively strong.

13. If an argument has true premises and a true conclusion, we know that it is a perfectly good argument.

14. A statement may legitimately be spoken of as "valid" or "invalid."

15. An argument may legitimately be spoken of as "true" or "false."

1.5   Argument Forms: Proving Invalidity

This section explores the idea that the validity of a deductive argument is determined by the **argument form.** This idea was suggested in the arguments about wines and beverages presented in Table 1.1 in the previous section. All the arguments in the valid column have the same form, and all the arguments in the invalid column have the same form.

Yet, in the exercises at the end of that section we saw many cases of valid deductive arguments that did not have any recognizable form. How can we reconcile this fact with the claim that validity is determined by form? The answer is that these arguments are incomplete, so the form is not explicit. But once such arguments are completed and correctly phrased (which we address later in this book), the form becomes apparent. For example, consider the following valid argument:

> Geese are migratory waterfowl, so they fly south for the winter.

This argument is missing a premise:

> Migratory waterfowl fly south for the winter.

The argument can now be rephrased to make its form apparent:

> All geese are migratory waterfowl.
> All migratory waterfowl are birds that fly south for the winter.
> Therefore, all geese are birds that fly south for the winter.

The form of the argument is

> All *A* are *B*.
> All *B* are *C*.
> _____
> All *A* are *C*.

This form is valid, and it captures the reasoning process of the argument. If we assume that the *A*s (whatever they might be) are included in the *B*s, and that the *B*s (whatever they might be) are included in the *C*s, then the *A*s must necessarily be included in the *C*s. This necessary relationship between the *A*s, *B*s, and *C*s is what makes the argument valid. This is what we mean when we say that the validity of a deductive argument is determined by its form.

Since validity is determined by form, it follows that any argument that has this valid form is a valid argument. Thus, we might substitute "daisies" for *A*, "flowers" for *B*, and "plants" for *C* and obtain the following valid argument:

> All daisies are flowers.
> All flowers are plants.
> Therefore, all daisies are plants.

Any argument such as this that is produced by uniformly substituting terms or statements in place of the letters in an argument form is called a **substitution instance** of that form.

Let us now consider an invalid argument form:

> All *A* are *B*.
> All *C* are *B*.
> _____
> All *A* are *C*.

In this argument form, if we assume that the *A*s are in the *B*s and that the *C*s are in the *B*s, it does not *necessarily* follow that the *A*s are in the *C*s. It would not follow if the

*A*s were in one part of the *B*s and the *C*s were in another part, as the following diagram illustrates:

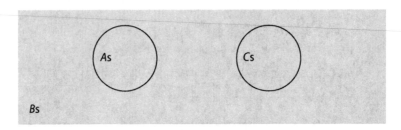

This diagram suggests that we can prove the form invalid if we can find a substitution instance having actually true premises and an actually false conclusion. In such a substitution instance the *A*s and the *C*s would be separated from each other, but they would both be included in the *B*s. If we substitute "cats" for *A*, "animals" for *B*, and "dogs" for *C*, we have such a substitution instance:

All *A* are *B*.	All cats are animals.	True
All *C* are *B*.	All dogs are animals.	True
All *A* are *C*.	Therefore, all cats are dogs.	False

This substitution instance proves the form invalid, because it provides a concrete example of a case where the *A*s are in the *B*s, the *C*s are in the *B*s, but the *A*s are *not* in the *C*s.

Now, since the form is invalid, can we say that any argument that has this form is invalid? Unfortunately, the situation with invalid forms is not quite as simple as it is with valid forms. Every substitution instance of a valid form is a valid argument, but it is not the case that every substitution instance of an invalid form is an invalid argument. The reason is that some substitution instances of invalid forms are also substitution instances of valid forms.* However, we can say that any substitution instance of an invalid form is an invalid argument *provided* that it is not a substitution instance of any valid form. Thus we will say that an argument actually *has* an invalid form if it is a substitution instance of that form and it is not a substitution instance of any valid form.

The fact that some substitution instances of invalid forms are also substitution instances of valid forms means simply that we must exercise caution in identifying the

---

*For example, the following valid argument is a substitution instance of the invalid form we have been discussing:

All bachelors are persons.
All unmarried men are persons.
Therefore, all bachelors are unmarried men.

However, because "bachelors" is equivalent in meaning to "unmarried men," the argument is also a substitution instance of this valid form:

All *A* are *B*.
All *A* are *B*.
All *A* are *A*.

form of an argument. However, cases of ordinary language arguments that can be interpreted as substitution instances of both valid and invalid forms are so rare that this book chooses to ignore them. With this in mind, consider the following argument:

> All romantic novels are literary pieces.
> All works of fiction are literary pieces.
> Therefore, all romantic novels are works of fiction.

This argument clearly has the invalid form just discussed. This invalid form captures the reasoning process of the argument, which is obviously defective. Therefore, the argument is invalid, and it is invalid precisely because it has an invalid form.

Counterexample Method

A substitution instance having true premises and a false conclusion (like the cats-and-dogs example just constructed) is called a counterexample, and the method we have just used to prove the romantic-novels argument invalid is called the **counterexample method.** It consists of isolating the form of an argument and then constructing a substitution instance having true premises and a false conclusion. This proves the form invalid, which in turn proves the argument invalid. The counterexample method can be used to prove the invalidity of any invalid argument, but it cannot prove the validity of any valid argument. Thus, before the method is applied to an argument, the argument must be known or suspected to be invalid in the first place. Let us apply the counterexample method to the following invalid categorical syllogism:

> Since some employees are not social climbers and all vice presidents are employees, we may conclude that some vice presidents are not social climbers.

This argument is invalid because the employees who are not social climbers might not be vice presidents. Accordingly, we can *prove* the argument invalid by constructing a substitution instance having true premises and a false conclusion. We begin by isolating the form of the argument:

> Some E are not S.
> All V are E.
> _____
> Some V are not S.

Next, we select three terms to substitute in place of the letters that will make the premises true and the conclusion false. The following selection will work:

> E = animals
> S = mammals
> V = dogs

The resulting substitution instance is this:

> Some animals are not mammals.
> All dogs are animals.
> Therefore, some dogs are not mammals.

The substitution instance has true premises and a false conclusion and is therefore, by definition, invalid. Because the substitution instance is invalid, the form is invalid, and therefore the original argument is invalid.

In applying the counterexample method to categorical syllogisms, it is useful to keep in mind the following set of terms: "cats," "dogs," "mammals," "fish," and "animals." Most invalid syllogisms can be proven invalid by strategically selecting three of these terms and using them to construct a counterexample. Because everyone agrees about these terms, everyone will agree about the truth or falsity of the premises and conclusion of the counterexample. Also, in constructing the counterexample, it often helps to begin with the conclusion. First, select two terms that yield a false conclusion, and then select a third term that yields true premises. Another point to keep in mind is that the word "some" in logic always means "at least one." For example, the statement "Some dogs are animals" means "At least one dog is an animal"—which is true. Also note that this statement does not imply that some dogs are not animals.

Not all deductive arguments, of course, are categorical syllogisms. Consider, for example, the following hypothetical syllogism:

> If the government imposes import restrictions, the price of automobiles will rise.
>   Therefore, since the government will not impose import restrictions, it follows that
>   the price of automobiles will not rise.

This argument is invalid because the price of automobiles might rise even though import restrictions are not imposed. It has the following form:

> If G, then P.
> Not G.
> Not P.

This form differs from the previous one in that its letters stand for complete statements. G, for example, stands for "The government imposes import restrictions." If we make the substitution

> G = Abraham Lincoln committed suicide.
> P = Abraham Lincoln is dead.

we obtain the following substitution instance:

> If Abraham Lincoln committed suicide, then Abraham Lincoln is dead.
> Abraham Lincoln did not commit suicide.
> Therefore, Abraham Lincoln is not dead.

Since the premises are true and the conclusion false, the substitution instance is clearly invalid. Therefore, the form is invalid, and this proves the original argument invalid.

When applying the counterexample method to an argument having a conditional statement as a premise (such as the one just discussed), it is recommended that the statement substituted in place of the conditional statement express some kind of necessary connection. In the Lincoln example, the first premise asserts the necessary connection between suicide and death. There can be no doubt about the truth of such a statement. Furthermore, if it should turn out that the conclusion is a conditional state-

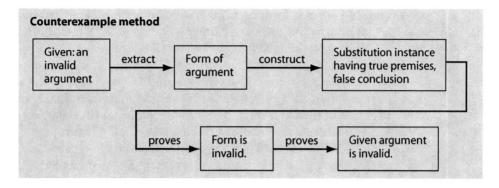

ment, note that one sure way of producing a false conditional statement is by joining a true antecedent with a false consequent. For example, the conditional statement "If Lassie is a dog, then Lassie is a cat" is clearly false.

Being able to identify the form of an argument with ease requires a familiarity with the basic deductive argument forms. The first task consists in distinguishing the premises from the conclusion. Always write the premises first and the conclusion last. The second task involves distinguishing what we may call "form words" from "content words." To reduce an argument to its form, leave the form words as they are, and replace the content words with letters. For categorical syllogisms, the words "all," "no," "some," "are," and "not" are form words, and for hypothetical syllogisms the words "if," "then," and "not" are form words. Additional form words for other types of arguments are "either," "or," "both," and "and." For various kinds of hybrid arguments, a more intuitive approach may be needed. Here is an example:

> All movie stars are actors who are famous, because all movie stars who are famous are actors.

If we replace "movie stars," "actors," and "famous" with the letters *M*, *A*, and *F*, this argument has the following form:

> All *M* who are *F* are *A*.
> ————————————
> All *M* are *A* who are *F*.

Here is one possible substitution instance for this form:

> All humans who are fathers are men.
> Therefore, all humans are men who are fathers.

Because the premise is true and the conclusion false, the form is invalid and so is the original argument.

Using the counterexample method to prove arguments invalid requires a little ingenuity because there is no rule that will automatically produce the required term or statement to be substituted into the form. Any term or statement will work, of course, provided that it yields a substitution instance that has premises that are indisputably true and a conclusion that is indisputably false. Ideally, the truth value of these statements should be known to the average individual; otherwise, the substitution instance cannot be depended on to prove anything. If, for example, *P* in the earlier hypothetical syllogism had been replaced by the statement "George Wilson is dead," the substitution instance would be useless, because nobody knows whether this statement is true or false.

The counterexample method is useful only for proving invalidity, because the only arrangement of truth and falsity that proves anything is true premises and false conclusion. If a substitution instance is produced having true premises and a true conclusion, it does *not* prove that the argument is valid. Furthermore, the method is useful only for deductive arguments because the strength and weakness of inductive arguments is only partially dependent on the form of the argument. Accordingly, no method that relates exclusively to the form of an inductive argument can be used to prove the argument weak.

EXERCISE 1.5

I. Use the counterexample method to prove the following categorical syllogisms invalid. In doing so, follow the suggestions given in the text.

★1. All galaxies are structures that contain black holes in the center, so all galaxies are quasars, since all quasars are structures that contain black holes in the center.

2. Some evolutionists are not people who believe in the Bible, for no creationists are evolutionists, and some people who believe in the Bible are not creationists.

3. No patents are measures that discourage research and development, and all patents are regulations that protect intellectual property. Thus, no measures that discourage research and development are regulations that protect intellectual property.

★4. Some farm workers are not people who are paid decent wages, because no illegal aliens are people who are paid decent wages, and some illegal aliens are not farm workers.

5. Some politicians are people who will stop at nothing to win an election, and no people who will stop at nothing to win an election are true statesmen. Hence, no politicians are true statesmen.

6. All meticulously constructed timepieces are true works of art, for all Swiss watches are true works of art and all Swiss watches are meticulously constructed timepieces.

★7. No patrons of fast-food restaurants are health-food addicts. Consequently, no patrons of fast-food restaurants are connoisseurs of fine desserts, since no connoisseurs of fine desserts are health-food addicts.

8. Some toxic dumps are sites that emit hazardous wastes, and some sites that emit hazardous wastes are undesirable places to live near. Thus, some toxic dumps are undesirable places to live near.

9. All persons who assist others in suicide are people guilty of murder. Accordingly, some individuals motivated by compassion are not persons guilty of murder, inasmuch as some people who assist others in suicide are individuals motivated by compassion.

★10. Some school boards are not groups that oppose values clarification, because some school boards are not organizations with vision, and some groups that oppose values clarification are not organizations with vision.

II. Use the counterexample method to prove each of the following arguments invalid.

★1. If animal species are fixed and immutable, then evolution is a myth. Therefore, evolution is not a myth, since animal species are not fixed and immutable.

2. If carbon dioxide is present in the atmosphere, then plants have a source of carbon. Hence, since plants have a source of carbon, carbon dioxide is present in the atmosphere.

3. If human rights are recognized, then civilization flourishes. If equality prevails, then civilization flourishes. Thus, if human rights are recognized, then equality prevails.

★4. If energy taxes are increased, then either the deficit will be reduced or conservation will be taken seriously. If the deficit is reduced, then inflation will be checked. Therefore, if energy taxes are increased, then inflation will be checked.

5. All homeless people who are panhandlers are destitute individuals. Therefore, all homeless people are destitute individuals.

6. Some wrestlers are colorful hulks, since some wrestlers are colorful and some wrestlers are hulks.

★7. All community colleges with low tuition are either schools with large enrollments or institutions supported by taxes. Therefore, all community colleges are institutions supported by taxes.

8. All merchandisers that are retailers are businesses that are inventory rotators. Therefore, all merchandisers are inventory rotators.

9. All diabetes victims are either insulin takers or glucose eliminators. Accordingly, some diabetes victims are glucose eliminators, since some diabetes victims are insulin takers.

★10. All FHA loans are living-standard enhancers for the following reasons. All reverse mortgages that are FHA loans are either living-standard enhancers or home equity depleters, and all reverse mortgages are home equity depleters.

1.6   Extended Arguments

The logical analysis of extended arguments, such as those found in editorials, essays, and lengthy letters to newspaper editors, involves numerous difficulties. Such arguments are often mixed together with fragments of reports, pieces of expository writing, illustrations, explanations, and statements of opinion. Proper analysis involves weeding out the extraneous material and isolating premises and conclusions. Another problem stems from the fact that lengthy arguments often involve complex arrangements of subarguments that feed into the main argument in various ways. Distinguishing one subargument from another is often a complicated task. And then there are some argumentative passages that involve completely separate strands of argumentation leading to separate conclusions. Again, distinguishing the strands and assigning premises to the right conclusion not only is problematic but often involves an element of creativity on the part of the analyst.

To facilitate the analysis of extended arguments, we will assign numerals to the various statements in the passage and use arrows to represent the inferential links. Example:

① The contamination of underground aquifers represents a pollution problem of catastrophic proportions. ② Half the nation's drinking water, which comes from these aquifers, is being poisoned by chemical wastes dumped into the soil for generations.

This argument is diagrammed as follows:

The diagram says that statement ②, the premise, supports statement ①, the conclusion.

In extended arguments we can identify two distinct patterns of argumentation, which we will name the vertical pattern and the horizontal pattern. The *vertical pattern* consists of a series of arguments in which a conclusion of a logically prior argument becomes a premise of a subsequent argument. Example:

① The selling of human organs, such as hearts, kidneys, and corneas, should be outlawed. ② Allowing human organs to be sold will inevitably lead to a situation in which only the rich will be able to afford transplants. This is so because ③ whenever something scarce is bought and sold as a commodity, the price always goes up. ④ The law of supply and demand requires it.

This argument is diagrammed as follows:

Vertical pattern

The diagram says that statement ①, which is the main conclusion, is supported by ②, which in turn is supported by ③, which in turn is supported by ④.

The *horizontal pattern* consists of a single argument in which two or more premises provide independent support for a single conclusion. If one of the premises were omitted, the other(s) would continue to support the conclusion in the same way. Example:

① The selling of human organs, such as hearts, kidneys, and corneas, should be outlawed. ② If this practice is allowed to get a foothold, people in desperate financial straits will start selling their own organs to pay their bills. Alternately, ③ those with a criminal bent will take to killing healthy young people and selling their organs on the black market. ④ In the final analysis, the buying and selling of human organs comes just too close to the buying and selling of life itself.

The diagram for this argument is as follows:

Horizontal pattern

This diagram says that statements ②, ③, and ④ support ① independently.

Two variations on the horizontal and vertical patterns occur when two or more premises support a conclusion *conjointly,* and when one or more premises support *multiple* conclusions. The first variation occurs when the premises depend on one another in such a way that if one were omitted, the support that the others provide would be diminished or destroyed. The following argument illustrates the occurrence of conjoint premises:

> ① Getting poor people off the welfare rolls requires that we modify their behavior patterns. ② The vast majority of people on welfare are high school dropouts, single parents, or people who abuse alcohol and drugs. ③ These behavior patterns frustrate any desire poor people may have to get a job and improve their condition in life.

Statement ① is the conclusion. Taken separately, statements ② and ③ provide little or no support for ①, but taken together they do provide support. That is, ② and ③ support ① *conjointly.* This relationship between the premises is illustrated by the use of the brace in the following diagram:

Conjoint premises

The next example illustrates the occurrence of a multiple conclusion:

> ① Dropping out of school and bearing children outside of marriage are two of the primary causes of poverty in this country. Therefore, ② to eliminate poverty we must offer incentives for people to get high school diplomas. Also, ③ we must find some way to encourage people to get married before they start having children.

In this passage statement ① supports both ② and ③. Since no single argument can have more than one conclusion, the passage is correctly evaluated as consisting of two arguments. For our purposes, however, we will treat it as if it were a single argument by joining the two conclusions with a brace:

Multiple conclusion

Our symbolism is now sufficiently developed to analyze most arguments found in editorials and letters to the editor of newspapers and magazines. Consider the following argument, taken from a newspaper editorial:

> ① Government mandates for zero-emission vehicles won't work because ② only electric cars qualify as zero-emission vehicles, and ③ electric cars won't sell. ④ They are too expensive, ⑤ their range of operation is too limited, and ⑥ recharging facilities are not generally available.
>
> (William Campbell, "Technology Is Not Good Enough")

We immediately see that ① is the main conclusion, and ② and ③ support ① conjointly. Also, ④, ⑤, and ⑥ support ③ independently. The argument pattern is as follows:

The next argument is taken from a letter to the editor:

> ① Rhinos in Kenya are threatened with extinction because ② poachers are killing them for their horn. Since ③ the rhino has no natural predators, ④ it does not need its horn to survive. Thus ⑤ there should be an organized program to capture rhinos in the wild and remove their horn. ⑥ Such a program would eliminate the incentive of the poachers.
>
> (Pamela C. Wagner, "Rhino Poaching")

First we search for the final conclusion. We select ⑤, because it is the ultimate point that the passage attempts to establish. Next we survey the premise and conclusion indicators. From this, we see that ② supports ① and ③ supports ④. Finally, we see that ①, ④, and ⑥ support ⑤. Yet these supporting statements depend on one another for their effect. Thus, they support the final conclusion conjointly. The argument pattern is as follows:

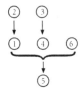

The next argument is taken from a magazine article:

> ① Skating is a wonderful form of exercise and relaxation, but ② today's rollerbladers are a growing menace and ③ something should be done to control them. ④ Rollerbladers are oblivious to traffic regulations as ⑤ they breeze through red lights and ⑥ skim down the wrong way on one-way streets. ⑦ They pose a threat to pedestrians because ⑧ a collision can cause serious injury. ⑨ Rollerbladers are

even a hazard to shopkeepers as ⑩ they zoom through stores and ⑪ damage merchandise.

(Joan Schmidt, "Hell—On Wheels")

After reading the argument, we see that ① is merely an introductory sentence, and ② and ③ together compose the main conclusion. Also, ④, ⑦, and ⑨ support the main conclusion independently, while ⑤ and ⑥ support ④ independently, ⑧ supports ⑦, and ⑩ and ⑪ support ⑨ independently. The diagram is as follows:

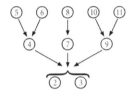

The next argument is taken from the science column of a newspaper:

① We can expect small changes to occur in the length of our calendar year for an indefinite time to come. ② This is true for two reasons. ③ First, the rotation of the earth exhibits certain irregularities. ④ And why is this so? ⑤ The rotation of any body is affected by its distribution of mass, and ⑥ the earth's mass distribution is continually subject to change. For example, ⑦ earthquakes alter the location of the tectonic plates. Also, ⑧ the liquid core of the earth sloshes as the earth turns, and ⑨ rainfall redistributes water from the oceans. The second reason is that ⑩ the motion of the tides causes a continual slowing down of earth's rotation. ⑪ Tidal motion produces heat, and ⑫ the loss of this heat removes energy from the system.

(Isaac Asimov, "As the World Turns")

Preliminary analysis reveals that the final conclusion is ①. Also, ② tells us that the supporting statements are divided into two basic groups, but since ② does not add any support, we can leave it out of the diagram. In the first group, ⑤ and ⑥ support ③ conjointly, while ⑦, ⑧, and ⑨ support ⑥ independently. ④ will not appear in the diagram, because it serves merely as a premise indicator. In the second group, ⑪ and ⑫ support ⑩ conjointly. Thus, the argument pattern is as follows:

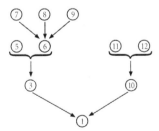

Our last example is taken from a letter to the editor of a newspaper:

① Community college districts save a great deal of money by hiring untenured part-time instructors, but ② the extensive use of these instructors is a disadvantage to the students. ③ Most part-time instructors are paid only 60 percent of what a full-time teacher earns, and as a result, ④ they are forced to teach five or six courses just to survive. ⑤ This detracts from the opportunity to consult with students outside the classroom. To make matters worse, ⑥ many part-timers are not even given office space. Furthermore, ⑦ the lower pay demoralizes the part-timer, and ⑧ the lack of tenure makes for constant financial insecurity. ⑨ Obviously these conditions render the instructor less receptive to student needs. Lastly, because ⑩ these part-timers are burning the candle from both ends, ⑪ they have no spare energy to improve their courses, and ⑫ many lack the enthusiasm to motivate their students. As a result, ⑬ the educational process is impaired.

(Gordon Dossett et al., "Part-Time College Instructors")

Preliminary analysis reveals that the main conclusion is not ① but ②. Also, we see three main reasons why part-timers are a disadvantage to students: They have little opportunity to consult with students, they are less receptive to student needs, and the educational process is impaired by ⑪ and ⑫. In the first main branch, the indicator "as a result" shows that ③ supports ④, and ④ and ⑥ independently support ⑤. In the second branch, ⑦ and ⑧ independently support ⑨. In the third, ⑩ supports both ⑪ and ⑫, which in turn support ⑬ independently. Here is the argument pattern:

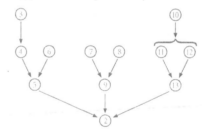

EXERCISE 1.6

I. The following arguments were abstracted from newspaper articles, editorials, and letters to the editor. Use the method presented in this section to construct argument patterns. If a statement is redundant or plays no role in the argument, do not include it in the pattern.

★1. ① The conditions under which many food animals are raised are unhealthy for humans. ② To keep these animals alive, large quantities of drugs must be administered. ③ These drugs remain in the animals' flesh and are passed on to the humans who eat it.

(Philip D. Oliver, "We Can Eat Ribs and Still Be Humane")

2. ① The development of carbon-embedded plastics, otherwise called "composits," is an important new technology because ② it holds the key for new aircraft and spacecraft designs. This is so because ③ these composits are not only stronger than steel but lighter than aluminum.

(Thomas H. Maugh II, "Composits—The Lightweight Champs of Aircraft Industry")

3. ① Homework stifles the thrill of learning in the mind of the student. ② It instills an oppressive learn-or-else discipline. ③ It quenches the desire for knowledge and the love of truth. For these reasons ④ homework should never be assigned.

(Colman McCarthy, "Homework's Tyranny Hobbles Promising Minds")

★4. ① When parents become old and destitute, the obligation of caring for them should be imposed on their children. ② Clearly, children owe a debt to their parents. ③ Their parents brought them into the world and cared for them when they were unable to care for themselves. ④ This debt could be appropriately discharged by having grown children care for their parents.

(Gary Jones, "The Responsibility of Parents")

5. ① Defending the war on drugs may not be fashionable, but the fact remains that ② hardcore drugs should remain illegal. ③ As long as hardcore drugs are illegal, they are harder to get, and ④ the social stigma of being arrested deters many users.

(Charles Van DeVenter, "I'm Proof: The War on Drugs Is Working")

6. ① The rain forest of Brazil produces oxygen for the whole world, yet ② it yields no monetary return to that country. Given that ③ the industrialized nations consume the most oxygen, ④ those nations ought to pay Brazil an annual fee for the use of its rain forest.

(Diane B. Robinson, letter to the editor)

★7. ① It appears that animals may be able to predict earthquakes. ② Prior to a major quake in China, hundreds of snakes suddenly appeared from hibernation and froze to death in the snow, ③ fish were seen leaping from rivers and lakes, and ④ cows and horses refused to enter barns. Also, ⑤ prior to a quake in Fremont, California, a flood of callers reported strange behavior from their pets and domestic animals.

(Michael Bowker, "Can Animals Really Predict Earthquakes?")

8. ① Contributions to relief organizations are often wasted. ② Food sent to war torn countries rarely reaches its destination, because ③ food distribution is controlled by the warring groups, and ④ these groups sell the food to buy weapons and ammunition.

(Michael Maren, "The Faces of Famine")

9. ① Research leading to the development of a scramjet engine is worthwhile. ② Commercial aircraft incorporating such an engine could cross the Pacific in as little as two hours. ③ This would relieve the fatigue of flights from New York to Tokyo. Also, ④ such an engine could power future orbiting spacecraft.

(T. A. Heppenheimer, "A Plane for Space")

★10. ① There is a lot of pressure on untenured college teachers to dumb down their courses. ② Administrators tend to rehire teachers who bring in more money, and ③ teachers who dumb down their classes do precisely this. Why? Because ④ easier classes attract more students, and ⑤ more students means more money for the school.

(Lynne Drury Lerych, "Meeting the Bottom Line in the College Biz")

II. The following arguments gradually increase in difficulty. Use the method presented in this section to construct argument patterns. If a statement is redundant or plays no role in the argument, do not include it in the pattern.

★1. ① Many people believe that the crime of bribery cannot extend to campaign contributions. ② From a legal standpoint, however, countless campaign contributions are in fact bribes. ③ A bribe is anything of value or advantage given with the intent to unlawfully influence the person to whom it is given in his official capacity. ④ A campaign contribution is certainly something of value or advantage. Furthermore, ⑤ every contribution from a lobbyist or special interest group is given with the intent to influence voting, and ⑥ thousands of such contributions are made in every important election.

(Daniel Hays Lowenstein, "Can Candidates Run for Political Office
Without Taking Bribes?")

2. ① America's farm policy desperately needs revamping. ② Seventy-three cents of every farm program dollar ends up in the pockets of the nation's super-farmers. As a result, ③ the mid-sized family farms are being squeezed out of existence. Also, ④ our farm policy courts environmental disaster. ⑤ Federal subsidies encourage farmers to use enormous amounts of fertilizer and pesticides. ⑥ These chemicals percolate down through the soil and pollute limited groundwater.

(Osha Gray Davidson, "Rise of America's Rural Ghetto")

3. ① Society values white lives more than black lives. This is clear from the fact that ② killers of whites are much more likely to be sentenced to death than killers of blacks. ③ Of the 1788 people currently on death row, 1713 were convicted of killing a white person. Yet ④ blacks are six times more likely to be murder victims than whites are. ⑤ In Florida, no one has ever been executed for murdering a black person, but ⑥ dozens have been executed for murdering white people.

(Los Angeles Times editorial, "Death and Race")

★4. ① Powerful new particle accelerators are important in high-energy physics, and ② they are worth their cost because ③ they will allow scientists to produce and capture significant quantities of Z particles. ④ Z particles result from the collision of positrons and electrons, and ⑤ particle accelerators are needed to achieve significant numbers of these collisions. ⑥ Z particles are thought to be the bearers of the weak nuclear force, and ⑦ learning the nature of this force may lead to the development of entirely new sources of energy.

(Lee Dye, "Linear Collider: Bold Gamble in Atomic Physics")

5. ① For years our country has been providing Japan unlimited access to our technology while getting little in return. ② Currently 7,000 Japanese graduate students study science and engineering in the U.S., ③ while only 1,000 Americans are engaged in similar studies in Japan. Also, ④ our government laboratories are open to the Japanese, but ⑤ Japanese laboratories are not open to Americans. ⑥ To remedy this imbalance, Japan should subsidize our universities, and also ⑦ it should help defray the costs of our laboratories.

(William C. Norris, "Technology Must Travel 2-Way Street")

6. ① All men crave material success because ② it serves as an insurance policy against sexual rejection. This is true because ③ women love men who are successful. ④ Both men and women want power, and ⑤ success is the form of power women feel most deprived of. Thus, ⑥ women try to achieve it vicariously through men. ⑦ As the 5-foot 6-inch Dustin Hoffman once put it, "When I was in high school, women wouldn't touch me with a 10-foot pole. Now I can't keep them away with a 10-foot pole."

(Warren Farrell, "Success Story: From Frog to Prince")

★7. ① Cigarette consumption could be easily reduced by simply outlawing tailor-made cigarettes. ② The manufacture of tailor-made cigarettes to American standards is a high-tech industry. ③ It cannot be done in small illicit labs like the processing of PCP, cocaine or heroin. ④ The availability of quality tobacco for hand-rolling would discourage the development of an illegal tailor-made market. ⑤ Most people would not pay the premium prices demanded by an illicit market for a product of unknown quality. ⑥ They could roll a high-quality product for themselves. ⑦ Truly addicted persons would continue to smoke no matter how inconvenient. But ⑧ most would give it up as too much bother before it became a deeply ingrained habit.

(Richard Sand, "An Easy Way to Reduce Cigarette Consumption")

8. ① Flesh food is not a necessity in the human diet, as ② nutritionally adequate alternatives are readily available. ③ Many people in the world thrive on a nonmeat diet. ④ Indeed, vegetarian Seventh-Day Adventists in this country live an average of six years longer than their meat-eating counterparts. ⑤ The National Academy of Science warns that our fat-laden diet is directly responsible for much of the heart disease and cancer that afflict so many. ⑥ At a time when people are starving in certain parts of the world, it should be noted that a steer must consume sixteen pounds of grain and soy to produce one pound of meat. ⑦ The grain and soybeans we feed our meat-producing animals would feed every hungry mouth in the world many times over. ⑧ Cattle are competing with humans for food. ⑨ Clearly, a reassessment of the whole concept of killing and eating animals is in order.

(Suzanne Sutton, "Killing Animals for Food—Time for a Second Look")

9. ① The argument has been made that to cut down on teenage drunk driving we should increase the federal excise tax on beer. ② Such a measure, however, would almost certainly fail to achieve its intended result. ③ Teenagers are notoriously insensitive to cost. ④ They gladly accept premium prices for the latest style in clothes or the most popular record albums. And then, ⑤ those who drink and drive already risk arrest and loss of driving privileges. ⑥ They would not think twice about paying a little more for a six-pack. Finally, ⑦ the situation is not as bleak as it has been made to appear. ⑧ The fatality rate for teenage drivers is lower today than it has been in years.

(James C. Sanders, "Increased U.S. Tax on Beer")

★10. ① It has been widely acknowledged that the quality of undergraduate education in this country is diminishing. ② An often unrecognized cause of this malady is the exploitative way that universities as employers treat their part-time and temporary faculty members. ③ In many universities there are no formal guidelines for evaluating the work of these instructors. As a result, ④ poor instructors who solicit the favor of the department chairman are often retained over better ones who do not. ⑤ Another factor is the low pay given to these instructors. ⑥ In order to survive, many of them must accept heavy teaching loads spread out over three or four institutions. ⑦ The quality of instruction can only suffer when faculty members stretch themselves so thin. Lastly, because ⑧ part-time and temporary faculty are rarely members of the faculty senate, ⑨ they have no voice in university governance. But ⑩ without a voice, the shoddy conditions under which they work are never brought to light.

(Michael Schwalbe, "Part-Time Faculty Members Deserve a Break")

11. ① Doctors who attend elderly people in nursing homes often prescribe tranquilizers to keep these people immobile. ② This practice is often unwarranted, and ③ it often impairs the health of the patients. ④ These tranquilizers often have damaging side effects in that ⑤ they accentuate the symptoms of senility, and ⑥ they increase the likelihood of a dangerous fall because ⑦ they produce unsteadiness in walking. Furthermore, since ⑧ these medications produce immobility, ⑨ they increase the risk of bedsores. ⑩ Doctors at the Center for Aging and Health say that physicians who care for the elderly are simply prescribing too much medication.

(Hal Willard, "At 90, the Zombie Shuffle")

12. ① All of us have encountered motorists who will go to any length to get a parking spot within 20 feet of the door they expect to enter. ② This obsession with good parking spots transcends all logic. ③ It might take 5 minutes to secure the ideal spot in a store parking lot, ④ while a more distant spot that is immediately available is only a 40-second walk from the door. ⑤ Waiting for that ideal spot also results in frenzied nerves and skyrocketing blood pressure. ⑥ Inevitably the occupant of the desired space will preen her hair before departing, and ⑦ all the while the cars backed up behind the waiting driver are blaring their horns. ⑧ Parking a little farther away is usually easier and safer

because ⑨ you can pull out more quickly, and ⑩ it avoids damage to car doors by adjacent parkers.

(Gwinn Owens, "A Ridiculous Addiction")

★13. ① The state has a right to intervene on behalf of unborn children, and ② this right should be implemented immediately. ③ While it may be true that a mere fetus has no rights, ④ surely a born child does have rights, and ⑤ these rights project backward to the time it was in the womb. This is true because ⑥ what happens to the child in the womb can have an impact throughout the child's life. ⑦ It is well known that alcohol and drug abuse by expectant mothers cause birth defects, and ⑧ these defects are not correctable after birth. ⑨ Granted, an expectant mother has the right to treat her own body as she chooses, but ⑩ this right does not extend to her unborn child. ⑪ Once a pregnant woman decides to give birth, she effectively transfers part of her rights over to her unborn child. ⑫ Unfortunately, however, the unborn child is incapable of securing these rights for itself. Thus, ⑬ the intervention of a higher power is justified.

(Alan Dershowitz, "Drawing the Line on Prenatal Rights")

14. ① A manned trip to Mars is a justified scientific goal because ② it affords a unique opportunity to explore the origins of the solar system and the emergence of life. However, ③ from a scientific standpoint, an initial landing on the tiny Martian moons, Phobos and Deimos, would be more rewarding than a landing on the planet itself. Because ④ the Martian terrain is rugged, ⑤ humans would not be able to venture far, ⑥ nor could they operate a robot vehicle without the use of a satellite, since ⑦ Mars's mountains would block their view. ⑧ Explorers on Phobos and Deimos could easily send robot vehicles to the planet's surface. ⑨ Using Mars's moons as a base would also be better than unmanned exploration directed from the Houston space center. Because ⑩ the distance is so great, ⑪ radio signals to and from Mars can take as long as an hour. Thus, ⑫ driving an unmanned rover from Earth, step by step, would be a time-consuming operation. ⑬ Sample returns to Earth would take months instead of hours, and ⑭ follow-on missions would be years apart instead of days, further slowing the process of exploration.

(S. Fred Singer, "The Case for Going to Mars")

15. ① There are lots of problems with the U.S. airline system, but ② deregulation isn't one of them. ③ Airline deregulation has delivered most of what it promised when enacted in 1978. ④ It has held down fares, ⑤ increased competition, ⑥ and raised the industry's efficiency. ⑦ Despite claims to the contrary, airline safety has not suffered. And, ⑧ with some exceptions, service to some cities and towns has improved. ⑨ On average, fares are lower today than in 1980. ⑩ Morrison and Winston estimate that fares are 20% to 30% below what they would be under regulation. ⑪ Competition has increased because ⑫ prior to deregulation airlines had protected routes. ⑬ After deregulation this changed. ⑭ Efficiency has also improved. ⑮ After deregulation the percentage of occupied seats jumped by 10% and miles traveled by 32%. ⑯ Despite fears that

airlines would cut unprofitable service to small communities, most smaller cities and towns experienced a 20% to 30% increase in flight frequency. Lastly, ⑰ travel on U.S. airlines remains among the safest forms of transportation. ⑱ Between 1975 and 1985, deaths resulting from crashes totaled fewer than 3000.

(Robert J. Samuelson, "Let's Not Regulate the Deregulated Airlines")

III. Turn to the editorial pages of a newspaper and select an editorial that contains an argument. Keep in mind that some editorials are really reports and contain no arguments at all. Also, few editorials are as neat and straightforward as the selections presented in Parts I and II of this exercise. Guest editorials on the opinion-editorial page (usually opposite the editorial page) are often better written than those on the editorial page. Analyze the argument (or arguments) according to the method presented in this section. Begin by placing a numeral at the beginning of each statement. Compound statements having components that are claimed to be true may be broken up into parts and the parts enumerated accordingly. Numerals should usually be placed after genuine premise and conclusion indicators even when they occur in the middle of a statement. Do *not*, however, break up conditional statements into antecedent and consequent. Proceed to identify the main conclusion (or conclusions) and determine how the other statements provide support. Any statement that does not play a direct role in the argument should be left out of the final argument pattern.

Summary

Logic is the study of the evaluation of arguments, which are lists of statements consisting of one or more premises and one conclusion. Premises can be distinguished from conclusion by the occurrence of indicator words ("hence," "therefore," "since," and so on) or an inferential relation among the statements. Because not all groups of statements are arguments, it is important to be able to distinguish arguments from nonarguments. This is done by attending to indicator words, the presence of an inferential relation among the statements, and typical kinds of nonarguments. Typical nonarguments include warnings, loosely associated statements, reports, expository passages, illustrations, conditional statements, and explanations.

Arguments are customarily described as deductive or inductive. Deductive arguments are those in which the conclusion is claimed to follow necessarily from the premises, while inductive arguments are those in which the conclusion is claimed to follow only probably from the premises. The two can be distinguished by attending to special indicator words ("it necessarily follows that," "it probably follows that," and so on), the actual strength of the inferential relation, and typical forms or styles of deductive and inductive argumentation. Typical deductive arguments include arguments based on mathematics, arguments from definition, and categorical, hypothetical, and disjunctive syllogisms. Typical inductive arguments include predictions, arguments from analogy, generalizations, arguments from authority, arguments based on signs, and causal inferences.

The evaluation of arguments involves two steps: evaluating the link between premises and conclusion, and evaluating the truth of the premises. Deductive arguments in which the conclusion actually follows from the premises are said to be valid, and those that also have true premises are said to be sound. Inductive arguments in which the conclusion actually follows from the premises are said to be strong, and those that also have true premises are said to be cogent. The terms "true" and "false" apply not to arguments, but to statements. The truth and falsity of premises and conclusion is only indirectly related to validity, but any deductive argument having true premises and a false conclusion is invalid.

The validity of a deductive argument is determined by the form of the argument. An argument form that allows for a substitution instance having true premises and a false conclusion is an invalid form, and any argument having that form is an invalid argument. This fact leads to the counterexample method for proving invalidity. This method consists in identifying the form of a given invalid argument and then constructing a counterexample having premises that are indisputably true and a conclusion that is indisputably false.

The structure of longer arguments may be disclosed by the application of a method consisting of arrows and braces that show how the various premises support intermediate conclusions, and how the latter in turn support the main conclusion. Four basic argument patterns are the vertical pattern, horizontal pattern, conjoint premises, and multiple conclusion.

Answers to Selected Exercises

Exercise 1.1

I.

1. **P:** Titanium combines readily with oxygen, nitrogen, and hydrogen, all of which have an adverse effect on its mechanical properties.

   C: Titanium must be processed in their absence.

4. **P:** When individuals voluntarily abandon property, they forfeit any expectation of privacy in it that they might have had.

   C: A warrantless search and seizure of abandoned property is not unreasonable under the Fourth Amendment.

7. **P_1:** After October 1963, when Hurricane Flora devastated the island and killed more than a thousand people, the Cuban government overhauled its civil defense system.

   P_2: It was so successful that when six powerful hurricanes thumped Cuba between 1996 and 2002 only 16 people died.

   P_3: And when Hurricane Ivan struck Cuba in 2004 there was not a single casualty, but the same storm killed at least 70 people in other Caribbean countries.

   C: Cuba's record on disaster prevention is impressive.

10. **P_1:** Punishment, when speedy and specific, may suppress undesirable behavior.

    P_2: Punishment cannot teach or encourage desirable alternatives.

    C: It is crucial to use positive techniques to model and reinforce appropriate behavior that the person can use in place of the unacceptable response that has to be suppressed.

13. **P_1:** Private property helps people define themselves.

    P_2: Private property frees people from mundane cares of daily subsistence.

    P_3: Private property is finite.

    C: No individual should accumulate so much property that others are prevented from accumulating the necessities of life.

16. **P_1:** The nations of planet earth have acquired nuclear weapons with an explosive power equal to more than a million Hiroshima bombs.

    P_2: Studies suggest that explosion of only half these weapons would produce enough soot, smoke, and dust to blanket the earth, block out the sun, and bring on a nuclear winter that would threaten the survival of the human race.

    C: Radioactive fallout isn't the only concern in the aftermath of nuclear explosions.

19. **P_1:** Antipoverty programs provide jobs for middle-class professionals in social work, penology, and public health.

    P_2: Such workers' future advancement is tied to the continued growth of bureaucracies dependent on the existence of poverty.

    C: Poverty offers numerous benefits to the nonpoor.

22. P: Take the nurse who alleges that physicians enrich themselves in her hospital through un-
         necessary surgery; the engineer who discloses safety defects in the braking systems of a
         fleet of new rapid-transit vehicles; the Defense Department official who alerts Congress to
         military graft and overspending: All know that they pose a threat to those whom they de-
         nounce and that their own careers may be at risk.

    C: The stakes in whistle-blowing are high.

25. P_1: It is generally accepted that by constantly swimming with its mouth open, the shark is
         simply avoiding suffocation.

    P_2: This assures a continuous flow of oxygen-laden water into the shark's mouth, over its gills,
         and out through the gill slits.

    C: Contrary to the tales of some scuba divers, the toothy, gaping grin on the mouth of an
         approaching shark is not necessarily anticipatory.

28. P_1: Anyone familiar with our prison system knows that there are some inmates who behave
         little better than brute beasts.

    P_2: If the death penalty had been truly effective as a deterrent, such prisoners would long ago
         have vanished.

    C: The very fact that these prisoners exist is a telling argument against the efficacy of capital
         punishment as a deterrent.

II.

   1. College sports are as much driven by money as are professional sports.

   4. Business majors are robbing themselves of the true purpose of collegiate academics, a sacrifice
      that outweighs the future salary checks.

   7. The religious intolerance of television preachers must not be tolerated.

  10. Protecting the environment requires that we limit population growth.

Exercise 1.2

I.

   1. Nonargument; explanation.

   4. Nonargument; illustration.

   7. Argument (conclusion: If stem-cell research is restricted, then people will die prematurely).

  10. Nonargument; report.

  13. Nonargument; opinion.

  16. Nonargument; piece of advice.

  19. Argument (conclusion: For organisms at the sea surface, sinking into deep water usually means death).

  22. Argument (conclusion: Atoms can combine to form molecules whose properties generally are
      very different from those of the constituent atoms).

  25. Nonargument; explanation.

  28. Argument (conclusion: A person never becomes truly self-reliant).

  31. This passage could be both an argument and an explanation (conclusion: In areas where rats are
      a problem, it is very difficult to exterminate them with bait poison).

  34. Nonargument; loosely associated statements.

II.

   1. Nonargument.

   4. Nonargument.

   7. Argument (conclusion: The poor quality of parenting and the lack in continuity of adult care
      provided to many U.S. children contribute to a passivity and a sense of helplessness that hobbles
      individuals for the remainder of their lives).

  10. Nonargument.

VI.

1. Sufficient: If something is a tiger, then it is an animal.
4. Necessary: If a person has no racket, then he/she cannot play tennis. *Or*, If a person plays tennis, then he/she has a racket.
7. Sufficient: If leaves burn, then smoke is produced.
10. Necessary: If a person does not open the door, then he/she cannot cross the threshold. *Or*, If a person crosses the threshold, then he/she has opened the door.

Exercise 1.3

I.

1. Deductive (argument based on mathematics; also, conclusion follows necessarily from the premises).
4. Deductive (categorical syllogism; also, conclusion follows necessarily from the premises).
7. Inductive (causal inference; also, conclusion follows only probably from the premise).
10. Inductive (argument from analogy; also, conclusion follows only probably from the premise).
13. Inductive (argument from authority; also, conclusion follows only probably from the premise).
16. Deductive (conclusion follows necessarily from the premise).
19. Inductive (causal inference; also, conclusion follows only probably from the premises).
22. Deductive (conclusion follows necessarily from the premise; this example might also be interpreted as an argument from definition—the definition of "refraction").
25. Inductive (causal inference: The dog's familiarity with the visitor caused the dog to be silent).
28. Inductive (causal inference; also, the word "may" suggests a probabilistic inference).

Exercise 1.4

I.

1. Valid, unsound; false premises, false conclusion.
4. Valid, sound; true premises, true conclusion.
7. Invalid, unsound; true premise, true conclusion.
10. Valid, unsound; false premise, false conclusion.
13. Invalid, unsound; true premises, true conclusion.

II.

1. Strong, cogent; true premise, probably true conclusion.
4. Weak, uncogent; true premise, probably false conclusion.
7. Strong, uncogent; false premise, probably true conclusion.
10. Strong, cogent; true premise, probably true conclusion.
13. Weak, uncogent; true premises, probably false conclusion.

III.

1. Deductive, valid.
4. Deductive, valid.
7. Inductive, weak.
10. Deductive, invalid.
13. Inductive, weak.
16. Deductive, invalid.
19. Inductive, strong.

Exercise 1.5

I.

1. All *G* are *S*.   All cats are animals. (T)
   All *Q* are *S*.   All dogs are animals. (T)
   All *G* are *Q*.   All cats are dogs. (F)

4. No *I* are *P*.

Some *I* are not *F*.

Some *F* are not *P*.

No fish are mammals. (T)

Some fish are not cats. (T)

Some cats are not mammals. (F)

7. No *P* are *H*.

No *C* are *H*.

No *P* are *C*.

No dogs are fish. (T)

No mammals are fish. (T)

No dogs are mammals. (F)

10. Some *S* are not *O*.

Some *G* are not *O*.

Some *S* are not *G*.

Some dogs are not fish. (T)

Some animals are not fish. (T)

Some dogs are not animals. (F)

II.

1. If *A* then *E*.

Not *A*.

Not *E*.

If George Washington was assassinated, then
George Washington is dead. (T)

George Washington was not assassinated. (T)

George Washington is not dead. (F)

4. If *E*, then either *D* or *C*.

If *D*, then *I*.

If *E*, then *I*.

If Tom Cruise is a man, then he is either
a mouse or a human. (T)

If Tom Cruise is a mouse, then he has a tail. (T)

If Tom Cruise is a man, then he has a tail. (F)

7. All *C* with *L* are either
S or *I*.

All *C* are *I*.

All cats with fur are either mammals or dogs. (T)

All cats are dogs. (F)

10. All *R* that are *F* are either
L or *H*.

All *R* are *H*.

All *F* are *L*.

All cats that are mammals are either
dogs or animals. (T)

All cats are animals. (T)

All mammals are dogs. (F)

Exercise 1.6

I.

1.   4.   7.   10.

II.

Note: Possible variations exist for ⑤, ⑥, and ⑦.

2

Informal Fallacies

3.1 Fallacies in General

A **fallacy** is a defect in an argument that consists in something other than false premises alone. The fallacies introduced in this chapter involve defective patterns of arguing that occur so often they have been given specific names. Such defects comprise either mistakes in reasoning or the creation of an illusion that makes a bad argument appear good. The term *non sequitur* ("it does not follow") is another name for fallacy. Both deductive and inductive arguments may contain fallacies; if they do, they are either unsound or uncogent, depending on the kind of argument. Conversely, if an argument is unsound or uncogent, it has one or more false premises or it contains a fallacy (or both).

Fallacies are usually divided into two groups: formal and informal. A **formal fallacy** is one that may be identified by merely examining the form or structure of an argument. Fallacies of this kind are found only in deductive arguments that have identifiable forms. Chapter 1 presented some of these forms: categorical syllogisms, disjunctive syllogisms, and hypothetical syllogisms. The following categorical syllogism contains a formal fallacy:

> All bullfights are grotesque rituals.
> All executions are grotesque rituals.
> Therefore, all bullfights are executions.

This argument has the following form:

> All *A* are *B*.
> All *C* are *B*.
> ———————
> All *A* are *C*.

By merely examining this form, one can see that it is invalid. The fact that *A*, *B*, and *C* stand respectively for "bullfights," "grotesque rituals," and "executions" is irrelevant in detecting the fallacy. The problem may be traced to the second premise. If the letters *C* and *B* are interchanged, the form becomes valid, and the original argument, with the same change introduced, also becomes valid (but unsound).

Here is an example of a formal fallacy that occurs in a hypothetical syllogism:

If apes are intelligent, then apes can solve puzzles.
Apes can solve puzzles.
Therefore, apes are intelligent.

This argument has the following form:

If A then B.
B.
———————
A.

In this case, if A and B are interchanged in the first premise, the form becomes valid, and the original argument, with the same change, also becomes valid. This fallacy and the one that precedes it will be discussed in later chapters.

In distinguishing formal from informal fallacies, remember that formal fallacies occur only in deductive arguments. Thus, if a given argument is inductive, it cannot contain a formal fallacy. Also, keep an eye out for standard deductive argument forms such as categorical syllogisms and hypothetical syllogisms. If such an argument is invalid because of an improper arrangement of terms or statements, it commits a formal fallacy. Section 1.5 investigated some of these forms and gave instruction on distinguishing the form from the content of an argument. All of the exercises at the end of that section commit formal fallacies.

Informal fallacies are those that can be detected only by examining the content of the argument. Consider the following example:

The Brooklyn Bridge is made of atoms.
Atoms are invisible.
Therefore, the Brooklyn Bridge is invisible.

To detect this fallacy one must know something about bridges—namely, that they are large visible objects, and even though their atomic components are invisible, this does not mean that the bridges themselves are invisible.

Or consider this example:

A chess player is a person.
Therefore, a bad chess player is a bad person.

To detect this fallacy one must know that the meaning of the word "bad" depends on what it modifies, and that being a bad chess player is quite different from being a bad person.

The various informal fallacies accomplish their purpose in so many different ways that no single umbrella theory covers them all. Some fallacies work by getting the reader or listener to feel various emotions, such as fear, pity, or camaraderie, and then attaching a certain conclusion to those emotions. Others attempt to discredit an opposing argument by associating it with certain pejorative features of its author. And then there are those that appeal to various dispositions on the part of the reader or listener, such as superstition or mental laziness, to get him or her to accept a conclusion. By studying the typical ways in which arguers apply these techniques, one is less likely to be fooled by the fallacious arguments posed by others or to stumble blindly into fallacies when constructing arguments for one's own use.

Since the time of Aristotle, logicians have attempted to classify the various informal fallacies. Aristotle himself identified thirteen and separated them into two groups. The work of subsequent logicians has produced dozens more, rendering the task of classifying them even more difficult. The presentation that follows divides twenty-two informal fallacies into five groups: fallacies of relevance, fallacies of weak induction, fallacies of presumption, fallacies of ambiguity, and fallacies of grammatical analogy. The final section of the chapter considers the related topics of detecting and avoiding fallacies in the context of ordinary language.

EXERCISE 3.1

Determine whether the fallacies committed by the following arguments are formal fallacies or informal fallacies.

★1. If Rasputin was really mad, then he deceived Czar Nicholas II. Rasputin was not really mad. Therefore, he did not deceive Czar Nicholas II.

2. Everything that runs has feet. The Columbia River runs very swiftly. Therefore, the Columbia River has feet.

3. All people who believe we create our own reality are people who lack social responsibility. All people governed by selfish motives are people who lack social responsibility. Therefore, all people who believe we create our own reality are people governed by selfish motives.

★4. The ship of state is like a ship at sea. No sailor is ever allowed to protest orders from the captain. For the same reason, no citizen should ever be allowed to protest presidential policies.

5. Renowned violinist Pinchas Zukerman has said, "When it comes to vodka, Smirnoff plays second fiddle to none." We must therefore conclude that Smirnoff is the best vodka available.

6. If the Chinese government systematically kills its unwanted orphans, then the Chinese government is immoral. The Chinese government is indeed immoral. Therefore, the Chinese government systematically kills its unwanted orphans.

★7. Sarah Jessica Parker, Ben Affleck, and Julia Roberts are Democrats. Therefore, it must be the case that all Hollywood stars are Democrats.

8. Venezuelan President Hugo Chavez argues that the United States has no right to decide what's good or bad for the whole world. But who is this Chavez? He's nothing but an autocratic demagogue who assaults democracy at every opportunity. Clearly his arguments are nonsense.

9. If plastic guns are sold to the public, then terrorists will carry them aboard airliners undetected. If plastic guns are sold to the public, then airline hijackings will increase. Therefore, if terrorists carry plastic guns aboard airliners undetected, then airline hijackings will increase.

★10. Some corporate mergers are arrangements that produce layoffs. Some arrangements that produce layoffs are occasions of economic unrest. Therefore, some corporate mergers are occasions of economic unrest.

3.2   Fallacies of Relevance

The **fallacies of relevance** share the common characteristic that the arguments in which they occur have premises that are *logically* irrelevant to the conclusion. Yet the premises may appear to be *psychologically* relevant, so the conclusion may *seem* to follow from the premises, even though it does not follow logically. In a good argument the premises provide genuine evidence in support of the conclusion. In an argument that commits a fallacy of relevance, on the other hand, the connection between premises and conclusion is emotional. To identify a fallacy of relevance, therefore, one must be able to distinguish genuine evidence from various forms of emotional appeal.

1. Appeal to Force
(*Argumentum ad Baculum*: Appeal to the "Stick")

The fallacy of **appeal to force** occurs whenever an arguer poses a conclusion to another person and tells that person either implicitly or explicitly that some harm will come to him or her if he or she does not accept the conclusion. The fallacy always involves a threat by the arguer to the physical or psychological well-being of the listener or reader, who may be either an individual or a group of people. Obviously, such a threat is logically irrelevant to the subject matter of the conclusion, so any argument based on such a procedure is fallacious. The *ad baculum* fallacy often occurs when children argue with one another:

> *Child to playmate: Sesame Street* is the best show on TV; and if you don't believe it, I'm going to call my big brother over here and he's going to beat you up.

But it occurs among adults as well:

> *Secretary to boss:* I deserve a raise in salary for the coming year. After all, you know how friendly I am with your wife, and I'm sure you wouldn't want her to find out what's been going on between you and that sexpot client of yours.

The first example involves a physical threat, the second a psychological one. While neither threat provides any genuine evidence that the conclusion is true, both provide evidence that someone might be injured. If the two types of evidence are confused with each other, both arguer and listener may be deluded into thinking that the conclusion is supported by evidence, when in fact it is not.

The appeal to force fallacy usually accomplishes its purpose by psychologically impeding the reader or listener from acknowledging a missing premise that, if acknowl-

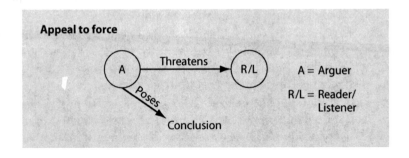

edged, would be seen to be false or at least questionable. The two examples just given can be interpreted as concealing the following premises, both of which are most likely false:

> If my brother forces you to admit that *Sesame Street* is the best show on TV, then *Sesame Street* is in fact the best show.

> If I succeed in threatening you, then I deserve a raise in salary.

The conclusion of the first argument is that *Sesame Street* is the best show on TV. But just because someone is forced into saying that it is does not mean that such is the case. Similarly, the conclusion of the second argument is that the secretary deserves a raise in salary. But if the boss is threatened into raising the secretary's salary, this does not mean that the secretary deserves a raise. Many of the other informal fallacies can be interpreted as accomplishing their purpose in this way.

2. Appeal to Pity (*Argumentum ad Misericordiam*)

The **appeal to pity** fallacy occurs when an arguer attempts to support a conclusion by merely evoking pity from the reader or listener. This pity may be directed toward the arguer or toward some third party. Example:

> *Taxpayer to judge:* Your Honor, I admit that I declared thirteen children as dependents on my tax return, even though I have only two. But if you find me guilty of tax evasion, my reputation will be ruined. I'll probably lose my job, my poor wife will not be able to have the operation that she desperately needs, and my kids will starve. Surely I am not guilty.

The conclusion of this argument is "Surely I am not guilty." Obviously, the conclusion is not *logically* relevant to the arguer's set of pathetic circumstances, although it is *psychologically* relevant. If the arguer succeeds in evoking pity from the listener or reader, the latter is likely to exercise his or her desire to help the arguer by accepting the argument. In this way the reader or listener may be fooled into accepting a conclusion that is not supported by any evidence. The appeal to pity is quite common and is often used by students on their instructors at exam time and by lawyers on behalf of their clients before judges and juries.

Of course, some arguments that attempt to evoke sympathetic feelings from the reader or listener are not fallacious. We might call them *arguments from compassion*. Such arguments differ from the fallacious appeal to pity in that, in addition to evoking

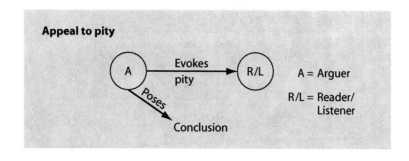

compassion on behalf of some person, they supply information about why that person is genuinely deserving of help or special consideration. Whenever possible these nonfallacious arguments should show that the person in question is a victim of circumstances and not responsible for the dire straits he finds himself in, that the recommended help or special consideration is not illegal or inappropriate, and that it will genuinely help the person in question. In contrast to such arguments, the appeal to pity proceeds by ignoring all of these considerations and attempts to support a conclusion by merely evoking pity from the reader or listener.

3. Appeal to the People (*Argumentum ad Populum*)

Nearly everyone wants to be loved, esteemed, admired, valued, recognized, and accepted by others. The **appeal to the people** uses these desires to get the reader or listener to accept a conclusion. Two approaches are involved: one of them direct, the other indirect.

The *direct approach* occurs when an arguer, addressing a large group of people, excites the emotions and enthusiasm of the crowd to win acceptance for his or her conclusion. The objective is to arouse a kind of mob mentality. This is the strategy used by nearly every propagandist and demagogue. Adolf Hitler was a master of the technique, but speech makers at Democratic and Republican national conventions also use it with some measure of success. Waving flags and blaring music add to the overall effect. Because the individuals in the audience want to share in the camaraderie, the euphoria, and the excitement, they find themselves accepting a variety of conclusions with ever-increasing fervor.

An appeal to negative emotions, such as suspicion and fear, can also generate a mob mentality. These emotions have produced many lynchings, and they led to the internment of Japanese Americans during World War II. Also, the direct approach is not limited to oral discourse. The same effect can be accomplished in writing. By using such emotionally charged phrasing as "fighter of communism," "champion of the free enterprise system," and "defender of the working man," polemicists can awaken the same kind of mob mentality as they would if they were speaking.

In the *indirect approach* the arguer aims his or her appeal not at the crowd as a whole but at one or more individuals separately, focusing on some aspect of their relationship to the crowd. The indirect approach includes such specific forms as the bandwagon argument, the appeal to vanity, and the appeal to snobbery. All are standard techniques of the advertising industry.

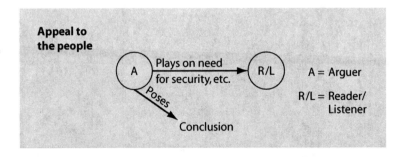

Here is an example of the **bandwagon argument:**

> Of course you want to buy Zing toothpaste. Why, 90 percent of America brushes with Zing.

The idea is that you will be left behind or left out of the group if you do not use the product.

The **appeal to vanity** often associates the product with someone who is admired, pursued, or imitated, the idea being that you, too, will be admired and pursued if you use it. The recent television and billboard ads for the U.S. Marine Corps provide an example. The ads show a strong, handsome man in uniform holding a gleaming sword, and the caption reads:

> The Few, the Proud, the Marines.

The message is that if you join the Marines, then you, too, will be admired and respected, just like the handsome man in the uniform.

The **appeal to snobbery** depends on a similar kind of association.

> A Rolls-Royce is not for everyone. If you qualify as one of the select few, this distinguished classic may be seen and driven at British Motor Cars, Ltd.
> (By appointment only, please.)

Needless to say, the indirect approach is used not only by advertisers:

> *Mother to child:* You want to grow up and be just like Wonder Woman, don't you? Then eat your liver and carrots.

These examples illustrate how the indirect version of the appeal to the people can overlap the false cause fallacy, which is presented in Section 3.3. Thus, the previous example might be interpreted to suggest that eating liver and carrots will *cause* one to become just like Wonder Woman. If so, the fallacy could be identified as false cause.

Both the direct and indirect approaches of the *ad populum* fallacy have the same basic structure:

> You want to be accepted/included in the group/loved/esteemed....Therefore, you should accept XYZ as true.

In the direct approach the arousal of a mob mentality produces an immediate feeling of belonging. Each person feels united with the crowd, and this feeling evokes a sense of strength and security. When the crowd roars its approval of the conclusions that are then offered, anyone who does not accept them automatically cuts himself or herself off from the crowd and risks the loss of his or her security, strength, and acceptance. The same thing happens in the indirect approach, but the context and technique are somewhat subtler.

4. Argument Against the Person (*Argumentum ad Hominem*)

This fallacy always involves two arguers. One of them advances (either directly or implicitly) a certain argument, and the other then responds by directing his or her attention not to the first person's argument but to the first person *himself.* When this occurs, the second person is said to commit an **argument against the person.**

The argument against the person occurs in three forms: the *ad hominem* abusive, the *ad hominem* circumstantial, and the *tu quoque.* In the **ad hominem abusive,** the second person responds to the first person's argument by verbally abusing the first person. Example:

> Before he died, poet Allen Ginsberg argued in favor of legalizing pornography. But Ginsberg's arguments are nothing but trash. Ginsberg was a marijuana-smoking homosexual and a thoroughgoing advocate of the drug culture.

Because Ginsberg's being a marijuana-smoking homosexual and advocate of the drug culture is irrelevant to whether the premises of this argument support the conclusion, the argument is fallacious.

Not all cases of the *ad hominem* abusive are so blunt, but they are just as fallacious. Example:

> William Buckley has argued in favor of legalizing drugs such as cocaine and heroin. But Buckley is just another one of those upper-crust intellectuals who is out of touch with real America. No sensible person should listen to his pseudosolutions.

Again, whether Buckley is an upper-crust intellectual has nothing to do with whether his premises support his conclusion.

The **ad hominem circumstantial** begins the same way as the *ad hominem* abusive, but instead of heaping verbal abuse on his or her opponent, the respondent attempts to discredit the opponent's argument by alluding to certain circumstances that affect the opponent. By doing so the respondent hopes to show that the opponent is predisposed to argue the way he or she does and should therefore not be taken seriously. Here is an example:

> The Dalai Lama argues that China has no business in Tibet and that the West should do something about it. But the Dalai Lama just wants the Chinese to leave so he can return as leader. Naturally he argues this way. Therefore, we should reject his arguments.

The author of this argument ignores the substance of the Dalai Lama's argument and attempts to discredit it by calling attention to certain circumstances that affect the Dalai Lama—namely, that he wants to return to Tibet as its leader. But the fact that the Dalai Lama happens to be affected by these circumstances is irrelevant to whether

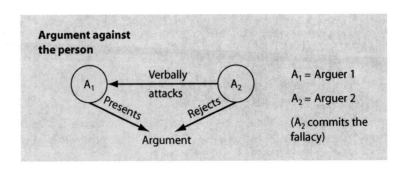

his premises support a conclusion. The *ad hominem* circumstantial is easy to recognize because it always takes this form: "Of course Mr. X argues this way; just look at the circumstances that affect him."

The **tu quoque** ("you too") fallacy begins the same way as the other two varieties of the *ad hominem* argument, except that the second arguer attempts to make the first appear to be hypocritical or arguing in bad faith. The second arguer usually accomplishes this by citing features in the life or behavior of the first arguer that conflict with the latter's conclusion. In effect, the second arguer says, "How dare you argue that I should stop doing *X;* why, you do (or have done) *X* yourself." Example:

> *Child to parent:* Your argument that I should stop stealing candy from the corner store is no good. You told me yourself just a week ago that you, too, stole candy when you were a kid.

Obviously, whether the parent stole candy is irrelevant to whether the parent's premises support the conclusion that the child should not steal candy.

Keep in mind that the purpose of an *ad hominem* argument is to discredit another person's argument by placing its author in a bad light. Thus, for the fallacy to be committed, there must always be two arguers (at least implicitly). If it should turn out that the person being attacked is not an arguer, then the personal comments made by the attacker may well be relevant to the conclusion that is drawn. In general, personal observations are relevant to conclusions about what kind of person someone is (good, bad, stingy, trustworthy, and so forth) and whether a person has done something. Example:

> International terrorist Osama bin Laden planned the destruction of the World Trade Center, killing thousands of innocent people, and he supports terrorist causes all over the world. Bin Laden is therefore a wicked and irresponsible person.

The conclusion is not that Bin Laden's argument is bad but that Bin Laden himself is bad. Because the premises give relevant support to this conclusion, the argument commits no fallacy. Another example:

> Shakespeare cannot possibly have written the thirty-six plays attributed to him, because the real Shakespeare was a two-bit country businessman who barely finished the fourth grade in school and who never left the confines of his native England.

The conclusion is not that some argument of Shakespeare's is bad but that Shakespeare did not write certain plays. Again, since the premises are relevant to this conclusion, the argument commits no *ad hominem* fallacy.

Determining what kind of person someone is includes determining whether that person is trustworthy. Thus, personal comments are often relevant in evaluating whether a person's proclamations or statements, unsupported by evidence, warrant our belief. Examples of such statements include promises to do something, testimony given by a witness, and testimonials in support of a product or service. Here is an example of an argument that discredits a witness:

> Mickey has testified that he saw Freddy set fire to the building. But Mickey was recently convicted on ten counts of perjury, and he hates Freddy with a passion and would love to see him sent to jail. Therefore, you should not believe Mickey's testimony.

This argument commits no fallacy. The conclusion is not that you should reject Mickey's argument but rather that you should reject his testimony. Testimony is not argument, and the fact that the witness is a known liar and has a motive to lie now is relevant to whether we should believe him. Furthermore, note that the conclusion is not that Mickey's statement is literally false but rather that we should not *believe* the statement. It is quite possible that Mickey really did see Freddy set fire to the building and that Mickey's statement to that effect is true. But if our only reason for believing this statement is the mere fact that Mickey has made it, then given the circumstances, we are not justified in that belief. Personal factors are never relevant to truth and falsity as such, but they are relevant to believability.

Yet there is often a close connection between truth and believability, and this provides one of the reasons why *ad hominem* arguments are often effective. In evaluating any argument there are always two issues to be considered: the quality of the reasoning and the truth of the premises. As noted, both are irrelevant to the personal characteristics of the arguer. But whether we *accept* the premises as true may depend on the credibility of the arguer. Knowing that the arguer is biased or has a motive to lie may provide good grounds for distrusting the premises. Another reason why *ad hominem* arguments are effective is that they engage the emotions of readers and listeners and thereby motivate them to transfer their negative feelings about the arguer onto the argument.

5. Accident

The fallacy of **accident** is committed when a general rule is applied to a specific case it was not intended to cover. Typically, the general rule is cited (either directly or implicitly) in the premises and then wrongly applied to the specific case mentioned in the conclusion. Two examples:

> Freedom of speech is a constitutionally guaranteed right. Therefore, John Q. Radical should not be arrested for his speech that incited the riot last week.

> Property should be returned to its rightful owner. That drunken sailor who is starting a fight with his opponents at the pool table lent you his .45-caliber pistol, and now he wants it back. Therefore, you should return it to him now.

In the first example, the general rule is that freedom of speech is normally guaranteed, and the specific case is the speech made by John Q. Radical. Because the speech incited

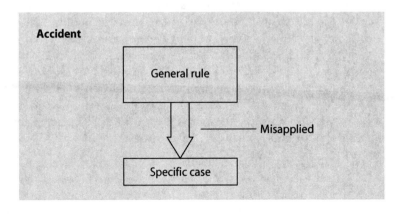

a riot, the rule does not apply. In the second example, the general rule is that property should be returned to its rightful owner, and the specific case is the sailor who wants his gun returned. The rule does not apply, because the return of the property might result in serious injury or death.

The fallacy of accident gets its name from the fact that one or more accidental features of the specific case make it an exception to the rule. In the first example the accidental feature is that the speech incited a riot; in the second example the accidental features are that the sailor is drunk, that he is starting a fight, and that the property in question is dangerous.

6. Straw Man

The **straw man** fallacy is committed when an arguer distorts an opponent's argument for the purpose of more easily attacking it, demolishes the distorted argument, and then concludes that the opponent's real argument has been demolished. By so doing, the arguer is said to have set up a straw man and knocked it down, only to conclude that the real man (opposing argument) has been knocked down as well. Example:

> Mr. Goldberg has argued against prayer in the public schools. Obviously Mr. Goldberg advocates atheism. But atheism is what they used to have in Russia. Atheism leads to the suppression of all religions and the replacement of God by an omnipotent state. Is that what we want for this country? I hardly think so. Clearly Mr. Goldberg's argument is nonsense.

Like the argument against the person fallacy, the straw man fallacy involves two arguers. Mr. Goldberg, who is the first arguer, has presented an argument against prayer in the public schools. The second arguer then attacks Goldberg's argument by equating it with an argument for atheism. He then attacks atheism and concludes that Goldberg's argument is nonsense. Since Goldberg's argument had nothing to do with atheism, the second argument commits the straw man fallacy.

As this example illustrates, the kind of distortion the second arguer resorts to is often an attempt to exaggerate the first person's argument or make it look more extreme than it really is. Here are two more examples:

> The garment workers have signed a petition arguing for better ventilation on the work premises. Unfortunately, air-conditioning is expensive. Air ducts would have to be run throughout the factory, and a massive heat exchange unit installed on the roof. Also, the cost of operating such a system during the summer would be astronomical. In view of these considerations the petition must be rejected.

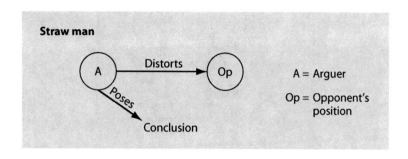

> The student status committee has presented us with an argument favoring alcohol privileges on campus. What do the students want? Is it their intention to stay boozed up from the day they enter as freshmen until the day they graduate? Do they expect us to open a bar for them? Or maybe a chain of bars all over campus? Such a proposal is ridiculous!

In the first argument, the petition is merely for better ventilation in the factory—maybe a fan in the window during the summer. The arguer exaggerates this request to mean an elaborate air-conditioning system installed throughout the building. He then points out that this is too expensive and concludes by rejecting the petition. A similar strategy is used in the second argument. The arguer distorts the request for alcohol privileges to mean a chain of bars all over campus. Such an idea is so patently outlandish that no further argument is necessary.

7. Missing the Point (*Ignoratio Elenchi*)

All the fallacies we have discussed thus far have been instances of cases where the premises of an argument are irrelevant to the conclusion. **Missing the point** illustrates a special form of irrelevance. This fallacy occurs when the premises of an argument support one particular conclusion, but then a different conclusion, often vaguely related to the correct conclusion, is drawn. Whenever one suspects that such a fallacy is being committed, he or she should be able to identify the *correct* conclusion, the conclusion that the premises *logically* imply. This conclusion must be significantly different from the conclusion that is actually drawn. Examples:

> Crimes of theft and robbery have been increasing at an alarming rate lately. The conclusion is obvious: We must reinstate the death penalty immediately.

> Abuse of the welfare system is rampant nowadays. Our only alternative is to abolish the system altogether.

At least two correct conclusions are implied by the premise of the first argument: either "We should provide increased police protection in vulnerable neighborhoods" or "We should initiate programs to eliminate the causes of the crimes." Reinstating the death

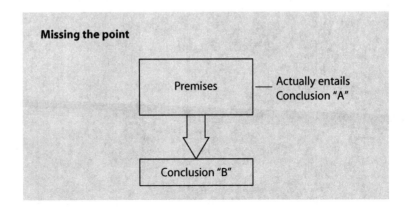

penalty is not a logical conclusion at all. Among other things, theft and robbery are not capital crimes. In the second argument the premises logically suggest some systematic effort to eliminate the cheaters rather than eliminating the system altogether.

Ignoratio elenchi means "ignorance of the proof." The arguer is ignorant of the logical implications of his or her own premises and, as a result, draws a conclusion that misses the point entirely. The fallacy has a distinct structure all its own, but in some ways it serves as a catchall for arguments that are not clear instances of one or more of the other fallacies. An argument should not be identified as a case of missing the point, however, if one of the other fallacies fits.

8. Red Herring

This fallacy is closely associated with missing the point (*ignoratio elenchi*). The **red herring** fallacy is committed when the arguer diverts the attention of the reader or listener by changing the subject to a different but sometimes subtly related one. He or she then finishes by either drawing a conclusion about this different issue or by merely presuming that some conclusion has been established. By so doing, the arguer purports to have won the argument. The fallacy gets its name from a procedure used to train hunting dogs to follow a scent. A red herring (or bag of them) is dragged across the trail with the aim of leading the dogs astray. Since red herrings have an especially potent scent (caused in part by the smoking process used to preserve them), only the best dogs will follow the original scent.

To use the red herring fallacy effectively, the arguer must change the original subject of the argument without the reader or listener noticing it. One way of doing this is to change the subject to one that is subtly related to the original subject. Here are two examples of this technique:

> Environmentalists are continually harping about the dangers of nuclear power. Unfortunately, electricity is dangerous no matter where it comes from. Every year hundreds of people are electrocuted by accident. Since most of these accidents are caused by carelessness, they could be avoided if people would just exercise greater caution.

> There is a good deal of talk these days about the need to eliminate pesticides from our fruits and vegetables. But many of these foods are essential to our health. Carrots are an excellent source of vitamin A, broccoli is rich in iron, and oranges and grapefruit have lots of vitamin C.

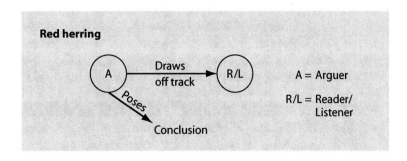

Both arguments commit the red herring fallacy. In the first, the original issue is whether nuclear power is dangerous. The arguer changes this subject to the danger of electrocution and proceeds to draw a conclusion about that. The new subject is clearly different from the possibility of nuclear explosion or meltdown, but the fact that both are related to electricity facilitates the arguer's goal of leading someone off the track. In the second argument, the original issue is pesticides, and the arguer changes it to the value of fruits and vegetables in one's diet. Again, the fact that the second topic is related to the first assists the arguer in committing the fallacy. In neither case does the arguer draw a conclusion about the original topic, but by merely diverting the attention of the reader or listener, the arguer creates the presumption of having won the argument.

A second way of using the red herring effectively is to change the subject to some flashy, eye-catching topic that is virtually guaranteed to distract the listener's attention. Topics of this sort include sex, crime, scandal, immorality, death, and any other topic that might serve as the subject of gossip. Here is an example of this technique:

> Professor Conway complains of inadequate parking on our campus. But did you
>   know that last year Conway carried on a torrid love affair with a member of the
>   English Department? The two used to meet every day for clandestine sex in the
>   copier room. Apparently they didn't realize how much you can see through that
>   fogged glass window. Even the students got an eyeful. Enough said about Conway.

The red herring fallacy can be confused with the straw man fallacy because both have the effect of drawing the reader/listener off the track. This confusion can usually be avoided by remembering the unique ways in which they accomplish this purpose. In the straw man, the arguer begins by distorting an opponent's argument and concludes by knocking down the distorted argument. In the red herring, the arguer ignores the opponent's argument (if there is one) and subtly changes the subject. Thus, to distinguish the two fallacies, one should attempt to determine whether the arguer has knocked down a distorted argument or simply changed the subject. Also keep in mind that straw man always involves two arguers, at least implicitly, whereas a red herring often does not.

Both the red herring and straw man fallacies are susceptible of being confused with missing the point, because all three involve a similar kind of irrelevancy. To avoid this confusion, one should note that both red herring and straw man proceed by generating a new set of premises, whereas missing the point does not. Straw man draws a conclusion from new premises that are obtained by distorting an earlier argument, and red herring, if it draws any conclusion at all, draws one from new premises obtained by changing the subject. Missing the point, however, draws a conclusion from the original premises. Also, in the red herring and straw man, the conclusion, if there is one, is *relevant* to the premises from which it is drawn; but in missing the point, the conclusion is *irrelevant* to the premises from which it is drawn. Finally, remember that missing the point serves in part as a kind of catchall fallacy, and a fallacious argument should not be identified as a case of missing the point if one of the other fallacies clearly fits.

EXERCISE 3.2

I. Identify the fallacies of relevance committed by the following arguments, giving a brief explanation for your answer. If no fallacy is committed, write "no fallacy."

★1. The position open in the accounting department should be given to Frank Thompson. Frank has six hungry children to feed, and his wife desperately needs an operation to save her eyesight.

2. Erica Evans, who takes orders at the local Taco Bell, argues persuasively in favor of increasing the minimum wage. But this is exactly what you would expect. Erica is paid the minimum wage, and if the minimum wage is increased, then her own salary will go up. Obviously Erica's arguments are worthless.

3. The school board argues that our schools are in desperate need of repair. But the real reason our students are falling behind is that they spend too much time with their computers. Becoming educated means a lot more than learning how to point and click. The school board should send a letter to the parents urging them to monitor their kids' computer time.

★4. Whoever thrusts a knife into another person should be arrested. But surgeons do precisely this when operating. Therefore, surgeons should be arrested.

5. You should read Irving Stone's latest novel right away. It's sold over a million copies, and practically everyone in the Manhattan cocktail circuit is talking about it.

6. Friedrich Nietzsche's philosophy is not worth the paper it's printed on. Nietzsche was an immoral reprobate who went completely insane from syphilis before he died.

★7. Surely you welcome the opportunity to join our protective organization. Think of all the money you will lose from broken windows, overturned trucks, and damaged merchandise in the event of your not joining.

8. Senator Barrow advocates increased Social Security benefits for the poor. It is regrettable that the senator finds it necessary to advocate socialism. Socialism defeats initiative, takes away promised rewards, and leads directly to inefficiency and big government. It was tried for years in Eastern Europe, and it failed miserably. Clearly, socialism is no good.

9. Something is seriously wrong with high school education these days. After ten years of decline, SAT scores are still extremely low, and high school graduates are practically incapable of reading and writing. The obvious conclusion is that we should close the schools.

★10. The editors of the *Daily Register* have accused our company of being one of the city's worst water polluters. But the *Daily Register* is responsible for much more pollution than we are. After all, they own the Western Paper Company, and that company discharges tons of chemical residue into the city's river every day.

11. If 20 percent of adult Americans are functionally illiterate, then it's no wonder that morons get elected to public office. In fact, 20 percent of adult Americans *are* functionally illiterate. Therefore, it's no wonder that morons get elected to public office.

12. Ladies and gentlemen, today the lines of battle have been drawn. When the din of clashing armor has finally died away, the Republican party will emerge

victorious! We are the true party of the American people! We embody the values that all real Americans hold sacred! We cherish and protect our founding fathers' vision that gave birth to the Constitution! We stand for decency and righteousness; for self-determination and the liberty to conduct our affairs as each of us freely chooses! In the coming election, victory will be ours, so help us God!

★13. We've all heard the argument that too much television is the reason our students can't read and write. Yet many of today's TV shows are excellent. *Grey's Anatomy* unveils the personal lives of interns at an urban hospital, *Law and Order* explores ethical issues in our criminal justice system, and *American Idol* uncovers hidden musical talent. Today's TV is just great!

14. Surely architect Norris is not responsible for the collapse of the Central Bank Tower. Norris has had nothing but trouble lately. His daughter eloped with a child molester, his son committed suicide, and his alcoholic wife recently left for Las Vegas with his retirement savings.

15. The First Amendment to the Constitution prevents the government from interfering with the free exercise of religion. The liturgical practice of the Religion of Internal Enlightenment involves human sacrifice. Therefore, it would be wrong for the government to interfere with this religious practice.

★16. Former antiterrorism czar Richard Clark argues in his book that the Iraq war was a terrible mistake and that it undermines the war on terrorism. But it's clear that Clark makes these outlandish claims merely to drum up sales for his book. Thus, we really shouldn't take his arguments seriously.

17. Professor Pearson's arguments in favor of the theory of evolution should be discounted. Pearson is a cocaine-snorting sex pervert and, according to some reports, a member of the Communist party.

18. Rudolf Höss, commandant of the Auschwitz concentration camp, confessed to having exterminated one million people, most of whom were Jews, in the Auschwitz gas chamber. We can only conclude that Höss was either insane or an extremely evil person.

★19. TV commentator Larry Kudlow argues that government should get off the back of the American businessman. Obviously, Kudlow wants to abolish government altogether. Yet without government there would be no defense, no judicial system, no Social Security, and no health and safety regulations. None of us wants to forgo these benefits. Thus, we can see that Kudlow's argument is absurd.

20. I know that some of you oppose the appointment of David Cole as the new sales manager. On further consideration, however, I am confident you will find him well qualified for the job. If Cole is not appointed, it may become necessary to make severe personnel cutbacks in your department.

21. Animal rights activists say that animals are abused in biomedical research labs. But consider this: Pets are abused by their owners every day. Probably 25 percent of pet owners should never get near animals. Some cases of abuse are enough to make you sick.

★22. Of course you want to buy a pair of Slinky fashion jeans. Slinky jeans really show off your figure, and all the Hollywood starlets down on the Strip can be seen wearing them these days.

23. Actress Andie MacDowell says that it's healthy to drink milk. But the dairy industry pays MacDowell thousands of dollars to make these ads. Therefore, we should not take her testimonials too seriously.

24. Dr. Morrison has argued that smoking is responsible for the majority of health problems in this country and that every smoker who has even the slightest concern for his or her health should quit. Unfortunately, however, we must consign Dr. Morrison's argument to the trash bin. Only yesterday I saw none other than Dr. Morrison himself smoking a cigar.

★25. Mr. Rhodes is suffering from amnesia and has no recollection whatever of the events of the past two weeks. We can only conclude that he did not commit the crime of murdering his wife a week ago, as he has been accused of doing.

II. Answer "true" or "false" to the following statements:

1. In the appeal to force, the arguer physically attacks the listener.

2. In the direct variety of the appeal to the people, the arguer attempts to create a kind of mob mentality.

3. If an arguer attempts to discredit court room testimony or a promise by pointing out that the witness or the person making the promise is a liar, then the arguer commits an *argumentum ad hominem* (argument against the person) fallacy.

4. The *argumentum ad hominem* always involves two arguers.

5. In the *argumentum ad hominem* circumstantial, the circumstances cited by the second arguer are intended precisely to malign the character of the first arguer.

6. In the *tu quoque* fallacy, the arguer threatens the reader or listener.

7. In the fallacy of accident, a general rule is applied to a specific case where it does not fit.

8. In the straw man fallacy, an arguer often distorts another person's argument by making it look more extreme than it really is.

9. Whenever one suspects that a missing the point fallacy is being committed, one should be able to state the conclusion that is logically implied by the premises.

10. In the red herring fallacy, the arguer attempts to lead the reader or listener off the track.

III. Identify the arguments in the following dialogue, then discuss each of them in terms of the fallacies presented in this section. You should be able to find at least one case of each fallacy.

"Thanks for saving us a seat," Jodie says to her friend Frank, as she and Liz sit down with coffee cups in hand in the crowded cafeteria.

"No problem," Frank says.

"We were late getting out of Professor Conklin's social problems class," Jodie says disgustedly. "He's such a jerk! He always keeps us late, and he's the most arrogant snob I've ever met."

"I've heard that," Frank says. "What's he covering in class now?"

"Sexual harassment in the workplace," Jodie replies. "But that *is* a real problem these days."

"How so?"

"Well, my friend Amelia is a dispatcher for a trucking company, and she's told me about dozens of times she's been a victim of sexual harassment. The truckers have *Playboy* centerfolds tacked up all over the place, they constantly leer at her, they're always asking her for dates. One of them even pats her rear when she leans over at the drinking fountain."

Frank laughs. "Well, there is such a thing as the First Amendment, which supposedly guarantees freedom of expression. You wouldn't want to deny these guys their freedom of expression, would you?"

"Freedom of expression, my eye!" explodes Jodie, looking incredulously at Frank. "Patting someone's rear isn't freedom of expression, it's abusive physical contact. So it's not protected by the First Amendment. Men! The trouble with you, Frank, is you're a typical man. If you were a woman, you'd see these things for what they are," she says, looking at Liz for support.

Liz nods her head in strong agreement.

"Well," says Frank, "I think your friend is lucky to have a job, what with all the people out of work these days. I've got a friend who's spent half his retirement savings just putting food on the table for his family, after losing his job. He was in the construction business, which is dead right now. And in other parts of the country it's even worse. You should tell Amelia to quit complaining."

"Stop giving me the runaround," demands Jodie, offended. "The trouble with you men is, you always look at women as sex objects. That makes sexual harassment inevitable."

"What do you mean?" protests Frank. "It's you women who treat us men like sex objects. What about all your makeup and perfume? And the tight pants and all the see-through stuff you wear? You think men are just a pack of animals—nothing but instinct—and you think that will make us fall for you. Isn't that how you see us?"

"I won't dignify that with a reply," fumes Jodie. "Anyone who isn't blind can see that Amelia's being victimized by those truckers. If you can't see it, maybe pouring this hot coffee over your thick head will wake you up!" she threatens.

"Calm down," says Frank with a startled look. "Everyone is beginning to stare at us. Okay, suppose I agree that Amelia is a victim. The question is, what do we do about it?"

"To begin with," says Jodie firmly, "the trucking company should transfer Amelia out of dispatch and give her a better job, like executive secretary in the regional office. Her husband ran out on her recently, leaving her with all five kids— and little Tommy needs braces. She could really use the extra money."

"You're joking!" Frank laughs sarcastically. "Didn't you tell me once that Amelia never finished high school and is functionally illiterate? She could never handle a job like that."

Thinking for a moment, Jodie then replies, "Well, maybe you're right. But at least the company should adopt a policy forbidding all forms of sexual harassment. Maybe that would make the truckers see how abusive they are, and then they might stop acting that way. Practically every company in the country has such a policy, but Amelia's bosses are dragging their feet."

"Okay. But then how do you define sexual harassment?" Frank asks. "'Cause if you can't define it, any policy is useless."

"Well, I don't exactly know," Jodie hesitates. "I'll have to think about that."

"Aha! I knew it!" exclaims Frank, triumphantly. "You can't define it, which means you don't even know if it exists! If you weren't such a radical feminist, you would see that all these claims of sexual harassment are hooey."

"Me, radical?" Jodie explodes. "The truth is you're a radical sexist. What you're saying is, women are only chattel, like they were 200 years ago, and men can use or abuse them any way they please. Liz, that's what he's saying, isn't it?"

"Absolutely," Liz affirms.

"What a crazy argument," says Frank scornfully. "What you're saying is, we should abolish all distinctions between men and women and create a unisex society in which everyone acts like a bunch of robots. Isn't that right, Liz?"

"No, not at all," insists Liz. "She's trying to—"

"You're completely insane, Frank," Jodie interrupts, rising determinedly from her chair, "and your arguments are wacko!" She then throws the remains of her coffee at Frank. The other students who have been listening to the heated argument rise up shouting, "Right on, Jodie!" Some begin chanting, "End sex harassment! End sex harassment!" As more students join the demonstration, they surround Frank, gesturing crudely.

Angry and humiliated, he breaks away and dashes out the door.

3.3 Fallacies of Weak Induction

The **fallacies of weak induction** occur not because the premises are logically irrelevant to the conclusion, as is the case with the eight fallacies of relevance, but because the connection between premises and conclusion is not strong enough to support the conclusion. In each of the following fallacies, the premises provide at least a shred of evidence in support of the conclusion, but the evidence is not nearly good enough to cause a reasonable person to believe the conclusion. Like the fallacies of relevance, however, the fallacies of weak induction often involve emotional grounds for believing the conclusion.

9. Appeal to Unqualified Authority (*Argumentum ad Verecundiam*)

We saw in Chapter 1 that an argument from authority is an inductive argument in which an arguer cites the authority or testimony of another person in support of some conclusion. The **appeal to unqualified authority** fallacy is a variety of the argument from authority and occurs when the cited authority or witness lacks credibility. There are several reasons why an authority or witness might lack credibility. The person might lack the requisite expertise, might be biased or prejudiced, might have a motive

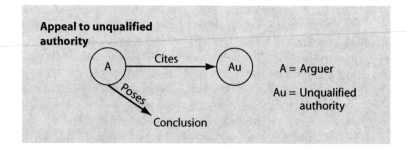

to lie or disseminate "misinformation," or might lack the requisite ability to perceive or recall. The following examples illustrate these reasons:

> Dr. Bradshaw, our family physician, has stated that the creation of muonic atoms of deuterium and tritium hold the key to producing a sustained nuclear fusion reaction at room temperature. In view of Dr. Bradshaw's expertise as a physician, we must conclude that this is indeed true.

This conclusion deals with nuclear physics, and the authority is a family physician. Because it is unlikely that a physician would be an expert in nuclear physics, the argument commits an appeal to unqualified authority.

> David Duke, former Grand Wizard of the Ku Klux Klan, has stated, "Jews are not good Americans. They have no understanding of what America is." On the basis of Duke's authority, we must therefore conclude that the Jews in this country are un-American.

As an authority, David Duke is clearly biased, so his statements cannot be trusted.

> James W. Johnston, Chairman of R. J. Reynolds Tobacco Company, testified before Congress that tobacco is not an addictive substance and that smoking cigarettes does not produce any addiction. Therefore, we should believe him and conclude that smoking does not in fact lead to any addiction.

If Mr. Johnston had admitted that tobacco is addictive, it would have opened the door to government regulation, which could put his company out of business. Thus, because Johnston had a clear motive to lie, we should not believe his statements.

> Old Mrs. Furguson (who is practically blind) has testified that she saw the defendant stab the victim with a bayonet while she was standing in the twilight shadows 100 yards from the incident. Therefore, members of the jury, you must find the defendant guilty.

Here the witness lacks the ability to perceive what she has testified to, so her testimony is untrustworthy.

Of course if an authority is credible, the resulting argument will contain no fallacy. Example:

> The county tax collector issued a press release stating that property tax revenues are higher this year than last. Therefore, we conclude that these revenues are indeed higher this year.

Normally a county tax collector would be considered a qualified expert in the area of tax revenues, so assuming the tax collector has no reason to lie, this argument is inductively strong.

In deciding whether a person is a qualified authority, one should keep two important points in mind. First, the person might be an authority in more than one field. For example, a chemist might also be an authority in biology, or an economist might also be an authority in law. The second point is that there are some areas in which practically no one can be considered an authority. Such areas include politics, morals, and religion. For example, if someone were to argue that abortion is immoral because a certain philosopher or religious leader has said so, the argument would be weak regardless of the authority's qualifications. Many questions in these areas are so hotly contested that there is no conventional wisdom an authority can depend on.

10. Appeal to Ignorance
(*Argumentum ad Ignorantiam*)

When the premises of an argument state that nothing has been proved one way or the other about something, and the conclusion then makes a definite assertion about that thing, the argument commits an **appeal to ignorance.** The issue usually involves something that is incapable of being proved or something that has not yet been proved. Example:

> People have been trying for centuries to provide conclusive evidence for the claims of astrology, and no one has ever succeeded. Therefore, we must conclude that astrology is a lot of nonsense.

Conversely, the following argument commits the same fallacy.

> People have been trying for centuries to disprove the claims of astrology, and no one has ever succeeded. Therefore, we must conclude that the claims of astrology are true.

The premises of an argument are supposed to provide positive evidence for the conclusion. The premises of these arguments, however, tell us nothing about astrology; rather, they tell us about what certain unnamed and unidentified people have tried unsuccessfully to do. This evidence may provide some slight reason for believing the conclusion, but certainly not sufficient reason.

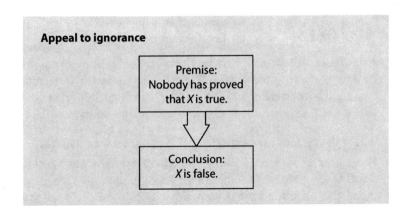

Appeal to ignorance

Premise:
Nobody has proved
that *X* is true.

Conclusion:
X is false.

These examples do, however, lead us to the first of two important exceptions to the appeal to ignorance. The first stems from the fact that if qualified researchers investigate a certain phenomenon within their range of expertise and fail to turn up any evidence that the phenomenon exists, this fruitless search by itself constitutes positive evidence about the question. Consider, for example, the following argument:

> Teams of scientists attempted over several decades to detect the existence of the luminiferous aether, and all failed to do so. Therefore, the luminiferous aether does not exist.

The premises of this argument are true. Given the circumstances, it is likely that the scientists in question would have detected the aether if in fact it did exist. Since they did not detect it, it probably does not exist. Thus, we can say that the given argument is inductively strong (but not deductively valid).

As for the two arguments about astrology, if the attempts to prove or disprove the astrological claims had been done in a systematic way by qualified experts, the arguments would more likely be good. Exactly what is required to qualify someone to investigate astrological claims is, of course, difficult to say. But as these arguments stand, the premises state nothing about the qualifications of the investigators, and so the arguments remain fallacious.

It is not always necessary, however, that the investigators have *special* qualifications. The kinds of qualifications needed depend on the situation. Sometimes the mere ability to see and report what one sees is sufficient. Example:

> No one has ever seen Mr. Andrews drink a glass of wine, beer, or any other alcoholic beverage. Probably Mr. Andrews is a nondrinker.

Because it is highly probable that if Mr. Andrews were a drinker, somebody would have seen him drinking, this argument is inductively strong. No special qualifications are needed to be able to see someone take a drink.

The second exception to the appeal to ignorance relates to courtroom procedure. In the United States and a few other countries, a person is presumed innocent until proven guilty. If the prosecutor in a criminal trial fails to prove the guilt of the defendant beyond reasonable doubt, counsel for the defense may justifiably argue that his or her client is not guilty. Example:

> Members of the jury, you have heard the prosecution present its case against the defendant. Nothing, however, has been proved beyond a reasonable doubt. Therefore, under the law, the defendant is not guilty.

This argument commits no fallacy because "not guilty" means, in the legal sense, that guilt beyond a reasonable doubt has not been proved. The defendant may indeed have committed the crime of which he or she is accused, but if the prosecutor fails to prove guilt beyond a reasonable doubt, the defendant is considered "not guilty."

11. Hasty Generalization (Converse Accident)

Hasty generalization is a fallacy that affects inductive generalizations. In Chapter 1 we saw that an inductive generalization is an argument that draws a conclusion about all members of a group from evidence that pertains to a selected sample. The fallacy oc-

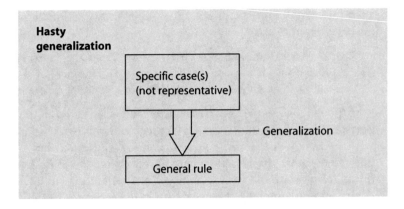

curs when there is a reasonable likelihood that the sample is not representative of the group. Such a likelihood may arise if the sample is either too small or not randomly selected. Here are two examples:

> After only one year the alternator went out in Mr. O'Grady's new Chevrolet. Mrs. Dodson's Oldsmobile developed a transmission problem after six months. The obvious conclusion is that cars made by General Motors are just a pile of junk these days.

> Ten Arab fundamentalists hijacked planes and crashed them into the World Trade Center in New York City. The message is clear: Arabs are nothing but a pack of religious fanatics prone to violence.

In these arguments a conclusion about a whole group is drawn from premises that mention only a few instances. Because such small, atypical samples are not sufficient to support a general conclusion, each argument commits a hasty generalization. The second example indicates how hasty generalization plays a role in racial and religious prejudice.

The mere fact that a sample is small, however, does not necessarily mean that it is atypical. On the other hand, the mere fact that a sample is large does not guarantee that it is typical. In the case of small samples, various factors may intervene that render such a sample typical of the larger group. Examples:

> Ten milligrams of substance Z was fed to four mice, and within two minutes all four went into shock and died. Probably substance Z, in this amount, is fatal to mice in general.

> On three separate occasions I drank a bottle of Figowitz beer and found it flat and bitter. Probably I would find every bottle of Figowitz beer flat and bitter.

Neither of these arguments commits the fallacy of hasty generalization, because in neither case is there any likelihood that the sample is atypical of the group. In the first argument the fact that the mice died in only two minutes suggests the existence of a causal connection between eating substance Z and death. If there is such a connection, it would hold for other mice as well. In the second example the fact that the taste of beer typically remains constant from bottle to bottle causes the argument to be strong, even though only three bottles were sampled.

In the case of large samples, if the sample is not random, it may not be typical of the larger group. Example:

> One hundred thousand voters from Orange County, California, were surveyed on their choice for governor, and 68 percent said they intend to vote for the Republican candidate. Clearly the Republican candidate will be elected.

Even though the sample cited in this argument is large, the argument commits a hasty generalization. The problem is that Orange County is overwhelmingly Republican, so the mere fact that 68 percent intend to vote for the Republican candidate is no indication of how others in the state intend to vote. In other words, the survey was not conducted randomly, and for this reason the argument is fatally flawed. The need for randomness in samples is discussed further in Chapter 12 of this book.

Hasty generalization is otherwise called "converse accident" because it proceeds in a direction opposite to that of accident. Whereas accident proceeds from the general to the particular, converse accident moves from the particular to the general. The premises cite some characteristic affecting one or more atypical instances of a certain class, and the conclusion then applies that characteristic to all members of the class.

12. False Cause

The fallacy of **false cause** occurs whenever the link between premises and conclusion depends on some imagined causal connection that probably does not exist. Whenever an argument is suspected of committing the false cause fallacy, the reader or listener should be able to say that the conclusion depends on the supposition that X causes Y, whereas X probably does not cause Y at all. Examples:

> During the past two months, every time that the cheerleaders have worn blue ribbons in their hair, the basketball team has been defeated. Therefore, to prevent defeats in the future, the cheerleaders should get rid of those blue ribbons.

> Successful business executives are paid salaries in excess of $100,000. Therefore, the best way to ensure that Ferguson will become a successful executive is to raise his salary to at least $100,000.

> There are more laws on the books today than ever before, and more crimes are being committed than ever before. Therefore, to reduce crime we must eliminate the laws.

The first argument depends on the supposition that the blue ribbons caused the defeats, the second on the supposition that a high salary causes success, and the third on the supposition that laws cause crime. In no case is it likely that any causal connection exists.

The first argument illustrates a variety of the false cause fallacy called *post hoc ergo propter hoc* ("after this, therefore on account of this"). This variety of the fallacy presupposes that just because one event precedes another event, the first event causes the second. Obviously, mere temporal succession is not sufficient to establish a causal connection. Nevertheless, this kind of reasoning is quite common and lies behind most forms of superstition. (Example: "A black cat crossed my path and later I tripped and sprained my ankle. It must be that black cats really are bad luck.")

The second and third arguments illustrate a variety of the false cause fallacy called *non causa pro causa* ("not the cause for the cause"). This variety is committed when

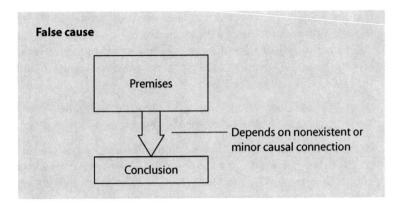

what is taken to be the cause of something is not really the cause at all and the mistake is based on something other than mere temporal succession. In reference to the second argument, success as an executive causes increases in salary—not the other way around—so the argument mistakes the cause for the effect. In reference to the third argument, the increase in crime is, for the most part, only coincidental with the increase in the number of laws. Obviously, the mere fact that one event is coincidental with another is not sufficient reason to think that one caused the other.

A third variety of the false cause fallacy, and one that is probably committed more often than either of the others in their pure form, is *oversimplified cause*. This variety occurs when a multitude of causes is responsible for a certain effect but the arguer selects just one of these causes and represents it as if it were the sole cause. Here are some examples:

> The quality of education in our grade schools and high schools has been declining for years. Clearly, our teachers just aren't doing their job these days.

> Today, all of us can look forward to a longer life span than our parents and grandparents. Obviously we owe our thanks to the millions of dedicated doctors who expend every effort to ensure our health.

In reference to the first argument, the decline in the quality of education is caused by many factors, including lack of discipline in the home, lack of parental involvement, too much television, and drug use by students. Poor teacher performance is only one of these factors and probably a minor one at that. In the second argument, the efforts of doctors are only one among many factors responsible for our longer life span. Other, more important factors include a better diet, more exercise, reduced smoking, safer highways, and more stringent occupational safety standards.

The oversimplified cause fallacy is usually motivated by self-serving interests. Sometimes the arguer wants to take undeserved credit for himself or herself or give undeserved credit to some movement with which he or she is affiliated. At other times, the arguer wants to heap blame on an opponent or shift blame from himself or herself onto some convenient occurrence. Instances of the fallacy can resemble either the *post hoc* or the *non causa pro causa* varieties in that the alleged cause can occur either prior to or concurrently with the effect. It differs from the other varieties of false cause fallacy in that the single factor selected for credit or blame is often partly responsible for the effect, but responsible to only a minor degree.

The last variety of false cause we will consider is called the *gambler's fallacy*. This fallacy is committed whenever the conclusion of an argument depends on the supposition that independent events in a game of chance are causally related. Here is an example:

> A fair coin was flipped five times in a row, and each time it came up heads. Therefore, it is extremely likely that it will come up tails on the next flip.

In fact, it is no more likely that the coin will come up tails on the next flip than it was on the first flip. Each flip is an independent event, so earlier flips have no causal influence on later ones. Thus, the fact that the earlier flips came up heads does not increase the likelihood that the next flip will come up tails.

For the gambler's fallacy to be committed, the events must be independent or nearly independent. Such events include rolls of a pair of fair (unloaded) dice, spins of a fair roulette wheel, and selections of lottery winning numbers. Events are not completely independent whenever the skill of the gambler affects the outcome. Thus, poker, blackjack, and horse-race betting provide less-than-perfect candidates for the gambler's fallacy.

The false cause fallacy is often convincing because it is often difficult to determine whether two phenomena are causally related. A lengthy time lapse between the operation of the cause and the occurrence of the effect can exacerbate the problem. For example, the thirty-year interval between exposure to asbestos and the onset of asbestosis impeded the recognition of a causal connection. Also, when two events are causally related, determining the degree of relatedness may be hard. Thus, there may be some connection between the electromagnetic field produced by high voltage transmission lines and leukemia, but the connection may be extremely slight. Finally, when a causal connection is recognized, it may be difficult to determine which is the cause and which is the effect. For example, an allergic reaction may be connected with an episode of anxiety, but it may be hard to tell if the reaction causes the anxiety or if the anxiety causes the reaction.

The realm of human action constitutes another area in which causal connections are notoriously difficult to establish. For example, the attorneys for accused murderer Dan White argued that Twinkies, Coke, and potato chips caused him to kill San Francisco mayor George Moscone. Other attorneys have blamed their clients' crimes on PMS, rap music, childhood abuse, mental retardation, and hallucinations. The complex nature of human motivation renders all such causal claims difficult to evaluate. The situation may become even worse when a whole nation of people are involved. Thus, the recent drop in crime rates has been attributed to "three strikes" laws, but it is difficult to say whether this or some other factor is really responsible.

One point that should be kept in mind when establishing causal connections is that statistical correlations by themselves often reveal little about what is actually going on. For example, if all that we knew about smoking and lung cancer was that the two frequently occur together, we might conclude any number of things. We might conclude that both have a common cause, such as a genetic predisposition, or we might conclude that lung cancer is a disease contracted early in life and that it manifests itself in its early stages by a strong desire for tobacco. Fortunately, in this case we have more evidence than a mere statistical correlation. This additional evidence inclines us to believe that the smoking is a cause of the cancer.

13. Slippery Slope

The fallacy of **slippery slope** is a variety of the false cause fallacy. It occurs when the conclusion of an argument rests on an alleged chain reaction and there is not sufficient reason to think that the chain reaction will actually take place. Here is an example:

> Immediate steps should be taken to outlaw pornography once and for all. The continued manufacture and sale of pornographic material will almost certainly lead to an increase in sex-related crimes such as rape and incest. This in turn will gradually erode the moral fabric of society and result in an increase in crimes of all sorts. Eventually a complete disintegration of law and order will occur, leading in the end to the total collapse of civilization.

Because there is no good reason to think that the mere failure to outlaw pornography will result in all these dire consequences, this argument is fallacious. An equally fallacious counterargument is as follows:

> Attempts to outlaw pornography threaten basic civil rights and should be summarily abandoned. If pornography is outlawed, censorship of newspapers and news magazines is only a short step away. After that there will be censorship of textbooks, political speeches, and the content of lectures delivered by university professors. Complete mind control by the central government will be the inevitable result.

Both arguments attempt to persuade the reader or listener that the welfare of society rests on a "slippery slope" and that a single step in the wrong direction will result in an inevitable slide all the way to the bottom.

The slippery slope fallacy can involve various kinds of causality. For example, someone might argue that removing a single brick from a building would set off a chain reaction leading to the destruction of the building, or that chopping down a tall tree would set off a cascade of falling trees leading to the destruction of the forest. These arguments depend on pure physical causality. On the other hand, someone might argue that starting a rumor about the health of the economy would set off a chain reaction leading to the collapse of the stock market. Such an argument would depend on the kind of causality found in interpersonal communications. Or someone might argue that planting a seed of doubt in a person's mind about the faithfulness of his or her spouse would gnaw away at that person, leading to the breakup of the marriage. Such an argument would depend on the kind of causality that links mental states.

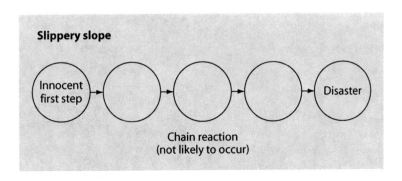

Deciding whether a slippery slope fallacy has been committed can be difficult when one is uncertain whether the alleged chain reaction will or will not occur. This question is discussed in Section 3.5. But many slippery slopes rest on a mere emotional conviction on the part of the arguer that a certain action or policy is bad, and the arguer attempts to trump up support for his or her position by citing all sorts of dire consequences that will result if the action is taken or the policy followed. In such cases there is usually little problem in identifying the argument as a slippery slope.

14. Weak Analogy

This fallacy affects inductive arguments from analogy. As we saw in Chapter 1, an argument from analogy is an argument in which the conclusion depends on the existence of an analogy, or similarity, between two things or situations. The fallacy of **weak analogy** is committed when the analogy is not strong enough to support the conclusion that is drawn. Example:

> Harper's new car is bright blue, has leather upholstery, and gets excellent gas mileage. Crowley's new car is also bright blue and has leather upholstery. Therefore, it probably gets excellent gas mileage, too.

Because the color of a car and the choice of upholstery have nothing to do with gasoline consumption, this argument is fallacious.

The basic structure of an argument from analogy is as follows:

> Entity A has attributes $a, b, c,$ and z.
> Entity B has attributes a, b, c.
> Therefore, entity B probably has attribute z also.

Evaluating an argument having this form requires a two-step procedure: (1) Identify the attributes $a, b, c, \ldots$ that the two entities A and B share, and (2) determine how the attribute z, mentioned in the conclusion, relates to the attributes $a, b, c, \ldots$ If some causal or systematic relation exists between z and $a, b,$ or c, the argument is strong; otherwise, it is weak. In the example argument, the two entities share the attributes of being cars; the attributes entailed by being a car, such as having four wheels; and the attributes of color and upholstery material. Because none of these attributes is systematically or causally related to good gas mileage, the argument is fallacious.

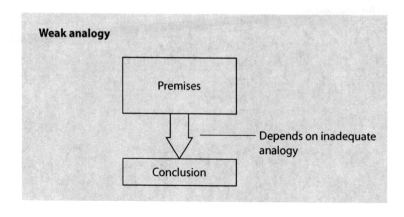

■ EMINENT LOGICIANS

William of Ockham ca. 1285–1347

© The Granger Collection, New York

The English philosopher and theologian, William of Ockham, was born in or near the village of Ockham not far from London. Little is known about his childhood, and his biographers are not even certain about the year of his birth, with estimates running from 1280 to 1290. However, they are certain that while Ockham was still a small boy, his parents delivered him to the nearest Franciscan monastery to be brought up in the monastic way of life. His parents' intentions were realized when he entered the Franciscan Order and was ordained in 1306.

Ockham studied theology at Oxford, possibly under Duns Scotus, and he lectured there. He also studied and taught at the University of Paris, where he wrote extensively on theology and philosophy. Ockham's theological views generated controversy among theologians of the day, some of whom vehemently opposed him. In 1324, he was called to Avignon, then the location of the papal court, to answer charges of heresy.

A panel of scholars had been appointed to review the charges made against Ockham, and he was obliged to remain at a Franciscan house in Avignon throughout the investigation, which lasted four years. During this time, the Franciscan minister general, Michael of Cesena, was called to Avignon, because he had become embroiled in a controversy with Pope John XXII over the issue of the poverty of Jesus and the apostles. Michael held that Jesus and the apostles did not own property but instead survived through goodwill offerings of people in the community. The Franciscans regarded themselves as emulating the model set by Jesus and the apostles, but the pope, who lived in luxury, obviously disagreed.

Though Ockham had more than enough problems of his own, the minister general asked him to research the issue to see which position was right—the pope's or the minister general's. Ockham ultimately came out on the side of the minister general, claiming that the pope was a heretic and had no business even being pope. This got the Avignon Franciscans into a great deal of trouble, and to extricate themselves they purloined several horses and rode out of town in the middle of the night. Ludwig of Bavaria, the Holy Roman Emperor, gave them protection, and Ockham lived out the rest of his life in Munich. While there he turned his attention to politics and political philosophy. He was a staunch advocate of the separation of church and state, claiming that the pope had no right to intervene in state affairs. The pope retaliated by excommunicating him.

Ockham is best known for endorsing a principle of parsimony that has come to be called "Ockham's razor." This principle states that, among alternative explanations, the simplest one is the best. Ockham emphasized the importance of keeping the number of entities hypothesized in an explanation to an absolute minimum. In the area of logic, he is known for his theory of truth conditions for categorical propositions, for work in the foundations of inductive reasoning, for preliminary work on a three-valued logic, and for developing a close approximation to what would later come to be known as De Morgan's rule.

As an illustration of when the requisite systematic or causal relation does and does not exist, consider the following arguments:

> The flow of electricity through a wire is similar to the flow of water through a pipe. Obviously a large-diameter pipe will carry a greater flow of water than a pipe of small diameter. Therefore, a large-diameter wire should carry a greater flow of electricity than a small-diameter wire.

> The flow of electricity through a wire is similar to the flow of water through a pipe. When water runs downhill through a pipe, the pressure at the bottom of the hill is greater than it is at the top. Thus, when electricity flows downhill through a wire, the voltage should be greater at the bottom of the hill than at the top.

The first argument is good and the second is fallacious. Both arguments depend on the similarity between water molecules flowing through a pipe and electrons flowing through a wire. In both cases there is a systematic relation between the diameter of the pipe/wire and the amount of flow. In the first argument this systematic relation provides a strong link between premises and conclusion, and so the argument is a good one. But in the second argument a causal connection exists between difference in elevation and increase in pressure that holds for water but not for electricity. Water molecules flowing through a pipe are significantly affected by gravity, but electrons flowing through a wire are not. Thus, the second argument is fallacious.

The theory and evaluation of arguments from analogy is one of the most complex and elusive subjects in all of logic. Additional material on arguments from analogy appears in Section 3.5 and Chapter 9 of this text.

EXERCISE 3.3

I. Identify the fallacies of weak induction committed by the following arguments, giving a brief explanation for your answer. If no fallacy is committed, write "no fallacy."

★1. The *Daily News* carried an article this morning about three local teenagers who were arrested on charges of drug possession. Teenagers these days are nothing but a bunch of junkies.

2. If a car breaks down on the freeway, a passing mechanic is not obligated to render emergency road service. For similar reasons, if a person suffers a heart attack on the street, a passing physician is not obligated to render emergency medical assistance.

3. There must be something to psychical research. Three famous physicists— Oliver Lodge, James Jeans, and Arthur Stanley Eddington—took it seriously.

★4. The secretaries have asked us to provide lounge areas where they can spend their coffee breaks. This request will have to be refused. If we give them lounge areas, next they'll be asking for spas and swimming pools. Then it will be racquetball courts, tennis courts, and fitness centers. Expenditures for these facilities will drive us into bankruptcy.

5. The accumulation of pressure in a society is similar to the buildup of pressure in a boiler. If the pressure in a boiler increases beyond a critical point, the

boiler will explode. Accordingly, if a government represses its people beyond a certain point, the people will rise up in revolt.

6. A few minutes after Governor Harrison finished his speech on television, a devastating earthquake struck southern Alaska. For the safety of the people up there, it is imperative that Governor Harrison make no more speeches.

★7. No one has ever been able to prove the existence of extrasensory perception. We must therefore conclude that extrasensory perception is a myth.

8. Lester Brown, universally respected author of the yearly *State of the World* report, has said that the destruction of tropical rain forests is one of the ten most serious worldwide problems. Thus, it must be the case that this is indeed a very serious problem.

9. America's business leaders are all a bunch of crooks. Just look at the facts. Dennis Kowslowski ripped off millions of dollars from Tyco Corporation, Jeffrey Skilling and Andy Fastow did the same with Enron, Bernie Ebbers defrauded the investors of WorldCom, and the Rigas family stole millions from Adelphia.

★10. Iranian President Mahmoud Ahmadinejad says that the holocaust is a fairy tale promoted for the purpose of garnering sympathy for Israel. In view of Ahmadinejad's apparent expertise in this area, we must conclude that the holocaust is indeed a fairy tale, just as he says.

11. Probably no life exists on Venus. Teams of scientists have conducted exhaustive studies of the planet's surface and atmosphere, and no living organisms have been found.

12. We don't dare let the animal rights activists get their foot in the door. If they sell us on the idea that dogs, cats, and dolphins have rights, next it will be chickens and cows. That means no more chicken Kiev or prime rib. Next it will be worms and insects. This will lead to the decimation of our agricultural industry. The starvation of the human race will follow close behind.

★13. No one would buy a pair of shoes without trying them on. Why should anyone be expected to get married without premarital sex?

14. No one has proved conclusively that America's nuclear power plants constitute a danger to people living in their immediate vicinity. Therefore, it is perfectly safe to continue to build nuclear power plants near large metropolitan centers.

15. There are more churches in New York City than in any other city in the nation, and more crimes are committed in New York City than anywhere else. So, if we are to eliminate crime, we must abolish the churches.

II. Answer "true" or "false" to the following statements:

1. If an arguer cites a statement by a recognized expert in support of a conclusion and the statement falls within the expert's range of expertise, then the arguer commits an appeal to unqualified authority.

2. If an arguer cites a statement in support of a conclusion and the statement reflects the strong bias of its author, then the arguer commits an appeal to unqualified authority.

3. In the appeal to ignorance, the arguer accuses the reader or listener of being ignorant.

4. If an attorney for the defense in an American or Canadian criminal trial argues that the prosecution has proved nothing beyond a reasonable doubt about the guilt of the defendant, then the attorney commits an appeal to ignorance.

5. Hasty generalization always proceeds from the particular to the general.

6. The *post hoc ergo propter hoc* variety of the false cause fallacy presumes that X causes Y merely because X happens before Y.

7. If an argument concludes that X causes Y simply because X and Y occur over the same time interval, then the argument commits the *non causa pro causa* variety of the false cause fallacy.

8. If the conclusion of an argument depends on the occurrence of a chain reaction of events, and there is good reason to believe that the chain reaction will actually occur, the argument commits a slippery slope fallacy.

9. The fallacy of weak analogy always depends on an alleged similarity between two things or situations.

10. If an argument from analogy depends on a causal or systematic relationship between certain attributes, and there is good reason to believe that this relationship exists, then the argument commits no fallacy.

III. Identify the fallacies of relevance and weak induction committed by the following arguments. If no fallacy is committed, write "no fallacy."

★1. On our first date, George had his hands all over me, and I found it nearly impossible to keep him in his place. A week ago Tom gave me that stupid line about how, in order to prove my love, I had to spend the night with him. Men are all alike. All any of them want is sex.

2. Tagging by graffiti artists has become a terrible problem in recent years. Obviously our schools are stifling the creative spirit of these young people.

3. North Korean dictator Kim Jong Il has promised not to let any of his nuclear weapons fall into the hands of terrorists. But Kim is erratic, dishonest, corrupt, and possibly even insane. Therefore, we should not trust his promises for a minute.

★4. House speaker Nancy Pelosi has argued strongly against oil and gas exploration in the Arctic National Wildlife Refuge. But what would you expect? She represents the city of San Francisco, which is loaded with environmentalists. If she didn't take this position, she would be run out of office. Thus, her arguments on this issue really have no merit.

5. What the farmer sows in the spring he reaps in the fall. In the spring he sows $8-per-bushel soybeans. Therefore, in the fall he will reap $8-per-bushel soybeans.

6. World-renowned physicist Stephen Hawking claims that black holes do not gobble up everything that falls into them without leaving a trace, but that something is always left behind. Given Hawking's stature as a scientist and the

many years he has worked on this problem, we should conclude that this is indeed the case.

★7. Emily has bought over 100 tickets on the weekly state lottery, and she has never won anything. Therefore, the likelihood increases every week that she will win something if she continues to buy tickets.

8. Johnny, of course I deserve the use of your bicycle for the afternoon. After all, I'm sure you wouldn't want your mother to find out that you played hooky today.

9. Practically everyone downloads music free of charge from the Internet these days. Therefore, you should have no qualms about doing this yourself.

★10. Ellen Quinn has argued that logic is not the most important thing in life. Apparently Ellen advocates irrationality. It has taken two million years for the human race to achieve the position that it has, and Ellen would throw the whole thing into the garbage. What utter nonsense!

11. When water is poured on the top of a pile of rocks, it always trickles down to the rocks on the bottom. Similarly, when rich people make lots of money, we can expect this money to trickle down to the poor.

12. Extensive laboratory tests have failed to prove any deleterious side effects of the new painkiller lexaprine. We conclude that lexaprine is safe for human consumption.

★13. Environmentalists accuse us of blocking the plan to convert Antarctica into a world park. In fact, nothing could be further from the truth. Antarctica is a huge continent teeming with life. It is the home of millions of penguins, seals, sea birds, and sea lions. Also, great schools of finfish and whales inhabit its coastal waters.

14. Media host Howard Stern claims that leaders of the religious right are nothing but a pack of racketeers bent on destroying every vestige of free speech, and he gives numerous reasons to support this claim. But Stern is just a vulgar, smut-mouthed freak who will say anything for shock value. Nobody should listen to this nonsense.

15. The operation of a camera is similar in many ways to the operation of an eye. If you are to see anything in a darkened room, the pupils of your eyes must first dilate. Accordingly, if you are to take a photograph (without flash) in a darkened room, the aperture of the camera lens must first be increased.

★16. Certainly Miss Malone will be a capable and efficient manager. She has a great figure, a gorgeous face, and tremendous poise and she dresses very fashionably.

17. James Dobson, director of Focus on the Family, says that men have the divine obligation to lead their families, and women have the divine obligation to submit to their husband's authority. Given Dobson's apparent ability to receive messages from God, we must conclude that this statement is absolutely true.

18. Dear Internal Revenue Service: I received a notice that my taxes are being audited for last year. But you have no right to do this. The deadline for filing a return was April 15, and I filed my tax return on April 12—a full three days before the deadline.

★19. To prevent dangerous weapons from being carried aboard airliners, those seeking to board must pass through a magnetometer and submit to a possible pat-down search. Therefore, to prevent alcohol and drugs from being carried into rock concerts, those entering should submit to similar search procedures.

20. Mr. Flemming's arguments against the rent control initiative on the September ballot should be taken with a grain of salt. As a landlord he would naturally be expected to oppose the initiative.

21. India is suffering a serious drought, thousands of children are dying of starvation in their mothers' arms, and homeless beggars line the streets of the major cities. Surely we must give these poor downtrodden people the chance of bettering their condition in America, the land of wealth and opportunity.

★22. Members of the jury, you have heard Shirley Gaines testify that the defendant did not offer to perform acts of prostitution for the undercover police officer. But Gaines is a known prostitute herself and a close friend of the defendant. Also, only a year ago she was convicted of twelve counts of perjury. Therefore, you should certainly discount Gaines's testimony.

23. It is ridiculous to hear that man from Peru complaining about America's poverty. Peru has twice as much poverty as America has ever had.

24. Angela complains that the problems on the algebra test were too hard. But have you ever seen the way Angela flirts with that good-looking quarterback on the football team? She's constantly batting those long, black eyelashes at him, and her tight-fitting sweaters leave nothing to the imagination. Angela should pay more attention to her studies.

★25. Nobody has ever proved that immoral behavior by elected officials erodes public morality. Therefore, we must conclude that such behavior does not erode public morality.

26. Freedom of speech is guaranteed by the First Amendment. Therefore, your friend was acting within his rights when he shouted "Fire! Fire!" in that crowded theater, even though it was only a joke.

27. No one, on encountering a watch lying on a forest trail, would expect that it had simply appeared there without having been made by someone. For the same reason, no one should expect that the universe simply appeared without having been made by some being.

★28. On Monday I drank ten rum and Cokes, and the next morning I woke up with a headache. On Wednesday I drank eight gin and Cokes, and the next morning I woke up with a headache. On Friday I drank nine bourbon and Cokes, and the next morning I woke up with a headache. Obviously, to prevent further headaches I must give up Coke.

29. Radio entertainer Rush Limbaugh claims there is not a shred of evidence to prove that nicotine is addictive or that cigarettes cause emphysema, lung cancer, or any other disease. Given Limbaugh's apparent expertise in medical science, we can only conclude that what he says about nicotine and cigarettes is true.

30. Some of the parents in our school district have asked that we provide bilingual education in Spanish. This request will have to be denied. If we provide this service, then someone will ask for bilingual education in Greek. Then it will be German, French, and Hungarian. Polish, Russian, Chinese, Japanese, and Korean will follow close behind. We certainly can't accommodate all of them.

IV. Identify the arguments in the following dialogue, then discuss each of them in terms of the fallacies presented in this section and the previous section. You should be able to find at least one case of each fallacy.

"Hi! Glad you could make it," Ralph says to his friend Claudia at a Friday night party. "Hey, you just missed a great discussion that Tom, Ruben, and I were having about abduction by extraterrestrials. Ruben just left, but he said he's been reading this book by Whitley Strieber—I think it's called *Transformation*—in which Strieber describes being kidnapped by creatures from outer space."

"Good grief! You don't actually believe that nonsense, do you?" Claudia asks incredulously.

"Well, I don't think Strieber would lie. Also, Ruben told us an amazing personal story. He was out camping a year ago, and after he'd killed off a couple of six-packs of Moosehead, he says he saw a UFO. So, I think we have to conclude there really are UFOs."

"What a joke!" Claudia laughs scornfully. "Ruben was probably hallucinating. By the way, didn't he fail most of his classes last semester? His parents are spending a fortune for his education, and all he does is party, sleep, and ignore his studies. I think that's immoral. As for Strieber, does he give any evidence?"

"As a matter of fact, he does," Ralph replies smugly. "Apparently, a few years ago, he was driving with his wife on some country road, when both of them experienced an unusual blackout. When they woke up, they were thirty-five miles further down the road, and they had no recollection of how they got there. Later, both began having dreams about extraterrestrials performing experiments on them while they were on board their spacecraft. Extraterrestrials must have abducted them, then hypnotized them so they wouldn't remember what had happened."

"Oh yeah, now I remember who Strieber is," answers Claudia, caustically. "He's that weirdo who dreams up all kinds of fantastic stories just so he can write books about them and make lots of money. If you give that sickie one minute of your time, then you're crazier than he is."

"I think you're prejudiced," Ralph says. "Why, recent surveys show that 64 percent of the American public believe in UFOs, and the number is growing every day. That alone should convince you they're real."

"You've got to be kidding," Claudia mutters, shaking her head in disbelief.

"Well then, consider this," insists Ralph. "There are hundreds of people out there who've had similar dreams and the same unaccounted-for time lapses. They can't all be fantasizing."

"I know that Strieber is a kook," Claudia persists, "so all the others must be, too."

"Now, now, aren't we jumping to conclusions?" her friend asks condescendingly.

"Not at all. First it was UFOs and little green men. Now those little creatures are abducting people and experimenting on them. Before long they'll be manipulating our genes and trying to infiltrate the human race. In the end, everyone will suspect everyone else of being an alien, mass terror will prevail, and civilization will collapse!" Claudia exclaims in mock horror.

"Don't be a fool!" Ralph barks, irritated. "The problem with you is, you're an agnostic. Obviously, you're saying we should refuse to believe in anything we can't clearly see or touch. So, logically, God doesn't exist, and there is no immortal soul. Tom, that's what she's saying, isn't it?"

"More or less," Tom agrees halfheartedly.

"Again, not at all," Claudia responds. "What I'm saying is, people have to be just a little bit critical about what they believe. Apparently you believe any cockamamie story that comes your way. You're just so gullible. If you keep it up, everyone and their dog will take you for a ride."

"Oh yeah? If I were you, I'd take a close look at my own beliefs," Ralph gibes. "Didn't I see you reading the astrology column just the other day? Nobody in their right mind believes in astrology. Maybe I should start screaming 'Claudia believes in astrology! Claudia believes in astrology!' Then everyone will gawk at you, and that sexy physics major you're dying to get a date with will think you're a nut."

"Oh, shut up!" says Claudia, blushing. "I may read the astrology column, but I certainly don't believe it. I just read it for fun. But, the fact is, during the past twenty-five years there have been thousands of alleged sightings of UFOs, and not a single one has led to any solid evidence of their existence. What do you make of that?"

"I think we should look at this situation the other way around," Ralph says. "Up until now, nobody has shown that UFOs *don't* exist, so I think we should give those people who claim they have seen them the benefit of the doubt. We should believe in UFOs and extraterrestrials until the sightings are proved false."

"Well, okay. Let's suppose, just for the sake of argument, that I admit the existence of UFOs and their little green drivers. How are we supposed to respond to them? What are we supposed to do?" Claudia asks.

"For starters, we should extend an open invitation to them," answers Ralph. "They may come from a dying planet where millions of their compatriots desperately struggle for survival. Their sun may be burning out, their water supply exhausted, and their soil poisoned with toxic chemicals. Surely they deserve a second chance on a new planet."

"Maybe so," Claudia says in a patronizing tone. "And now that you mention it, we probably have a legal obligation to let them in. Our current immigration laws say that we have to admit at least ten thousand applicants annually, from every major nation. If those aliens would just sign the right papers, we'd have to give them permanent residency. However, what worries me is, they may have the wrong intentions. After all, didn't they conduct experiments on those people they abducted?"

"Yes, but don't we experiment on animals? If the animals don't complain, why should we? Also, medical experimentation often leads to wonderful new cures. I'm certain we have nothing to worry about," says Ralph, proud of his logic.

"Humph! I hope you're right. Well, I've got to go now—and don't let any green men kidnap you," Claudia says with a barb.

"And you, either," Ralph answers.

3.4 Fallacies of Presumption, Ambiguity, and Grammatical Analogy

The **fallacies of presumption** include begging the question, complex question, false dichotomy, and suppressed evidence. These fallacies arise not because the premises are irrelevant to the conclusion or provide insufficient reason for believing the conclusion but because the premises presume what they purport to prove. *Begging the question* presumes that the premises provide adequate support for the conclusion when in fact they do not, and *complex question* presumes that a question can be answered by a simple "yes," "no," or other brief answer when a more sophisticated answer is needed. *False dichotomy* presumes that an "either . . . or . . ." statement presents jointly exhaustive alternatives when in fact it does not, and *suppressed evidence* presumes that no important evidence has been overlooked by the premises when in fact it has.

The **fallacies of ambiguity** include *equivocation* and *amphiboly*. These fallacies arise from the occurrence of some form of ambiguity in either the premises or the conclusion (or both). As we saw in Section 2.1, an expression is ambiguous if it is susceptible to different interpretations in a given context. The words "light" and "bank" are ambiguous, as is the statement "Tuna are biting off the Washington coast." When the conclusion of an argument depends on a shift in meaning of an ambiguous word or phrase or on the wrong interpretation of an ambiguous statement, the argument commits a fallacy of ambiguity.

The **fallacies of grammatical analogy** include *composition* and *division*. Arguments that commit these fallacies are grammatically analogous to other arguments that are good in every respect. Because of this similarity in linguistic structure, such fallacious arguments may appear good yet be bad.

15. Begging the Question (*Petitio Principii*)

The fallacy of **begging the question** is committed whenever the arguer creates the illusion that inadequate premises provide adequate support for the conclusion by leaving out a possibly false (shaky) key premise, by restating a possibly false premise as the conclusion, or by reasoning in a circle. The Latin name for this fallacy, *petitio principii*, means "request for the source." The actual source of support for the conclusion is not apparent, and so the argument is said to beg the question. After reading or hearing the argument, the observer is inclined to ask, "But how do you know *X*?" where *X* is the needed support.

The first, and most common, way of committing this fallacy is by leaving a possibly false key premise out of the argument while creating the illusion that nothing more is needed to establish the conclusion. Examples:

> Murder is morally wrong. This being the case, it follows that abortion is morally wrong.

> Of course humans and apes evolved from common ancestors. Just look how similar they are.

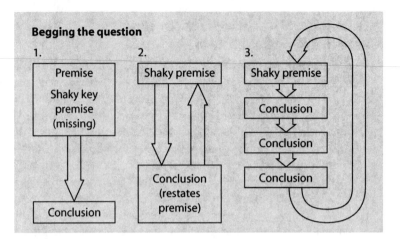

It's obvious that the poor in this country should be given handouts from the government. After all, these people earn less than the average citizen.

Clearly, terminally ill patients have a right to doctor-assisted suicide. After all, many of these people are unable to commit suicide by themselves.

The first of these arguments begs the question "How do you know that abortion is a form of murder?" The second begs the question "Does the mere fact that humans and apes look similar imply that they evolved from common ancestors?" And the third and fourth beg the questions "Just because the poor earn less than the average citizen, does this imply that the government should give them handouts?" and "Just because terminally ill patients cannot commit suicide by themselves, does it follow that they have a right to a doctor's assistance?"

These questions indicate that something has been left out of the original arguments. Thus, the first argument is missing the premise "Abortion is a form of murder"; the second is missing the premise "If humans and apes look similar, then they have common ancestors"; and so on. These premises are crucial for the soundness of the arguments. If the arguer is unable to establish the truth of these premises, then the arguments prove nothing. However, in most cases of begging the question, this is precisely the reason why such premises are left unstated. The arguer is *not* able to establish their truth, and by employing rhetorical phraseology such as "of course," "clearly," "this being the case," and "after all," the arguer hopes to create the illusion that the stated premise, by itself, provides adequate support for the conclusion when in fact it does not.

The same form of begging the question often appears in arguments concerning religious topics to justify conclusions about the existence of God, the immortality of the soul, and so on. Example:

The world in which we live displays an amazing degree of organization. Obviously this world was created by an intelligent God.

This argument begs the question "How do you know that the organization in the world could only have come from an intelligent creator?" Of course the claim that it did come from an intelligent creator may well be true, but the burden is on the arguer to prove it. Without supporting reasons or evidence, the argument proves nothing. Yet most people who are predisposed to believe the conclusion are likely to accept the argument as a good one. The same can be said of most arguments that beg the question, and this fact suggests another reason why arguers resort to this fallacy: Such arguments tend to reinforce preexisting inclinations and beliefs.

The second form of *petitio principii* occurs when the conclusion of an argument merely restates a possibly false premise in slightly different language. In such an argument, the premise supports the conclusion, and the conclusion tends to reinforce the premise. Examples:

> Capital punishment is justified for the crimes of murder and kidnapping because it is quite legitimate and appropriate that someone be put to death for having committed such hateful and inhuman acts.

> Anyone who preaches revolution has a vision of the future for the simple reason that if a person has no vision of the future he could not possibly preach revolution.

In the first argument, saying that capital punishment is "justified" means the same thing as saying that it is "legitimate and appropriate," and in the second argument the premise and the conclusion say exactly the same thing. However, by repeating the same thing in slightly different language, the arguer creates the illusion that independent evidence is being presented in support of the conclusion, when in fact it is not. Both arguments contain rhetorical phraseology ("hateful and inhuman," "*simple* reason," and "could not possibly") that help effect the illusion. The first argument begs the question "How do you know that capital punishment really is legitimate and appropriate?" and the second begs the question "How do you know that people who preach revolution really do have a vision of the future?"

The third form of *petitio principii* involves circular reasoning in a chain of inferences having a first premise that is possibly false. Example:

> Ford Motor Company clearly produces the finest cars in the United States. We know they produce the finest cars because they have the best design engineers. This is true because they can afford to pay them more than other manufacturers. Obviously they can afford to pay them more because they produce the finest cars in the United States.

On encountering this argument, the attentive reader is inclined to ask, "Where does this reasoning begin? What is its source?" Since the argument goes in a circle, it has no beginning or source, and as a result it proves nothing. Of course, in this example the circularity is rather apparent, so the argument is not likely to convince anyone. Cases in which circular reasoning may convince involve long and complex arguments having premises that depend on one another in subtle ways and a possibly false key premise that depends on the conclusion.

In all cases of begging the question, the arguer uses some linguistic device to create the illusion that inadequate premises provide adequate support for a conclusion. Without such an illusion, the fallacy is not committed. Thus, the following arguments commit no fallacy:

No dogs are cats.
Therefore, no cats are dogs.

London is in England and Paris is in France.
Therefore, Paris is in France and London is in England.

In both of these examples, the premise amounts to little more than a restatement of the conclusion. Yet both arguments are sound because they are valid and have true premises. No fallacy is committed, because no illusion is created to make inadequate premises appear as adequate. We will study arguments of this sort in Chapters 4 and 7.

Here is another example:

Rome is in Germany or Rome is in Germany.
Therefore, Rome is in Germany.

This argument is valid, but it is unsound because it has a false premise. However, it commits no fallacy because, again, no illusion is created to cover anything up. Arguments having this form also appear in Chapter 7.

As with these examples, arguments that beg the question are normally valid. This is easy to see. Any argument that includes the conclusion as one of the premises is clearly valid, and those forms of the fallacy that leave a key premise out of the argument become valid when that key premise is introduced. The problem with arguments that beg the question is that they are usually unsound, or at least not clearly sound, because the premise needed to provide adequate support for the conclusion is, at best, of uncertain truth value. Because such arguments presume the truth of this premise, begging the question is called a fallacy of presumption.

16. Complex Question

The fallacy of **complex question** is committed when two (or more) questions are asked in the guise of a single question and a single answer is then given to both of them. Every complex question presumes the existence of a certain condition. When the respondent's answer is added to the complex question, an argument emerges that establishes the presumed condition. Thus, although not an argument as such, a complex question involves an implicit argument. This argument is usually intended to trap the respondent into acknowledging something that he or she might otherwise not want to acknowledge. Examples:

Have you stopped cheating on exams?

Where did you hide the marijuana you were smoking?

Let us suppose the respondent answers "yes" to the first question and "under the bed" to the second. The following arguments emerge:

You were asked whether you have stopped cheating on exams. You answered, "Yes." Therefore, it follows that you have cheated in the past.

You were asked where you hid the marijuana you were smoking. You replied, "Under the bed." It follows that you were in fact smoking marijuana.

On the other hand, let us suppose that the respondent answers "no" to the first question and "nowhere" to the second. We then have the following arguments:

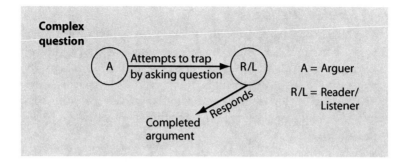

> You were asked whether you have stopped cheating on exams. You answered, "No." Therefore, you continue to cheat.

> You were asked where you hid the marijuana you were smoking. You answered, "Nowhere." It follows that you must have smoked all of it.

Obviously, each of the questions is really two questions:

> Did you cheat on exams in the past? If you did cheat in the past, have you stopped now?

> Were you smoking marijuana? If you were smoking it, where did you hide it?

If respondents are not sophisticated enough to identify a complex question when one is put to them, they may answer quite innocently and be trapped by a conclusion that is supported by no evidence at all; or, they may be tricked into providing the evidence themselves. The correct response lies in resolving the complex question into its component questions and answering each separately.

The fallacy of complex question should be distinguished from another kind of question known in law as a leading question. A *leading question* is one in which the answer is in some way suggested in the question. Whether or not a question is a leading one is important in the direct examination of a witness by counsel. Example:

> Tell us, on April 9, did you see
>   the defendant shoot the
>   deceased?   (leading question)
> Tell us, what did you see on
>   April 9?   (straight question)

Leading questions differ from complex questions in that they involve no logical fallacies—that is, they do not attempt to trick the respondent into admitting something he or she does not want to admit. To distinguish the two, however, one sometimes needs to know whether prior questions have been asked. Here are some additional examples of complex questions:

> Are you going to be a good little boy and eat your hamburger?
> Is George Hendrix still telling lies?
> How long must I put up with your snotty behavior?
> When are you going to stop talking nonsense?

17. False Dichotomy

The fallacy of **false dichotomy** is committed when a disjunctive ("either . . . or . . .") premise presents two unlikely alternatives as if they were the only ones available, and the arguer then eliminates the undesirable alternative, leaving the desirable one as the conclusion. Such an argument is clearly valid, but since the disjunctive premise is false, or at least probably false, the argument is typically unsound. The fallacy is often committed by children when arguing with their parents, by advertisers, and by adults generally. Here are three examples:

> Either you let me attend the Dixie Chicks concert or I'll be miserable for the rest of my life. I know you don't want me to be miserable for the rest of my life, so it follows that you'll let me attend the concert.

> Either you use Ultra Guard deodorant or you risk the chance of perspiration odor. Surely you don't want to risk the chance of perspiration odor. Therefore, you will want to use Ultra Guard deodorant.

> Either you buy only American-made products or you don't deserve to be called a loyal American. Yesterday you bought a new Toyota. It's therefore clear that you don't deserve to be called a loyal American.

In none of these arguments does the disjunctive premise present the only alternatives available, but in each case the arguer tries to convey that impression. For example, in the first argument, the arguer tries to convey the impression that he or she either goes to the concert or faces a lifetime of misery, and that no other alternatives are possible. Clearly, however, this is not the case.

The fallacious nature of false dichotomy lies in the illusion created by the arguer that the disjunctive premise presents jointly exhaustive alternatives. If it did, the premise would be true of necessity. For example, the statement "Either Reno is in Nevada, or it is not in Nevada" presents jointly exhaustive alternatives and is true of necessity. But in the fallacy of false dichotomy, not only do the two alternatives fail to be jointly exhaustive, but they are not even likely. As a result, the disjunctive premise is false, or at least probably false. Thus, the fallacy amounts to making a false or probably false premise appear true.

If one of the alternatives in the disjunctive premise is true, then the fallacy is not committed. For example, the following argument is valid and sound:

> Either Seattle is in Washington, or it is in Oregon.
> Seattle is not in Oregon.
> Therefore, Seattle is in Washington

False dichotomy is otherwise called "false bifurcation" and the "either-or fallacy." Also, in most cases the arguer expresses only the disjunctive premise and leaves it to the reader or listener to supply the missing statements:

> Either you buy me a new mink coat, or I'll freeze to death when winter comes.
> Either I continue smoking, or I'll get fat and you'll hate to be seen with me.

The missing premise and conclusion are easily introduced.

18. Suppressed Evidence

Chapter 1 explained that a cogent argument is an inductive argument with good reasoning and true premises. The requirement of true premises includes the proviso that the premises not ignore some important piece of evidence that outweighs the presented evidence and entails a very different conclusion. If an inductive argument does indeed ignore such evidence, then the argument commits the fallacy of **suppressed evidence.** Consider, for example, the following argument:

> Most dogs are friendly and pose no threat to people who pet them. Therefore, it would be safe to pet the little dog that is approaching us now.

If the arguer ignores the fact that the little dog is excited and foaming at the mouth (which suggests rabies), then the argument commits a suppressed evidence fallacy. This fallacy is classified as a fallacy of presumption because it works by creating the presumption that the premises are both true and complete when in fact they are not.

Perhaps the most common occurrence of the suppressed evidence fallacy appears in inferences based on advertisements. Nearly every ad neglects to mention certain negative features of the product advertised. As a result, an observer who sees or hears an advertisement and then draws a conclusion from it may commit the fallacy of suppressed evidence. Example:

> The ad for Kentucky Fried Chicken says, "Buy a bucket of chicken and have a barrel of fun!" Therefore, if we buy a bucket of that chicken, we will be guaranteed to have lots of fun.

The ad fails to state that the fun does not come packaged with the chicken but must be supplied by the buyer. Also, of course, the ad fails to state that the chicken is loaded with fat and that the buyer's resultant weight gain may not amount to a barrel of fun. By ignoring these facts, the argument based on the ad is fallacious.

Another way that an arguer can commit the suppressed evidence fallacy is by ignoring important events that have occurred with the passage of time that render an inductive conclusion improbable. Here is an example:

> During the past sixty years, Poland has enjoyed a rather low standard of living. Therefore, Poland will probably have a low standard of living for the next sixty years.

This argument ignores the fact that Poland was part of the Soviet bloc during most of the past sixty years, and this fact accounts for its rather low standard of living. However, following the collapse of the Soviet Union, Poland became an independent nation, and its economy is expected to improve steadily during the next sixty years.

Yet another form of suppressed evidence is committed by arguers who quote passages out of context from sources such as the Bible, the Constitution, and the Bill of Rights to support a conclusion that the passage was not intended to support. Consider, for example, the following argument against gun control:

> The Second Amendment to the Constitution states that the right of the people to keep and bear arms shall not be infringed. But a law controlling handguns would infringe the right to keep and bear arms. Therefore, a law controlling handguns would be unconstitutional.

In fact, the Second Amendment reads, "A well regulated militia being necessary to the security of a free state, the right of the people to keep and bear arms shall not be infringed." In other words, the amendment states that the right to bear arms shall not be infringed when the arms are necessary for the preservation of a well-regulated militia. Because a law controlling handguns (pistols) would have little effect on the preservation of a well-regulated militia, it is unlikely that such a law would be unconstitutional.

The suppressed evidence fallacy is similar to the form of begging the question in which the arguer leaves a key premise out of the argument. The difference is that suppressed evidence leaves out a premise that requires a *different* conclusion, while that form of begging the question leaves out a premise that is needed to support the *stated* conclusion. However, because both fallacies proceed by leaving a premise out of the argument, there are cases where the two fallacies overlap.

19. Equivocation

The fallacy of **equivocation** occurs when the conclusion of an argument depends on the fact that a word or phrase is used, either explicitly or implicitly, in two different senses in the argument. Such arguments are either invalid or have a false premise, and in either case they are unsound. Examples:

> Some triangles are obtuse. Whatever is obtuse is ignorant. Therefore, some triangles are ignorant.

> Any law can be repealed by the legislative authority. But the law of gravity is a law. Therefore, the law of gravity can be repealed by the legislative authority.

> We have a duty to do what is right. We have a right to speak out in defense of the innocent. Therefore, we have a duty to speak out in defense of the innocent.

> A mouse is an animal. Therefore, a large mouse is a large animal.

In the first argument "obtuse" is used in two different senses. In the first premise it describes a certain kind of angle, while in the second it means dull or stupid. The second argument equivocates on the word "law." In the first premise it means statutory law, and in the second it means law of nature. The third argument uses "right" in two senses. In the first premise "right" means morally correct, but in the second it means a

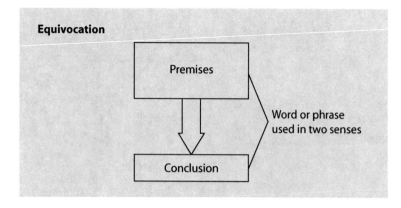

just claim or power. The fourth argument illustrates the ambiguous use of a relative word. The word "large" means different things depending on the context. Other relative words that are susceptible to this same kind of ambiguity include "small," "good," "bad," "light," "heavy," "difficult," "easy," "tall," and "short."

To be convincing, an argument that commits an equivocation must use the equivocal word in ways that are subtly related. Of the examples just given, only the third might fulfill this requirement. Since both uses of the word "right" are related to ethics, the unalert observer may not notice the shift in meaning. Another technique is to spread the shift in meaning out over the course of a lengthy argument. Political speech makers often use phrases such as "equal opportunity," "gun control," "national security," and "environmental protection" in one way at the beginning of a speech and in quite another way at the end. A third technique consists in using such phrases one way in a speech to one group and in a different way in a speech to an opposing group. If the same people are not present at both speeches, the equivocation is not detected.

20. Amphiboly

The fallacy of **amphiboly** occurs when the arguer misinterprets an ambiguous statement and then draws a conclusion based on this faulty interpretation. The original statement is usually asserted by someone other than the arguer, and the ambiguity usually arises from a mistake in grammar or punctuation—a missing comma, a dangling modifier, an ambiguous antecedent of a pronoun, or some other careless arrangement of words. Because of this ambiguity, the statement may be understood in two clearly distinguishable ways. The arguer typically selects the unintended interpretation and proceeds to draw a conclusion based on it. Here are some examples:

> The tour guide said that standing in Greenwich Village, the Empire State Building could easily be seen. It follows that the Empire State Building is in Greenwich Village.

> John told Henry that he had made a mistake. It follows that John has at least the courage to admit his own mistakes.

> Professor Johnson said that he will give a lecture about heart failure in the biology lecture hall. It must be the case that a number of heart failures have occurred there recently.

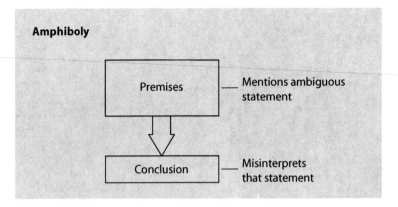

The premise of the first argument contains a dangling modifier. Is it the observer or the Empire State Building that is supposed to be standing in Greenwich Village? The factually correct interpretation is the former. In the second argument the pronoun "he" has an ambiguous antecedent; it can refer either to John or to Henry. Perhaps John told Henry that *Henry* had made a mistake. In the third argument the ambiguity concerns what takes place in the biology lecture hall; is it the lecture or the heart failures? The correct interpretation is probably the former. The ambiguity can be eliminated by inserting commas ("Professor Johnson said that he will give a lecture, about heart failure, in the biology lecture hall") or by moving the ambiguous modifier ("Professor Johnson said that he will give a lecture in the biology lecture hall about heart failure"). Ambiguities of this sort are called *syntactical ambiguities*.

Two areas where cases of amphiboly cause serious problems involve contracts and wills. The drafters of these documents often express their intentions in terms of ambiguous statements, and alternate interpretations of these statements then lead to different conclusions. Examples:

> Mrs. Hart stated in her will, "I leave my 500-carat diamond necklace and my pet chinchilla to Alice and Theresa." Therefore, we conclude that Alice gets the necklace and Theresa gets the chinchilla.

> Mr. James signed a contract that reads, "In exchange for painting my house, I promise to pay David $5,000 and give him my new Cadillac only if he finishes the job by May 1." Therefore, since David did not finish until May 10, it follows that he gets neither the $5,000 nor the Cadillac.

In the first example the conclusion obviously favors Alice. Theresa is almost certain to argue that the gift of the necklace and chinchilla should be shared equally by her and Alice. Mrs. Hart could have avoided the dispute by adding either "respectively" or "collectively" to the end of the sentence. In the second example, the conclusion favors Mr. James. David will argue that the condition that he finish by May 1 affected only the Cadillac and that he therefore is entitled to the $5,000. The dispute could have been avoided by properly inserting a comma in the language of the promise.

Amphiboly differs from equivocation in two important ways. First, equivocation is always traced to an ambiguity in the meaning of a *word* or *phrase*, whereas amphiboly involves a syntactical ambiguity in a *statement*. The second difference is that amphiboly usually involves a mistake made by the arguer in interpreting an ambiguous statement made by someone else, whereas the ambiguity in equivocation is typically the arguer's own creation. If these distinctions are kept in mind, it is usually easy to distinguish amphiboly from equivocation. Occasionally, however, the two fallacies occur together, as the following example illustrates:

> The *Great Western Cookbook* recommends that we serve the oysters when thoroughly stewed. Apparently the delicate flavor is enhanced by the intoxicated condition of the diners.

First, it is unclear whether "stewed" refers to the oysters or to the diners, and so the argument commits an amphiboly. But if "stewed" refers to the oysters it means "cooked," and if it refers to the diners it means "intoxicated." Thus, the argument also involves an equivocation.

21. Composition

The fallacy of **composition** is committed when the conclusion of an argument depends on the erroneous transference of an attribute from the parts of something onto the whole. In other words, the fallacy occurs when it is argued that because the parts have a certain attribute, it follows that the whole has that attribute, too, and the situation is such that the attribute in question cannot be legitimately transferred from parts to whole. Examples:

> Maria likes anchovies. She also likes chocolate ice cream. Therefore, it is certain that she would like a chocolate sundae topped with anchovies.

> Each player on this basketball team is an excellent athlete. Therefore, the team as a whole is excellent.

> Each atom in this teacup is invisible. Therefore, this teacup is invisible.

> Sodium and chlorine, the atomic components of salt, are both deadly poisons. Therefore, salt is a deadly poison.

In these arguments the attributes that are transferred from the parts onto the whole are designated by the words "Maria likes," "excellent," "invisible," and "deadly poison," respectively. In each case the transference is illegitimate, and so the argument is fallacious.

Not every such transference is illegitimate, however. Consider the following arguments:

> Every atom in this teacup has mass. Therefore, this teacup has mass.

> Every component in this picket fence is white. Therefore, the whole fence is white.

In each case an attribute (having mass, being white) is transferred from the parts onto the whole, but these transferences are quite legitimate. Indeed, the fact that the atoms have mass is the very reason *why* the teacup has mass. The same reasoning extends to the fence. Thus, the acceptability of these arguments is attributable, at least in part, to the *legitimate* transference of an attribute from parts onto the whole.

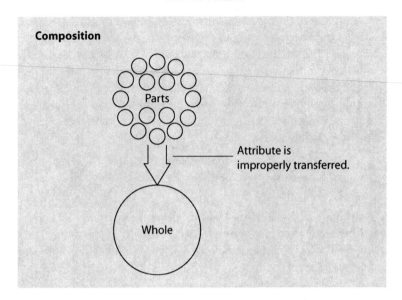

Composition

Parts

Attribute is
improperly transferred.

Whole

These examples illustrate the fact that the fallacy of composition is indeed an infor-mal fallacy. It cannot be discovered by a mere inspection of the form of an argument—that is, by the mere observation that an attribute is being transferred from parts onto the whole. In addition, detecting this fallacy requires a general knowledge of the situa-tion and of the nature of the attribute being transferred. The critic must be certain that, given the situation, the transference of this particular attribute is not allowed.

Further caution is required by the fact that composition is sometimes confused with hasty generalization. The only time this confusion is possible is when the "whole" is a class (such as the class of people in a city or the class of trees in a forest), and the "parts" are the members of the class. In such a case composition proceeds from the members of the class to the class itself. Hasty generalization, on the other hand, proceeds from the specific to the general. Because it is sometimes easy to mistake a statement about a class for a general statement, composition can be mistaken for hasty generalization. Such a mistake can be avoided if one is careful to keep in mind the distinction between these two kinds of statements. This distinction falls back on the difference between the **collec-tive** and the **distributive** predication of an attribute. Consider the following statements:

> Fleas are small.
> Fleas are numerous.

The first statement is a general statement. The attribute of being small is predicated distributively; that is, it is assigned (or distributed) to each and every flea in the class. Each and every flea in the class is said to be small. The second statement, on the other hand, is a statement about a class as a whole, or what we will call a "class statement." The attribute of being numerous is predicated collectively; in other words, it is as-signed not to the individual fleas but to the *class* of fleas. The meaning of the state-ment is not that each and every flea is numerous but that the class of fleas is large.

To distinguish composition from hasty generalization, therefore, the following procedure should be followed. Examine the conclusion of the argument. If the conclusion is a general statement—that is, a statement in which an attribute is predicated distributively to each and every member of a class—the fallacy committed is hasty generalization. But if the conclusion is a class statement—that is, a statement in which an attribute is predicated collectively to a class as a whole—the fallacy is composition. Example:

> Less gasoline is consumed by a car than by a truck. Therefore, less gasoline is consumed in the United States by cars than by trucks.

At first sight this argument might appear to proceed from the specific to the general and, consequently, to commit a hasty generalization. But in fact the conclusion is not a general statement at all but a class statement. The conclusion states that the whole class of cars uses less gas than does the whole class of trucks (which is false, because there are many more cars than trucks). Since the attribute of using less gasoline is predicated collectively, the fallacy committed is composition.

22. Division

The fallacy of **division** is the exact reverse of composition. As composition goes from parts to whole, division goes from whole to parts. The fallacy is committed when the conclusion of an argument depends on the erroneous transference of an attribute from a whole (or a class) onto its parts (or members). Examples:

> Salt is a nonpoisonous compound. Therefore, its component elements, sodium and chlorine, are nonpoisonous.

> This jigsaw puzzle, when assembled, is circular in shape. Therefore, each piece is circular in shape.

> The Royal Society is over 300 years old. Professor Thompson is a member of the Royal Society. Therefore, Professor Thompson is over 300 years old.

In each case the attribute, designated respectively by the terms "nonpoisonous," "circular in shape," and "over 300 years old," is illegitimately transferred from the whole or class onto the parts or members. As with the fallacy of composition, however, this kind of transference is not always illegitimate. The following arguments contain no fallacy:

> This teacup has mass. Therefore, the atoms that compose this teacup have mass.

> This field of poppies is uniformly orange. Therefore, the individual poppies are orange.

Obviously, one must be acquainted with the situation and the nature of the attribute being transferred to decide whether the fallacy of division is actually committed.

Just as composition can sometimes be confused with hasty generalization (converse accident), division can sometimes be confused with accident. As with composition, this confusion can occur only when the "whole" is a class. In such a case, division proceeds from the class to the members, whereas accident proceeds from the general to the specific. Thus, if a class statement is mistaken for a general statement, division may be mistaken for accident. To avoid such a mistake, one should analyze the premises of

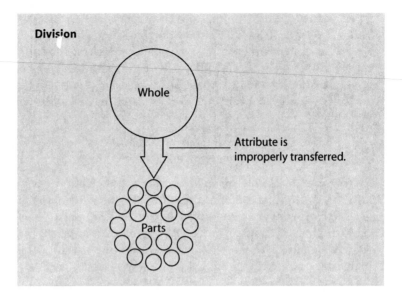

the argument. If the premises contain a general statement, the fallacy committed is accident; but if they contain a class statement, the fallacy is division. Example:

Stanley Steamers have almost disappeared.
This car is a Stanley Steamer.
Therefore, this car has almost disappeared.

The first premise is not a general statement but a class statement. The attribute of having almost disappeared is predicated collectively. Accordingly, the fallacy committed is division, not accident.

This example also illustrates how cases of division that involve class statements can include a subtle form of equivocation. In the conclusion, the word "disappeared" means fading from vision, as when the lights are turned down; but in the first premise it means rarely seen. The equivocation is a kind of secondary fallacy that results from the primary fallacy, which is division.

The next example shows how division turns up in arguments dealing with averages.

The average American family has 2.5 children.
The Jones family is an average American family.
Therefore, the Jones family has 2.5 children.

The statement "The average American family has 2.5 children" is not a general statement, but rather a class statement. The sense of the statement is not that each and every family has 2.5 children, but that the class of families is reducible to about 55 percent children and 45 percent adults. Thus, once again, the fallacy is division, and not accident.

In our account of composition and division, we have presented examples of arguments that commit these fallacies in conjunction with other, structurally similar arguments that do not. Because of the structural similarity between arguments that do and do not commit these fallacies, composition and division are classified as fallacies of grammatical analogy.

SUMMARY OF INFORMAL FALLACIES

Fallacies of Relevance

Appeal to force: Arguer threatens reader/listener.

Appeal to pity: Arguer elicits pity from reader/listener.

Appeal to the people (direct): Arguer arouses mob mentality.

Appeal to the people (indirect): Arguer appeals to reader/listener's desire for security, love, respect, etc.

Argument against the person (abusive): Arguer verbally abuses other arguer.

Argument against the person (circumstantial): Arguer presents other arguer as predisposed to argue this way.

Argument against the person (*tu quoque*): Arguer presents other arguer as hypocrite.

Accident: General rule is applied to a specific case it was not intended to cover.

Straw man: Arguer distorts opponent's argument and then attacks the distorted argument.

Missing the point: Arguer draws conclusion different from that supported by premises.

Red herring: Arguer leads reader/listener off track.

Fallacies of Weak Induction

Appeal to unqualified authority: Arguer cites untrustworthy authority.

Appeal to ignorance: Premises report that nothing is known or proved, and then a conclusion is drawn.

Hasty generalization: Conclusion is drawn from an atypical sample.

False cause: Conclusion depends on nonexistent or minor causal connection.

Slippery slope: Conclusion depends on unlikely chain reaction.

Weak analogy: Conclusion depends on defective analogy.

Fallacies of Presumption

Begging the question: Arguer creates the illusion that inadequate premises are adequate by leaving out a key premise, by restating the conclusion as a premise, or by reasoning in a circle.

Complex question: Multiple questions are concealed in a single question.

False dichotomy: "Either … or …" statement hides additional alternatives.

Suppressed evidence: Arguer ignores important evidence that requires a different conclusion.

Fallacies of Ambiguity

Equivocation: Conclusion depends on a shift in meaning of a word or phrase.

Amphiboly: Conclusion depends on the wrong interpretation of a syntactically ambiguous statement.

Fallacies of Grammatical Analogy

Composition: Attribute is wrongly transferred from parts to whole.

Division: Attribute is wrongly transferred from whole to parts.

EXERCISE 3.4

I. Identify the fallacies of presumption, ambiguity, and grammatical analogy committed by the following arguments, giving a brief explanation for your answer. If no fallacy is committed, write "no fallacy."

★1. Either we require forced sterilization of Third World peoples or the world population will explode and all of us will die. We certainly don't want to die, so we must require forced sterilization.

2. Every sentence in this paragraph is well written. Therefore, the paragraph is well written.

3. An athlete is a human being. Therefore, a good athlete is a good human being.

★4. James said that he saw a picture of a beautiful girl stashed in Stephen's locker. We can only conclude that Stephen has broken the rules, because girls are not allowed in the locker room.

5. Why is it so difficult for you to reach a decision?

6. Water will quench one's thirst. Water is composed of hydrogen and oxygen. Therefore, hydrogen and oxygen will quench one's thirst.

★7. People who lack humility have no sense of beauty, because everyone who has a sense of beauty also has humility.

8. Butane is combustible. Therefore, it burns.

9. Twenty years ago, Kung Fong, the great sumo wrestler, could have yanked up one of the fir trees in the new municipal arboretum with a single pull. Therefore, since Mr. Fong is as strong today as he was then, he could just as easily pull up one of those trees today.

★10. If Thomas gives Marie a ring, then Thomas and Marie will be engaged. Thomas did give Marie a ring. In fact, he phoned her just the other night. Therefore, Thomas and Marie are engaged.

11. Alex, I heard your testimony in court earlier today. Tell me, why did you lie on the witness stand?

12. Johnson is employed by the General Services Administration, and everyone knows that the GSA is the most inefficient branch of the government. Therefore, Johnson must be an inefficient worker.

★13. All men are mortal. Therefore, some day man will disappear from the earth.

14. Each and every cell in this carrot is 90 percent water. Therefore, the entire carrot is 90 percent water.

15. George said that he was interviewing for a job drilling oil wells in the supervisor's office. We can only conclude that the supervisor must have an awfully dirty office.

★16. During the fifty years that Mr. Jones worked, he contributed $90,000 to Social Security. Now that he is retired, he stands to collect $200,000 from the system. Obviously he will collect a much greater monetary value than he contributed.

17. Either you marry me right now or I'll be forced to leave you and never speak to you again. I'm sure you wouldn't want me to do that. Therefore, you'll marry me right now.

18. Either Meg Ryan or Britney Spears is a popular singer. Meg Ryan is not a popular singer. Therefore, Britney Spears is a popular singer.

★19. Switzerland is 48 percent Protestant. Heidi Gilsing is a Swiss. Therefore, Heidi Gilsing is 48 percent Protestant.

20. Picasso is the greatest artist of the twentieth century. We know that this is so because art critics have described him in these terms. These art critics are correct in their assessment because they have a more keenly developed sense of appreciation than the average person. This is true because it takes a more keenly developed sense of appreciation to realize that Picasso is the greatest artist of the twentieth century.

21. An atomic bomb causes more damage than a conventional bomb. Therefore, during World War II more damage was caused by atomic bombs than by conventional bombs.

★22. Sylvia, I saw you shopping for wine the other day. Incidentally, are you still drinking excessively?

23. The author warns about numerous computational errors in his accounting text. Therefore, he must have written it very carelessly.

24. Emeralds are seldom found in this country, so you should be careful not to misplace your emerald ring.

★25. Of course abortion is permissible. After all, a woman has a right to do as she pleases with her own body.

II. Answer "true" or "false" to the following statements:

   1. Arguments that commit the fallacy of begging the question are normally valid.

   2. The effect of begging the question is to hide the fact that a premise may not be true.

   3. The correct way of responding to a complex question is to divide the question into its component questions and answer each separately.

   4. False dichotomy always involves an "either . . . or . . ." statement, at least implicitly.

   5. The fallacy of equivocation arises from a syntactical defect in a statement.

   6. The fallacy of amphiboly usually involves the ambiguous use of a single word.

   7. Amphiboly usually arises from the arguer's misinterpreting a statement made by someone else.

   8. The fallacy of composition always proceeds from whole to parts.

   9. The fallacy of division always proceeds from parts to whole.

 10. A general statement makes an assertion about each and every member of a class.

 11. A class statement makes an assertion about a class as a whole.

 12. In the statement "Divorces are increasing," an attribute is predicated distributively.

 13. In the statement "Waistlines are increasing," an attribute is predicated distributively.

 14. Composition and division involve the distributive predication of an attribute.

 15. Equivocation and amphiboly are classified as fallacies of ambiguity.

III. Identify the fallacies of relevance, weak induction, presumption, ambiguity, and grammatical analogy committed by the following arguments, giving a brief explanation for your answer. If no fallacy is committed, write "no fallacy."

 ★1. In his *History of the American Civil War*, Jeffry Noland argues that the war had little to do with slavery. However, as a historian from Alabama, Noland could not possibly present an accurate account. Therefore, his arguments should be discounted.

  2. Mr. Wilson said that on July 4 he went out on the veranda and watched the fireworks go up in his pajamas. We conclude that Mr. Wilson must have had an exciting evening.

  3. Televangelist Jerry Falwell said that God's anger with feminism led to the destruction of the World Trade Center. Given Falwell's closeness to God, we have no alternative than to blame the feminists for this atrocity.

 ★4. A crust of bread is better than nothing. Nothing is better than true love. Therefore, a crust of bread is better than true love.

  5. Every member of the Delta Club is over 70 years old. Therefore, the Delta Club must be over 70 years old.

  6. Of course you should eat Wheaties. Wheaties is the breakfast of champions, you know.

★7. It's obvious that animals have rights. Just look at how powerless they are in comparison with modern humans.

8. The idea that black people in this country live in poverty is ridiculous. Look at Bill Cosby. He's a millionaire. And so are Denzel Washington and Oprah Winfrey.

9. No one has ever proved that the human fetus is not a person with rights. Therefore, abortion is morally wrong.

★10. California condors are rapidly disappearing. This bird is a California condor. Therefore, this bird should disappear any minute now.

11. When a car breaks down so often that repairs become pointless, the car is thrown on the junk heap. Similarly, when a person becomes old and diseased, he or she should be mercifully put to death.

12. The twenty-story Carson Building is constructed of concrete blocks. Each and every concrete block in the structure can withstand an earthquake of 9.5 on the Richter scale. Therefore, the building can withstand an earthquake of 9.5 on the Richter scale.

★13. Terrorists from the Middle East have crossed our borders and traveled through the country at will. Obviously the Immigration Service has not been doing its job.

14. This administration is not anti-German, as it has been alleged. Germany is a great country. It has contributed immensely to the world's artistic treasury. Goethe and Schiller made magnificent contributions to literature, and Bach, Beethoven, Wagner, and Brahms did the same in music.

15. Paul, it was great to see you at the party the other night. Everyone there was doing crack. Incidentally, how long have you been dealing that stuff?

★16. Duane Richards, CEO of the Western Fuels Association, an organization that supplies coal to electric utilities, says that there is no evidence that burning fossil fuels causes global warming. In view of Mr. Richards's wealth of expertise in the area of fossil fuels, we must conclude that what he says about global warming is true.

17. Senator Kennedy's arguments in favor of health care for the poor and aged should be ignored. Kennedy is a do-gooder who supports this kind of legislation only to get his name in the newspapers.

18. Professor Andrews, surely I deserve a B in logic. I know that I have gotten Fs on all the tests, but if you give me an F for my final grade, I will lose my scholarship. That will force me to drop out of school, and my poor, aged parents, who yearn to see me graduate, will be grief stricken for the rest of their lives.

★19. Molecules are in constant random motion. The Statue of Liberty is composed of molecules. Therefore, the Statue of Liberty is in constant random motion.

20. Either we have prayer in our public schools or the moral fabric of society will disintegrate. The choice should be obvious.

21. White sheep eat more than black sheep (because there are more of them). Therefore, this white sheep eats more than that black sheep.

★22. If someone rents a piece of land and plants crops on it, the landlord is never permitted to come and take those crops for himself when harvest time arrives. Similarly, if couples enlist the services of a surrogate mother to provide them with a baby, the mother should never be allowed to welch on the deal and keep the baby for herself once it is born.

23. Motives and desires exert forces on people, causing them to choose one thing over another. But force is a physical quantity, governed by the laws of physics. Therefore, human choices are governed by the laws of physics.

24. Each and every brick in the completely brick-faced Wainright Building has a reddish brown color. Therefore, the Wainright Building has a reddish brown color.

★25. Humanitarian groups have argued in favor of housing for the poor. Apparently what they want is another high-density project. Unfortunately, these projects have been tried in the past and have failed. In no time they turn into ghettos with astronomical rates of crime and delinquency. Chicago's Cabrini-Green is a prime example. Clearly, these humanitarian arguments are not what they seem.

26. Pauline said that after she had removed her new mink coat from the shipping carton she threw it into the trash. We conclude that Pauline has no appreciation for fine furs.

27. We know that induction will provide dependable results in the future because it has always worked in the past. Whatever has consistently worked in the past will continue to work in the future, and we know that this is true because it has been established by induction.

★28. What goes up must come down. The price of housing has been going up for years. Therefore, it will surely come down soon.

29. Mr. Prime Minister, I am certain you will want to release the members of our National Liberation Group whom you currently hold in prison. After all, I'm sure you will want to avoid having car bombs go off in the centers of your most heavily populated cities.

30. San Diego has the same latitude as Yuma, Arizona, and San Diego enjoys moderate temperatures through the summer months. Therefore, probably Yuma enjoys moderate temperatures through the summer months.

★31. We're all familiar with the complaint that over 40 million Americans are without health insurance. But America's doctors, nurses, and hospitals are among the best in the world. Thousands of people come from abroad every year to be treated here. Clearly there is nothing wrong with our health care system.

32. Real estate mogul Donald Trump argues that good management is essential to any business. But who is he to talk? Trump's own mismanagement drove Trump Hotels and Casino Resorts into bankruptcy twice in twelve years.

33. The farmers of our state have asked that we introduce legislation to provide subsidies for soybeans. Unfortunately, we will have to turn down their request. If we give subsidies to the soybean farmers, then the corn and wheat growers

will ask for the same thing. Then it will be the cotton growers, citrus growers, truck farmers, and cattle raisers. In the end, the cost will be astronomical.

★34. The travel brochure states that walking up O'Connell Street, the statue of Parnell comes into view. Apparently that statue has no trouble getting around.

35. Criminals are basically stupid, because anyone who isn't basically stupid wouldn't be a criminal.

36. Professor Glazebrooks's theory about the origin of the Martian craters is undoubtedly true. Rudolph Orkin, the great concert pianist, announced his support of the theory in this morning's newspaper.

★37. Mr. Franklin has lost at the craps table for the last ten throws of the dice. Therefore, it is extremely likely that he will win on the next throw.

38. Raising a child is like growing a tree. Sometimes violent things, such as cutting off branches, have to be done to force the tree to grow straight. Similarly, corporal punishment must sometimes be inflicted on children to force them to develop properly.

39. Good steaks are rare these days, so don't order yours well done.

★40. The Book of Mormon is true because it was written by Joseph Smith. Joseph Smith wrote the truth because he was divinely inspired. We know that Joseph Smith was divinely inspired because the Book of Mormon says that he was, and the Book of Mormon is true.

41. The students attending Bradford College come from every one of the fifty states. Michelle attends Bradford College. Therefore, Michelle comes from every one of the fifty states.

42. Rhubarb pie is a dessert. Therefore, whoever eats rhubarb pie eats a dessert.

★43. The vast majority of car accidents occur within twenty miles of one's home. Apparently it is much more dangerous to drive close to home than far away from home.

44. Either you're with us or you're with the terrorists. The choice should be easy.

45. Nobody has ever proved that weapons of mass destruction do not exist in Iraq. Therefore, those weapons must be in that country somewhere.

★46. On Friday I took Virginia out to dinner. She told me that if I wasn't interested in a serious relationship, I should forget about dating her. On Saturday I took Margie to a film. When we discussed it afterward over a drink, she couldn't understand why I wasn't interested in babies. Women are all alike. All they want is a secure marriage.

47. Dozens of species of plants and animals are being wiped out every year, even though we have laws to prevent it. Clearly, we should repeal the Endangered Species Act.

48. People are driving their cars like maniacs tonight. There must be a full moon.

★49. A line is composed of points. Points have no length. Therefore, a line has no length.

50. Are you in favor of the ruinous economic policy of the Democratic Platform Committee?

IV. Identify the arguments in the following dialogue, then discuss each of them in terms of the fallacies presented in this section and the previous section. You should be able to find at least one case of each fallacy.

"Thanks for giving me a lift home," Paul says to his friend Steve, as they head toward the freeway.

"No problem; it's on my way," says Steve.

"Uh oh," warns Paul suddenly, "watch out ahead. Looks like the police have pulled somebody over."

"Thanks," Steve says. "Hope they don't beat the guy up."

"Not a chance," says Paul. "Why would you say that?"

"You're an optimist," answers Steve. "Most cops are animals; they beat up on anybody they want to. You remember Rodney King, don't you? Those cops in L.A. put King in the hospital for no reason at all. That should prove I'm right."

"I think you're overreacting," Paul says. "Daryl Gates, the L.A. police chief at the time, said the King incident was an aberration. Since he was chief, I think we should take him at his word."

"But Gates was a lunatic who refused to acknowledge even our most basic rights," Steve persists. "Also, if you recall, he was forced to resign after the King incident. I know we don't live in L.A., but our police department is just as bad as theirs. So you can bet that our friend back there is just as abusive as any of them."

"Wait a minute," Paul argues. "As far as I know, nobody has ever proved that our police force is the slightest bit violent. You've no right to draw such a conclusion."

"Well, listen to this," Steve counters, as he changes lanes and turns onto the freeway. "About a week ago, I was with my friend Casey. When I left him, he was perfectly okay, but he was picked up for going through a stop sign on the way home. I saw him a couple of days later, and he had a big bruise under his right eye. The cop who stopped Casey must have hit him with his baton."

"Hold on. Did you ask Casey what happened?"

"No. I didn't have to," says Steve, a bit righteously. "I asked Casey's wife what happened between Casey and the cop, and she said he hit him. Those were her exact words, so that was good enough for me. I bet the cop's a maniac."

"Good grief," answers his friend. "How long will it take you to get over your warped view of things?"

"My way of looking at things isn't warped," Steve insists. "The problem is, you and I are both white. If you were black, you'd see things differently. Police brutality toward African Americans is way out of hand."

"Well," counters Paul, "a study done recently by an independent agency might interest you. According to that study, for every African American whom the police use force against, there's a white person they also use force against. That proves the police treat African Americans no worse than they do whites."

"I've never heard of that study, but it seems to me there must be something wrong with it," insists Steve.

"Well, the results of that study are borne out in my experience," says Paul. "I've been pulled over three or four times in the past couple of years, and the officers have always been extremely courteous. I can only conclude that the vast majority of these allegations of police brutality are the product of fertile imaginations."

"Again, your naïveté amazes me," Steve answers, dumbfounded. "First of all, you forget that you're white and you drive a new Mercedes. Don't you think that makes a difference? In fact, that's the trouble with all these arguments that downplay police brutality. They're all concocted by white people."

"Well, the fact remains that we have a major crime problem in this country," Paul argues. "Combating crime requires a few concessions, and you do want to combat crime, don't you?"

"Sure," Steve replies grudgingly, "but at what expense? Do innocent people have to get their heads bashed in?"

"Well, I think what it comes down to is this," says Paul. "Either you allow the police to use whatever force they find necessary, or the criminals will take over this country. Now you certainly don't want that to happen, do you?"

"No, but that's the crucial question," Steve says, exiting from the freeway. "When and how much force is necessary?"

"Well, you remember when the police apprehended that serial killer a few weeks ago? When the police made the arrest, the killer attacked them. So, the police can use force when attacked."

"I agree," responds Steve thoughtfully. "But what about the way the police treated those peaceful right-to-lifers who were demonstrating in front of the abortion clinic the other day? Many of them were elderly and posed no physical threat. But the cops used those contraptions—what do you call them, nimchucks, nomchucks, I don't know—to squeeze the old folks' wrists, causing great pain and injury, and they hit the old people on the head with their batons. Do you think that was necessary?"

"Of course it was," answers Paul, agitatedly. "Those people attacked the police—they hurled epithets at them."

"Honestly, I don't know how we've managed to stay friends all these years," Steve says with some frustration. "By the way, do you know what it says on the back of all police cars? It says 'To Protect and Serve.' Now if you hired a servant to take care of you, you'd get rid of him if he disobeyed you. Right?"

"Probably."

"Well, isn't it true," Steve asks, "that whenever a police officer disobeys one of us taxpayers, that officer should be fired?"

"That may be stretching it a bit," Paul laughs.

"But seriously," continues Steve, "I think what we need is some screening device to keep violent types from ever becoming cops."

"Well, you'll be happy to know that exactly such a device has been used for the past twenty-one years," Paul states. "Before entering the police academy, every applicant goes through a battery of psychological tests that positively eliminates all the macho types and the ones prone to violence. This ensures the individual officers are nonviolent, so we know the entire police force is nonviolent."

"Hmm. Maybe your so-called solution is really the problem," Steve suggests, as he pulls up in front of Paul's house. "We've had psychological testing for twenty-one years, and all that time, police violence has been on the rise. Perhaps we should get rid of the testing program."

"Well, I don't know about the logic of that," Paul muses, stepping out of the car. "But like you said, we've been friends for a long time, so I guess we can disagree. Thanks for the ride and the discussion. See you tomorrow!"

"Sure," Steve murmurs. "Tomorrow."

3.5   Fallacies in Ordinary Language

This section addresses two topics. The first concerns the challenge of detecting the fallacies of others in ordinary language, and the second relates to the goal of avoiding fallacies in one's own arguments.

Detecting Fallacies

Most of the informal fallacies that we have seen thus far have been clear-cut, easily recognizable instances of a specific mistake. When fallacies occur in ordinary usage, however, they are often neither clear-cut nor easily recognizable. The reason is that there are innumerable ways of making mistakes in arguing, and variations inevitably occur that may not be exact instances of any specifically named fallacy. In addition, one fallacious mode of arguing may be mixed with one or more others, and the strands of reasoning may have to be disentangled before the fallacies can be named. Yet another problem arises from the fact that arguments in ordinary language are rarely presented in complete form. A premise or conclusion often is left unexpressed, which may obscure the nature of the evidence that is presented or the strength of the link between premises and conclusion.

Consider, for example, the following letter that appeared in a newspaper:

> God, I am sick of "women's rights"! Every time one turns on the news we hear about some form of discrimination against some poor female who wants to be a fireman—or some "remark" that suggests or implies women are inferior to men.
>
> I, for one, do not want to be rescued by a "woman fireman," especially if I am a 6-foot-2 male and she is a 5-foot-6 female.
>
> Why is it that women find their "role" so degrading? What is wrong with being a wife and mother, staying home while the male goes out and "hunts for food" and brings it home to his family?
>
> I don't think women have proven themselves to be as inventive, as capable (on the average) of world leadership, as physically capable, or as "courageous" as men. They have yet to fight a war (the average American woman) and let's face it ladies, who wants to?
>
> Whether a person is female, black, white, handicapped—whatever—*ability* is what counts in the final analysis. Women cannot demand "equality"—no one can—unless it is earned.
>
> When push comes to shove and a damsel is in distress, she is hard-pressed to protect herself and usually has to be rescued by a man. Until I can move a piano, beat off a potential robber or rapist, or fight a war, I am quite content to be a woman, thank you.
>
> (Patricia Kelley)

This letter presents numerous fallacies. The phrase "poor female who wants to be a fireman" suggests a mild *ad hominem* abusive, and equating women's rights in general with the right to be a firefighter suggests a straw man. The second paragraph commits another straw man fallacy by supposing that the job of firefighter inevitably entails such activities as climbing up ladders and rescuing people. Surely there are many male firefighters who cannot do this. The same paragraph also can be interpreted as begging the question: Do women who want to be firefighters want the specific job of rescuing tall men?

The third paragraph throws out a red herring. The issue is whether women have the right to be considered for a job of their choice and whether they must be paid as much as a man in the same situation. Whether there is something wrong with being a wife and mother is quite a different issue. Also, the reference to men hunting for food suggests a possible begging of the question: Are we still locked into a "hunter-gatherer" social structure?

The paragraph about whether women have proved themselves to be as inventive, capable, and courageous as men begs yet another question: Assuming, for the sake of argument, that this is true, have women been allowed to occupy roles in society where such inventiveness, capability, and courageousness can be demonstrated? Furthermore, this paragraph commits a red herring fallacy and/or misses the point: Even if women have not proved this, what does that have to do with the issue? Most jobs do not require any high degree of inventiveness or courage or a capacity for world leadership.

The paragraph about ability begs yet another question: Is it in fact the case that women have less ability? I am not aware that anything of the sort has ever been proved. Finally, the last paragraph throws out another red herring. What does moving pianos and beating off rapists have to do with most jobs or the question of equal pay for equal work?

Probably the single most important requirement for detecting fallacies in ordinary language is alertness. The reader or listener must pay close attention to what the arguer is saying. What is the conclusion? What are the reasons given in support of the conclusion? Are the reasons relevant to the conclusion? Do the reasons support the conclusion? If the reader or listener is half asleep or lounging in that passive, drugged-out state that attends much television viewing, then none of these questions will receive answers. Under those circumstances the reader or listener will never be able to detect informal fallacies, and he or she will accept even the worst reasoning without the slightest hesitation.

Avoiding Fallacies

Why do people commit informal fallacies? Unfortunately, this question admits of no simple, straightforward answer. The reasons underlying the commission of fallacies are complex and interconnected. However, we can identify three factors that lead to most of the informal mistakes in reasoning. The first is intent. Many fallacies are committed intentionally. The arguer may know full well that his or her reasoning is defective but goes ahead with it anyway because of some benefit for himself or herself or some other person. All of the informal fallacies we have studied can be used for that purpose, but some of them are particularly well suited to it. These include the appeal to force, appeal to pity, appeal to the people, straw man, *ad hominem*, complex question, false dichotomy, and suppressed evidence. Here is such a case of appeal to force:

> I deserve a chocolate sundae for dessert, and if you don't buy me one right now, I'll start screaming and embarrass you in front of all of the people in this restaurant.

And here is a case of false dichotomy that conveys the appearance of being intentionally committed:

> Either you take me on a Caribbean cruise, or I'll have a nervous breakdown. It's up to you.

The key to avoiding fallacies that are intentionally committed probably lies in some form of moral education. The arguer must come to realize that using intellectually dishonest means to acquire something he or she does not deserve is just another form of cheating.

The situation becomes more complicated, however, when the sought-after goal is morally justified. Arguers sometimes use fallacious reasoning intentionally to trick a person into doing something that is really for that person's own good. Here is a false dichotomy of that sort:

> Either you control your eating and get regular exercise, or you'll have a heart attack and die. The choice is yours.

Given the beneficial consequences of controlled eating and regular exercise, some moral philosophers will find nothing wrong with this argument. Others will contend that manipulating someone into doing something violates human dignity. In either case, such arguments are logically unacceptable.

The second factor that leads to the commission of informal fallacies is a careless mental posture combined with an emotional disposition favoring or opposing some person or thing. The careless mental posture opens the door, so to speak, to fallacious reasoning, and the emotional disposition pushes the arguer through it. Even people who are thoroughly versed in the informal fallacies occasionally succumb to the deadly combination of mental carelessness and emotional impetus. For example, arguments such as the following *ad hominem* abusive can sometimes be heard in the halls of university philosophy departments:

> Professor Ballard's argument in favor of restructuring our course offering isn't worth a hoot. But what would you expect from someone who publishes in such mediocre journals? And did you hear Ballard's recent lecture on Aristotle? It was total nonsense.

When people who should know better are confronted with the fact that their argument commits a common fallacy, they often admit with embarrassment that they have not been thinking and then revise their argument according to logical principles. In contrast, people who are not familiar with the distinction between good and fallacious reasoning will likely deny that there is anything wrong with their argument. Thus, the key to avoiding fallacies that arise from mental carelessness lies in developing a thorough familiarity with the informal fallacies, combined with a habitual realization of how emotions affect people's reasoning. Everyone should realize that unchecked emotions are an open invitation to illogical reasoning, and they can lead a person to commit quite blindly every one of the fallacies we have studied thus far.

The third factor that leads to the commission of informal fallacies is far more difficult to contend with than the first two. It consists in the influence of what we might call the "worldview" of the arguer. By worldview we mean a cognitive network of beliefs, attitudes, habits, memories, values, and other elements that conditions and renders meaningful the world in which we live. Beginning in infancy, our worldview emerges quietly and unconsciously from enveloping influences—culture, language, gender, religion, politics, and social and economic status. As we grow older, it continues to develop through the shaping forces of education and experience. Once it has taken root, our worldview determines how each of us sizes up the world in which we live. Given a set of circumstances, it indicates what is reasonable to believe and what is unreasonable.

In connection with the construction and evaluation of arguments, an arguer's worldview determines the answer to questions about importance, relevance, causal connections, the qualifications of authorities, whether a sample is typical or atypical of a group, what can and cannot be taken for granted, and other factors. However, because these determinations inevitably involve unexamined presuppositions, the arguer's worldview can lead to the commission of informal fallacies. All of the fallacies we have studied so far are likely candidates, but the ones especially susceptible are appeal to pity, straw man, missing the point, appeal to unqualified authority, hasty generalization, false cause, slippery slope, weak analogy, begging the question, false dichotomy, and suppressed evidence.

Thus, a person with a victim mentality may think that his pathetic circumstances really justify some favorable treatment; an uncritical conservative may cite with complete confidence the authority of Rush Limbaugh; a person with a racist worldview may conclude that the errant behavior of a handful of Asians, African Americans, or Hispanics really is typical of the larger class; a person with a liberal worldview may quite innocently distort an opponent's argument by equating it with fascism; a pro-life arguer may consider it obvious that the fetus is a person with rights, while a pro-choice arguer may take it for granted that the fetus is not a person with rights, and so on. Consider, for example, the following argument from analogy:

> A court trial is like a professional football game. In a professional football game, the most important thing is winning. Similarly, in a trial, the most important thing is winning.

This argument is consistent with the worldview of many, if not most, lawyers. Lawyers are trained as advocates, and when they enter a courtroom they see themselves going into battle for their clients. In any battle, winning is the most important objective. But this viewpoint presupposes that truth and justice are either unattainable in the courtroom or of secondary importance. Thus, while many lawyers would evaluate this argument as nonfallacious, many nonlawyers would reject it as a weak analogy.

For another example, consider the following causal inference:

> After enslaving most of Eastern Europe for nearly fifty years, the evil Soviet empire finally collapsed. Obviously God listened to our prayers.

This argument reflects the worldview of many theists. It presupposes that there is a God, that God listens to prayers, that God is affected by prayers, that God has the power to influence the course of history, and that God does influence the course of history. While the theist is likely to consider this argument a good one, the atheist will reject it as a blatant case of false cause.

To avoid fallacies that arise from the influence of worldviews, the arguer must acknowledge and critique his or her presuppositions. Doing so inclines the arguer to couch his or her arguments in language that takes those presuppositions into account. The result is nearly always an argument that is more intelligently crafted, and, it is hoped, more persuasive. However, the task of recognizing and critiquing one's presuppositions is not easy. Presuppositions are intrinsically linked to one's worldview, and many people are not even aware that they have a worldview. The reason is that worldviews are formed through a process that is largely unconscious. Thus, the arguer must first recognize that he or she has a worldview and must then exercise constant vigilance over the presuppositions it comprises.

Even after one's presuppositions have been exposed and thoroughly critiqued, however, there is no guarantee that one's arguments will agree with the arguments of others who have critiqued their worldviews. This is because a person's worldview reflects the unique perspective that person has on the world. No two people share exactly the same perspective. Nevertheless, disclosing and critiquing the presuppositions in one's worldview lays a foundation for meaningful communication with other reasonable arguers, and it provides a context of reasonableness for working out disagreements.

In summary, the three factors that are probably responsible for most informal fallacies are intent, mental carelessness combined with emotional dispositions, and unexamined presuppositions in the arguer's worldview. However, these factors rarely occur in isolation. In the vast majority of cases, two or all three conspire to produce fallacious reasoning. This fact exacerbates the difficulty in avoiding informal fallacies in one's own arguments and in detecting fallacies in the arguments of others.

Now let us consider some cases of real-life arguments in light of the factors we have just discussed. All are taken from letters to the editors of newspapers and magazines. The first relates to affirmative action programs:

> I'm a nonracist, nonsexist, white male born in 1969, who has never owned a slave, treated anyone as inferior because of his or her race, or sexually harassed a female co-worker. In other words, I don't owe women or minorities a thing. Since when are people required to pay for the sins of their predecessors simply because they belong to the same race or gender?
>
> (Ben Gibbons)

The author of this argument presupposes that racist and sexist patterns in society have not benefited him in any way. Among other things, he presupposes that his white ancestors in no way benefited from their being white and that none of these benefits passed down to him. On the other hand, given that he has received such benefits, he may presuppose that he is not obligated to pay any of them back. Of course, none of these things may have occurred, but the author should at least address these issues. Because he does not address them, the argument begs the question.

The next argument relates to second-hand smoke from cigarettes:

> Now, besides lung cancer and other nasty business, second-hand smoke causes deafness and impotence. Was second-hand smoke a problem when people heated their homes solely by fireplaces? How about those romantic teepees with the smoke hole at the top? And what about fireplaces in new homes? Let's have some research

about the problems caused by these as well as barbecues. A little cancer with your
hot dog, anyone?

(Pat Sharp)

This argument seems to commit the fallacy of equivocation. The arguer begins by
using "second-hand smoke" to refer to the smoke from burning tobacco, and then
uses the term to refer to the smoke from fireplaces, teepee fires, and barbecues. Smoke
from burning tobacco is clearly not the same thing as smoke from burning wood or
charcoal. Alternately, the argument might be seen to beg the question: "But do people
burn tobacco in their fireplaces and barbecues?" These fallacies probably arise either
from the intentions of the author or from carelessness in failing to distinguish the two
kinds of second-hand smoke. In either event, the author is probably hostile to government efforts to control second-hand tobacco smoke in confined areas.

The next argument deals with gun control:

> Detroit, the seventh largest city and one with strict gun laws, had 596 homicides last
> year. In the same year Phoenix, the ninth largest city and one that at the time did
> not require gun owners to be licensed, had 136 homicides. Criminals don't fear the
> toothless criminal-justice system, but they do fear armed citizens.

(Paul M. Berardi)

This argument commits a false cause fallacy. The author presupposes that the availability of guns caused Phoenix to have a lower homicide rate than Detroit. The arguer
also presupposes that Detroit and Phoenix are comparable as to homicide rate merely
because they are roughly the same size. As a result, the argument involves a weak analogy and also begs the question. The additional factors of emotion and intent may also
be present. The arguer probably hates the prospect of gun control, and he may be fully
aware of the fact that Phoenix and Detroit are not comparable for his purpose, but he
went ahead with the comparison anyway.

The next argument deals with religious fundamentalism:

> If we compromise God's word, we compromise the truth. To say that the fundamen-
> talist is a loud shrill voice drowning out religious moderation implies that diluted
> truth is better than absolute truth.

(Gerald Gleason)

This argument begs the question. The arguer presupposes that there is a God, that
God has spoken, that God has revealed his intentions to fundamentalist preachers,
and that those preachers accurately report the word of God. The argument also seems
to reflect an emotional disposition in favor of religious fundamentalism.

The last argument we will consider relates to English as the official U.S. language:

> This great country has been held together for more than 200 years because of one
> simple thing: the English language.
>   There are two things we must do: Make English the official language of the
> United States and do away with bilingual education.

(David Moisan)

This argument misses the point. The arguer presupposes that making English the official
language would guarantee that all citizens speak it and that doing away with bilingual

education would accelerate the learning process of immigrant children. The argument may also reflect the fear that many feel in connection with the changes U.S. society is experiencing as a result of recent immigration.

EXERCISE 3.5

I. Most of the following selections were taken from letters to the editors of newspapers and magazines. Identify any fallacies that may be committed, giving a brief explanation for your answer. Then, if a fallacy is identified, discuss the possible factors that led the arguer to commit the fallacy.

★1. Exporting cigarettes [to Asia] is good business for America; there is no reason we should be prohibited from doing so. Asians have been smoking for decades; we are only offering variety in their habit. If the Asians made tobacco smoking illegal, that would be a different situation. But as long as it is legal, the decision is up to the smokers. The Asians are just afraid of American supremacy in the tobacco industries.

(Pat Monohan)

2. When will these upper-crust intellectuals realize that the masses of working people are not in cozy, cushy, interesting, challenging, well-paying jobs, professions and businesses? My husband is now 51; for most of the last 33 years he has worked in the same factory job, and only the thought of retiring at 62 has sustained him. When he reaches that age in 11 years, who will tell him that his aging and physically wracked body must keep going another two years? My heart cries out for all the poor souls who man the assembly lines, ride the trucks or work in the fields or mines, or in the poorly ventilated, hot-in-summer, cold-in-winter factories and garages. Many cannot afford to retire at 62, 65, or even later. Never, never let them extend the retirement age. It's a matter of survival to so many.

(Isabel Fierman)

3. Women in military combat is insane. No society in its right mind would have such a policy. The military needs only young people and that means the only women who go are those in their child-bearing years. Kill them off and society will not be able to perpetuate itself.

(Jack Carman)

★4. Dear Ann: I've read that one aspirin taken every other day will reduce the risk of heart attack. Why not take two and double the protection?

(Boston)

5. The American Civil Liberties Union did a study that found that in the last 80 years it believes twenty-five innocent people have been executed in the United States. This is unfortunate. But, there are innocent people who die each year in highway accidents. Out of 40,000 deaths, how many deaths are related to driving while intoxicated? How many more thousands are injured and incur financial ruin or are invalids and handicapped for the remainder of their lives?

(Mahlon R. Braden)

6. Mexico's president expresses legitimate concern when he questions supplying oil to Americans who are unwilling to apply "discipline" in oil consumption. In view of the fact that his country's population is expected to double in only twenty-two years, isn't it legitimate for us to ask when Mexicans will apply the discipline necessary to control population growth and quit dumping their excess millions over our borders?

(Wayne R. Bartz)

★7. A parent would never give a ten-year-old the car keys, fix him or her a martini, or let him or her wander at night through a dangerous part of town. The same holds true of the Internet. Watch what children access, but leave the Net alone. Regulation is no substitute for responsibility.

(Bobby Dunning)

8. How would you feel to see your children starving and have all doors slammed in your face? Isn't it time that all of us who believe in freedom and human rights stop thinking in terms of color and national boundaries? We should open our arms and hearts to those less fortunate and remember that a time could come when we might be in a similar situation.

(Lorna Doyle)

9. A capital gains tax [reduction] benefits everyone, not just the "rich," because everyone will have more money to invest or spend in the private economy, resulting in more jobs and increasing prosperity for all. This is certainly better than paying high taxes to a corrupt, self-serving and incompetent government that squanders our earnings on wasteful and useless programs.

(David Miller)

★10. After reading "Homosexuals in the Churches," I'd like to point out that I don't know any serious, capable exegetes who stumble over Saint Paul's denunciation of homosexuality. Only a fool (and there seem to be more and more these days) can fail to understand the plain words of Romans, Chapter one. God did not make anyone "gay." Paul tells us in Romans 1 that homosexuals become that way because of their own lusts.

(LeRoy J. Hopper)

11. When will they ever learn—that the Republican Party is not for the people who voted for it?

(Alton L. Stafford)

12. Before I came to the United States in July, 1922, I was in Berlin where I visited the famous zoo. In one of the large cages were a lion and a tiger. Both respected each other's strength. It occurred to me that it was a good illustration of "balance of power." Each beast followed the other and watched each other's moves. When one moved, the other did. When one stopped, the other stopped.

In today's world, big powers or groups of powers are trying to maintain the status quo, trying to be as strong as or stronger than the other. They realize a conflict may result in mutual destruction. As long as the countries believe there is a balance of power we may hope for peace.

(Emilie Lackow)

★13. Doctors say the birth of a baby is a high point of being a doctor. Yet a medical survey shows one out of every nine obstetricians in America has stopped delivering babies.

Expectant mothers have had to find new doctors. In some rural areas, women have had to travel elsewhere to give birth.

How did this happen? It's part of the price of the lawsuit crisis.

The number of lawsuits Americans file each year is on the rise. Obstetricians are among the hardest hit—almost three out of four have faced a malpractice claim. Many have decided it isn't worth the risk.

(Magazine ad by the Insurance Information Institute)

14. The conservative diatribe found in campus journalism comes from the mouths of a handful of affluent brats who were spoon-fed through the '80s. Put them on an ethnically more diverse campus, rather than a Princeton or a Dartmouth, and then let us see how long their newspapers survive.

(David Simons)

15. I see that our courts are being asked to rule on the propriety of outlawing video games as a "waste of time and money."

It seems that we may be onto something here. A favorable ruling would open the door to new laws eliminating show business, spectator sports, cocktail lounges, the state of Nevada, public education and, of course, the entire federal bureaucracy.

(A. G. Dobrin)

★16. The death penalty is the punishment for murder. Just as we have long jail terms for armed robbery, assault and battery, fraud, contempt of court, fines for speeding, reckless driving and other numerous traffic violations, so must we have a punishment for murder. Yes, the death penalty will not deter murders any more than a speeding ticket will deter violating speed laws again, but it is the punishment for such violation!

(Lawrence J. Barstow)

17. Would you rather invest in our nation's children or Pentagon waste? The choice is yours.

(Political ad)

18. My gun has protected me, and my son's gun taught him safety and responsibility long before he got hold of a far more lethal weapon—the family car. Cigarettes kill many times more people yearly than guns and, unlike guns, have absolutely no redeeming qualities. If John Lennon had died a long, painful and expensive death from lung cancer, would you have devoted a page to a harangue against the product of some of your biggest advertisers—the cigarette companies?

(Silvia A. DeFreitas)

★19. If the advocates of prayers in public schools win on this issue, just where will it end? Perhaps next they will ask for prayers on public transportation? Prayers by government workers before they start their job each day? Or maybe, mandatory prayers in public restaurants before starting each meal might be a good idea.

(Leonard Mendelson)

20. So you want to ban smoking in all eating establishments? Well, you go right ahead and do that little thing. And when the 40 percent of smokers stop eating out, the restaurants can do one of two things: close, or raise the price of a $20 dinner 40 percent to $28.

(Karen Sawyer)

21. Pigeons are forced to leave our city to battle for life. Their struggle is an end-less search for food. What manner of person would watch these hungry crea-tures suffer from want of food and deny them their survival? These helpless birds are too often ignored by the people of our city, with not the least bit of compassion shown to them. Pigeons are God's creatures just as the so-called human race is. They need help.

(Leslie Ann Price)

★22. You take half of the American population every night and set them down in front of a box watching people getting stabbed, shot and blown away. And then you expect them to go out into the streets hugging each other?

(Mark Hustad)

23. So you think that putting the worst type of criminal out of his misery is wrong. How about the Americans who were sent to Korea, to Vietnam, to Beirut, to Central America? Thousands of good men were sacrificed supposedly for the good of our country. At the same time we were saving and protecting Charles Manson, Sirhan Sirhan [Robert Kennedy's murderer], and a whole raft of oth-ers too numerous to mention.

(George M. Purvis)

24. The fact is that the hype over "acid rain" and "global warming" is just that: hype. Take, for example, Stephen Schneider, author of *Global Warming*. In his current "study" he discusses a "greenhouse effect of catastrophic proportions," yet twenty years ago Schneider was a vocal proponent of the theory of a "new ice age."

(Urs Furrer)

★25. Just as our parents did for us, my husband and I rely solely on Christian Sci-ence for all the health needs of our four sons and find it invaluable for the quick cure of whatever ailments and contagions they are subject to. One par-ticular healing that comes to mind happened several years ago when our youngest was a toddler. He had a flu-type illness that suddenly became quite serious. We called a Christian Science practitioner for treatment and he was completely well the next morning.

(Ellen Austin)

26. As somebody who has experienced the tragedy of miscarriage—or sponta-neous abortion—at eight weeks, I greatly resent the position that a fetus is not

a baby. I went through the grief of losing a baby, and no one should tell me otherwise.

(Ann Fons)

27. How can we pledge allegiance to the flag of the United States of America and not establish laws to punish people who burn the flag to make a statement? We are a people who punish an individual who libels another person but will not seek redress from an individual who insults every citizen of this great country by desecrating the flag.

(William D. Lankford)

★28. The notion of "buying American" is as misguided as the notion of buying Wisconsin, or Oshkosh, Wisconsin, or South Oshkosh, Wisconsin. For the same reasons that Wisconsin increases its standard of living by trading with the rest of the nation, America increases its standard of living by trading with the rest of the world.

(Phillip Smith)

29. We've often heard the saying, "Far better to let 100 guilty men go free than to condemn one innocent man." What happens then if we apply the logic of this argument to the question, "Is a fetus an unborn human being?" Then is it not better to let 100 fetuses be born rather than to mistakenly kill one unborn human being? This line of reasoning is a strictly humanist argument against abortion.

(James Sebastian)

30. In our society it is generally considered improper for a man to sleep, shower, and dress amid a group of women to whom he normally would be sexually attracted. It seems to me, then, to be equally unacceptable that a gay man sleep, shower, and dress in a company of men to whom, we assume, he would be no less sexually attracted.

(Mark O. Temple)

★31. I say "bravo" and "right on!" Now we have some real-life humane heroes to look up to! These brave people [a group of animal liberators] went up against the insensitive bureaucratic technology, and won, saving former pet animals from senseless torture.

   If researchers want to experiment, let them use computers, or themselves—but not former pet animals! I know it's bad enough they use monkeys and rats, but if those animals are bred knowing nothing else but these Frankensteins abusing them it's different (but not better) than dogs or cats that have been loved and petted all their lives to suddenly be tortured and mutilated in the name of science. End all animal research! Free all research animals!

   Right on, animal liberators!

(Linda Magee)

32. Dear Ann: Recently I was shopping downtown in 20-below-zero weather. A stranger walked up to me and said, "I wonder how many beautiful rabbits died so you could have that coat?" I noticed she was wearing a down coat, so I asked

if the geese they got the down from to make her coat were still alive. She looked surprised. Obviously she had never given it a thought.

If people are so upset about cruelty to animals, why don't they go after the folks who refuse to spend the money to have their pets neutered and spayed? Thousands of dogs are put to death every year because the animal pounds can't feed and house them. Talk about cruelty to animals—that's the best example there is.

("Baby It's Cold Outside")

33. I prayed for the U.S. Senate to defeat the prayer amendment—and it did. There is a God.

(Richard Carr)

★34. People of the Philippines, I have returned! The hour of your redemption is here! Rally to me! Let the indomitable spirit of Bataan and Corregidor lead on! As the lines of battle roll forward to bring you within the zone of operations, rise and strike! For future generations of your sons and daughters, strike! Let no heart be faint! Let every arm be steeled! The guidance of divine God points the way! Follow in his name to the Holy Grail of righteous victory!

(General Douglas MacArthur)

35. As the oldest of eleven children (all married), I'd like to point out our combined family numbers more than 100 who vote only for pro-life candidates. Pro-lifers have children, pro-choicers do not.

(Mrs. Kitty Reickenback)

36. I am 12 years old. My class had a discussion on whether police used unnecessary force when arresting the people from Operation Rescue.

My teacher is an ex-cop, and he demonstrated police holds to us. They don't hurt at all unless the person is struggling or trying to pull away. If anybody was hurt when they were arrested, then they must have been struggling with the officers trying to arrest them.

(Ben Torre-Bueno)

★37. As corporate farms continue to gobble up smaller family farms, they control a larger percentage of the grain and produce raised in the United States. Some have already reached a point in size where, if they should decide to withhold their grain and produce from the marketplace, spot shortages could occur and higher prices would result. The choice is to pay us family farmers now or pay the corporations later.

(Delwin Yost)

38. If you buy our airline ticket now you can save 60 percent, and that means 60 percent more vacation for you.

(Radio ad)

39. Why all the flap about atomic bombs? The potential for death is always with us. Of course, if you just want something to worry about, go ahead. Franklin D. Roosevelt said it: "The only thing we have to fear is fear itself."

(Lee Flemming Reese)

★**40.** September 17 marked the anniversary of the signing of the U.S. Constitution. How well have we, the people, protected our rights? Consider what has happened to our private-property rights.

"Property has divine rights, and the moment the idea is admitted into society that property is not as sacred as the laws of God, anarchy and tyranny begin." John Quincy Adams, 1767–1848, Sixth President of the United States.

Taxes and regulations are the two-edged sword which gravely threatens the fabric of our capitalistic republic. The tyranny of which Adams speaks is with us today in the form of government regulators and regulations which have all but destroyed the right to own property. Can anarchy be far behind?

(Timothy R. Binder)

41. Evolution would have been dealt serious setbacks if environmentalists had been around over the eons trying to save endangered species.

Species are endangered because they just do not fit the bigger picture any more as the world changes. That's not bad. It's just life.

In most cases we have seen the "endangered species" argument is just a ruse; much deeper motives usually exist, and they are almost always selfish and personal.

(Tom Gable)

42. The problem that I have with the pro-choice supporters' argument is that they make "choice" the ultimate issue. Let's face facts. No one has absolute freedom of choice sanctioned by the law. One can choose to rob a bank, but it's not lawful. Others can choose to kill their one-year-old child, but it is not legal. Why then should a woman have the legal right to take the life of her unborn child?

(Loretta S. Horn)

★**43.** If a car or truck kills a person, do politicians call for car control or truck control? And call in all cars/trucks?

If a child burns down a house do we have match control or child control and call in all of each?

Gun control and confiscation is equally as pathetic a thought process in an age of supposed intelligence.

(Pete Hawes)

44. I was incensed to read in your article about the return of anti-Semitism that New York City Moral Majority Leader Rev. Dan C. Fore actually said that "Jews have a God-given ability to make money, almost a supernatural ability . . ." I find it incredibly ironic that he and other Moral Majority types conveniently overlook the fact that they, too, pack away a pretty tidy sum themselves through their fund-raising efforts. It is sad that anti-Semitism exists, but to have this prejudice voiced by leaders of religious organizations is deplorable. These people are in for quite a surprise come Judgment Day.

(John R. Murks)

45. Are Americans so stupid they don't realize that every time they pay thousands of dollars for one of those new "economical" Japanese cars, they are simultaneously making the U.S. bankrupt and giving the Japanese enough money to buy all of America?

(Sylvia Petersen Young)

★46. Why are people so shocked that Susan Smith apparently chose to kill her children because they had become an inconvenience? Doesn't this occur every day in abortion clinics across the country? We suspect Smith heard very clearly the message many feminists have been trying to deliver about the expendable nature of our children.

(Kevin and Diana Cogan)

47. What's wrong with kids today? Answer: nothing, for the majority of them. They are great.

Witness the action of two San Diego teenage boys recently, when the Normal Heights fire was at its worst. They took a garden hose to the roof of a threatened house—a house belonging to four elderly sisters, people they didn't even know. They saved the house, while neighboring houses burned to the ground.

In the Baldwin Hills fire, two teenage girls rescued a blind, retired Navy man from sure death when they braved the flames to find him, confused, outside his burning house. He would probably have perished if they hadn't run a distance to rescue him.

(Theodore H. Wickham)

48. Now that Big Brother has decided that I must wear a seatbelt when I ride in a car, how long will it take before I have to wear an inner tube when I swim in my pool, a safety harness when I climb a ladder, and shoes with steel-reinforced toecaps when I carry out the garbage?

(G. R. Turgeon)

★49. Dear Ann: I was disappointed in your response to the girl whose mother used the strap on her. The gym teacher noticed the bruises on her legs and backside and called it "child abuse." Why are you against strapping a child when the Bible tells us in plain language that this is what parents should do?

The Book of Proverbs mentions many times that the rod must be used. Proverbs 23:13 says: "Withhold not correction from the child for if thou beatest him with the rod he shall not die." Proverbs 23:14 says: "Thou shalt beat him with the rod and shalt deliver his soul from death."

There is no substitute for a good whipping. I have seen the results of trying to reason with kids. They are arrogant, disrespectful and mouthy. Parents may wish for a more "humane" way, but there is none. Beating children is God's way of getting parents to gain control over their children.

(Davisville, W.Va.)

50. The Fourth Amendment guarantees our right to freedom from unreasonable search and seizure. It does not prohibit *reasonable* search and seizure. The matter of sobriety roadblocks to stop drunk drivers boils down to this: Are such roadblocks reasonable or unreasonable? The majority of people answer:

"Reasonable." Therefore, sobriety roadblocks should not be considered to be unconstitutional.

(Haskell Collier)

51. The Supreme Court recently ruled that a police department in Florida did not violate any rights of privacy when a police helicopter flew over the back yard of a suspected drug dealer and noticed marijuana growing on his property. Many people, including groups like the Anti-Common Logic Union, felt that the suspect's right to privacy outweighed the police department's need to protect the public at large.

The simple idea of sacrificing a right to serve a greater good should be allowed in certain cases. In this particular case the danger to the public wasn't extremely large; marijuana is probably less dangerous than regular beer. But anything could have been in that back yard—a load of cocaine, an illegal stockpile of weapons, or other major threats to society.

(Matt Cookson)

★52. I am 79 and have been smoking for 60 years. My husband is 90 and has inhaled my smoke for some 50 years with no bad effects.

I see no reason to take further steps to isolate smokers in our restaurants and public places, other than we now observe.

Smokers have taken punishment enough from neurotic sniffers, some of whom belong in bubbles. There are plenty of injudicious fumes on our streets and freeways.

(Helen Gans)

53. The mainstream press finds itself left behind by talk radio, so they try to minimize its importance. Americans are finding the true spirit of democracy in community and national debate. Why should we be told what to believe by a news weekly or the nightly news when we can follow public debate as it unfolds on talk radio?

(Adam Abbott)

54. The issue is not whether we should subsidize the arts, but whether anyone should be able to force someone else to subsidize the arts. You and I are free to *give* any amount of our money to any artistic endeavor we wish to support. When the government gets involved, however, a group of bureaucrats is given the power to *take* our money and give it to the arts they wish to support. We are not consulted. That is not a way to promote a responsible culture. That is tyranny.

(Jerry Harben)

★55. Who are these Supreme Court justices who have the guts to OK the burning of our flag?

If the wife or daughter of these so-called justices were raped, could the rapist be exonerated because he took the First Amendment? That he was just expressing himself? How about murder in the same situation?

(Robert A. Lewis)

56. I have one question for those bleeding hearts who say we should not have used the atomic bomb: If the nation responsible for the Rape of Nanking, the Manchurian atrocities, Pearl Harbor and the Bataan Death March had invented the bomb first, don't you think they would have used it? So do I.

(Bill Blair)

57. Since when did military service become a right, for gays or anyone else? The military has always been allowed to discriminate against people who don't meet its requirements, including those who are overweight or too tall or too short. There is an adequate supply of personnel with the characteristics they need. And there is no national need for gays in the military.

(William R. Cnossen)

★58. There is something very wrong about the custom of tipping. When we go to a store, we don't decide what a product is worth and pay what we please; we pay the price or we leave. Prices in coffee bars and restaurants should be raised, waiters should be paid a decent wage, and the words "no tipping" should be clearly visible on menus and at counters.

(George Jochnowitz)

59. Most Americans do not favor gun control. They know that their well-being depends on their own ability to protect themselves. So-called "assault rifles" are used in few crimes. They are not the weapon of choice of criminals, but they are for people trying to protect themselves from government troops.

(Larry Herron)

60. Holding a gun, a thief robs John Q. Public of thousands of dollars. Holding a baby, an unmarried mother robs taxpayers of thousands of dollars. If one behavior is considered a crime, then so should the other.

(Louis R. Ward)

II. Turn to the editorial pages of a newspaper or the letters column of a magazine and find an instance of a fallacious argument in the editorials or letters to the editor. Identify the premises and conclusion of the argument and write an analysis at least one paragraph in length identifying the fallacy or fallacies committed and the factors that may have led the arguer to commit them.

Summary

A fallacy is a mistake in an argument that arises from something other than merely false premises. Usually fallacies involve defects in reasoning or the creation of an illusion that makes a bad argument appear good. Fallacies can be either formal or informal. A formal fallacy is one that can be detected by analyzing the form of an argument; such fallacies affect only deductive arguments. An informal fallacy is one that can be identified only by analyzing the content of an argument; such fallacies can affect both deductive and inductive arguments.

The fallacies of relevance occur when the premises of an argument are not relevant to the conclusion. Cases of such irrelevance occur in premises that threaten the observer, elicit pity from the observer, create a mob mentality in a group of observers, appeal to the observer's desire for security, verbally abuse an opposing arguer, present an opposing arguer as predisposed to argue as he does, present an opposing arguer as a hypocrite, misapply a general rule, distort an opponent's argument, or lead the observer off the track. A kind of catchall fallacy, missing the point, occurs when an arguer draws a conclusion different from the one implied by the premises.

The fallacies of weak induction occur when the premises, although possibly relevant to the conclusion, provide insufficient support for the conclusion. Cases of such inadequate support occur when the arguer cites an authority who is not qualified, draws a conclusion from premises that give no positive evidence, draws a conclusion from an atypical sample, depends on a nonexistent or minor causal connection, depends on a chain reaction that is unlikely to occur, or draws a conclusion from an analogy that is not close enough to support it.

The fallacies of presumption occur when the premises presume what they purport to prove. Such presumptions occur when the arguer creates the illusion that inadequate premises are adequate, asks a question that comprises two or more questions, uses a disjunctive statement that falsely claims to exhaust the available alternatives, or ignores important evidence that requires a different conclusion.

The fallacies of ambiguity occur when the conclusion depends on some form of linguistic ambiguity. Either a word or phrase is used in more than one sense or the wrong interpretation is given to an ambiguous statement.

The fallacies of grammatical analogy occur when a defective argument appears good owing to a grammatical similarity to some argument that is not fallacious. Such grammatical similarities occur in arguments that wrongly transfer an attribute from parts to a whole or from a whole to its parts.

Fallacies that occur in real-life argumentation are harder to detect than those in manufactured examples because they may not exactly fit the structure of the named fallacies and because several fallacies can be woven together in a single passage. Three factors that underlie the commission of fallacies in real-life argumentation are the intent of the arguer, mental carelessness combined with unchecked emotions, and unexamined presuppositions in the arguer's worldview.

Answers to Selected Exercises

Exercise 3.1
1. Formal fallacy.
4. Informal fallacy.

7. Informal fallacy.
10. Formal fallacy.

Exercise 3.2
I.
1. Appeal to pity.
4. Accident.
7. Appeal to force.
10. *Tu quoque* (you, too).
13. Red herring.

16. *Ad hominem* circumstantial.
19. Straw man.
22. Appeal to the people, indirect variety.
25. Missing the point.

Exercise 3.3
I.
1. Hasty generalization (converse accident).
4. Slippery slope.

III.
1. Hasty generalization.
4. *Ad hominem* circumstantial.
7. False cause (gambler's fallacy).
10. Straw man.
13. Red herring.

7. Appeal to ignorance.
10. Appeal to unqualified authority.
13. Weak analogy.

16. Missing the point.
19. Weak analogy.
22. No fallacy.
25. Appeal to ignorance.
28. False cause.

Exercise 3.4
I.
1. False dichotomy.
4. Amphiboly.
7. Begging the question.
10. Equivocation.
13. Composition.

16. Suppressed evidence.
19. Division.
22. Complex question.
25. Begging the question.

III.

1. *Ad hominem* circumstantial.
4. Equivocation.
7. Begging the question.
10. Division.
13. False cause (oversimplified cause).
16. Appeal to unqualified authority.
19. Composition.
22. Weak analogy.
25. Straw man.

28. Accident.
31. Red herring.
34. Amphiboly.
37. False cause (gambler's fallacy).
40. Begging the question.
43. Missing the point or suppressed evidence.
46. Hasty generalization.
49. Composition.

Exercise 3.5

I.

1. Missing the point or begging the question.
4. Composition.
7. No fallacy? Weak analogy?
10. Appeal to unqualified authority. The statement "Only a fool . . ." involves an *ad hominem* abusive.
13. False cause, suppressed evidence, begging the question. There is little or no evidence of any causal connection between malpractice suits and the decision of some obstetricians to leave the field. An unmentioned factor is the inconvenience of being on call twenty-four hours per day waiting for patients to deliver. There is also little or no evidence of any genuine "lawsuit crisis."
16. Begging the question? (Strange argument!)
19. Slippery slope.
22. False cause? No fallacy?
25. False cause.
28. Suppressed evidence? Begging the question? No fallacy? The Commerce Clause of the U.S. Constitution and pertinent federal legislation prohibit unfair trade practices between states. No equivalent regulations exist for international trade.
31. Appeal to the people (direct variety). Also appeal to pity?
34. Appeal to the people (direct variety)?
37. False dichotomy? No fallacy?
40. Appeal to unqualified authority, slippery slope.
43. Several cases of weak analogy. Also, a possible case of *ad hominem* abusive.
46. Begging the question; straw man.
49. Appeal to unqualified authority. The last paragraph suggests a hasty generalization.
52. Hasty generalization. *Ad hominem* abusive? Also, begging the question or red herring?
55. Weak analogy.
58. Weak analogy? No fallacy?

3

Analogy and Legal
and Moral Reasoning

9.1   Analogical Reasoning

Analogical reasoning may be the most fundamental and the most common of all rational processes. It stands at the basis of many ordinary decisions in life. For example, a woman wanting to buy a can of soup might deliberate between Campbell's and Brand X and, after recalling that other varieties of Campbell's were good, decide in favor of that brand. A man contemplating a haircut might recall that a friend got an especially good cut at the Golden Touch and as a result decide to go there himself. A woman selecting a plant for her garden might observe that gardenias grow well at the house next door and conclude that gardenias would grow well at her house, too. A man thinking of reading a novel by Stephen King might recall that King's last three novels were thrilling and conclude that his latest novel would also be thrilling.

Analogical reasoning is reasoning that depends on a comparison of instances. If the instances are sufficiently similar, the decision reached in the end is usually a good one; but if they are not sufficiently similar, the decision may not be good. When such a reasoning process is expressed in words, the result is an argument from analogy (see Chapter 1). Simple arguments from analogy have the following structure:

> Entity A has attributes $a, b, c,$ and z.
> Entity B has attributes a, b, c.
> Therefore, entity B probably has attribute z also.

If the attributes a, b, and c are connected in some important way to z (that is, are relevant to z), the argument is usually strong. If they are not so connected (that is, are irrelevant to z), the argument is usually weak.

Analogical arguments are closely related to generalizations. In a generalization, the arguer begins with one or more instances and proceeds to draw a conclusion about all the members of a class. The arguer may then apply the generalization to one or more members of this class that were not noted earlier. The first stage of such an inference is inductive, and the second stage is deductive. For example, the man thinking of reading the latest Stephen King novel might argue that because the last three novels by King were thrilling, all King novels are thrilling (inductive argument). Applying this generalization to the latest novel, he might then conclude that it too will be thrilling (deductive argument). In an argument from analogy, on the other hand, the arguer proceeds directly from one or more individual instances to a conclusion about another individual instance without appealing to any intermediate generalization. Such an argument is purely inductive. Thus, the arguer might conclude directly from reading three earlier King novels that the latest one will be thrilling.

In any argument from analogy, the items that are compared are called *analogues*. Thus, if one should argue that Britney Spears's latest CD is probably good because her two previous CDs were good, the three CDs are the analogues. The two earlier CDs are called the *primary analogues,* and the latest CD is called the *secondary analogue.* With these definitions in mind, we may now examine a set of principles that are useful for evaluating most arguments from analogy. They include (1) the relevance of the similarities shared by the primary and secondary analogues, (2) the number of similarities, (3) the nature and degree of disanalogy, (4) the number of primary analogues, (5) the diversity among the primary analogues, and (6) the specificity of the conclusion.

1. *Relevance of the similarities.* Suppose a certain person—let us call her Lucy—is contemplating the purchase of a new car. She decides in favor of a Chevrolet because she wants good gas mileage and her friend Tom's new Chevy gets good gas mileage. To support her decision, Lucy argues that both cars have a padded steering wheel, tachometer, vinyl upholstery, tinted windows, CD player, and white paint. Lucy's argument is weak because these similarities are irrelevant to gas mileage. On the other hand, if Lucy bases her conclusion on the fact that both cars have the same-size engine, her argument is relatively strong, because engine size is relevant to gas mileage.

2. *Number of similarities.* Suppose, in addition to the same-size engine, Lucy notes further similarities between the car she intends to buy and Tom's car: curb weight, aerodynamic body, gear ratio, and tires. These additional similarities, all of which are relevant to gas mileage, tend to strengthen Lucy's argument. If, in addition, Lucy notes that she and Tom both drive about half on city streets and half on freeways, her argument is strengthened even further.

3. *Nature and degree of disanalogy.* On the other hand, if Lucy's car is equipped with a turbocharger, if Lucy loves to make jackrabbit starts and screeching stops, if Tom's car has overdrive but Lucy's does not, and if Lucy constantly drives on congested freeways while Tom drives on relatively clear freeways, Lucy's argument is weakened. These differences are called *disanalogies.* Depending on how they relate to the conclusion, disanalogies can either weaken or strengthen an argument. If we suppose instead that Tom's car has the turbocharger, that Tom loves jackrabbit starts, and so on, then Lucy's argument is strengthened, because these disanalogies tend to reduce Tom's gas mileage.

4. *Number of primary analogues.* Thus far, Lucy has based her conclusion on the similarity between the car she intends to buy and only one other car—Tom's. Now suppose that Lucy has three additional friends, that all of them drive cars of the same model and year as Tom's, and that all of them get good gas mileage.

These additional primary analogues strengthen Lucy's argument because they lessen the likelihood that Tom's good gas mileage is a freak incident. On the other hand, suppose that two of these additional friends get the same good gas mileage as Tom but that the third gets poor mileage. As before, the first two cases tend to strengthen Lucy's argument, but the third now tends to weaken it. This third case is called a *counteranalogy* because it supports a conclusion opposed to that of the original analogy.

5. *Diversity among the primary analogues.* Suppose now that Lucy's four friends (all of whom get good mileage) all buy their gas at the same station, have their cars tuned up regularly by the same mechanic, put the same friction-reducing additive in their oil, inflate their tires to the same pressure, and do their city driving on uncongested, level streets at a fuel-maximizing 28 miles per hour. Such factors would tend to reduce the probability of Lucy's conclusion, because it is possible that one or a combination of them is responsible for the good mileage and that this factor (or combination of them) is absent in Lucy's case. On the other hand, if Lucy's friends buy their gas at different stations, have their cars tuned up at different intervals by different mechanics, inflate their tires to different pressures, drive at different speeds on different grades, and have different attitudes toward using the oil additive, then it is less likely that the good gas mileage they enjoy is attributable to any factor other than the model and year of their car.

6. *Specificity of the conclusion.* Lucy's conclusion is simply that her car will get "good" mileage. If she now changes her conclusion to state that her car will get gas mileage "at least as good" as Tom's, then her argument is weakened. Such a conclusion is more specific than the earlier conclusion and is easier to falsify. Thus, if her mileage were only one-tenth of a mile per gallon less than Tom's, her conclusion would turn out to be false. Now suppose that Lucy changes her conclusion to state that her car will get exactly the same gas mileage as Tom's. This conclusion is even more specific than the "at least as good" conclusion, and it is easier still to falsify. Thus, such a conclusion renders Lucy's argument much weaker than her original argument.

Let us now use these six principles to evaluate an argument from analogy. Suppose that you want to shade a bedroom window from the intense western sun. To accomplish this purpose, you decide to plant some trees, but the trees must be narrow ones that will grow approximately 25 feet tall. Recalling that a friend has some Italian cypresses that are almost exactly 25 feet tall, you conclude that this variety of tree will do the job. Thus far, your argument is based on a single similarity, the species of the tree. Because this similarity is very relevant to height, your argument is fairly strong. Now if, in addition, it turns out that your friend lives in the same city and has the same kind of soil as you, your argument is strengthened. However, if it happens that your friend has a knack for growing trees while you have a knack for killing them, your argument is weakened.

To this set of facts, suppose we add the observation that four of your neighbors have Italian cypresses and that all of their trees are approximately 25 feet tall. This fact tends to strengthen your argument. Also, if all four neighbors planted their trees in different years, use different kinds of fertilizers on them, and give them different amounts of water, your argument is further strengthened. Finally, should you broaden your conclusion to state that your trees will grow between 22 and 28 feet tall, your argument is strengthened even further. But if you narrow your conclusion to state that your trees will grow to between 24½ and 25½ feet tall, your argument is weakened.

9.2   Legal Reasoning

Many of the arguments used by lawyers in the United States and Canada to support a case at trial are analogical arguments. The reason is that the legal systems of these countries were derived many years ago from the English system, and an essential feature of the English system is its dependence on precedent. According to the requirement of precedent, similar cases must be decided similarly. Thus, in arguing a case, a lawyer will often attempt to show that the case is analogous to some earlier case that was decided in a favorable way. Sometimes, even today, these precedents go back to early English law.

For example, suppose you own a factory and one of your machines, a drill press, breaks down, causing the entire operation to come to a halt. Urgently you call a repair company and explain the whole situation. The spokesperson for the company promises to have the drill press back in operation within two days. Unfortunately, there are delays, and two weeks elapse before the drill press is repaired. In the meantime your company loses an additional $10,000 in profits. Because you relied on the spokesperson's assurance that the drill press would be fixed in two days, you demand that the repair company reimburse you for the additional lost profits. When the repair company refuses your demand, you file suit.

The lawyer who argues your case will probably make reference to a much earlier case, *Hadley v. Baxendale,* decided in Gloucester, England, in 1854. In that case the operation of a mill was halted because of a broken crankshaft, and the owner of the mill (Hadley) employed a shipping company (Baxendale) to return the crankshaft to the manufacturer. Hadley informed Baxendale that the broken crankshaft had interrupted the operation of the mill, and Baxendale replied that the broken crankshaft would be in the hands of the manufacturer within one day. As it turned out, the shipment was delayed by several days, and Hadley incurred lost profits from the additional time the mill was shut down. Hadley demanded reimbursement from Baxendale, and when Baxendale refused, Hadley filed suit. The court ruled that Baxendale should pay only if he foresaw when he agreed to do the work that delays would result in lost profits for Hadley.

Applying this result to the drill press case, your lawyer will argue that because the repair company was informed that delays in repairing the drill press would result in lost profits, it should reimburse you for the losses incurred.

In the early days, much of English law resulted directly from judges' rendering decisions in particular cases. This judge-made law is otherwise called common law. However, today many of our laws are not the direct product of judges but rather of legislative bodies. These laws, called *statutes,* are codified in books that are periodically revised. Can it be said that precedent plays a central role in decisions involving statutory law in the same way that it does in decisions involving common law? The answer is a definite yes. Statutory laws are invariably phrased in relatively general language, and precedent is required to determine how the statutes should be interpreted and applied.

Consider, for example, a "law" that we are all familiar with, the First Amendment to the U.S. Constitution, which provides for freedom of speech and religious expression. Suppose that you decide, in reliance on the First Amendment, to pass out religious pamphlets on a downtown street corner. Suppose further that most of the people you hand your pamphlets to merely glance at them and then throw them on the street and that the gathering litter makes the area look like a garbage dump. To prevent the litter, the police tell you that you can hand out your pamphlets only in the vicinity of public garbage cans, so that those who do not want the pamphlets can properly dispose of them. You object that such a restriction violates your First Amendment rights, and you take the issue to court.

In presenting your case, your lawyer will argue that the case is analogous to other cases where the state attempted to limit not the content of religious expression, but the time, place, and manner of its expression. Next, your lawyer will note that in such cases the state is allowed to restrict the expression only if the restriction is "narrowly tailored" to serve a "significant government interest." Finally, your lawyer will attempt to show that your case is analogous to cases in which the government failed to prove that the restriction was so tailored.

As these examples illustrate, many of the arguments that occur in law are arguments from analogy, and the principles developed at the beginning of this section can be used to evaluate them. The first principle, which deals with the relevance of the similarities, has an obvious application to legal arguments. Suppose, for example, that two cases are similar in that each involves a burning building, the building in each case is located in Chicago, and in each case ten people died. The comparison is pointless if the issue in the first case is whether an insurance company is liable to pay damages while the issue in the second is whether somebody is guilty of arson.

The second and third principles, which deal with the number of similarities and the nature and degree of disanalogy, are also applicable. If a preceding case resembles the case at hand in virtually all important details, then the preceding case is said to be "on point" and, given certain other requirements (discussed shortly), will dictate the outcome of the case to be decided. As for the nature and degree of disanalogy, if a preceding case deals with fraud by a stockbroker while the case to be decided deals with fraud by a real estate broker, the precedent may be more or less controlling, depending on such circumstances as applicable statutory law.

As applied to legal analogies, the fourth principle (number of primary analogues) usually determines how well established a legal precedent is. If fifty previous courts have followed a certain rule, the precedent is stronger (everything else being equal) than if only two courts have followed that rule. The fifth principle (diversity of primary analogues) is also applicable. If a certain rule turns up in a broad range of cases, it provides a stronger precedent (other things being equal) than a rule that turns up in a narrow range of cases. For example, the principle underlying the inadmissibility of hearsay testimony is well established because it appears in a broad cross section of cases.

Finally, the sixth principle states that the more specific a conclusion is, the weaker the argument becomes. Suppose, in an earlier case, a person is awarded half a million dollars for injuries inflicted by a surgeon who, during an appendix operation, left a stethoscope in the body opening. The argument that another person injured in the same way by another doctor should be awarded *exactly* the same amount of money is relatively weak in comparison with the argument that the person should be awarded *approximately* the same amount of money.

Analogical arguments that occur in law differ from the fairly simple analogies considered earlier in at least two important ways. In the analogy dealing with gas mileage, the modes of similarity that linked the analogues (number of engine cylinders, curb weight, and the like) were clearly defined by conventional thinking, and their relevance to the conclusion had been established by scientific principles. In law, however, clarity of this sort is seldom to be found. Modes of similarity between cases are often the result of highly creative thinking by lawyers and judges, and the relevance of these similarities to the proposed conclusion is nearly always debatable. These differences render analogical arguments in law considerably more elusive than those dealing with subjects such as gas mileage.

The other difference between simple analogical arguments and those found in law is that the primary analogues in law (earlier cases) do not all have equal weight. The reason is that our courts operate in different jurisdictions. The system of federal courts is totally separate from the system of state courts. As a result, a case that might have considerable weight as a precedent in one system might have little or no weight in the other. In addition, within these systems there are different circuits, and a case that is controlling in one circuit may not be in another. Lastly, within these systems, the courts exist on different levels. For example, within the federal system there are the district courts, courts of appeals, and the U.S. Supreme Court. A case that is binding on a lower court may not be binding on a higher court.

Let us now illustrate the process of legal reasoning with a hypothetical example. Suppose a certain vagrant—let us call him Blake—attempted to earn some pocket change by breaking into a cigarette vending machine and stealing the cash. The police apprehended Blake in the act, and the district attorney charged him with burglary. Blake had one prior conviction for breaking into a cigarette machine.

The first thing that any lawyer would do with this case is to recall the definition of "burglary." According to the traditional definition, "burglary" means "the trespassory breaking and entering of a dwelling house of another at night with the intent to commit a felony therein." Under many modern statutes, "dwelling house" has been replaced by "structure" and "at night" has been deleted.

There is little doubt that Blake has broken into a structure. The question is, is a cigarette machine the kind of structure intended by the statute? A second question is, did Blake intend to commit a felony when he broke into the cigarette machine? To answer these questions a lawyer would consult additional statutes and relevant cases. Let us suppose that our jurisdiction has a statute that defines felony theft as theft of $400 or more. Also, let us suppose that the cash box of this particular machine contained $450 but most similar machines can hold no more than $350.

As for cases, let us suppose that our jurisdiction has two controlling precedents. In *People v. Harris,* Harris broke into a warehouse with the intent of stealing its contents. The warehouse contained microwave ovens valued at $10,000, and Harris was found guilty of burglary. In *People v. Sawyer,* Sawyer broke into a newspaper vending machine with the intent to steal the cash in the cash box. The maximum capacity of the cash box was $20, and Sawyer was found not guilty of burglary.

Relying on these facts and preceding cases, the district attorney might present the following argument to the judge (or jury):

> In breaking into the cigarette machine, Blake is guilty of burglary for the following reasons. In *People v. Harris,* the defendant was found guilty of burglary for breaking into a warehouse. A cigarette vending machine is like a warehouse in that it contains goods stored for resale. Furthermore, like a warehouse, people's livelihoods depend on the goods stored therein. Also, the vending machine contained over $400, and Blake intended to steal this money. Stealing over $400 is a felony. Therefore, Blake intended to commit a felony when he broke into the machine. Also, by placing his hand into the machine, he "entered" it. A cigarette machine differs from a newspaper machine in that it can hold goods valued much more than a stack of newspapers. Thus, all the requirements are met for conviction.

Defense counsel, on the other hand, might argue as follows:

> In breaking into the cigarette machine, Blake is not guilty of burglary, for the following reasons. The original crime of burglary extended only to dwelling houses because people live in dwelling houses and it is important that their lives be protected. Modern law has extended the kind of structure requisite for burglary to include warehouses because people work and live in them. A cigarette machine is unlike a warehouse in that a person is not capable of working and living in it. Also, for the crime of burglary to be committed, the burglar must enter the structure. A cigarette machine differs from a warehouse in that a person is not capable of entering it with his whole body.
>
> On the contrary, a cigarette vending machine is very similar to a newspaper vending machine in that it contains relatively small quantities of products for resale. In *People v. Sawyer,* the defendant was found not guilty of burglary in breaking into a newspaper vending machine. Finally, Blake was familiar with cigarette machines (he broke into one once before), and he therefore knew that their cash boxes are usually limited to holding less than $400. Therefore, when he broke into this particular machine, Blake intended to steal less than $400, and therefore he did not intend to commit a felony.

In deciding whether Blake is guilty, the judge or jury will have to evaluate these analogical arguments by determining which analogies are the strongest.

Sometimes lawyers and judges are confronted with cases for which there is no clear precedent. Such cases are called *cases of first impression,* and the attempt to deal with them by appeal to analogous instances involves even more creativity than does the attempt to deal with ordinary cases. In deciding cases of first impression, judges often resort to moral reasoning, and they grope for any analogy that can shed light on the issue. The reasoning process in such a decision often involves a sequence of analogies followed by disanalogies and counteranalogies. These analogies present the issue in a continually shifting light, and the experience of coming to grips with them expands the outlook of the reasoner. New perspectives are created, attitudes are changed, and worldviews are altered.

9.3   Moral Reasoning

As in law, arguments from analogy are also useful in deciding moral questions. Such arguments often occur in the context of a dialogue. As an example of a dialogue that includes several arguments from analogy, consider the following one between two fictional characters, Jason and Deirdre. The dialogue deals with the morality and legality of fetal abuse.

"Jason, I read an article in this morning's newspaper about fetal abuse—you know, expectant mothers who take drugs or drink alcohol during pregnancy and cause damage to their fetus. The article said that 11 percent of all babies currently born in this country have traces of alcohol or illegal drugs in their blood. I think such women should be shot!"

"I can see that you're pretty worked up about this, Deirdre, but don't you think you're being a bit prudish? After all, what's so bad about a little alcohol or a few drugs?"

"I can't believe you said that!" Deirdre scolds. "The alcohol and drugs cause permanent brain damage to the fetus and leave the child maimed for life. Many of these kids will grow up retarded, and many will become criminals and end up in jail. The burden on society will be incredible! Women who treat their unborn child in this way are utterly immoral, and they ought to be sent to jail."

"Let's take these claims one at a time," Jason responds. "First, why do you think feeding alcohol or drugs to a fetus is immoral, Deirdre?"

"Because I think the fetus has rights."

"But wait a minute," counters Jason. "According to *Roe v. Wade*, the mother can abort the fetus. That must mean the fetus has no right to life; and if it has no right to life, surely it has no rights at all."

Deirdre scratches her head. "It seems to me you're overlooking something," she says. "When a mother intends to abort her fetus, it's one thing. But when she intends to bring it to term, it's quite another thing. It's almost as if she has extended a contract to the fetus. Look, suppose I tell a house painter, 'You paint my house, and I'll pay you $1,000.' If the painter fulfills his end of the bargain but I refuse to pay, clearly I am doing something wrong. In the same way, the mother who intends to bear her child in effect tells the fetus, 'You agree to grow and develop in a normal way, and I'll provide you with a healthy environment.' If the fetus grows and develops normally and then the mother feeds it drugs, she welshes on the deal."

Mom has a contract with her fetus.

"I agree with you about the house painter," Jason answers. "But it seems to me that you can only enter into contracts with human beings. You don't enter into contracts with dogs and cats, and you don't enter into contracts with fetuses, either."

"A fetus is very much like a complete human being, though," Deirdre replies. "It's made up of human flesh and blood, it has the same genetic code as a human being, and as it develops, it has the same organization of internal organs as a human being and it even looks like a human being. Isn't this enough?"

"And because of these similarities you think the fetus has rights?"

"Yes, I do."

"Well, I think your analogy is nice," Jason replies, "but I don't think the similarities you cite are relevant to your conclusion. The reason human beings have rights and can enter into contracts is because they are rational and have the power of speech. They demonstrate these powers by proving theorems in geometry and engaging in conversations. I've never seen a fetus do either of these things."

"No," replies Deirdre, "but neither do people when they're asleep. Do you think a sleeping person is not human? Would you take a sleeping person and sweep him out the door like a clump of dust because he wasn't at that moment demonstrating rational powers?"

"Of course not," Jason replies. "But unlike a sleeping person, a fetus has *never* demonstrated rational powers."

"But neither has a newborn baby," Deirdre argues. "When do you think a newborn baby becomes human? Does it happen at the moment it's born? Was it not a human being one hour before birth? Isn't a tomato growing on a vine as much a tomato one day before it ripens as it is when it's ripe? Isn't an apple growing on a tree as much an apple when it's green as it is after it turns red?"

When does a fetus become human?

"That's a good analogy," says Jason.

"Also, even if a fetus can't be proved beyond any uncertainty to be fully human, don't you think it should be given the benefit of the doubt? When a person falls through the ice on a frozen lake, don't the rescuers who pull the person out rush him to a hospital even though no signs of life remain? Isn't the person, whether dead or alive, treated as if he were still alive? Similarly, shouldn't a fetus, who shows no signs of rationality, be treated as if it had rationality?"

"Perhaps," Jason answers, "but I have trouble attributing humanity or personhood to a mere lump of flesh. This wart on the back of my hand is made of human flesh and blood, and its cells carry the same genetic code as I. Of course it's not shaped like a human being, but neither is a fetus in the early stages of development. Does this mean that I should consider this wart to be human or a person?"

"So what you're saying," Deirdre replies, "is that the fetus is just a part of its mother's body, like that wart is part of yours?"

"Exactly," he says. "And that means the fetus can have no rights or interests distinct from those of the mother, any more than someone's liver can have rights distinct from the person who has the liver. When an alcoholic abuses his liver by excessive alcohol consumption, we don't say that he is immoral and incarcerate him for liver abuse. Similarly, we don't say that smokers are immoral for abusing their lungs and put them in jail for lung abuse. Accordingly, we shouldn't call pregnant women immoral and put them in jail for fetal abuse."

"Your analogy has one fatal flaw," Deirdre answers with a smile. "If the fetus is merely part of its mother's body, then it would have exactly the same genetic code as the mother. Every ordinary body part—heart, liver, lungs, and so on—carries the same genes as the host organism. But the fetus has a unique genetic code. Also, it's meant to develop and separate from the body of its host, unlike a liver or a lung. Therefore, a fetus is not merely a part of the mother's body."

A fetus has its own genes.

"Well, perhaps you're right," Jason says. "But I have a better analogy. The fetus is like a seed planted in the ground or a group of cells growing in a petri dish. Imagine you were walking down the street and a little seed shouted up at you, 'Help! Get me out of this soil! It's too acidic!' What would you do? Would you reach down, lift the seedling up, and transplant it elsewhere? Of course not. You'd say to the seed, 'Be quiet! It's lucky you found any soil at all to grow in.' Isn't that what you'd say?"

"Maybe I would," she says, "but not if I expected the seed to grow into a human being. And incidentally, don't ever accuse me of anthropomorphizing! I think a far better analogy is that of someone who perpetrates a battery on another person. I was reading about a famous case where a man approached a woman in her sleep and gave her a kiss on the cheek. The man was someone the woman despised, and when she woke up and found out what had happened, she was so furious that she sued the man for battery—and she won. A battery, you know, is any intentionally produced harmful or offensive contact. The case establishes the principle that the target of a battery need not be aware of it at the time it happens. Now if a kiss can be a battery, how much more so is being drowned in drugs and booze? The fetus might not be able to sue till after it's born, but the battery was nevertheless committed before birth."

"Very clever," Jason responds. "However, I don't think you can say someone's asleep if that person has never been awake. A fetus has never been awake."

"I see you're still harping on whether the fetus has human thought processes," replies Deirdre. "Well, consider this. After the child is born, everyone agrees it's a full-fledged human being. When that child enters the world with drugs in its body, we can appropriately ask where those drugs came from. The answer, of course, is the mother. Thus, the mother has given drugs not to a mere fetus but to a real child.

Mom is like a drug dealer.

The situation would be exactly the same as if a common drug dealer had given drugs to the kid. Thus, the mother should be treated the same way as any drug dealer."

"I think you've got me there," Jason admits. "But your analogy holds only for kids who are actually born with drugs or alcohol in their system. What about fetuses who are fed drugs or alcohol weeks before birth but who are delivered without any trace of them?"

"Suppose," replies Deirdre, "a doctor who is treating a pregnant woman periodically injects cocaine into the fetus using a long hypodermic needle. Not only would everyone consider the doctor fiendish and immoral, but the doctor would be liable for civil and criminal sanctions. Is the mother who feeds cocaine to her fetus any different from this doctor?"

"Interesting point," says Jason. "I expect, however, that the doctor would be subject to liability for acting without the mother's consent—not for acting without the fetus's consent."

"I hope you're wrong," says Deirdre. "But you know how I feel about these fetal abusers? I see a child in a playpen near a window. Outside the window other kids are playing on the grass. The child in the playpen is excited and happy when it sees them and can't wait until it's big enough to go out and join them. Then one day the mother comes in with a baseball bat and smashes the child's legs, and the child is never able to walk from that day on. That's what fetal abuse does, as far as I'm concerned."

"Getting a little emotional, aren't we, Deirdre?"

"Maybe. But I don't think morality is something devoid of feeling. Morality concerns life and life is feeling, and the two can't be separated."

"Well, even if I agreed with you that fetal abuse is immoral, that doesn't mean I think it should be made illegal. I know our criminal laws are closely tied to public morality, but that's true only up to a point. I think making fetal abuse a crime might be going too far."

"Why is that?" asks Deirdre.

"Because it's so invasive," Jason responds. "Like a rapist, the state would be invading the most private aspects of a woman's life. Also, it would be patronizing. The state would be treating the pregnant woman like an errant, recalcitrant child who's done something wrong and needs to be punished."

"But there is a long history of state intervention in the lives of people who are a danger to themselves or others," Deirdre observes. "For example, people who attempt suicide are sometimes institutionalized to prevent them from killing themselves. Also, mental deviants are often committed to mental institutions for their own benefit. The theory is that, if these people were in their right minds, they would want the state to do exactly that. Women who abuse their fetuses are very similar to mental deviants. If these women were in their right minds, they would want the state to intercede and prevent them from injuring their fetuses."

The state protects citizens from deviants.

"Still," replies Jason, "I think a law criminalizing fetal abuse would be unenforceable. It would be just like the law against alcohol during prohibition. That law was eventually repealed because, among other things, it was impossible to enforce. A law against fetal abuse would suffer the same fate. It would require that police officers snoop into the homes and bedrooms of every pregnant woman reasonably suspected of abusing her fetus. Such action would violate one of our most cherished values, the right to privacy, and it would require massive additions to our police force."

"Yes," answers Deirdre, "but the problem is so significant that I think something must be done. You can look at the whole of society as a single human body grown large. Women who abuse their unborn children are like spiders who inject venom into the body of society. This venom creates a sore that lasts for seventy years or more. Now I ask you, what person threatened by such a spider would not go to any lengths to prevent its bite? What rational person would stand idle, let the spider inject its venom, and then tolerate the resulting canker for seventy years?"

"Yes," agrees Jason, "but unfortunately, getting rid of fetal abuse is harder than simply brushing off a spider. I think the solution is to stress educational programs and provide prenatal care for every expectant mother. After all, you catch more flies with honey than you do with vinegar. Such programs might reduce the problem of fetal abuse to a point where it becomes tolerable."

Honey catches more flies than vinegar.

"I think any amount of fetal abuse is intolerable," Deirdre replies.

"Society is like a water supply," Jason says. "Public health officials test it for contaminants and find microscopic amounts of this and microscopic amounts of that. If these amounts are within acceptable limits, they pronounce the water supply potable. Yes, the thought of any fetal abuse is disturbing, but we can never eliminate it entirely. The best we can hope for is to reduce it to a point where it won't cripple society as a whole."

"Perhaps you're right," concludes Deirdre, "but the thought of that child in the playpen still bothers me."

This dialogue contains numerous analogies and counteranalogies. The modes of similarity between the many primary analogues and the secondary analogues (the fetus, women who commit fetal abuse, laws against fetal abuse, and so on) are never relevant beyond dispute, and the nature and degree of disanalogy rarely has undisputed consequences. However, the dialogue serves to illustrate the subtle effect that analogies have on our thought processes and the power they have to alter our attitudes and perspectives.

EXERCISE 9

I. Evaluate the arguments from analogy contained in the dialogue between Jason and Deirdre. First, identify the primary and secondary analogues in each analogy and counteranalogy. Next, list the similarities between the primary and secondary analogues and note their relevance to the conclusion. Add any additional similarities you can think of. Finally, identify the disanalogies associated with each analogy or counteranalogy and evaluate their effectiveness in destroying the original analogy.

II. Work the following problems.

★1. Jessica has long admired Rachel's near-perfect body, and she notes that Rachel works out on a Roboflex exercise machine. Jessica concludes that if she buys a Roboflex for herself, she will be able to duplicate Rachel's results. How do the following facts bear on Jessica's argument?

   a. Roboflex recently changed its corporate headquarters from Ohio to Illinois.

   b. Jessica and Rachel are siblings.

   c. Rachel is 25 years old, but Jessica is 32.

   d. Jessica is 40 pounds overweight, but Rachel was only 10 pounds overweight when she started using her Roboflex.

   e. Whenever Jessica makes up her mind to do something, she always sticks with it longer than Rachel does.

   f. Jessica knows of five other women who work out on a Roboflex, and these women all look as good as Rachel.

   g. These women are all between the ages of 24 and 26.

   h. Jessica discovers four additional women between the ages of 31 and 33 who work out on a Roboflex, and these women look nearly as good as Rachel.

   i. Jessica changes her conclusion to state that she will look almost as good as Rachel.

   j. Jessica changes her conclusion to state that she will look better than Rachel.

2. Harold needs to have his rugs cleaned, and his friend Veronica reports that Ajax Carpet Service did an excellent job on her rugs. From this, Harold concludes that Ajax will do an equally good job on his rugs. How do the following facts bear on Harold's argument?

   a. Veronica hired Ajax several times, and Ajax always did an excellent job.

   b. Veronica's rugs are wool, whereas Harold's are nylon.

   c. Veronica's carpets never had any stains on them before they were cleaned, but Harold's have several large stains.

   d. Veronica always had her rugs cleaned in mid-October, whereas Harold wants his done just a week before Easter.

   e. Harold knows of six additional people who have had their carpets cleaned by Ajax, and all six have been very pleased.

   f. All six own rugs made of different material.

   g. All six were born in Massachusetts.

   h. Ajax has recently undergone a change in management.

   i. The Environmental Protection Agency recently banned the cleaning solution Ajax has used for many years.

   j. Harold changes his conclusion to state that Ajax will get his carpets approximately as clean as it has gotten Veronica's.

3. Kristin is president of a corporation that operates a chain of clothing stores, and she faces the task of hiring a manager to replace a man who retired from one of the stores. The former manager increased sales by 15 percent every year for the past five years. Kristin concludes that Roger Benson, a recent graduate of Wharton School of Business, will duplicate the former manager's performance. How do the following facts bear on Kristin's argument?

   a. The manager who retired was a graduate of Wharton.

   b. The manager who retired liked tennis and drove a Jaguar, whereas Benson dislikes tennis and drives a BMW.

   c. Unlike the manager who retired, Benson formerly managed a shoe store, where he increased sales 20 percent for each of the two years he was there.

   d. A labor dispute has recently erupted in the store Benson will manage.

   e. The manager who retired was an alcoholic, whereas Benson is a moderate drinker.

   f. The government has approved a 10 percent increase in federal income taxes that takes effect at the beginning of the year.

   g. Three additional stores owned by Kristin's company are managed by recent Wharton graduates, and all three managers have increased sales by 18 percent for each of the past three years.

   h. These three stores are located in the city's three wealthiest suburbs.

   i. The store Benson will manage is located in a neighborhood that has recently begun to decline.

   j. Kristin changes her conclusion to state that Benson will increase sales by at least 10 percent for the first year.

★4. Sam has planned a one-day fishing trip in Alaska. He intends to fish off Rocky Point, where he fished last year. Because he caught five fish in a one-day outing last year, Sam concludes that he will catch five fish this year. How do the following facts bear on Sam's argument?

   a. Last year Sam used a wooden boat, but this year he will use a fiberglass boat.

    b. Sam used herring for bait last year, but this year he will use anchovies.

    c. Sam fished with four friends last year, and each of them caught more than five fish on that day.

    d. This year Sam will fish on July 15, but last year he fished on August 1.

    e. Last year these four friends caught an average of five fish per day from July 15 to August 1.

    f. These four friends are women.

    g. These four friends used various kinds of bait—herring, squid, anchovies, and artificial lures.

    h. It is now July 12. Yesterday, ten people fished off Rocky Point, and none caught any fish.

    i. A fleet of commercial fishing boats has been fishing the area near Rocky Point for the first time.

    j. Sam changes his conclusion to state that he will catch at least one fish.

5. Susan is considering a job as public relations specialist with the Chamber of Commerce. Her friend Terry took such a job one year ago, and within nine months her annual salary was $50,000. Susan argues that if she takes this job, then her annual salary will be at least $50,000 within nine months. How do the following facts bear on Susan's argument?

    a. Susan is beautiful and outgoing, whereas Terry is average looking and introverted.

    b. Susan is a Democrat, but Terry is a Republican.

    c. Like Terry, Susan is 5 feet 4 inches tall and has blonde hair.

    d. Susan's parents are elementary school teachers, but Terry's parents are prominent businesspeople.

    e. One year ago, Cindy, April, Elizabeth, and Jackie accepted jobs as public relations specialists with the Chamber of Commerce, and today all are earning $44,000.

    f. April is a Republican, Cindy is a Democrat, Elizabeth is a Libertarian, and Jackie is a member of the Peace and Freedom Party.

    g. Cindy, April, Elizabeth, and Jackie are beautiful and outgoing.

    h. Susan has five years of experience as a public relations specialist, whereas Terry, when she was hired, had only two years of experience in that area.

    i. There is a shortage of public relations specialists in the local job pool.

    j. Susan changes her conclusion to state that after nine months she will be earning at least $47,000.

6. Paul is searching for a puppy that will grow up to be friendly with his children. His friend Barbara has an Airedale that is good with her children. From this, Paul concludes that an Airedale puppy would make a good choice. How do the following facts bear on Paul's argument?

    a. Barbara's dog is a female, but Paul plans to get a male.

    b. Tim, Ed, and Irene have male Airedales that are friendly with their children.

c. Tim's, Ed's, and Irene's dogs all came from the same litter.

d. Fran, Penny, and Bob have Airedales that snap at their children.

e. Fran's, Penny's and Bob's Airedales all came from different litters.

f. The puppy that Paul plans to get was born in June, just as Barbara's was.

g. The puppy that Paul plans to get is of the same subspecies as Barbara's dog.

h. The puppy that Paul plans to get had a littermate that was vicious and had to be destroyed. Barbara's dog had no such littermates.

i. Paul plans to give his dog special training, but Barbara's dog received no such training.

j. Paul changes his conclusion to state that if he gets an Airedale puppy, it will grow up at least to tolerate children.

★7. Laura is considering taking Calculus I from Professor Rogers. Her friend Gina took Professor Rogers for this class and got an A. Laura concludes that she, too, will get an A from Professor Rogers. How do the following facts bear on Laura's argument?

a. Gina earned straight A's in high school math, whereas Laura got B's.

b. Laura took precalculus in high school, but Gina took no precalculus class.

c. Laura is a Buddhist, whereas Gina is a Protestant.

d. Kevin, Toni, and Samantha took precalculus in high school, and all of them received A's in Professor Rogers's Calculus I class.

e. Kevin, Toni, and Samantha all have different majors.

f. Kevin, Toni, and Samantha attended Franklin High School.

g. Laura attended Roosevelt High School.

h. Kevin, Toni, and Samantha took precalculus from different instructors.

i. Laura and Gina earned equal scores on the college math entrance exam.

j. Laura changes her conclusion to state that she will receive an A+ in Professor Rogers's class.

8. Andrew is thinking about buying stock in E-Tron, a new company that sells electronic equipment over the Internet. Six months ago, he bought shares in E-Boot, a new company that sells shoes over the Internet, and the price of the stock doubled in two months. Andrew argues that if he buys E-Tron, the stock will double in two months. How do the following facts bear on Andrew's argument?

a. Stocks in Internet companies have been in a steep decline for the past two weeks, whereas they were rising six months ago.

b. E-Tron will be run by the same management team that runs E-Boot.

c. During the past year, the stock of five other new companies that sell over the Internet doubled within two months of their initial offering.

d. These five companies market Swiss chocolates, tires, appliances, furniture, and luggage.

e. A survey was taken of E-Boot customers, and 90 percent said they would not consider buying electronic equipment over the Internet.

f. Two other companies that market jewelry and lingerie over the Internet have done poorly.

g. America Online, the most widely used Net service provider, just increased its monthly service charge by 50 percent.

h. E-Boot is incorporated in New Jersey, whereas E-Tron is incorporated in Delaware.

i. E-Boot introduced its products with a major ad campaign, whereas E-Tron plans no such campaign.

j. Andrew changes his conclusion to state that E-Tron stock will triple within the next two months.

9. According to the doctrine of adverse possession, a person occupying a piece of land in a way that is open, notorious, and hostile to the owner's rights can claim ownership of the land after a certain number of years of continuous occupancy. In this connection, Dr. Wacko, a mad scientist, hauled telescopes and radio antennas to the top of Mica Peak every night for twenty years to detect extraterrestrial life. At the end of the period he petitioned the court for a decree stating that he owned Mica Peak under the theory of adverse possession. Tom Bell, the owner of Mica Peak, attempts to defeat Dr. Wacko's petition.

Construct two arguments, one supporting Dr. Wacko's position, the other supporting Tom Bell's position. The statutory period for adverse possession in this jurisdiction is twenty years, and there are two controlling cases:

Crick v. Hoskins: Crick occupied a house in Centerville that was owned by Hoskins. She lived in the house continuously, mowed the lawn weekly, and parked her car in front. After twenty years she petitioned the court for a decree stating that she owned the property under the theory of adverse possession, and the court granted the decree against the objections of Hoskins.

Raymond v. McBride: Raymond set up a large tent on a piece of rural property owned by McBride and lived in it for nine months each year. During the remaining three months, heavy snow made the property inaccessible. After twenty years Raymond petitioned the court for a decree stating that he owned the property under the theory of adverse possession, and the court denied Raymond's petition.

★10. The Fourth Amendment to the U.S. Constitution prohibits unreasonable searches and seizures. A *search* is defined as a "violation of a person's reasonable expectation of privacy by the police." Legal issues dealing with searches often turn on the question of whether the person who was searched had a reasonable expectation of privacy at the time and place the search was conducted. In this connection, consider the following set of facts. Maxie was lining up drug contacts from his cell phone while he was driving on the freeway. Without obtaining a search warrant, federal agents intercepted one of his messages and used it to locate Maxie's car and arrest Maxie. Maxie argues that the federal agents violated his reasonable expectation of privacy, and the government denies it.

Your task is to construct two arguments, one supporting Maxie's position, the other supporting the position of the federal agents. There are three controlling cases in this jurisdiction:

U.S. v. Taylor: Federal agents suspected Taylor of illegal distribution of firearms. Without obtaining a search warrant, they planted a listening device on the phone in Taylor's home and used the evidence obtained to arrest Taylor. The court ruled that their action violated Taylor's reasonable expectation of privacy and disallowed the evidence.

U.S. v. Weber: Without obtaining a search warrant, federal agents operating inside U.S. borders intercepted a radio transmission from a plane flying over Mexico. The message mentioned drugs, and it disclosed the location of a landing strip inside the United States. Using this information, the agents met the plane and arrested its pilot for drug smuggling. The court ruled that their action did not violate the pilot's reasonable expectation of privacy.

U.S. v. Robinson: Federal agents were using a telescope to conduct surveillance on the resident of a distant apartment building. Inadvertently they noticed some teenagers smoking crack in a car parked in the lot near the building, and they proceeded to arrest them. The court ruled that their action did not violate the teenagers' reasonable expectation of privacy.

11. The First Amendment to the U.S. Constitution states that Congress shall make no law abridging the freedom of speech or the right to peaceable assembly. This "law" applies to states (and cities) as a result of the adoption of the Fourteenth Amendment. In reliance on the First Amendment, a group of gays and lesbians apply for a permit to march on Gay Freedom Day. Similar parades in other cities have been calm and orderly, but the police chief denies a parade permit to this group.

   Construct two arguments, one supporting the position of the group, the other supporting the position of the police chief. There are three controlling cases in this jurisdiction:

   Lester v. City: Police seized an art collection displayed in a public park, because it depicted heterosexuals in nude poses. The court ruled that the display was protected by the First Amendment.

   Byron v. City: Police denied a parade permit to a Nazi group that wanted to march on Hitler's birthday. The court ruled that the denial violated the group's rights under the First Amendment.

   Stone v. City: Police closed down a theater showing an erotic gay film, because they claimed that the film promoted the spread of AIDS. The court ruled that the action of the police was allowed under the First Amendment.

12. *Constructive eviction* is a legal doctrine by which a landlord who substantially interferes with a tenant's use and enjoyment of the premises will be considered to have evicted the tenant. Such a landlord cannot collect rent from the tenant. In this connection, Isabel signed a lease for an apartment owned by Carolyn. A clause in the lease stated that all tenants must keep noise to a minimum dur-

ing evening hours. After moving in, Isabel found that another tenant played his stereo all night long at ear-splitting levels. Carolyn declined to enforce the noise clause in the lease. After one week without sleep, Isabel moved out, and Carolyn now sues Isabel for rent.

Construct two arguments, one supporting Isabel's position, the other supporting Carolyn's. There are two controlling cases in this jurisdiction:

Garvin v. Linder: Linder rented an apartment from Garvin, and the lease stated that Garvin would provide heat during the winter. When winter arrived, Garvin provided heat for only one hour per day, and the inside temperature sometimes dropped to 50°F. Linder moved out, and Garvin sued Linder for rent. The court ruled in favor of Linder.

Quincy v. Fulton: Fulton rented a tenth-floor apartment from Quincy. Shortly thereafter, Quincy decided to have repairs made on the elevator, causing it to be shut down for a month. Because Fulton had arthritis, he had great difficulty climbing ten flights of stairs. Fulton moved out, and Quincy sued Fulton for rent. The court ruled in favor of Quincy.

★13. A negligent person who causes an injury to another person is liable for the latter's injuries. Because it is sometimes very difficult to determine the causal extent of a negligent action, courts have developed the theory of proximate cause, which limits the scope of liability. In this connection, Liz Shaffer negligently failed to maintain the brakes on her car, and as a result her car crashed into one driven by Mary Vassar. Mary was taken to the hospital for bumps and bruises, but while she was there, doctors mistakenly amputated her perfectly healthy leg. Mary sues Liz for loss of her leg.

Construct two arguments, one supporting Mary's position, the other supporting Liz's position. The only issue is whether Liz proximately caused the loss of the leg. There are two controlling cases in this jurisdiction:

Sacco v. Lane: Lane negligently used gasoline to light his barbecue in a strong wind. The flames from the barbecue ignited nearby trees and then spread to ten houses in the neighborhood, burning them to the ground. The court ruled that Lane was liable for damage to the houses.

Hunt v. Gomez: Hunt was a passenger in a taxi driven by Gomez. Gomez was drunk and negligently let Hunt out at the wrong corner. While Hunt was walking home, a worker dropped a brick from a building that was under construction, injuring Hunt. Hunt sued Gomez for injury resulting from the falling brick. The court ruled in favor of Gomez.

14. Lynn Dodd, age twenty, has become a member of New Age Enlightenment, a religious cult group. The group has convinced Lynn to sell all her worldly possessions and give the proceeds to the group. The group forbids any contact between Lynn and her relatives and friends. On one occasion Lynn's parents encountered Lynn on a street corner, and they tried to persuade her to leave the group and return home, but she refused. The parents fear that some form of mind control is being used to keep Lynn in the group, and they plan a rescue operation.

Write a dialogue, similar to the dialogue in the text, examining the morality and legality of such an operation. Include in your dialogue analogies between the proposed rescue operation and the following: rescuing an adult who has been hypnotized by captors, kidnapping someone against his or her will, rescuing a child who has been kidnapped, spiriting away a novice who has joined a Jesuit seminary or Franciscan convent, coercing an alcoholic to enter a detoxification center, forcing a child to attend a certain school, preventing someone from committing suicide, forcing a child to attend a certain church, rescuing an eighteen-year-old from a Nazi youth group, removing one's daughter from the Girl Scouts, and any other pertinent analogy that comes to mind.

15. During fifteen years of marriage, James and Leslie Knox had not succeeded in having a baby. As a last resort, they tried in vitro fertilization. Doctors surgically removed nine eggs from Leslie and fertilized them with James's sperm. The embryos were then placed in a freezer until the proper time for them to be implanted in Leslie's womb. In the meantime, James and Leslie came to realize that their marriage was going nowhere, and they decided to get a divorce. The couple has had no trouble arriving at a settlement concerning the house, cars, bank accounts, and other possessions, but they cannot agree on the disposition of the frozen embryos. James is adamant about not wanting to have any children by Leslie, and he wants the embryos destroyed. Leslie, on the other hand, realizing that she is getting older, thinks that the frozen embryos offer her the best chance of having a baby, and she wants them implanted.

Write a dialogue, similar to the one in the text, examining the moral and/or legal ramifications of this dispute. Include in your dialogue analogies between this situation and the following: killing a fetus, killing a baby, forcing your wife to have an abortion, having an abortion against the wishes of your husband, owning a dog or cat, owning a child, determining custody of a child upon divorce, dividing a bank account, determining ownership of a unique and valuable painting produced jointly by two people, implanting an embryo in a surrogate mother, and any other analogies that come to mind, including analogies that show that the embryos have or do not have rights and analogies that illustrate the investment that James and Leslie have in the embryos.

Summary

An argument from analogy is an inductive argument that rests on a similarity between two things. Because one of these things (the primary analogue) has a certain attribute, it is argued that the other (the secondary analogue) does also. Six factors that bear on the strength of an argument from analogy are the relevance of the similarities shared by the primary and secondary analogues, the number of similarities, the nature and degree of disanalogy, the number of primary analogues, the diversity among the primary analogues, and the specificity of the conclusion. Legal and moral reasoning provide a natural vehicle for studying the function of analogical arguments in real-life situations. The analogy between precedent cases and the case at hand may determine the outcome of a trial, and analogies are effective in characterizing elusive moral situations.

Answers to Selected Exercises

Exercise 9

II.

1. a. Has no effect.
   b. Strengthens.
   c. Weakens.
   d. Weakens.
   e. Strengthens.
   f. Strengthens.
   g. Weakens.
   h. Strengthens.
   i. Strengthens.
   j. Weakens.

4. a. Has no effect.
   b. Weakens.
   c. Strengthens.
   d. Weakens.
   e. Strengthens.
   f. Has no effect.
   g. Strengthens.
   h. Weakens.
   i. Weakens.
   j. Strengthens.

7. a. Weakens.
   b. Strengthens.
   c. Has no effect.
   d. Strengthens.
   e. Strengthens.
   f. Weakens.
   g. Weakens.
   h. Strengthens.
   i. Strengthens.
   j. Weakens.

10. Hint: For Maxie's argument, concentrate on the similarities between a home and a car (a car is an extended living space with heating, air conditioning, stereo, telephone, and so on), the dissimilarities between a plane and a car (greater difficulty in controlling, ease of crossing international borders, greater danger in operating, and so on). Also, people outside U.S. borders are not accorded the same constitutional protections as people inside, and a phone message normally suggests greater privacy than a radio message. In addition, the teenagers parked in the lot were acting in plain view, and a telescope only enhances ordinary sense perception (so there was no search). Maxie, on the other hand, was talking while speeding down the freeway and was thus not acting in plain view (in the same sense), and a radio receiver (used by the agents) does not enhance ordinary sense perception.

    For the agents' argument, concentrate on the similarities between a car and a plane (both are means of transportation, both can cross state lines, both are relatively hard to keep track of, and so on) and the dissimilarities between a car or plane and a house (houses do not move, so it will stay in place while a search warrant is obtained). Also, cell phones use radio transmitters just like planes, both the cell phone message and the radio message from the plane were received inside U.S. borders, and the cell phone message was received inadvertently, just as the radio message from the plane and the image through the telescope were (thus making it impossible to plan ahead for a search warrant). Also, in a sense, Maxie *was* acting in plain view: A lip reader traveling in an adjacent car might interpret his message. Lastly, controlling illicit drugs is a high priority for the government.

13. Hint: Couch your arguments in terms of foreseeability.

For Liz's argument note that there were several events that intervened between the car accident and the amputation: Mary's being taken to the hospital, Mary's being treated by doctors for bumps and bruises, Mary's apparent mix-up with some other patient scheduled for leg amputation, the doctors' failure to check Mary's proper identity before operating, etc. Liz did not directly control any of these events, and therefore she could not have foreseen them. Liz could not have foreseen what hospital Mary would be taken to, the fact that Mary would be mixed up with another patient, etc. Because Liz should not be held liable for an event utterly unforeseen to her, she should not be liable for Mary's amputated leg. The facts are similar to those in *Gomez v. Hunt,* where Gomez could not foresee the exact route that Hunt would take when walking home, the fact that a worker would drop a brick, the fact that the brick would strike Hunt, etc. The facts are dissimilar to those in *Sacco v. Lane,* where Lane was in direct control over the flames in the barbecue, and it was those very same flames that spread to the houses.

For Mary's argument note that Liz initiated a chain of events that flowed naturally from the car accident to the amputation. Once the car accident occurred, it was foreseeable that Mary would be taken to the hospital; once Mary was in the hospital it was foreseeable that mix-ups would occur (after all, mix-ups occur in hospitals every day); given the nature of these mix-ups, it was foreseeable that Mary's leg would be amputated. Granted, Liz might not have been able to foresee each event in the chain, but once an event occurred, someone familiar with it could have foreseen the next event. Therefore, given that each event was foreseeable by *someone*—at least some hypothetical person—Liz should be held liable. The events are similar to those in *Sacco v. Lane.* When the flames were leaping from the barbecue, it was foreseeable that they would ignite the trees; once the trees were aflame, it was foreseeable that a house would be ignited, then another house, etc. Lane would not have been able to foresee the whole chain of events at the time he was tending the barbecue, but once one event occurred, the next was foreseeable. Also, even though the wind constituted an intervening event, Lane was still held liable. Finally, the facts are dissimilar to those in *Gomez v. Hunt.* When Hunt was walking home, he was in complete control over his own actions. He freely chose to walk past the building under construction, and he should have been on the lookout for falling objects. The fact that he was struck by a falling brick was partly the result of his own failure to observe. On the contrary, from the time of the accident until the amputation, Mary was in the hands of others: the person who took her to the hospital, nurses in the hospital, etc. In no sense was the amputation the result of Mary's free choices.

4

Causality and Mill's Methods

10.1 **"Cause" and Necessary and Sufficient Conditions**

A knowledge of causal connections plays a prominent role in our effort to control the environment in which we live. We insulate our homes because we know insulation will prevent heat loss, we vaccinate our children because we know vaccination will protect them from polio and diphtheria, we practice the piano and violin because we know that by doing so we may become proficient on them, and we cook our meat and fish because we know that doing so will make them edible.

When the word "cause" is used in ordinary English, however, it is seriously affected by ambiguity. For example, when we say that sprinkling water on the flowers will cause them to grow, we mean that water is required for growth, not that water alone will do the job—sunshine and the proper soil are also required. On the other hand, when we say that taking a swim on a hot summer day will cause us to cool off, we mean that the dip by itself *will* do the job, but we understand that other things will work just as well, such as taking a cold shower, entering an air-conditioned room, and so on.

To clear up this ambiguity affecting the meaning of "cause," adopting the language of sufficient and necessary conditions is useful. When we say that electrocution is a cause of death, we mean "cause" in the sense of *sufficient* condition. Electrocution is sufficient to produce death, but there are other methods equally effective, such as poisoning, drowning, and shooting. On the other hand, when we say that the presence of clouds is a cause of rain, we mean "cause" in the sense of *necessary* condition. Without clouds, rain cannot occur, but clouds alone are not sufficient. Certain combinations of pressure and temperature are also required.

Sometimes "cause" is used in the sense of necessary *and* sufficient condition, as when we say that the action of a force causes a body to accelerate or that an increase in voltage causes an increase in electrical current. For a body to accelerate, nothing more and nothing less is required than for it to be acted on by a net force; and for an electrical current to increase through a resistive circuit, nothing more and nothing less is required than an increase in voltage.

Thus, as these examples illustrate, the word "cause" can have any one of three different meanings:

1. Sufficient condition
2. Necessary condition
3. Sufficient and necessary condition

Sometimes the context provides an immediate clue to the sense in which "cause" is being used. If we are trying to *prevent* a certain phenomenon from happening, we usually search for a cause that is a necessary condition, and if we are trying to *produce* a certain phenomenon, we usually search for a cause that is a sufficient condition. For example, in attempting to prevent the occurrence of smog around cities, scientists try to isolate a necessary condition or group of necessary conditions that, if removed, will eliminate the smog. And in their effort to produce an abundant harvest, farmers search for a sufficient condition that, given sunshine and rainfall, will increase crop growth.

Another important point is that whenever an event occurs, at least *one* sufficient condition is present and *all* the necessary conditions are present. The conjunction of the necessary conditions *is* the sufficient condition that actually produces the event. For example, the necessary conditions for lighting a match are heat (produced by striking) and oxygen. Combining these two necessary conditions gives the sufficient condition. In other words, striking the match in the presence of oxygen is sufficient to ignite it. In cases where the sufficient condition is also a necessary condition, there is only one necessary condition, which is identical with the sufficient condition.

We can now summarize the meaning of cause in the sense of a sufficient condition and a necessary condition:

A is a sufficient condition for B: A's occurrence requires B's occurrence.
A is a necessary condition for B: B's occurrence requires A's occurrence.

According to these statements, if *A* occurs and *B* does not occur, then *A* is not a sufficient condition for *B*, and if *B* occurs and *A* does not occur, then *A* is not a necessary condition for *B*. Thus:

A is not a sufficient condition for B: A is present when B is absent.
A is not a necessary condition for B: A is absent when B is present.

These results will serve as important rules in the material that follows.

10.2   Mill's Five Methods

In his *System of Logic,* the nineteenth-century philosopher John Stuart Mill compiled five methods for identifying causal connections between events. These he called the method of agreement, the method of difference, the joint method of agreement and difference, the method of residues, and the method of concomitant variation. In the years that have elapsed since the publication of Mill's *Logic,* the five methods have received a good deal of philosophical criticism. Today most logicians agree that the methods fall short of the claims made for them by Mill, but the fact remains that the methods function implicitly in many of the inductive inferences we make in ordinary life.

In addition to criticizing these methods, modern logicians have introduced many variations that have multiplied their number beyond the original five. Some of these variations have resulted from the fact that Mill himself failed to distinguish causes that are sufficient conditions from causes that are necessary conditions. The account that follows introduces this distinction into the first three methods, but apart from that, it remains faithful to Mill's own presentation.

Method of Agreement

Suppose that five people eat dinner in a certain restaurant, and a short while later all five become sick. Suppose further that these people ordered an assortment of items from the menu, but the only food that all of them ordered was vanilla ice cream for dessert. In other words, all of the dinners were in agreement only as to the ice cream. Such a situation suggests that the ice cream caused the sickness. The **method of agreement** consists in a systematic effort to find a single factor (such as the ice cream) that is common to several occurrences for the purpose of identifying that factor as the cause of a phenomenon present in the occurrences (such as the sickness).

The method of agreement identifies a cause in the sense of a necessary condition. To see how this method works, let us develop the restaurant example a bit further.

> Five people eat dinner in a restaurant. Jack has salad, french fries, a hamburger, ice cream, and mixed vegetables; Bob has salad, french fries, soup, ice cream, fish, and mixed vegetables; Mary has a hamburger, soup, and ice cream; Tim has fish, mixed vegetables, ice cream, salad, and soup; and Gail has mixed vegetables, fish, ice cream, french fries, and salad. Afterwards all of them became sick from something they ate. What food caused the sickness?

If we let occurrences 1 through 5 stand for Jack, Bob, Mary, Tim, and Gail, respectively, and let A through G represent salad, soup, french fries, a hamburger, fish, ice cream, and mixed vegetables, respectively, we can construct a table that reflects what these five people ate (Table 10.1). In this table an asterisk means that a certain food was eaten, and a dash means that it was not eaten.

Table 10.1

| | Possible necessary conditions | | | | | | | Phenomenon (sickness) |
Occurrence	A	B	C	D	E	F	G	
1	*	-	*	*	-	*	*	*
2	*	*	*	-	*	*	*	*
3	-	*	-	*	-	*	-	*
4	*	*	-	-	*	*	*	*
5	*	-	*	-	*	*	*	*

Now, since the method of agreement identifies a cause in the sense of a necessary condition, we begin by eliminating from this table the conditions that are not necessary for the occurrence of the phenomenon. In doing so, we use the rule that a condition is not necessary for the occurrence of a phenomenon if that condition is absent when the phenomenon is present. Thus, occurrence 1 eliminates condition *B* and condition *E*; occurrence 2 eliminates *D*; occurrence 3 eliminates *A, C, E* (again), and *G*; occurrence 4 eliminates *C* (again) and *D* (again); and occurrence 5 eliminates *B* (again) and *D* (again). This leaves only *F* (the ice cream) as a possible necessary condition. The conclusion is therefore warranted that the ice cream caused the sickness of the diners.

This conclusion follows only probably for two reasons. First, it is quite possible that some condition was overlooked in compiling conditions *A* through *G*. For example, if the ice cream was served with contaminated spoons, then the sickness of the diners could have been caused by that condition and not by the ice cream. Second, if more than one of the foods were contaminated (for example, both soup and french fries), then the sickness could have been caused by this combination of foods and not by the ice cream. Thus, the strength of the argument depends on the nonoccurrence of these two possibilities.

It is also important to realize that the conclusion yielded by Table 10.1 applies directly only to the five diners represented in the five occurrences, and not to everyone who may have eaten in the restaurant. Thus, if some food other than those listed in the table—for example, spaghetti—was contaminated, then only if they avoided both spaghetti and ice cream could the other diners be assured of not getting sick. But if, among all the foods in the restaurant, only the ice cream was contaminated, the conclusion would extend to the other patrons as well. This last point illustrates the fact that a conclusion reached by the method of agreement has limited generality. It applies directly only to those occurrences listed, and only indirectly, through a second inductive inference, to others.

Furthermore, because the conclusion yields a cause in the sense of a necessary condition, it does not assert that anyone who ate the ice cream would get sick. Many people have a natural immunity to food poisoning. What the conclusion says is that patrons who did not eat the ice cream would not get sick—at least not from the food. Thus, the method of agreement has a certain limited use. Basically what it says, in reference to the example, is that the ice cream is a highly suspect factor in the sickness of the patrons, and if investigators want to track down the cause of the sickness, this is where they should begin.

An example of an actual use of the method of agreement is provided by the discovery of the beneficial effects of fluoride on teeth. It was noticed several decades ago that people in certain communities were favored with especially healthy teeth. In researching the various factors these communities shared, scientists discovered that all had a high level of natural fluoride in their water supply. The scientists concluded from this evidence that fluoride causes teeth to be healthy.

Method of Difference

For an example of how this method works, let us modify our earlier case of people becoming sick from eating food in a restaurant. Instead of five people, suppose that identical twins, who have identical susceptibilities to food poisoning, go to that restaurant for dinner. They both order identical meals except that one orders ice cream for dessert while the other does not. The ice cream is the only way that the two meals differ. Later the twin who ordered the ice cream gets sick, whereas the other twin does not. The natural conclusion is that the ice cream caused the sickness.

■ EMINENT LOGICIANS

John Stuart Mill 1806–1873

© CORBIS

John Stuart Mill, who would become the most important English-speaking philosopher of the nineteenth century, was born in London to the philosopher and historian James Mill and his wife, Harriet Barrow. From a very early age the father took charge of his son's education, imposing on him an unusually strict course of studies. The boy began studying Greek at age three; he began Latin, geometry and algebra at eight; and by fourteen he had read most of the Latin and Greek classics. Also, by that time he had developed a thorough knowledge of history, scholastic and Aristotelian logic, and higher-level mathematics. At seventeen he accepted a position with the East India Company, a private corporation that virtually ruled all of India. He remained there for twenty-five years, eventually becoming chief examiner, which put him largely in charge of the company.

When he was twenty Mill suffered an acute attack of depression that lasted for several months. Although he managed to continue his work, everything seemed worthless to him at that time. This condition was most likely brought on by the severity of his educational upbringing, which had attended to his intellect but left his emotional life a desert. Gradually he pulled himself out by reading the poetry of William Wordsworth. Four years later Mill met Harriet Taylor, with whom he became emotionally but not sexually intimate (she was married at that time). Taylor would exert a profound influence on him for the rest of his life. After the death of her husband, nineteen years after she and Mill first met, they were married.

Today John Stuart Mill is widely known for his essay "On Liberty" and his book *Utilitarianism.* The essay is a sustained argument in favor of freedom of speech and the maximization of individual liberty against the strictures of government. *Utilitarianism* further develops the ethical theory promoted by James Mill and Jeremy Bentham. As perfected by John Stuart Mill, this theory holds that we should always perform the action that produces the greatest happiness for the greatest number of people. This work was important, among other reasons, for creating an ethical theory that was not based on any theology or religion. Mill also wrote extensively on women's rights, and when he was later elected to a three-year term in Parliament, he became the first member to urge that women receive the right to vote.

Mill's greatest work was his *System of Logic,* which went through eight editions during his lifetime. In that book Mill argues that deductive argumentation, far from being the paradigmatic form of reasoning most philosophers take it to be, is largely bereft of value because it never yields any new knowledge. Also, it is essentially dependent on induction. Thus, it is really induction that should be studied as the primary engine of scientific discovery.

In 1858 Harriet Taylor died from a lung infection while the couple were visiting Avignon, France. Nearly inconsolable, Mill bought a house there so he could be near her grave. He died in Avignon fifteen years later, and his body was buried alongside hers.

The **method of difference** consists in a systematic effort to identify a single factor that is present in an occurrence in which the phenomenon in question is present, and absent from an occurrence in which the phenomenon is absent. The method is confined to investigating exactly two occurrences, and it identifies a cause in the sense of a sufficient condition. For a clearer illustration of how this method works, let us add a few details to the twin example:

> A pair of twins, Jane and Jan, have dinner in a restaurant. The twins have identical susceptibilities to food poisoning. Jane orders soup, salad, chicken, carrots, rice, and ice cream. Jan orders soup, salad, chicken, carrots, rice, and no ice cream. Later, Jane gets sick from something she ate, but Jan does not. What food caused Jan's sickness?

If we let Jane and Jan stand for occurrences 1 and 2, respectively, and let A stand for the specific susceptibility to food poisoning shared by Jane and Jan, and B through G stand for soup, salad, chicken, carrots, rice, and ice cream, respectively, we can produce Table 10.2. Again, an asterisk indicates that a certain condition is present, and a dash indicates it is absent.

Table 10.2

	Possible sufficient conditions							Phenomenon (sickness)
Occurrence	A	B	C	D	E	F	G	
1	*	*	*	*	*	*	*	*
2	*	*	*	*	*	*	-	-

As with the method of agreement, we proceed to eliminate certain conditions, but in this case we use the rule that a condition is not sufficient for the occurrence of a phenomenon if it is present when the phenomenon is absent. Accordingly, occurrence 2 eliminates A, B, C, D, E, and F. This leaves only G as the sufficient condition for the phenomenon. Thus, G (ice cream) is the cause of Jan's sickness.

Since the result yielded by the method of difference applies to only the one occurrence in which the phenomenon is present (in this case, Jane), it is often less susceptible to generalization than is the method of agreement, which usually applies to several occurrences. Thus, the mere fact that the ice cream may have caused Jane to become sick does not mean that it caused other patrons who ate ice cream to get sick. Perhaps these other people have a higher resistance to food poisoning than Jane or Jan. But given that the others are similar to Jane and Jan in relevant respects, the result can often be generalized to cover these others as well. At the very least, if others in the restaurant became sick, the fact that the ice cream is what made Jane sick suggests that this is where investigators should begin when they try to explain what made the others sick.

The conclusion yielded by the method of difference is only probable, however, even for the one occurrence to which it directly applies. The problem is that it is impossible for two occurrences to be literally identical in every respect but one. The mere fact that two occurrences occupy different regions of space, that one is closer to the wall than the other, amounts to a difference. Such differences may be insignificant, but therein lies the possibility for error. It is not at all obvious how insignificant differ-ences should be distinguished from significant ones. Furthermore, it is impossible to make an exhaustive list of all the possible conditions; but without such a list there is no assurance that significant conditions have not been overlooked.

The objective of the method of difference is to identify a sufficient condition among those that are *present* in a specific occurrence. Sometimes, however, the *absence* of a factor can count as something positive that must be taken into account. Suppose, for example, that both of the twins who dined in the restaurant are allergic to dairy prod-ucts, but they can avoid an allergic reaction by taking Lactaid tablets. Suppose further that both twins ordered ice cream for dessert, but only Jan took the tablets. After the meal, Jane got sick. We can attribute Jane's sickness to the absence of the Lactaid.

We can illustrate this situation by modifying Table 10.2 as follows. Let A stand for the allergy to dairy products, let B through G stand for the same foods as before, and let H stand for Lactaid tablets. Then $\sim H$ will stand for the *absence* of Lactaid (the sym-bol $\sim$ means "not"). As before, let occurrence 1 stand for Jane, and occurrence 2 for Jan (see Table 10.3).

Table 10.3

| | Possible sufficient conditions | | | | | | | | Phenomenon |
Occurrence	A	B	C	D	E	F	G	~H	(sickness)
1	*	*	*	*	*	*	*	*	*
2	*	*	*	*	*	*	*	-	-

Using the same rule for elimination as with Table 10.2, we see that occurrence 2 eliminates A through G as sufficient conditions. This leaves $\sim H$ (the absence of Lac-taid) as the cause of Jane's sickness. In this case, the ice cream is not identified as the cause, because Jan (occurrence 2) ate ice cream (G) but did not get sick.

The method of difference has a wide range of applicability. For example, a farmer might fertilize one part of a field but not the other part to test the benefit of using fer-tilizer. If the fertilized part of the crop turns out to be fuller and healthier than the nonfertilized part, then the farmer can conclude that the improvement was caused by the fertilizer. On the other hand, a cook might leave some ingredient out of a batch of biscuits to determine the importance of that ingredient. If the biscuits turn out dry and crunchy, the cook can attribute the difference to the absence of that ingredient.

Joint Method of Agreement and Difference

To illustrate the joint method, we can once again modify the example of the diners who got sick by eating food in a restaurant. In place of the original five diners and the pair of twins, suppose that six people eat dinner in the restaurant. Among the first three, suppose that a variety of meals are eaten but that only ice cream is consumed by all, and later all three get sick. And among the other three, suppose that a variety of meals are eaten but that none of these diners eats any ice cream, and later none of them gets sick. The conclusion is warranted that the ice cream is what made the first three diners sick.

The **joint method of agreement and difference** consists of a systematic effort to identify a single condition that is present in two or more occurrences in which the phenomenon in question is present and that is absent from two or more occurrences in which the phenomenon is absent, but never present when the phenomenon is absent nor absent when the phenomenon is present. This condition is then taken to be the cause of the phenomenon in the sense of a necessary and sufficient condition. To see more clearly how this method works, let us add some details to the example:

> Six people eat dinner in a restaurant. Liz has soup, a hamburger, ice cream, french fries, and mixed vegetables. Tom has salad, soup, fish, mixed vegetables, and ice cream. Andy has salad, a hamburger, french fries, and ice cream. Sue has french fries, a hamburger, and salad. Meg has fish and mixed vegetables. Bill has french fries, a hamburger, and soup. Later Liz, Tom, and Andy get sick from something they ate, but Sue, Meg, and Bill do not. What food made the first three diners sick?

Let occurrences 1 through 6 stand for Liz, Tom, Andy, Sue, Meg, and Bill, respectively. And let *A* through *G* stand for salad, soup, a hamburger, fish, ice cream, french fries, and mixed vegetables (see Table 10.4).

Table 10.4

	Possible necessary or sufficient conditions							Phenomenon (sickness)
Occurrence	*A*	*B*	*C*	*D*	*E*	*F*	*G*	
1	-	*	*	-	*	*	*	*
2	*	*	-	*	*	-	*	*
3	*	-	*	-	*	*	-	*
4	*	-	*	-	-	*	-	-
5	-	-	-	*	-	-	*	-
6	-	*	*	-	-	*	-	-

In the first three occurrences the phenomenon is present, so we proceed by eliminating possible necessary conditions. Using the rule that a condition is not necessary if it is absent when the phenomenon is present, occurrence 1 eliminates *A* and *D*, occurrence 2 eliminates *C* and *F*, and occurrence 3 eliminates *B*, *D* (again), and *G*. This leaves only *E* as the necessary condition. Next, in the last three occurrences the phenomenon is absent, so we use the rule that a condition is not sufficient if it is present when the phenomenon is absent. Occurrence 4 eliminates *A*, *C*, and *F*; occurrence 5 eliminates *D* and *G*; and occurrence 6 eliminates *B*, *C* (again), and *F* (again). This leaves only *E* as the sufficient condit.on. Thus, condition *E* (ice cream) is the cause in the sense of both a necessary and sufficient condition of the sickness of the first three diners.

Since the joint method yields a cause in the sense of both a necessary and sufficient condition, it is usually thought to be stronger than either the method of agreement by itself, which yields a cause in the sense of a necessary condition, or the method of difference by itself, which yields a cause in the sense of a sufficient condition. However, when any of these methods is used as a basis for a subsequent inductive generalization, the strength of the conclusion is proportional to the number of occurrences that are included. Thus, an application of the method of agreement that included, say, one hundred occurrences might offer stronger results than an application of the joint method that included, say, only six occurrences. By similar reasoning, multiple applications of the method of difference might offer stronger results than a single application of the joint method.

As with the other methods, the conclusion yielded by the joint method is only probable because some relevant condition may have been overlooked in producing the table. If, for example, both salad and soup were contaminated, then the ice cream could not be identified as a necessary condition for the sickness, and if one of the last three diners was naturally immune, then the ice cream could not be identified as a sufficient condition. Obviously the attempt to extend the results of this example to other patrons of the restaurant who may have gotten sick is fraught with other difficulties.

Lastly, we note that even though the name of the joint method suggests that it results from a mere combination of the method of agreement with the method of difference, this is not the case—at least not as Mill presented it. Such a combination would consist of one occurrence in which the phenomenon is present, one occurrence in which the phenomenon is absent and which differs from the former occurrence as to only one condition, and one occurrence in which the phenomenon is present and which agrees with the first occurrence in only one condition. However, according to Mill, the joint method requires "two or more" occurrences in which the phenomenon is present, and "two or more" occurrences in which the phenomenon is absent.* His further description of the method accords with the foregoing account.

Method of Residues

This method and the one that follows are used to identify a causal connection between two conditions without regard for the specific kind of connection. Both methods may be used to identify conditions that are sufficient, necessary, or both sufficient and necessary. The **method of residues** consists of separating from a group of causally connected conditions and phenomena those strands of causal connection that are already known, leaving the required causal connection as the "residue." Here is an example:

> After occupying his new house Mr. Smith found it drafty. He traced the source of the draft to three conditions: a broken window in the garage, a crack under the front door, and a broken damper in the fireplace. When the window was replaced he noticed an improvement, and a further improvement when weather stripping was installed on the door. He concluded that the draft that remained was caused by the broken damper in the fireplace.

The method of residues as illustrated in this example may be diagramed as follows:

*A System of Logic, Book III, Chapter VIII, Sect. 4, Third Canon.

$$(A\ B\ C)\ \text{causes}\ (a\ b\ c.)$$

A causes *a*.

B causes *b*.

Therefore, *C* causes *c*.

In reference to the draft example, $(A\ B\ C)$ is the combination of possible conditions producing $(a\ b\ c)$, the total draft. When *A* (the broken window) is separated out, it is found to cause *a* (a portion of the draft). When *B* (the crack) is separated out, it is found to cause *b* (another portion of the draft). The conclusion is that *C* (the broken damper) causes *c* (the remaining portion of the draft). The conclusion follows only probably because it is quite possible that a fourth source of the draft was overlooked. Here is another example:

> After realizing a loss of $100,000 a department store's chief accountant could suggest only three causes: an excessive number of clerks, increases in utility rates, and damage to merchandise caused by a flood. These expenses were estimated at $25,000, $30,000, and $10,000, respectively. Since no other ordinary sources could be found, the accountant attributed the remaining $35,000 to shoplifting.

In this case $(A\ B\ C\ D)$ is the combination of conditions consisting of the number of clerks, the utility rate increases, the flood, and shoplifting; and $(a\ b\ c\ d)$ is the total loss of $100,000. After *A*, *B*, and *C* are separated out, the conclusion is that *D* (shoplifting) caused *d* (the remaining loss). Because the estimates might have been incorrect and because additional sources of financial loss might have been overlooked, the conclusion is only probable.

Some procedures that, at least on the face of it, appear to use the method of residues come closer to being deductive than inductive. A case in point is the procedure used to determine the weight of the cargo carried by a truck. First, the empty truck is put on a scale and the weight recorded. Then the truck is loaded and the truck together with the cargo is put on the same scale. The weight of the cargo is the difference between the two weights. If, to this procedure, we add the rather unproblematic assumptions that weight is an additive property, that the scale is accurate, that the scale operator reads the indicator properly, that the truck is not altered in the loading process, and a few others, the conclusion about the weight of the cargo follows deductively.

To distinguish deductive from inductive uses of the method of residues, we must take into account such factors as the role of mathematics. If the conclusion depends on a purely arithmetical computation, the argument is probably best characterized as deductive. If not, then it is probably inductive.

Method of Concomitant Variation

The **method of concomitant variation** identifies a causal connection between two conditions by matching variations in one condition with variations in another. According to one formulation, increases are matched with increases and decreases with decreases. Example:

In attempting to diagnose Mrs. Thompson's high blood pressure, a cardiologist noticed a correlation between fluctuations in blood pressure and certain brain
waves. As the blood pressure increased, so did the intensity of the brain waves,
and as the blood pressure decreased, the intensity of the brain waves decreased.
The cardiologist concluded that the two conditions were causally related.

The method of concomitant variation as illustrated in this example may be diagramed
as follows:

$(A\ B\ C)$ is coincident with $(X\ Y\ Z.)$

$(A\ B+\ C)$ is coincident with $(X\ Y+\ Z.)$

$(A\ B-\ C)$ is coincident with $(X\ Y-\ Z.)$

Therefore, B is causally connected to Y.

Here, $(A\ B\ C)$ is a set of observable conditions such as cholesterol level, liver function, and basal metabolism, with B representing blood pressure; and $(X\ Y\ Z)$ is another set of observable conditions with Y representing certain brain waves. In the
second and third rows, $B+$ and $B-$ represent increases and decreases in blood pressure, and $Y+$ and $Y-$ represent increases and decreases in the intensity of the brain
waves. The conclusion asserts that either B causes Y, Y causes B, or B and Y have a
common cause. Determining which is the case requires further investigation; of
course, if B occurs earlier in time than Y, then Y does not cause B, and if Y occurs earlier in time than B, then B does not cause Y.

The blood pressure example matches increases in one condition with increases in
another. For an example that matches increases in one condition with decreases in another, consider the following:

A sociologist studying divorce noticed a correlation between changes in the national
divorce rate and fluctuations in the gross domestic product. As the GDP increases,
the divorce rate decreases, and when the GDP sags, the divorce rate goes up. The
sociologist concluded that the two phenomena are causally connected.

This second version of the method of concomitant variation may be diagramed as
follows:

$(A\ B\ C)$ is coincident with $(X\ Y\ Z.)$

$(A\ B+\ C)$ is coincident with $(X\ Y-\ Z.)$

$(A\ B-\ C)$ is coincident with $(X\ Y+\ Z.)$

Therefore, B is causally connected to Y.

In this example $(A\ B\ C)$ is a set of economic conditions such as stock exchange in-
dexes, interest rates, and commodity prices, with B representing gross domestic product; and $(X\ Y\ Z)$ is a set of social conditions such as birth rates, employment rates,
and immigration numbers, with Y representing the national divorce rate. The conclusion is that B is somehow causally connected to Y. However, in this example an even

stronger conclusion could probably be drawn—namely, that decreases in the GDP cause increases in the divorce rate, and not conversely. That changes in economic prosperity (which is indicated by GDP) should affect the divorce rate is quite plausible, but the converse is less so.

At this point we should note that the existence of a mere correlation between two phenomena is never sufficient to identify a causal connection. In addition, the causal connection suggested by the correlation must at least make sense. Consider the following example:

> After an in-depth study researchers discovered a correlation between the price of pork belly futures on the Chicago Mercantile Exchange and earthquake activity in Japan. As the number and intensity of the quakes increased, the futures prices also increased, and vice versa. The researchers concluded that the two phenomena were causally connected.

The argument is clearly weak. Because it is virtually inconceivable that either phenomenon could cause a change in the other, or that changes in both could have a common cause, it is most likely that the correlation is purely coincidental.

The method of concomitant variation is useful when it is impossible for a condition to be either wholly present or wholly absent, as was required for the use of the first three of Mill's methods. Many conditions are of this sort—for example, the temperature of the ocean, the price of gold, the incidence of crime, the size of a mountain glacier, a person's cholesterol level, and so on. If some kind of correlation can be detected between variations in conditions such as these, the method of concomitant variation asserts that the two are causally connected. The method has been used successfully in the past to help establish the existence of causal connections between smoking and lung cancer, nuclear radiation and leukemia, and alcohol consumption and cirrhosis of the liver.

10.3   Mill's Methods and Science

Mill's methods closely resemble certain scientific methods that are intended to establish causal connections and correlations. For example, the method of difference is virtually identical to the method of controlled experiment employed in such fields as biology, pharmacology, and psychology. A controlled experiment is one that involves two groups of subjects, an experimental group and a control group. The experimental group includes the subjects that receive a certain treatment, and the control group includes the subjects that do not receive the treatment but are otherwise subjected to the same conditions as the experimental group.

The simplest type of controlled experiment involves an experimental group and a control group each consisting of just one member. Example:

> Two mice were used in a controlled experiment to determine whether a certain substance was carcinogenic. The two mice had identical genes, were the same age, were placed in identical cages in the same location, were subjected to the same environmental conditions, and were fed the same food, over the same period of time. One mouse was injected with the suspected carcinogen, and the other was

not. After two months, the injected mouse developed cancerous tumors, but the other mouse did not.

To summarize the results of this experiment we can construct a table just like the one for the method of difference. If we let occurrence 1 represent the injected mouse and occurrence 2 the mouse that was not injected, and let *A* through *F* represent the conditions common to the two mice (genes, age, cage, etc.) and *G* represent the injection, we have Table 10.5. Using the rule that a condition is not sufficient if it is present when the phenomenon is absent, occurrence 2 eliminates *A* through *F*, leaving *G* (the suspected carcinogen) as the cause of the phenomenon.

Table 10.5

	Possible sufficient conditions							Phenomenon (tumors)
Occurrence	A	B	C	D	E	F	G	
1	*	*	*	*	*	*	*	*
2	*	*	*	*	*	*	-	-

The principal drawback of this experiment is that the suspected carcinogen was given to only one mouse. As a result, the experiment offers relatively weak evidence that *any* mouse injected with this substance would develop tumors. Perhaps the injected mouse had some hidden defect that would have caused tumors even without the injection. Scientists address this problem by increasing the size of the experimental group and the control group. Thus, suppose the same experiment were performed on one hundred mice, of which fifty were injected and fifty were not. Suppose that after two months all fifty injected mice developed tumors and none of the control subjects did. Such a result would constitute much stronger evidence that the injected substance was carcinogenic.

This expanded experiment can be considered to be a case of multiple uses of Mill's method of difference. Since the method of difference always involves just two occurrences, mouse #1 could be matched with mouse #51 for one use of the method, mouse #2 with mouse #52 for a second use of the method, and so on. Although this expanded experiment might look like a case of the joint method, it is not (at least not a successful one). Any successful application of the joint method includes occurrences in which certain conditions are absent when the phenomenon is present. Those conditions are then eliminated as possible necessary conditions. The expanded experiment with the mice includes no such occurrences.

This fact points up an important difference between Mill's joint method and his method of difference. The purpose of the method of difference is to determine whether a *preselected* condition is the cause of a phenomenon. This preselected condition is present in one of the two occurrences and absent from the other. On the other hand, the purpose of the joint method is to determine which condition, among a selected *class* of conditions, is a cause of a phenomenon. The joint method applies rules for sufficient conditions and necessary conditions to (one hopes) reduce the class of conditions to just one.

Returning to the expanded experiment with the mice, let us suppose that only forty of the mice in the experimental group developed tumors, and none of those in the control group did. From Mill's standpoint, this would be equivalent to forty uses of the method of difference yielding positive results and ten yielding negative results. On the basis of such an outcome, the experimenter might conclude that the likelihood of the suspected carcinogen producing tumors in mice was 80 percent (40 ÷ 50).

Controlled experiments such as the one involving a hundred mice are often conducted on humans, but with humans it is never possible to control the circumstances to the degree that it is with mice. Humans cannot be put in cages or fed exactly the same food for any length of time, are not genetically identical to other humans, and so forth. Also, humans react to their environment in ways that cannot be anticipated or controlled. To correct this deficiency, statistical methods are applied to the results to enable the drawing of a conclusion.

For example, an experiment could be conducted to test the effectiveness of some new drug on children with attention deficit/hyperactivity disorder (ADHD). Fifty children with ADHD could be selected, with twenty-five being placed at random in the experimental group and twenty-five in the control group. The children in the experimental group would be given the drug, probably in a classroom situation, and the children in the control group would be given a placebo (sugar pill). This could be done on a "double blind" basis, so that neither the children nor the people conducting the experiment would know in advance who was getting the drug. The objective is to control the conditions as much as possible. Then the negative behavior of each of the fifty children would be recorded over a period, say, of an hour. Each time a child was out of his or her seat, disturbed others, fidgeted, failed to follow instructions, and so forth, the incident would be noted.

The results of such an experiment would be expected to follow what is called a normal probability distribution (bell-shaped curve). (Further discussion of normal probability distribution is presented in Chapter 12.) One curve would represent the experimental group, another curve the control group. Assuming the drug is effective, the two curves would be displaced from one another, but they would probably overlap in part, as indicated in Figure 10.1. This means that certain children in the experimental group exhibited more negative behaviors than certain children in the control group,

Figure 10.1

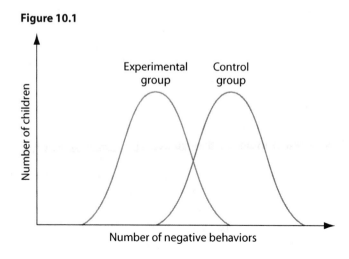

but most of the children in the experimental group exhibited fewer negative behaviors than most of the children in the control group. Then statistical methods would be applied to the two curves to determine the effectiveness of the drug. Such an experiment is similar to Mill's method of difference except that instead of the phenomenon (negative behavior) being wholly present in some occurrences, it is present in varying degrees. In this sense, the experiment resembles the method of concomitant variation.

In some kinds of scientific research on humans, controlling the circumstances to any significant degree is nearly impossible. Such research includes investigations that cover a long period or investigations in which the health of the subjects is at issue and legal or moral restrictions come into play. Example:

> A nutritionist wanted to determine the effect of fifteen vitamin and mineral supplements on atherosclerosis (artery disease). Because the effect was expected to require several years to develop, the nutritionist ran an ad in a health publication for individuals who had ingested these substances on a regular basis for five years. Eighty people answered the ad and reported which substances they had taken and how much of each. These people were then examined. Some showed no evidence of the disease, while others manifested the disease in varying degrees. After analyzing the data, the nutritionist concluded that certain vitamins and minerals offer protection against atherosclerosis.

The procedure followed by the nutritionist is very similar to Mill's joint method of agreement and difference. The objective is to identify a cause among a preselected class of possible conditions, some of which are accompanied by the phenomenon (atherosclerosis), and some of which are not. The major difference between the nutritionist's procedure and Mill's joint method is that the nutritionist took account of varying degrees in which the conditions and the phenomenon were present in the eighty occurrences. In this sense, again, the nutritionist's procedure was similar to Mill's method of concomitant variation. However, the nutritionist may also have taken into account various combinations of conditions, a consideration that lies beyond the power of the joint method by itself.

The procedure illustrated in this example is not an experiment but a study. More precisely, it is a *retrospective study* because it examines subjects who have already fulfilled the requirements of the examination—as opposed to a *prospective study*, where the subjects are expected to fulfill the requirements in the future. For a prospective study, the nutritionist could select a group of subjects and follow their future vitamin and mineral intake for five years. Such a study, however, would be more costly, and if the nutritionist instructed the subjects to ingest certain vitamins and minerals and avoid others, the study could involve legal or moral implications.

Another kind of study found widely in the social sciences uses what is called the *correlational method*, which closely replicates Mill's method of concomitant variation. Example:

> A psychology professor was interested in the relationship between IQ scores and grade point average. The professor randomly selected one hundred graduating seniors, obtained their GPAs from the registrar, and asked them to take an IQ test. All of them complied. Then the professor compared the scores of each student

with his or her GPA. The professor found that in general higher IQ scores corresponded with higher GPAs.

The results of this study indicate a positive correlation between IQ score and GPA. If the study showed that students with higher IQs had, in general, lower GPAs, this would indicate a negative correlation. Once a study of this sort is done, the next step is to compute the *correlation coefficient,* which is a number between +1.00 and −1.00 that expresses the degree of correlation. If it turned out that the student with the highest IQ score also had the highest GPA, the student with the next highest IQ score had proportionately the next highest GPA, and so on, so that the IQ-GPA graph was a straight line, then the correlation coefficient would be +1.00. This would reflect a perfect positive correlation.

On the other hand, if it turned out that the student with the highest IQ score had the lowest GPA, the student with the next highest IQ score had proportionately the next lowest GPA, and so on, so that, once again, the IQ-GPA graph was a straight line, then the correlation coefficient would be −1.00. This would reflect a perfect negative correlation. A correlation coefficient of 0.00 would mean that no correlation exists, which would be the case if the IQ scores corresponded randomly with the GPAs. A correlation coefficient of, say, +0.60 would mean that in general higher IQ scores corresponded positively with higher GPAs.

The outcome of this study can also be indicated graphically, with IQ score representing one coordinate on a graph, and GPA the other coordinate. The result for each student would then correspond to a point on the graph, such as the one in Figure 10.2. The graph of all the points is called a *scatter diagram.* A line that "best fits" the data can then be drawn through the scatter diagram. This line is called the *regression line,* and it can be used to produce a linear equation, $y = bx + a$, that describes the approximate relation between IQ score (x) and GPA (y). This equation can then be used to predict future GPAs. For example, suppose that an entering freshman student has an IQ of 116. This student's future GPA could be predicted to be approximately $116b + a$.

Hundreds of studies such as this one have been conducted to detect correlations between such factors as TV violence and aggression in children, self-esteem and intelligence, motivation and learning time, exposure to classical music and retention ability, and marijuana use and memory. However, such studies often fall short of establishing a causal connection between the two factors. For example, a positive cor-

Figure 10.2

relation between exposure to TV violence and aggression in children does not necessarily mean that exposure to TV violence causes aggression. It might be the case that children who tend to be violent are naturally attracted to violent TV shows. Or perhaps a third factor is the cause of both. But a positive correlation can at least suggest a causal connection.

Once a correlation is established, a controlled experiment can often be designed that will identify a causal connection. For example, in the case of TV violence, a group of children could be randomly divided into an experimental group and a control group. The experimental group could then be exposed to violent TV shows for a certain period, and the control group would be exposed to nonviolent shows for the same period. Later, the behavior of the children in both groups could be observed, with every act of aggression noted. If the experimental group displayed more acts of aggression than the control group, the conclusion might be drawn that TV violence causes aggression.

Experimental procedures resembling Mill's method of concomitant variation have also been used in the physical sciences to identify causal connections. For example, in the early part of the nineteenth century, Hans Christian Oerstead noticed that a wire carrying a current of electricity could deflect a nearby compass needle. As the current was increased, the amount of deflection increased, and as the current was decreased, the amount of deflection decreased. Also, if the current were reversed, the deflection would be reversed. Oerstead concluded that a current of electricity flowing through a wire causes a magnetic field to be produced around the wire.

Other applications of the method of concomitant variation have been used not so much to detect the existence of a causal connection (which may have already been known) as to determine the precise nature of a causal law. For example, in the latter part of the sixteenth century Galileo performed experiments involving spheres rolling down inclined planes. As the plane was incrementally lifted upward, the sphere covered greater and greater distances in a unit of time. Recognizing that the downward force on the sphere is proportional to the pitch of the plane, Galileo derived the law that the acceleration imparted to a body is directly proportional to the force acting on it. Galileo also noticed that whatever the angle of the plane, the distance covered by the ball increased exponentially with the time in which it was allowed to roll. For example, if the time was doubled, the distance was quadrupled. From this correlation he derived the law that the distance traveled by a falling body is proportional to the square of the time that it falls.

In the seventeenth century, Robert Boyle conducted experiments involving the pressure and volume of gases. Boyle constructed an apparatus that allowed him to compute the volume of a gas as he varied the pressure. He noted that as the pressure increased, the volume decreased, and as the pressure decreased, the volume increased. From this correlation he derived the law that the volume of a gas is inversely proportional to its pressure. A century later, Jacques Alexandre Charles observed a correlation between the temperature of a gas and its volume. As the temperature increased, the volume increased, and vice versa. This correlation provided the basis for Charles's law for gases.

Detecting correlations has also been important in astronomy. Early in the twentieth century, Henrietta Swan Leavitt recognized a correlation between the average brightness of certain variable stars, called Cepheids (pronounced sef'-ee-ids), and their periods of variation. Cepheids fluctuate in brightness over periods ranging from a day to several months, and Leavitt discovered that longer periods correspond with greater average brightness, and shorter periods with lesser average brightness. Once the distance of a few nearby Cepheids was determined, the distance of any Cepheid could then be computed from its average brightness and its period of variation. This correlation provided the first method available to astronomers for measuring the distance between our planet and galaxies other than our own.

EXERCISE 10

I. Identify the kind of causality intended by the following statements. Is the cause a sufficient condition, necessary condition, or both sufficient and necessary condition?

★1. Throwing a brick through a window will cause the window to break.

2. Heating an iron rod causes it to expand.

3. Slashing an inflated automobile tire with a knife will cause it to go flat.

★4. Releasing the shutter of a camera causes an image to appear on the film.

5. Pulling the trigger of a gun causes it to fire.

6. Wetting litmus paper with an acid causes it to turn red.

★7. Pouring water on a wood fire will cause it to be extinguished.

8. Eating contaminated food will cause one to become ill.

9. Stretching a spring causes it to exert an opposing force.

★10. Flipping the wall switch to the "up" position causes the overhead lights to go on.

II. The following problems pertain to Mill's methods. Answer each as directed.

★1. To determine the effectiveness of an oil additive, a testing firm purchased two cars of the same make, year, and model, and drove each a distance of 30,000 miles using the same kind of gasoline, the same kind of oil, the same driver, under the same road conditions. The oil in one engine included the additive, whereas the oil in the other engine did not. At the end of the test, the engines of both cars were dismantled, and it was found that the engine that contained the additive had less wear. The testing firm concluded that the oil additive caused the reduced wear. Construct a table that supports this conclusion. Which one of Mill's methods did the testing firm use? What sense of causality is involved in the conclusion?

2. An eighth-grade teacher had five pupils who read very well. These pupils were distinguished by the following features. Tom came from a large family, had professional parents who were not wealthy, had training in phonics, read novels, lived close to a library, and watched educational TV. Andy came from a family that was not large, had wealthy professional parents, watched educational TV, did not live close to a library, did not read novels, and had training in phonics. Cindy did not read novels, lived close to a library, had training in phonics, had wealthy professional parents, came from a large family, and did not watch educational TV. April had training in phonics, read novels, lived close to a library, watched educational TV, came from a large family, and had wealthy parents who were not professionals. Joe read novels, did not live close

to a library, had professional parents who were not wealthy, had training in phonics, watched educational TV, and came from a large family. What can the teacher conclude caused these children to be good readers? Construct a table that supports this conclusion. Which one of Mill's methods did the teacher use? What sense of causality is involved in the conclusion?

3. An administrator for the Internal Revenue Service noticed that tax revenues for a certain year were down by 14 percent. Of this amount, the administrator attributed 6 percent to an economic slowdown that year, 3 percent to higher interest rates that led to higher write-offs, and 2 percent to changes in the tax code. Unable to attribute the remaining 3 percent to any lawful factor, the administrator concluded that it resulted from increased cheating by the taxpayers. Which one of Mill's methods did the administrator use?

★4. The repair manager for a manufacturer of home computers noticed that a large number of units were being returned for repairs. The manager selected a sample of seven returned units and noticed that these units were distinguished by the following characteristics. Units 1 and 3 had type X circuitry and were shipped to coastal regions. Units 2 and 7 were sold to business customers, were manufactured in the Kansas City plant, and were shipped to coastal regions. Units 4 and 5 were used to play computer games and were manufactured in the Kansas City plant. Units 6 and 7 were shipped to large cities and had type X circuitry. Unit 4 was shipped to a large coastal city. Units 2 and 3 were shipped to large cities. Unit 5 was shipped to a coastal region and had type X circuitry. Unit 3 was sold to a business customer who used it to play computer games. Unit 1 was used to play computer games and was manufactured in the Kansas City plant. Finally, Unit 6 was sold to a business customer in a coastal region. Among these six distinguishing characteristics the manager concluded that salty air caused the computers to break down. Construct a table that supports this conclusion. Which one of Mill's methods did the manufacturer use? What sense of causality is involved in the conclusion?

5. A manufacturer of fishing equipment conducted a test of its products by giving them to eight fishermen who used them with the following results. Ed and Flo used a Hot Spot lure and caught no fish. Dan and Amy used a Trusty rod with a Husky reel, and Amy caught fish but Dan did not. Jake used a Sure Catch lure, a Best Bet rod, a Spiffy reel, and caught fish. Bill and Tim used a Husky reel, but only Bill caught fish. Kat used a Best Bet rod with a Husky reel and caught fish. Amy and Kat used a Sure Catch lure, but only Kat used monofilament line. Bill used a Trusty rod, monofilament line, and a Sure Catch lure. Flo and Tim used Best Bet rods, and both Tim and Dan used Dynamite lures. Finally, Flo used a Husky reel, Jake and Dan used monofilament line, and Ed used a Spiffy reel on a Trusty rod. What conclusion can the manufacturer draw about the power of this equipment to catch fish? Construct a table that supports this conclusion. Which one of Mill's methods did the manufacturer use? What sense of causality is involved in the conclusion?

6. Nancy was contemplating the purchase of a new oven for her kitchen, but she could not decide between an electric or a gas unit. Thus, she decided to conduct

an experiment using the ovens, one gas, one electric, of two friends who live in adjoining apartments. She mixed up two identical batches of brownies under identical conditions of relative humidity and identical altitudes, put them into identical baking dishes, and cooked them at the same temperature for exactly the same time. The brownies cooked in the electric oven came out moist, while the brownies cooked in the gas oven came out relatively dry. Nancy concluded that baking in the electric oven caused the brownies to be moist. Construct a table that supports this conclusion. Which one of Mill's methods did Nancy use? What sense of causality is involved in the conclusion?

★7. Mrs. Wilkins sometimes has trouble sleeping. In order to determine the cause, she decided to take note of her pre-bedtime behavior over the course of a week. On Monday she drank camomile tea, had a late dinner, took a hot bath, read from a book, took a walk, and slept well. On Tuesday she had a late dinner, read from a book, and slept poorly. On Wednesday she drank a glass of wine, got a massage, took a walk, and slept poorly. On Thursday she had a late dinner, drank a glass of wine, read from a book, took a hot bath, got a massage, and slept well. On Friday she read from a book, drank camomile tea, got a massage, had a late dinner, took a walk, and slept well. On Saturday she drank a glass of wine, got a massage, took a walk, drank camomile tea, took a hot bath, and slept well. On Sunday she read from a book, took a hot bath, drank camomile tea, and slept poorly. What can Mrs. Wilkins conclude is the cause of sleeping well? Construct a table that supports this conclusion. Which one of Mill's methods did Mrs. Wilkins use? What sense of causality is involved in the conclusion?

8. From a comparison of statistics a criminologist detected what he thought was a correlation between fluctuations in the employment rate and in crimes of theft. For every 2 percent increase in the employment rate, the rate of theft decreased by 1 percent, and for every 2 percent decrease in the employment rate, the theft rate increased by 1 percent. The criminologist concluded that unemployment causes crimes of theft. Which one of Mill's methods did the criminologist use?

9. A man developed an allergic reaction to an unknown food. His doctor asked him about foods that often cause allergic reactions, and the man replied that he had eaten coconut, chocolate, nuts, milk products, shellfish, peppers, eggs, and wheat products prior to suffering the reaction. The doctor told him to eliminate all of these foods from his diet; when he had done so, the reaction disappeared. The doctor then told him to introduce each of these foods back into his diet, one at a time. The man did so, and the reaction reappeared only when he ate milk products. The doctor concluded that milk products caused the allergic reaction. Construct a table that supports this conclusion. Which one of Mill's methods did the doctor use? What sense of causality is involved in the conclusion?

★10. A psychiatrist had six adult women patients who suffered blurred ego boundaries. These patients were distinguished by the following characteristics. Meg and Sue had been subjected to corporal punishment as children and both had siblings. Dot and Jane were adopted, had a male parent figure, and experienced sexual abuse. Lynn and Flo had siblings and a male parent figure, but only Flo had a domineering mother. Also, Lynn and Meg had experienced sexual abuse and were adopted, but only Meg had a domineering mother. Jane and Dot were uprooted often as children. Flo and Sue had experienced sexual abuse, but only Sue was raised in day-care centers. Jane and Dot each had a domineering mother, and each had been subjected to corporal punishment. Flo was uprooted often as a child and had been subjected to corporal punishment. Dot and Lynn were raised in day-care centers, Sue had a male parent figure, and Jane had siblings. What can the psychiatrist conclude is the cause of the blurred ego boundaries of these women? Construct a table that supports this conclusion. Which one of Mill's methods did the psychiatrist use? What sense of causality is involved in the conclusion?

11. A metallurgist added eight substances in various combinations to seven samples of molten aluminum for the purpose of producing aluminum alloys. The metallurgist was interested in producing an alloy that had a special resistance to corrosion. The samples were distinguished by the following characteristics. Samples 1, 2, and 3 contained both tin and copper, but only samples 1 and 2 were resistant. Samples 6 and 7 contained both silver and iron, but only sample 7 was resistant. Samples 4 and 5 contained sodium, but only sample 5 was resistant. In addition, samples 1 and 7 contained zinc, silicon, and nickel. Sample 2 contained sodium, iron, and silicon, and sample 5 contained silicon and copper. Finally, sample 3 contained nickel, and sample 4 contained zinc. Assuming no interaction occurs among these eight additives, what conclusion can the metallurgist draw about these additives? Construct a table that supports this conclusion. Which one of Mill's methods did the metallurgist use? What sense of causality is involved in the conclusion?

12. A doctor has five patients who suffer from an unusual form of cancer. The patients are distinguished by the following living conditions. Davis, Jones, and Ellis live in a smoggy area near high-tension power lines, and Smith and Frank smoke cigarettes and live downwind from a company that produces chemical defoliants for the military. Frank also lives near the nuclear power plant. Davis, Smith, and Ellis eat red meat every day and live near the nuclear power plant. Jones smokes cigarettes and lives downwind from the chemical defoliant company. Smith lives in a smoggy area, and Davis and Ellis live downwind from the defoliant company. What can the doctor conclude is the cause of the cancer? Construct a table that supports this conclusion. Which one of Mill's methods did the doctor use? What sense of causality is involved in the conclusion?

★13. Two of Mr. Andrews's rose bushes became infected with aphids. Mr. Andrews proceeded to spray one of the bushes with malathion insecticide but left the other bush untouched. The two bushes are both American Beauty, are five years old, have virtually identical locations, receive the same amount of water and sunlight, are planted in the same kind of soil, and receive the same degree of cultivation and the same amount of Bandini rose food. Within three days the aphids disappeared from the bush that was sprayed, but they continued to thrive on the other bush. Mr. Andrews concluded that the malathion killed the aphids on the bush that was sprayed. Construct a table that supports Mr. Andrews's conclusion. Which one of Mill's methods did Mr. Andrews use? What sense of causality is involved in the conclusion?

14. A sociologist conducted a study to determine if a correlation exists between grade point average at the time of graduation and income ten years after graduation. The sociologist visited the alumni office of a local university and obtained the names and addresses of those who had graduated ten years earlier. The sociologist then contacted those graduates and asked them to disclose their income and give permission for the university to disclose their graduating GPAs. Two hundred students replied to this inquiry. The sociologist then applied statistical methods to compute the correlation coefficient, which turned out to be +0.2. How does this study relate to Mill's methods? What does a correlation coefficient of +0.2 say about the correlation between GPA and income? Is such a study called a prospective study or a retrospective study? How do the two differ?

15. A cosmetics manufacturer tested a new cleansing cream on forty rabbits. The rabbits were virtually the same genetically and were the same age. Twenty of the rabbits were randomly placed in the experimental group and the other twenty were placed in the control group. A patch containing the cream was applied to the skin of each rabbit in the experimental group, and an identical patch containing a harmless substance was applied to the skin of each rabbit in the control group. Then, all forty rabbits were kept in the same room, at the same temperature, and under the same lighting conditions and were fed the same food. After five days, two of the rabbits in the experimental group developed a rash where the patch was applied, but none of the other rabbits did. The manufacturer concluded that there is a 10 percent likelihood that the cleansing cream will cause a rash on the skin of rabbits. How does this experiment relate to Mill's methods? What sense of causality is involved in the conclusion?

III. Identify the cause suggested by the information presented in the following tables. Is the cause a sufficient condition, necessary condition, or both sufficient and necessary condition? Can you identify the method?

★1.

Occurrence	Possible conditions					Phenomenon
	A	B	C	D	E	
1	*	-	*	*	*	*
2	*	*	*	*	-	*
3	*	-	*	*	*	*
4	*	*	-	*	*	*
5	-	*	*	*	-	*

2.

Occurrence	Possible conditions					Phenomenon
	A	B	C	D	E	
1	*	*	*	*	*	*
2	*	-	*	*	*	-

3.

Occurrence	A	B	C	D	E	F	Phenomenon
			Possible conditions				
1	*	-	-	*	-	-	-
2	-	*	*	*	-	-	*
3	*	-	*	*	*	-	*
4	-	*	-	-	-	*	-
5	*	-	-	-	*	-	-
6	*	*	*	-	*	-	*

★4.

Occurrence	A	B	C	D	E	Phenomenon
		Possible conditions				
1	*	*	*	*	-	*
2	-	-	*	-	*	*
3	*	-	-	-	*	-
4	-	*	-	*	*	*
5	*	*	-	-	-	-
6	-	*	*	-	-	-

5.

Occurrence	A	B	C	D	E	Phenomenon
		Possible conditions				
1	-	-	*	-	*	-
2	-	*	*	-	*	*
3	*	*	-	*	*	*
4	-	*	-	-	*	-
5	*	-	*	*	-	-
6	*	*	*	-	-	*

Summary

Causes can be described in terms of sufficient conditions, necessary conditions, and sufficient and necessary conditions. Mill's methods, named after the philosopher John Stuart Mill, are inductive techniques that allow us to identify causal connections. The method of agreement identifies necessary conditions, the method of difference identifies sufficient conditions present in a specific occurrence, and the joint method of agreement and difference identifies sufficient and necessary conditions. The method of residues and the method of concomitant variation identify causal connections without regard to the kind of causality involved. The methods of agreement, difference, and concomitant variation resemble certain methods used in the natural sciences and the social sciences to identify causal connections.

Answers to Selected Exercises

Exercise 10

I.

1. Sufficient condition. The window can also be broken by throwing a stone or baseball through it.
4. Necessary condition. For an image to appear on the film the camera must also be loaded and focused and there must be sufficient light.
7. Sufficient condition. The fire will also be extinguished if it is smothered.
10. Necessary condition. Electricity must also be supplied from the main lines.

II.

1. A = a certain make, B = a certain year, C = a certain model, D = driven 30,000 miles, E = a certain gasoline, F = a certain oil, G = a certain driver, H = certain road conditions, I = the additive.

	Possible conditions									Phenomenon (less wear)
Occurrence	**A**	**B**	**C**	**D**	**E**	**F**	**G**	**H**	**I**	
1	*	*	*	*	*	*	*	*	*	*
2	*	*	*	*	*	*	*	*	-	-

Method of difference, sufficient condition.

4. A = type X circuitry, B = shipped to a coastal region, C = sold to a business customer, D = manufactured in the Kansas City plant, E = used to play computer games, F = shipped to a large city.

Occurrence	Possible conditions						Phenomenon (returned)
	A	B	C	D	E	F	
1	*	*	-	*	*	-	*
2	-	*	*	*	-	*	*
3	*	*	*	-	*	*	*
4	-	*	-	*	*	*	*
5	*	*	-	*	*	-	*
6	*	*	*	-	-	*	*
7	*	*	*	*	-	*	*

Coastal region (salty air) is the cause in the sense of a necessary condition.

Method of agreement.

7. A = camomile tea, B = late dinner, C = hot bath, D = read book, E = walk, F = wine, G = massage.

Occurrence	Possible conditions							Phenomenon (slept well)
	A	B	C	D	E	F	G	
Mon	*	*	*	*	*	-	-	*
Tu	-	*	-	*	-	-	-	-
Wed	-	-	-	-	*	*	*	-
Th	-	*	*	*	-	*	*	*
Fri	*	*	-	*	*	-	*	*
Sat	*	-	*	-	*	*	*	*
Sun	*	-	*	*	-	-	-	-

None of the possible conditions is a cause of the phenomenon.

Joint method of agreement and difference.

10. A = corporal punishment, B = siblings, C = adopted, D = male parent figure, E = sexual abuse, F = domineering mother, G = uprooted often, H = day-care center.

Occurrence	Possible conditions								Phenomenon (blurred bound)
	A	B	C	D	E	F	G	H	
Meg	*	*	*	-	*	*	-	-	*
Sue	*	*	-	*	*	-	-	*	*
Dot	*	-	*	*	*	*	*	*	*
Jane	*	*	*	*	*	*	*	-	*
Lynn	-	*	*	*	*	-	-	*	*
Flo	*	*	-	*	*	*	*	-	*

Sexual abuse is the cause of the phenomenon in the sense of a necessary condition.

Method of agreement.

13. A = malathion, B = American Beauty, C = five years old, D = a certain location, E = a certain amount of water, F = a certain amount of sun, G = a certain kind of soil, H = a certain amount of cultivation, I = a certain amount of Bandini rose food.

| Occurrence | Possible conditions | | | | | | | | | Phenomenon (no aphids) |
	A	B	C	D	E	F	G	H	I	
1	*	*	*	*	*	*	*	*	*	*
2	-	*	*	*	*	*	*	*	*	-

Method of difference, sufficient condition.

III.

1. By the method of agreement, D is the cause in the sense of a necessary condition.
4. By an unnamed method, D is the cause in the sense of a sufficient condition.

5

Probability

Theories of Probability

Probability is a topic that is central to the question of induction, but like causality, it has different meanings. Consider the following statements:

> The probability of picking a spade from a full deck of cards is one-fourth.
>
> The probability that a twenty-year-old man will live to age seventy-five is .63.
>
> There is a high probability that Margaret and Peter will get married.

In each statement the word "probability" is used in a different sense. This difference stems from the fact that a different procedure is used in each case to determine or estimate the probability. To determine the probability of picking a spade from a deck of cards, a purely mathematical procedure is used. Given that there are fifty-two cards in a deck and thirteen are spades, thirteen is divided by fifty-two to obtain one-fourth. A different procedure is used to determine the probability that a twenty-year-old man will live to age seventy-five. For this, one must sample a large number of twenty-year-old men and count the number that live fifty-five more years. Yet a different procedure is used to determine the probability that Margaret and Peter will get married. This probability can only be estimated roughly, and doing so requires that we become acquainted with Margaret and Peter and with how they feel toward each other and toward marriage. These three procedures give rise to three distinct theories about probability: the classical theory, the relative frequency theory, and the subjectivist theory.

The **classical theory of probability** traces its origin to the work of the seventeenth-century mathematicians Blaise Pascal and Pierre de Fermat in determining the betting odds for a game of chance. The theory is otherwise called the *a priori theory of probability* because the computations are made independently of any sensory observation of actual events. According to the classical theory, the probability of an event A is given by the formula

$$P(A) = \frac{f}{n}$$

where f is the number of favorable outcomes and n is the number of possible outcomes. For example, in computing the probability of drawing an ace from a poker deck, the number of favorable outcomes is four (because there are four aces) and the number of possible outcomes is fifty-two (because there are fifty-two cards in the deck). Thus, the probability of that event is 4/52 or 1/13 (or .077).

It is important not to confuse the probability of an event's happening with the betting odds of its happening. For events governed by the classical theory, the fair betting odds that an event A will happen is given by the formula

$$\text{odds}(A) = f{:}u$$

where f is the number of favorable outcomes, and u is the number of unfavorable outcomes. For example, the fair betting odds of drawing an ace from a poker deck is 4 to 48, or 1 to 12, since there are four aces and 48 cards that are not aces. Or suppose that five horses are running a race; three are yours, two are your friend's, and there is an equal chance of any of the horses winning. The fair betting odds that one of your horses will win is 3 to 2, whereas the probability that one of your horses will win is 3/5.

Given that you and your friend accept these betting odds, if you bet $3 that one of your horses wins, and you win the bet, your friend must pay you $2. On the other hand, the odds that one of your friend's horses will win is 2 to 3, so if your friend bets $2 that one of her horses wins, and she wins the bet, then you must pay her $3.

Two assumptions are involved in computing probabilities and betting odds according to the classical theory: (1) that all possible outcomes are taken into account and (2) that all possible outcomes are equally probable. In the card example the first assumption entails that only the fifty-two ordinary outcomes are possible. In other words, it is assumed that the deck has not been altered, that the cards will not suddenly self-destruct or reproduce, and so on. In the racing example, the first assumption entails that no other horses are running in the race, and that none of the horses will simply vanish.

The second assumption, which is otherwise called the **principle of indifference,** entails for the card example that there is an equal likelihood of selecting any card. In other words, it is assumed that the cards are stacked evenly, that no two are glued together, and so on. For the horse race example, the second principle entails that each of the horses has an equal chance of winning.

Whenever these two assumptions can be made about the occurrence of an event, the classical theory can be used to compute its probability or the odds of its happening. Here are some additional examples:

P(a fair coin turning up heads) = 1/2	odds = 1:1
P(drawing a face card) = 12/52 = 3/13	odds = 12:40 = 3:10
P(a single die coming up "3") = 1/6	odds = 1:5
P(a single die coming up even) = 3/6 = 1/2	odds = 1:1

Strictly speaking, of course, the two assumptions underlying the classical theory are never perfectly reflected in any actual situation. Every coin is slightly off balance, as is every pair of dice. As a result, the probabilities of the various outcomes are never exactly equal. Similarly, the outcomes are never strictly confined to the normal ones entailed by the first assumption. When tossing a coin, there is always the possibility that the coin will land on edge, and in rolling dice there is the analogous possibility that one of them might break in half. These outcomes may not be possible in the *practical* sense, but they are *logically* possible in that they do not involve any contradiction. Because these outcomes are so unusual, however, it is reasonable to think that for all practical purposes the two assumptions hold and that therefore the classical theory is applicable.

There are many events, however, for which the two assumptions required by the classical theory obviously do not hold. For example, in attempting to determine the probability of a sixty-year-old woman dying of a heart attack within ten years, it would be virtually impossible to take account of all the possible outcomes. She might die of cancer, pneumonia, or an especially virulent case of the flu. She might be incapacitated by a car accident, or she might move to Florida and buy a house on the beach. Furthermore, none of these outcomes is equally probable in comparison with the others. To compute the probability of events such as these we need the relative frequency theory.

The **relative frequency theory of probability** originated with the use of mortality tables by life insurance companies in the eighteenth century. In contrast with the classical theory, which rests upon a priori computations, the relative frequency theory depends on actual observations of the frequency with which certain events happen. The probability of an event A is given by the formula

$$P(A) = \frac{f_o}{n_o}$$

where f_o is the number of *observed* favorable outcomes and n_o is the total number of *observed* outcomes. For example, to determine the probability that a fifty-year-old man will live five more years, a sample of 1,000 fifty-year-old men could be observed. If 968 were alive five years later, the probability that a fifty-year-old man will live an additional five years is 968/1000 or .968.

Similarly, if one wanted to determine the probability that a certain irregularly shaped pyramid with different colored sides would, when rolled, come to rest with the green side down, the pyramid could be rolled 1,000 times. If it came to rest with its green side down 327 times, the probability of this event happening would be computed to be .327.

The relative frequency method can also be used to compute the probability of the kinds of events that conform to the requirements of the classical theory. For example, the probability of a coin coming up heads could be determined by tossing the coin 100 times and counting the heads. If, after this many tosses, 46 heads have been recorded, one might assign a probability of .46 to this event. This leads us to an important point about the relative frequency theory: The results hold true only in the long run. It might be necessary to toss the coin 1,000 or even 10,000 times to get a close approximation. After 10,000 tosses one would expect to count close to 5,000 heads. If in fact only 4,623 heads have been recorded, one would probably be justified in concluding that the coin is off balance or that something was irregular in the way it had been tossed.

Strictly speaking, neither the classical method nor the relative frequency method can assign a probability to individual events. From the standpoint of these approaches only certain *kinds* or *classes* of events have probabilities. But many events in the actual world are unique—for example, Margaret's marrying Peter or Native Prancer's winning the fourth race at Churchill Downs. To interpret the probability of these events we turn to the subjectivist theory.

The **subjectivist theory of probability** interprets the meaning of probability in terms of the beliefs of individual people. Although such beliefs are vague and nebulous, they may be given quantitative interpretation through the odds that a person would accept on a bet. For example, if a person believes that a certain horse will win a race and he or she is willing to give 7 to 4 odds on that event happening, this means that he or she has assigned a probability of 7/(7+4) or 7/11 to that event. This procedure is unproblematic as long as the person is consistent in giving odds on the same event *not* happening. If, for example, 7 to 4 odds are given that an event will happen and 5 to 4 odds that it will not happen, the individual who gives these odds will inevitably lose. If 7 to 4 odds are given that an event *will* happen, no better than 4 to 7 odds can be given that the same event will *not* happen.

One of the difficulties surrounding the subjectivist theory is that one and the same event can be said to have different probabilities, depending on the willingness of different people to give different odds. If probabilities are taken to be genuine attributes of events, this would seem to be a serious problem. The problem might be avoided, though, either by interpreting probabilities as attributes of beliefs or by taking the average of the various individual probabilities as *the* probability of the event.

11.2   The Probability Calculus

The three theories discussed thus far—the classical theory, the relative frequency theory, and the subjectivist theory—provide separate procedures for assigning a probability to an event (or class of events). Sometimes one theory is more readily applicable, sometimes another. But once individual events have been given a probability, the groundwork has been laid for computing the probabilities of compound arrangements of events. This is done by means of what is called the **probability calculus.** In this respect the probability calculus functions analogously to the set of truth-functional rules in propositional logic. Just as the truth-functional rules allow us to compute the truth values of compound propositions from the individual truth values of the simple components, the rules of the probability calculus allow us to compute the probability of compound events from the individual probabilities of the simple events.

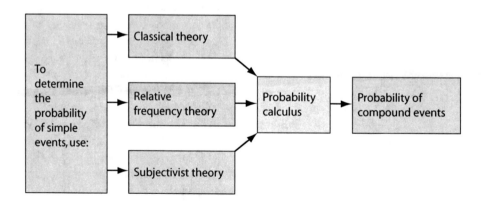

Two preliminary rules of the probability calculus are (1) the probability of an event that must necessarily happen is taken to be 1, and (2) the probability of an event that necessarily cannot happen is taken to be 0. For example, the event consisting of it either raining or not raining (at the same time and place) has a probability of 1, and the event consisting of it both raining and not raining (at the same time and place) has a probability of 0. These events correspond to statements that are tautological and self-contradictory, respectively. Contingent events, on the other hand, have probabilities greater than 0 but less than 1. For example, the probability that the Dow Jones Industrial Average will end a certain week at least five points higher than the previous week would usually be around 1/2, the probability that the polar ice cap will melt next year is very close to 0, and the probability that a traffic accident will occur somewhere tomorrow is very close to 1. Let us now consider six additional rules of the probability calculus.

1. Restricted Conjunction Rule

The **restricted conjunction rule** is used to compute the probability of two events occurring together when the events are *independent* of each other. Two events are said to be independent when the occurrence of one has no effect on the probability of the other one occurring. Examples include getting two heads from two tosses of a coin, drawing two hearts from a deck when the first is replaced before the second is drawn, and playing two sequential games of poker or roulette. The probability of two such events A and B occurring together is given by the formula

$$P(A \text{ and } B) = P(A) \times P(B)$$

For example, the probability of tossing two heads on a single throw of two coins is

$$P(H_1 \text{ and } H_2) = 1/2 \times 1/2 = 1/4$$

This result may be checked very easily by listing all the possible outcomes and comparing that number with the number of favorable outcomes:

Coin 1	Coin 2
H	H
H	T
T	H
T	T

Only one of the four possible outcomes shows both coins turning up heads.

Similarly, we may compute the probability of rolling two sixes with a pair of dice:

$$P(S_1 \text{ and } S_2) = 1/6 \times 1/6 = 1/36$$

Again, we may check the results by listing all the possible outcomes:

1-1	2-1	3-1	4-1	5-1	6-1
1-2	2-2	3-2	4-2	5-2	6-2
1-3	2-3	3-3	4-3	5-3	6-3
1-4	2-4	3-4	4-4	5-4	6-4
1-5	2-5	3-5	4-5	5-5	6-5
1-6	2-6	3-6	4-6	5-6	6-6

Since only one of the thirty-six possible outcomes shows two sixes together, the probability of this event is 1/36.

2. General Conjunction Rule

The **general conjunction rule** is used to compute the probability of two events occurring together whether or not the events are independent. When the events are independent, the general conjunction rule reduces to the restricted conjunction rule. Some examples of events that are not independent (that is, that are *dependent*) are drawing two spades from a deck on two draws when the first card drawn is not replaced, and selecting two or more window seats on an airplane. After the first card is drawn, the number of cards available for the second draw is reduced, and after one of the seats is taken on the plane, the number of seats remaining for subsequent choices is reduced. In other words, in both cases the second event is dependent on the first. The formula for computing the probability of two such events occurring together is

$$P(A \text{ and } B) = P(A) \times P(B \text{ given } A)$$

The expression $P(B \text{ given } A)$ is the probability that B will occur on the assumption that A has already occurred. Let us suppose, for example, that A and B designate the events of drawing two kings from a deck when the first card is not replaced before the second is drawn. If event A occurs, then only three kings remain, and the deck is also reduced to fifty-one cards. Thus, $P(B \text{ given } A)$ is 3/51. Since the probability of event A is 4/52, the probability of both events happening is the product of these two fractions, or 12/2652 (= 1/221).

For another illustration, consider an urn containing five red balls, six green balls, and seven yellow balls. The probability of drawing two red balls (without replacement) is computed as follows:

$$P(R_1 \text{ and } R_2) = 5/18 \times 4/17 = 20/306 = 10/153$$

If a red ball is selected on the first draw, this leaves four red balls from a total of seventeen. Thus, the probability of drawing a second red ball if one has already been drawn is 4/17.

For another example, consider the same urn with the same contents, but let us compute the probability of drawing first a green ball and then a yellow ball (without replacement):

$$P(G \text{ and } Y) = 6/18 \times 7/17 = 42/306 = 7/51$$

If a green ball is selected on the first draw, this affects the selection of a yellow ball on the second draw only to the extent of reducing the total number of balls to seventeen.

3. Restricted Disjunction Rule

The **restricted disjunction rule** is used to compute the probability of either of two events occurring when the events are *mutually exclusive*—that is, when they cannot both occur. Examples of such events include picking either an ace or a king from a deck of cards on a single draw or rolling either a six or a one on a single roll of a die. The probability is given by the formula

$$P(A \text{ or } B) = P(A) + P(B)$$

For example, the probability of drawing either a king or a queen (of any suit) from a deck of cards on a single draw is

$$P(K \text{ or } Q) = 4/52 + 4/52 = 8/52 = 2/13$$

For another example, consider an urn containing six black balls, four white balls, and two red balls. The probability of selecting either a black or red ball on a single draw is

$$P(B \text{ or } R) = 6/12 + 2/12 = 8/12 = 2/3$$

When the event in question is one that must *necessarily* occur, the probability is, of course, 1. Thus, the probability of obtaining either heads or tails on a single toss of a coin is

$$P(H \text{ or } T) = 1/2 + 1/2 = 1$$

The restricted disjunction rule may be combined with the restricted conjunction rule to compute the probability of getting either a five or a six on each of two consecutive rolls of a single die:

$$
\begin{aligned}
P[(F \text{ or } S)_1 \text{ and } (F \text{ or } S)_2] &= P(F \text{ or } S)_1 \times P(F \text{ or } S)_2 \\
&= (1/6 + 1/6) \times (1/6 + 1/6) \\
&= 1/3 \times 1/3 \\
&= 1/9
\end{aligned}
$$

Since getting a five and getting a six on a single die are mutually exclusive events, $P(F \text{ or } S)_1$ is evaluated using the restricted disjunction rule. The same is true of $P(F \text{ or } S)_2$. Then, since two rolls of a die are independent events, the conjunction of the two disjunctive events is evaluated by the restricted conjunction rule.

4. General Disjunction Rule

The **general disjunction rule** is used to compute the probability of either of two events whether or not they are mutually exclusive. The rule holds for any two events, but since its application is simplified when the events are independent, we will confine our attention to events of this kind. Examples of independent events that are not mutually exclusive include obtaining at least one head on two tosses of a coin, drawing at least one king from a deck on two draws when the first card is replaced before the second card is drawn, and getting at least one six when rolling a pair of dice. The formula for computing the probability of either of two such events is

$$P(A \text{ or } B) = P(A) + P(B) - P(A \text{ and } B)$$

If the events are independent, $P(A \text{ and } B)$ is computed using the restricted conjunction rule, and the general disjunction formula reduces to

$$P(A \text{ or } B) = P(A) + P(B) - [P(A) \times P(B)]$$

The general disjunction rule may be proved as follows. When A and B are nonexclusive, A occurs either with or without B, and B occurs either with or without A. Thus,

$$P(A) = P(A \text{ and } B) + P(A \text{ and not-}B)$$
$$P(B) = P(B \text{ and } A) + P(B \text{ and not-}A)$$

But A or B occurs in exactly three possible ways: A and not-B, B and not-A, and A and B. Thus,

$$P(A \text{ or } B) = P(A \text{ and not-}B) + P(B \text{ and not-}A) + P(A \text{ and } B)$$

Thus, when $P(A \text{ and } B)$ is subtracted from $P(A) + P(B)$, the difference is equal to $P(A \text{ or } B)$. [Note: $P(A \text{ and } B) = P(B \text{ and } A)$.]

For an example of the use of the general disjunction rule let us consider the probability of getting heads on either of two tosses of a coin. We have

$$P(H_1 \text{ or } H_2) = 1/2 + 1/2 - (1/2 \times 1/2)$$
$$= 1 - 1/4$$
$$= 3/4$$

For another example, consider the probability of getting at least one six when rolling a pair of dice. The computation is

$$P(S_1 \text{ or } S_2) = 1/6 + 1/6 - (1/6 \times 1/6)$$
$$= 2/6 - 1/36$$
$$= 11/36$$

The general disjunction rule may be combined with the restricted disjunction rule to compute the probability of getting either a three or a five when rolling a pair of dice. This is the probability of getting either a three or a five on the first die or either a three or a five on the second:

$$P[(T \text{ or } F)_1 \text{ or } (T \text{ or } F)_2] = P(T \text{ or } F)_1 + P(T \text{ or } F)_2 - [P(T \text{ or } F)_1 \times P(T \text{ or } F)_2]$$
$$= (1/6 + 1/6) + (1/6 + 1/6) - [(1/6 + 1/6) \times (1/6 + 1/6)]$$
$$= 2/6 + 2/6 - 4/36$$
$$= 20/36$$
$$= 5/9$$

Since getting a three or getting a five on a single throw are mutually exclusive events, $P(T \text{ or } F)_1$ is equal to the sum of the separate probabilities. The same is true for $P(T \text{ or } F)_2$.

The general disjunction rule may be combined with the general conjunction rule to compute the probability of drawing first a red ball and then a black ball on pairs of draws from either of two urns (without replacement). Suppose that the first urn contains two red balls, two black balls, and one green ball, and that the second urn contains three red balls, one black ball, and one white ball. The probability, giving two draws per urn, is

$$P[(R \text{ and } B)_1 \text{ or } (R \text{ and } B)_2]$$
$$= P(R \text{ and } B)_1 + P(R \text{ and } B)_2 - [P(R \text{ and } B)_1 \times P(R \text{ and } B)_2]$$
$$= (2/5 \times 2/4) + (3/5 \times 1/4) - [(2/5 \times 2/4) \times (3/5 \times 1/4)]$$
$$= 4/20 + 3/20 - (4/20 \times 3/20)$$
$$= 7/20 - 12/400$$
$$= 8/25$$

5. Negation Rule

The **negation rule** is useful for computing the probability of an event when the probability of the event *not* happening is either known or easily computed. The formula is as follows:

$$P(A) = 1 - P(\text{not-}A)$$

The formula can be proved very easily. By the restricted disjunction rule the probability of A or not-A is

$$P(A \text{ or not-}A) = P(A) + P(\text{not-}A)$$

But since A or not-A happens necessarily, $P(A \text{ or not-}A) = 1$. Thus,

$$1 = P(A) + P(\text{not-}A)$$

Rearranging the terms in this equation gives us the negation rule. For an example of the use of this rule, consider the probability of getting heads at least once on two tosses of a coin. The probability of the event *not* happening, which is the probability of getting tails on both tosses, is immediately computed by the restricted conjunction rule to be 1/4. Then, applying the negation rule, we have

$$P(H_1 \text{ or } H_2) = 1 - 1/4$$
$$= 3/4$$

The negation rule may also be used to compute the probabilities of disjunctive events that are *dependent*. In presenting the general disjunction rule we confined our attention to *independent* events. Let us suppose we are given an urn containing two black balls and three white balls. To compute the probability of getting at least one black ball on two draws (without replacement), we first compute the probability of the event not happening. This event consists in drawing two white balls, which, by the general conjunction rule, has the probability

$$P(W_1 \text{ and } W_2) = 3/5 \times 2/4 = 6/20$$

Now, applying the negation rule, the probability of getting at least one black ball on two draws is

$$P(B_1 \text{ or } B_2) = 1 - 6/20$$
$$= 14/20$$
$$= 7/10$$

For an example that is only slightly more complex, consider an urn containing two white, two black, and two red balls. To compute the probability of getting either a white or black ball on two draws (without replacement) we first compute the probability of the event not happening. This is the probability of getting red balls on both draws, which is

$$P(R_1 \text{ and } R_2) = 2/6 \times 1/5 = 2/30 = 1/15$$

Now, by the negation rule the probability of drawing either a white or black ball is

$$P(W \text{ or } B) = 1 - 1/15$$
$$= 14/15$$

6. Bayes's Theorem

Bayes's theorem, named after the eighteenth-century English clergyman Thomas Bayes, is a useful rule for evaluating the conditional probability of two or more mutually exclusive and jointly exhaustive events. The conditional probability of an event is the probability of that event happening given that another event has already happened, and it is expressed $P(A$ given $B)$. You may recall that an expression of this form occurred in the formulation of the general conjunction rule. When the number of mutually exclusive and jointly exhaustive events is limited to two, which we will designate A_1 and A_2, Bayes's theorem is expressed as follows:

$$P(A_1 \text{ given } B) = \frac{P(A_1) \times P(B \text{ given } A_1)}{[P(A_1) \times P(B \text{ given } A_1)] + [P(A_2) \times P(B \text{ given } A_2)]}$$

This limited formulation of Bayes's theorem may be proved as follows. Applying the general conjunction rule to the events A_1 and B, we have

$$P(A_1 \text{ and } B) = P(A_1) \times P(B \text{ given } A_1)$$

Applying the same rule to the same events written in the reverse order, we have

$$P(B \text{ and } A_1) = P(B) \times P(A_1 \text{ given } B)$$

Now, since $P(A_1$ and $B)$ is equal to $P(B$ and $A_1)$, we may set the right-hand side of these two equations equal to each other:

$$P(B) \times P(A_1 \text{ given } B) = P(A_1) \times P(B \text{ given } A_1)$$

Dividing both sides of this equation by $P(B)$, we have

$$P(A_1 \text{ given } B) = \frac{P(A_1) \times P(B \text{ given } A_1)}{P(B)} \tag{*}$$

Now, it can be easily proved using a truth table that B is logically equivalent to the expression $[(A_1$ and $B)$ or (not-A_1 and $B)]$. Furthermore, since A_1 and A_2 are mutually exclusive and jointly exhaustive, one and only one of them will happen. Thus, A_2 is simply another way of writing not-A_1. Accordingly, the former expression in brackets can be written $[(A_1$ and $B)$ or $(A_2$ and $B)]$, and since this expression is logically equivalent to B,

$$P(B) = P[(A_1 \text{ and } B) \text{ or } (A_2 \text{ and } B)]$$

Now, applying the general conjunction rule and the restricted disjunction rule to the right-hand side of this equation, we have

$$P(B) = [P(A_1) \times P(B \text{ given } A_1)] + [P(A_2) \times P(B \text{ given } A_2)]$$

Finally, substituting the right-hand side of this equation in place of $P(B)$ in the earlier equation marked (*), we have Bayes's theorem:

$$P(A_1 \text{ given } B) = \frac{P(A_1) \times P(B \text{ given } A_1)}{[P(A_1) \times P(B \text{ given } A_1)] + [P(A_2) \times P(B \text{ given } A_2)]}$$

For an illustration of the use of Bayes's theorem, suppose we are given one beige urn and four gray urns in a dimly lit room, so we cannot distinguish one color from the other. The beige urn contains eight red and two white balls, and each of the gray urns contains three red and seven white balls. Suppose that a red ball is drawn from one of these five urns. What is the probability that the urn was beige? In other words, we want to know the probability that the urn was beige given that a red ball was drawn. The events A_1 and A_2 in Bayes's theorem correspond to drawing a ball from either a beige urn or a gray urn. Substituting B and G for A_1 and A_2, respectively, we have

$$P(B \text{ given } R) = \frac{P(B) \times P(R \text{ given } B)}{[P(B) \times P(R \text{ given } B)] + [P(G) \times P(R \text{ given } G)]}$$

Now, since there are a total of five urns, the probability of randomly selecting the beige urn is 1/5, and the probability of randomly selecting one of the gray urns is 4/5. Finally, since each urn contains ten balls, the probability of drawing a red ball from the beige urn is 8/10, and the probability of drawing a red ball from the gray urn is 3/10. Thus, we have

$$P(B \text{ given } R) = \frac{1/5 \times 8/10}{(1/5 \times 8/10) + (4/5 \times 3/10)}$$

$$= \frac{8/50}{8/50 + 12/50} = \frac{8/50}{20/50} = 8/20 = .40$$

Bayes's theorem is quite practical because it allows us to change our probability estimates of ordinary events as new information is acquired. For an example of how Bayes's theorem is used for this purpose, consider the following example:

> Mr. Jones became seriously ill from ingesting defectively manufactured tablets of the painkiller novaprine. He intends to file a lawsuit against the most probable manufacturer of the tablets. After a brief investigation, he finds that 70 percent of the novaprine sold in this country is manufactured by Alpha Pharmaceuticals, and 30 percent is manufactured by Beta Pharmaceuticals.

From this information the probability that Alpha Pharmaceuticals manufactured the tablets is .70, in comparison with .30 for Beta Pharmaceuticals. Thus, Mr. Jones tentatively decides to file his lawsuit against Alpha. However, on further investigation Mr. Jones discovers the following:

> Of the novaprine manufactured by Alpha, 10 percent is sold on the East Coast and 90 percent on the West Coast, while 80 percent of Beta's novaprine is sold on the East Coast and 20 percent on the West Coast. Furthermore, Mr. Jones recalls that he purchased his novaprine on the East Coast.

Clearly this new information affects Mr. Jones's original probability estimate. We use Bayes's Theorem to recompute the probability that Alpha manufactured the defective tablets given that the tablets were purchased on the East Coast as follows:

$$P(A \text{ given } E) = \frac{P(A) \times P(E \text{ given } A)}{[P(A) \times P(E \text{ given } A)] + [P(B) \times P(E \text{ given } B)]}$$

For $P(A)$ and $P(B)$ we use the original probabilities of .70 and .30, respectively. The probability that the tablets were purchased on the East Coast given that they were manufactured by Alpha is .10, and the probability that they were purchased on the East Coast given that they were manufactured by Beta is .80. Thus, we have

$$P(A \text{ given } E) = \frac{.70 \times 10}{(.70 \times 10) + (.30 \times 80)} = \frac{.07}{.07 + .24} = .07/.31 = .23$$

The new information that Mr. Jones acquired has significantly affected the probability that Alpha manufactured the defective tablets. The probability has dropped from .70 to .23. With this new information, it is more likely that Beta manufactured the tablets, so Mr. Jones should now file his lawsuit against Beta. The probability for Beta is $1 - .23$, or .77.

The earlier probability for Alpha (.70) is called the *prior* probability, and the later figure (.23) is called the *posterior* probability. If Mr. Jones should acquire even more information, the posterior probability becomes a new prior, and it is used as the value for $P(A)$ in a subsequent application of Bayes's theorem.

Additional Applications

Most of the examples considered thus far have used the classical theory to determine the probability of the component events. But as was mentioned earlier, the probability calculus can also be used in conjunction with the relative frequency theory and the subjectivist theory. If we apply the relative frequency theory to the mortality tables used by insurance companies, we find that the probability of a twenty-five-year-old man living an additional forty years is .82, and the probability of a twenty-five-year-old woman living the same number of years is .88. To compute the probability of such a man and woman both living that long, we use the restricted conjunction rule and obtain $.82 \times 88 = .72$. For the probability that either of these people would live that long, we use the general disjunction rule and obtain

$$.82 + .88 - (.82 \times 88) = .98$$

Let us suppose that these two people are married and both would give 9 to 1 odds on their staying married for forty years. This translates into a probability of $9/(9 + 1)$ or .90. Using the restricted conjunction rule, the probability of this event happening is the product of the latter figure and the probability of their both living that long, or .65.

For an example involving the subjectivist theory, if the Philadelphia Eagles are given 7 to 5 odds of winning the NFC championship, and the New England Patriots are given 3 to 2 odds of winning the AFC championship, the probability that at least one of these teams will win is computed using the general disjunction rule. The odds translate respectively into probabilities of $7/12$ and $3/5$, and so the probability of the disjunction is $7/12 + 3/5 - (7/12 \times 3/5) = 5/6$. The probability that the two teams will meet in the Super Bowl (that both will win their conference championship) is, by the restricted conjunction rule, $7/12 \times 3/5 = 21/60$, or $7/20$. The probability that neither will play in the Super Bowl is, by the negation rule, $1 - 5/6 = 1/6$.

   The probability calculus can also be used to evaluate the strength of inductive arguments. Consider the following:

> The Philadelphia Eagles are given 7 to 5 odds of winning the NFC championship. The
> New England Patriots are given 3 to 2 odds of winning the AFC championship.
> Therefore, the Eagles and the Patriots will meet in the Super Bowl.

On the assumption that the premises are true, that is, on the assumption that the odds are reported correctly, the conclusion follows with a probability of 7/20 or .35. Thus, the argument is not particularly strong. But if the odds given in the premises should increase, the strength of the argument would increase proportionately. The premises of the following argument give different odds:

> The Philadelphia Eagles are given 7 to 2 odds of winning the NFC championship. The
> New England Patriots are given 8 to 3 odds of winning the AFC championship.
> Therefore, the Eagles and the Patriots will meet in the Super Bowl.

In this argument, if the premises are assumed true, the conclusion follows with a probability of $7/9 \times 8/11 = 56/99$, or .57. Thus, the argument is at least moderately strong.

   Lest this procedure be misinterpreted, however, we should recall a point raised in Chapter 1. The strength of an inductive argument depends not merely on whether the conclusion is probably true but on whether the conclusion follows probably from the premises. As a result, to evaluate the strength of an inductive argument it is not sufficient merely to know the probability of the conclusion on the assumption that the premises are true. One must also know whether the probability of the conclusion rests on the evidence given in the premises. If the probability of the conclusion does not rest on this evidence, the argument is weak regardless of whether the conclusion is probably true. The following argument is a case in point:

> All dogs are animals. Therefore, probably a traffic accident will occur somewhere
> tomorrow.

The conclusion of this argument is probably true independently of the premises, so the argument is weak.

   In this connection the analogy between deductive and inductive arguments breaks down. As we saw in Chapter 6, any argument having a conclusion that is necessarily true is deductively valid regardless of the content of its premises. But any inductive argument having a probably true conclusion is not strong unless the probability of the conclusion rests on the evidence given in the premises.

   A final comment is in order about the material covered in this chapter. Probability is one of those subjects about which there is little agreement among philosophers. Some philosophers defend each of the theories we have discussed as providing the only acceptable approach, and there are numerous views regarding the fine points of each. However, some philosophers argue that there are certain uses of "probability" that none of these theories can interpret. The statement "There is high probability that Einstein's theory of relativity is correct" may be a case in point. In any event, the various theories about the meaning of probability, as well as the details of the probability calculus, are highly complex subjects, and the brief account given here has merely scratched the surface.

EXERCISE 11

I. Compute probabilities or odds for the following simple events:

★1. What is the probability of rolling a five on a single roll of a die? What are the odds for this event?

2. From a sample of 9,750 Ajax trucks, 273 developed transmission problems within the first two years of operation. What is the probability that an Ajax truck will develop transmission problems within the first two years?

3. If the standard odds are 8 to 5 that the Chargers will beat the Lions, what is the probability that this event will happen?

★4. From a sample of 7,335 seventy-five-year-old women, 6,260 lived an additional five years. What is the probability that a seventy-five-year-old woman will live to age eighty?

5. What is the probability of picking a black jack from a poker deck (without jokers) on a single draw?

6. If the probability of the Red Sox beating the Tigers is 6/17, what are the odds for this event?

★7. Given an urn containing three red balls, four green balls, and five yellow balls, what is the probability of drawing a red ball on a single draw?

8. If the odds of the Broncos beating the Dolphins is 5 to 4, and you bet $10 on the Broncos, how much do you stand to win?

9. Given an urn containing four red balls, three green balls, and five yellow balls, what are the odds of drawing a red ball on a single draw?

★10. Suppose you give 1:6 odds that you can roll a "1" with a single fair die. If someone accepts your bet, how much could you expect to win after 100 rolls if you bet $1 on each roll?

II. Compute probabilities for the following compound events:

★1. What is the probability of getting either a six or a one from a single roll of a die?

2. What is the probability of getting heads on three successive tosses of a coin?

3. What is the probability of drawing either a king or a queen from a poker deck (no jokers) on a single draw?

★4. What is the probability of drawing two aces from a poker deck in two draws
   a. If the first card is replaced before the second is drawn?
   b. If the first card is not replaced before the second is drawn?

5. What is the probability of drawing at least one ace from a poker deck on two draws if the first card is replaced before the second is drawn?

6. What is the probability of getting at least one head on three tosses of a coin?

★7. What is the probability of getting at least one six on three rolls of a die?

8. If a pair of dice are rolled, what is the probability that the points add up to
   a. 5?
   b. 6?
   c. 7?

9. Given two urns, one containing two red, three green, and four yellow balls, the other containing four red, two green, and three yellow balls, if a single ball is drawn from each urn, what is the probability that

   a. Both are red?

   b. At least one is green?

   c. One is red, the other yellow?

   d. At least one is either red or yellow?

   e. Both are the same color?

★10. Given an urn containing three red, four green, and five yellow balls, if two balls are drawn from the urn (without replacement), what is the probability that

   a. Both are red?

   b. One is green, the other yellow?

   c. One is either red or green?

   d. At least one is green?

   e. Both have the same color?

11. What is the probability of drawing either an ace or a king (or both) on three draws (without replacement) from a poker deck? (Hint: Use the negation rule.)

12. What is the probability of drawing an ace and a king on three draws (without replacement) from a poker deck? (Hint: Use the negation rule.)

★13. The probability of a twenty-year-old man living to age seventy is .74, and the probability of a twenty-year-old woman living to the same age is .82. If a recently married couple, both age twenty, give 8 to 1 odds on their staying married for fifty years, what is the probability that

   a. At least one will live to age seventy?

   b. They will celebrate their golden wedding anniversary?

14. Assign a numerical value to the strength of the following argument: The odds are 5 to 3 that the Indians will win the American League pennant and 7 to 5 that the Cardinals will win the National League pennant. Therefore, the Indians and the Cardinals will meet in the World Series.

15. Assign a numerical value to the strength of the following argument: The Wilson family has four children. Therefore, at least two of the children were born on the same day of the week.

★16. We are given three new urns each containing seven red, five green, and three white balls, and two old urns each containing five red, three green, and seven white balls. The urns are identical except for an old or new date stamped beneath the base. If a single red ball is randomly drawn from one of these urns, was it most probably drawn from an old urn or a new urn? (Hint: For this exercise and the ones that follow, use Bayes's theorem.)

17. Knowing that your friend Angella studies for her tests only 40 percent of the time, you place an even bet with a third party that Angella will not study for her upcoming test. Later, you just happen to hear that Angella passed the test.

Should you retract your bet? Assume that Angella passes nine out of ten tests when she studies, and three out of ten when she does not.

18. A physician has diagnosed a patient as having either hepatitis or liver cancer (but not both). Statistics reveal that hepatitis occurs in the general population twice as frequently as liver cancer. Thus, the physician tentatively concludes that the patient probably has hepatitis. Later the physician conducts a test on the patient that turns out positive. On this test, nine out of ten cases of liver cancer trigger a positive outcome, and one out of six cases of hepatitis triggers a positive outcome. What is the new probability that the patient has liver cancer?

★19. Ms. Jones, a bookstore owner, wishes to send out an advertisement to potential customers. She estimates that 20 percent of the town's residents are recreational readers, and she knows that all of the residents are either recreational readers or TV addicts (but not both). Also, a TV repair person has told her that two of ten TV addicts are newspaper subscribers, and from a survey of her own customers she has learned that seven of ten recreational readers are newspaper subscribers. If Ms. Jones places an ad in the local newspaper, how effective will the ad be? (That is, what is the probability that a newspaper subscriber is a recreational reader?)

20. Mr. Andrews, a grape merchant, inquires about a certain wine that he tastes at a party. The host tells him that from a total of ten bottles of that wine, six came from the north vineyard and four came from the south vineyard. From this information, the merchant concludes that he should visit the north vineyard for a sample of the grapes. Later, he discovers that the wine in question came from a bottle labeled Classic Reserve, and 30 of 100 barrels of north vineyard wine were bottled with that label, while 130 of 200 barrels of south vineyard wine were bottled with that label. Given this new information, what is the probability that the wine came from the north vineyard?

Summary

Probability theory is a branch of mathematics that assigns a numerical figure to the probability of certain occurrences. It comprises the classical theory, which rests on a priori calculations; the relative frequency theory, which depends on empirical experimentation; and the subjectivist theory, which rests on the subjective beliefs of individual people. Once these theories are used to assign a numerical figure to the probability of a simple event, the rules of the probability calculus can be used to calculate the probability of compound events. The conjunction rules compute the probability of two events occurring together, the disjunction rules compute the probability of either of two events occurring, the negation rule computes the probability of an event not happening, the Bayes's theorem computes the conditional probability of two or more mutually exclusive and jointly exhaustive events.

Answers to Selected Exercises

Exercise 11

I.

1. 1/6   **4.** .853   **7.** 1/4 or .25   **10.** Approximately $17

II.

1. $P(6 \text{ or } 1) = P(6) + P(1) = 1/6 + 1/6 = 2/6 = 1/3$

4. a. $P(A_1 \text{ and } A_2) = P(A_1) \times P(A_2)$
$$= 4/52 \times 4/52$$
$$= 1/169 = .0059$$

b. $P(A_1 \text{ and } A_2) = P(A_1) \times P(A_2 \text{ given } A_1)$
$$= 4/52 \times 3/51$$
$$= 1/221 = .0045$$

7. First compute the probability of getting no sixes:
$$P(\text{no sixes}) = 5/6 \times 5/6 \times 5/6$$
$$= 125/216$$

Then use the negation rule:
$$P(\text{at least one six}) = 1 - P(\text{no sixes})$$
$$= 1 - 125/216$$
$$= 91/216 = .4213$$

10. a. $P(R_1 \text{ and } R_2) = P(R_1) \times P(R_2 \text{ given } R_1)$
$$= 3/12 \times 2/11$$
$$= 6/132 = .045$$

b. $P(Y \text{ and } G) = P(Y_1 \text{ and } G_2) + P(G_1 \text{ and } Y_2)$
$$= (5/12 \times 4/11) + (4/12 \times 5/11)$$
$$= 20/132 + 20/132$$
$$= 10/33 = .303$$

c. $P(R \text{ or } G) = 1 - P(Y_1 \text{ and } Y_2)$
$$= 1 - (5/12 \times 4/11)$$
$$= 1 - 20/132$$
$$= 28/33 = .848$$

d. $P(G_1 \text{ or } G_2) = 1 - P(\text{not } G)$

$= 1 - [P(R_1 \text{ and } R_2) + P(R_1 \text{ and } Y_2) + P(Y_1 \text{ and } R_2)$
$\quad + P(Y_1 \text{ and } Y_2)]$

$= 1 - [(3/12 \times 2/11) + (3/12 \times 5/11)$
$\quad + (5/12 \times 3/11) + (5/12 \times 4/11)]$

$= 1 - [6/132 + 15/132 + 15/132 + 20/132]$

$= 1 - 56/132$

$= 19/33 = .57$

e. $P(\text{same color}) = P(R_1 \text{ and } R_2) + P(G_1 \text{ and } G_2) + P(Y_1 \text{ and } Y_2)$

$= (3/12 \times 2/11) + (4/12 \times 3/11) + (5/12 \times 4/11)$

$= 6/132 + 12/132 + 20/132$

$= 19/66 = .288$

13. a. $P(M \text{ or } W) = P(M) + P(W) - P(M \text{ and } W)$

$= .74 + .82 - (.74 \times .82)$

$= .95$

b. $P(M \text{ and } W \text{ and } S) = P(M) \times P(W) \times P(S)$

$= .74 \times .82 \times 8/9$

$= .54$

16. $P(N \text{ given } R) = \dfrac{P(N) \times P(R \text{ given } N)}{[P(N) \times P(R \text{ given } N)] + [P(O) \times P(R \text{ given } O)]}$

$= \dfrac{3/5 \times 7/15}{[3/5 \times 7/15] + [2/5 \times 5/15]} = \dfrac{21/75}{21/75 + 10/75}$

$= \dfrac{21/75}{31/75} = 21/31 = .68$

Answer: new urn.

19. $P(R \text{ given } N) = \dfrac{P(R) \times P(N \text{ given } R)}{[P(R) \times P(N \text{ given } R)] + [P(T) \times P(N \text{ given } T)]}$

$= \dfrac{.2 \times .7}{(.2 \times .7) + (.8 \times .2)} = \dfrac{.14}{.14 + .16} = .14/.30 = .47$

6

Statistical Reasoning

12.1 Evaluating Statistics

In our day-to-day experience all of us encounter arguments that rest on statistical evidence. An especially prolific source of such arguments is the advertising industry. We are constantly told that we ought to sign up with a certain cell phone service because it has 30 percent fewer dropped calls, buy a certain kind of car because it gets 5 percent better gas mileage, and use a certain cold remedy because it is recommended by four out of five physicians. But the advertising industry is not the only source. We often read in the newspapers that some union is asking an increase in pay because its members earn less than the average or that a certain region is threatened with floods because rainfall has been more than the average.

To evaluate such arguments, we must be able to interpret the statistics on which they rest, but doing so is not always easy. Statements expressing averages and percentages are often ambiguous and can mean a variety of things, depending on how the average or percentage is computed. These difficulties are compounded by the fact that statistics provide a highly convenient way for people to deceive one another. Such deceptions can be effective even though they fall short of being outright lies. Thus, to evaluate arguments based on statistics one must be familiar not only with the ambiguities that occur in the language but with the devices that unscrupulous individuals use to deceive others.

This chapter touches on five areas that are frequent sources of such ambiguity and deception: problems in sampling, the meaning of "average," the importance of dispersion in a sample, the use of graphs and pictograms, and the use of percentages for the purpose of comparison. By becoming acquainted with these topics and with some of the misuses that occur, we improve our ability to determine whether a conclusion follows probably from a set of statistical premises.

12.2 Samples

Much of the statistical evidence presented in support of inductively drawn conclusions is gathered from analyzing samples. When a sample is found to possess a certain characteristic, it is argued that the group as a whole (the population) possesses that characteristic. For example, if we wanted to know the opinion of the student body at a certain university about whether to adopt an academic honor code, we could take a poll of 10 percent of the students. If the results of the poll showed that 80 percent of those sampled favored the code, we might draw the conclusion that 80 percent of the entire student body favored it. Such an argument would be classified as an inductive generalization.

The problem that arises with the use of samples has to do with whether the sample is representative of the population. Samples that are not representative are said to be **biased samples.** Depending on what the population consists of, whether machine parts or human beings, different considerations enter into determining whether a sample is biased. These considerations include (1) whether the sample is randomly selected, (2) the size of the sample, and (3) psychological factors.

A **random sample** is one in which every member of the population has an equal chance of being selected. The requirement that a sample be randomly selected applies to practically all samples, but sometimes it can be taken for granted. For example, when a physician draws a blood sample to test for blood sugar, there is no need to take a little bit from the finger, a little from the arm, and a little from the leg. Because blood is a circulating fluid, it can be assumed that it is homogenous in regard to blood sugar.

The randomness requirement requires more attention when the population consists of discrete units. Suppose, for example, that a quality-control engineer for a manufacturing firm needed to determine whether the components on a certain conveyor belt were within specifications. To do so, the engineer removed every tenth component for measurement. The sample obtained by such a procedure would not be random if the components were not randomly arranged on the conveyor belt. As a result of some malfunction in the manufacturing process it is quite possible that every tenth component was perfect and the rest were imperfect. If the engineer happened to select only the perfect ones, the sample would be biased. A selection procedure that would be more likely to ensure a random sample would be to roll a pair of dice and remove every component corresponding to a roll of ten. Since the outcome of a roll of dice is a random event, the selection would also be random. Such a procedure would be more likely to include defective components that turn up at regular intervals.

The randomness requirement presents even greater problems when the population consists of human beings. Suppose, for example, that a public opinion poll is to be conducted on the question of excessive corporate profits. It would hardly do to ask such a question randomly of the people encountered on Wall Street in New York City. Such a sample would almost certainly be biased in favor of the corporations. A less biased sample could be obtained by randomly selecting phone numbers from the telephone directory, but even this procedure would not yield a completely random sample. Among other things, the time of day in which a call is placed influences the kind of responses obtained. Most people who are employed full-time are not available during the day, and even if calls are made at night, a large percentage of the population have unlisted numbers.

A poll conducted by mail based on the addresses listed in the city directory would also yield a fairly random sample, but this method, too, has shortcomings. Many apartment dwellers are not listed, and others move before the directory is printed. Furthermore, none of those who live in rural areas are listed. In short, it is both difficult and expensive to conduct a large-scale public opinion poll that succeeds in obtaining responses from anything approximating a random sample of individuals.

A classic case of a poll that turned out to be biased in spite of a good deal of effort and expense occurred when the *Literary Digest* magazine undertook a poll to predict the outcome of the 1936 presidential election. The sample consisted of a large number of the magazine's subscribers together with other people selected from the telephone directory. Because four similar polls had picked the winner in previous years, the results of this poll were highly respected. As it turned out, however, the Republican candidate, Alf Landon, got a significant majority in the poll, but Franklin D. Roosevelt won the election by a landslide. The incorrect prediction is explained by the fact that the 1936 election occurred in the middle of the Depression, at a time when many people could afford neither a telephone nor a subscription to the *Digest*. These were the people who were overlooked in the poll, and they were also the ones who voted for Roosevelt.

Size is also an important factor in determining whether a sample is representative. Given that a sample is randomly selected, the larger the sample, the more closely it replicates the population. In statistics, this degree of closeness is expressed in terms of sampling error. The **sampling error** is the difference between the relative frequency with which some characteristic occurs in the sample and the relative frequency with which the same characteristic occurs in the population. If, for example, a poll were taken of a labor union and 60 percent of the members sampled expressed their intention to vote for Smith for president but in fact only 55 percent of the whole union intended to vote for Smith, the sampling error would be 5 percent. If a larger sample were taken, the error would be smaller.

Just how large a sample should be is a function of the size of the population and of the degree of sampling error that can be tolerated. For a sampling error of, say, 5 percent, a population of 10,000 would require a larger sample than would a population of 100. However, the ratio is not linear. To obtain the same precision, the sample for the larger population need not be 100 times as large as the one for the smaller population. When the population is very large, the size of the sample needed to ensure a certain precision levels off at a constant figure. Studies based on the Gallup poll show that a random sample of 400 will yield results of plus or minus 6 percent whether the population is 100,000 or 100 million. Additional figures for large populations are given in Table 12.1:

Table 12.1 Sample Size and Sampling Error*

Number of interviews	Margin of error (in percentage points)
4,000	±2
1,500	±3
1,000	±4
750	±4
600	±5
400	±6
200	±8
100	±11

*From Charles W. Roll Jr. and Albert H. Cantril, *Polls: Their Use and Misuse in Politics* (New York: Basic Books, 1972), p. 72.

As the table indicates, reducing the sampling error below 5 percent requires rather substantial increases in the size of the sample. The cost of obtaining large samples may not justify an increase in precision. The table also points up the importance of randomness. The sample in the 1936 *Literary Digest* poll was based on 2 million responses, yet the sampling error was huge because the sample was not randomly selected.

Statements of sampling error are often conspicuously absent from surveys used to support advertising claims. Marketers of products such as patent medicines have been known to take rather small samples until they obtain one that gives the "right" result. For example, twenty polls of twenty-five people might be taken inquiring about the preferred brand of aspirin. Even though the samples might be randomly selected, one will eventually be found in which twenty of the twenty-five respondents indicate their preference for Alpha brand aspirin. Having found such a sample, the marketing firm proceeds to promote this brand as the one preferred by four out of five of those sampled. The results of the other samples are, of course, discarded, and no mention is made of sampling error.

Psychological factors can also have a bearing on whether the sample is representative. When the population consists of inanimate objects, such as cans of soup or machine parts, psychological factors are usually irrelevant, but they can play a significant role when the population consists of human beings. If the people composing the sample think that they will gain or lose something by the kind of answer they give, their involvement will likely affect the outcome. For example, if the residents of a neighborhood were to be surveyed for annual income with the purpose of determining whether the neighborhood should be ranked among the fashionable areas in the city, we would expect the residents to exaggerate their answers. But if the purpose of the study were to determine whether the neighborhood could afford a special levy that would increase property taxes, we might expect the incomes to be underestimated.

The kind of question asked can also have a psychological bearing. Questions such as "How often do you brush your teeth?" and "How many books do you read in a year?" can be expected to generate responses that overestimate the truth, while "How many times have you been intoxicated?" and "How many extramarital affairs have you had?" would probably receive answers that underestimate the truth. Similar exaggerations can result from the way a question is phrased. For example, "Do you favor a reduction in welfare benefits as a response to rampant cheating?" would be expected to receive more affirmative answers than simply "Do you favor a reduction in welfare benefits?"

Another source of psychological influence is the personal interaction between the surveyor and the respondent. Suppose, for example, that a door-to-door survey were taken to determine how many people believe in God or attend church on Sunday. If the survey were conducted by priests and ministers dressed in clerical garb, one might expect a larger number of affirmative answers than if the survey were taken by nonclerics. The simple fact is that many people like to give answers that please the questioner.

To prevent this kind of interaction from affecting the outcome, scientific studies are often conducted under "double blind" conditions in which neither the surveyor nor the respondent knows what the "right" answer is. For example, in a double blind study to determine the effectiveness of a drug, bottles containing the drug would be mixed with other bottles containing a placebo (sugar tablet). The contents of each bottle would be matched with a code number on the label, and neither the person distributing the bottles nor the person recording the responses would know what the code is. Under these conditions the people conducting the study would not be able to influence, by some smile or gesture, the response of the people to whom the drugs are given.

Most of the statistical evidence encountered in ordinary experience contains no reference to such factors as randomness, sampling error, or the conditions under which the sample was taken. In the absence of such information, the person faced with evaluating the evidence must use his or her best judgment. If either the organization conducting the study or the people composing the sample have something to gain by the kind of answer that is given, the results of the survey should be regarded as suspect. And if the questions that are asked concern topics that would naturally elicit distorted answers, the results should probably be rejected. In either event, the mere fact that a study *appears* scientific or is expressed in mathematical language should never intimidate a person into accepting the results. Numbers and scientific terminology are no substitute for an unbiased sample.

12.3   The Meaning of "Average"

In statistics the word "average" is used in three different senses: mean, median, and mode. In evaluating arguments and inferences that rest on averages, we often need to know in precisely what sense the word is being used.

The **mean** value of a set of data is the arithmetical average. It is computed by dividing the sum of the individual values by the number of values in the set. Suppose, for example, that we are given Table 12.2 listing the ages of a group of people. To compute the mean age, we divide the sum of the individual ages by the number of people:

$$\text{mean age} = \frac{(1 \times 16) + (4 \times 17) + (1 \times 18) + (2 \times 19) + (3 \times 23)}{11} = 19$$

Table 12.2

Number of people	Age
1	16
4	17
1	18
2	19
3	23

The **median** of a set of data is the middle point when the data are arranged in ascending order. In other words, the median is the point at which there is an equal number of data above and below. In Table 12.2 the median age is 18 because there are five people above this age and five below.

The **mode** is the value that occurs with the greatest frequency. Here the mode is 17, because there are four people with that age and fewer people with any other age.

In this example, the mean, median, and mode differ but are all fairly close together. The problem for induction occurs when a great disparity among these values occurs. This sometimes occurs in the case of salaries. Consider, for example, Table 12.3,which

Table 12.3

Capacity	Number of personnel	Salary	
president	1	$275,000	
senior architect	2	150,000	
junior architect	2	80,000	
senior engineer	1	65,000	← mean
junior engineer	4	55,000	
senior draftsman	1	45,000	← median
junior draftsman	10	30,000	← mode

reports the salaries of a hypothetical architectural firm. Since there are twenty-one employees and a total of $1,365,000 is paid in salaries, the mean salary is $1,365,000/21, or $65,000. The median salary is $45,000 because ten employees earn less than this and ten earn more, and the mode, which is the salary that occurs most frequently, is $30,000. Each of these figures represents the "average" salary of the firm, but in different senses. Depending on the purpose for which the average is used, different figures might be cited as the basis for an argument.

For example, if the senior engineer were to request a raise in salary, the president could respond that his or her salary is already well above the average (in the sense of median and mode) and that therefore that person does not deserve a raise. If the junior draftsmen were to make the same request, the president could respond that they are presently earning the firm's average salary (in the sense of mode), and that for draftsmen to be earning the average salary is excellent. Finally, if someone from outside the firm were to allege that the firm pays subsistence-level wages, the president could respond that the average salary of the firm is a hefty $65,000. All of the president's responses would be true, but if the reader or listener were not sophisticated enough to distinguish the various senses of "average," he or she might be persuaded by the arguments.

In some situations, the mode is the most useful average. Suppose, for example, that you are in the market for a three-bedroom house. Suppose further that a real estate agent assures you that the houses in a certain complex have an average of three bedrooms and that therefore you will certainly want to see them. If the agent has used "average" in the sense of mean, it is possible that half the houses in the complex are four-bedroom, the other half are two-bedroom, and there are no three-bedroom houses at all. A similar result is possible if the agent has used average in the sense of median. The only sense of average that would be useful for your purposes is mode: If the modal average is three bedrooms, there are more three-bedroom houses than any other kind.

On other occasions a mean average is the most useful. Suppose, for example, that you have taken a job as a pilot on a plane that has nine passenger seats and a maximum carrying capacity of 1,350 pounds (in addition to yourself). Suppose further that you have arranged to fly a group of nine passengers over the Grand Canyon and that you must determine whether their combined weight is within the required limit. If a representative of the group tells you that the average weight of the passengers is

150 pounds, this by itself tells you nothing. If he means average in the sense of median, it could be the case that the four heavier passengers weigh 200 pounds and the four lighter ones weigh 145, for a combined weight of 1,530 pounds. Similarly, if the passenger representative means average in the sense of mode, it could be that two passengers weigh 150 pounds and that the others have varying weights in excess of 200 pounds, for a combined weight of over 1,700 pounds. Only if the representative means average in the sense of mean do you know that the combined weight of the passengers is 9 ✗ 50 or 1,350 pounds.

Finally, sometimes a median average is the most meaningful. Suppose, for example, that you are a manufacturer of a product that appeals to people under age thirty-five. To increase sales you decide to run an ad in a national magazine, but you want some assurance that the ad will be read by the right age group. If the advertising director of a magazine tells you that the average age of the magazine's readers is 35, you know virtually nothing. If the director means average in the sense of mean, it could be that 90 percent of the readers are over 35 and that the remaining 10 percent bring the average down to 35. Similarly, if the director means average in the sense of mode, it could be that 3 percent of the readers are exactly 35 and that the remaining 97 percent have ages ranging from 35 to 85. Only if the director means average in the sense of median do you know that half the readers are 35 or less.

12.4   Dispersion

Although averages often yield important information about a set of data, there are many cases in which merely knowing the average, in any sense of the term, tells us very little. The reason for this is that the average says nothing about how the data are distributed. For this, we need to know something about **dispersion,** which refers to how spread out the data are in regard to numerical value. Three important measures of dispersion are range, variance, and standard deviation.

Let us first consider the **range** of a set of data, which is the difference between the largest and the smallest values. For an example of the importance of this parameter, suppose that after living for many years in an intemperate climate, you decide to relocate in an area that has a more ideal mean temperature. On discovering that the annual mean temperature of Oklahoma City is 60°F you decide to move there, only to find that you roast in the summer and freeze in the winter. Unfortunately, you had ignored the fact that Oklahoma City has a temperature *range* of 130°, extending from a record low of −17° to a record high of 113°. In contrast, San Nicholas Island, off the coast of California, has a mean temperature of 61° but a range of only 40°, extending from 47° in the winter to 87° in the summer. The temperature ranges for these two locations are approximated in Figure 12.1.

Even granting the importance of the range of the data in this example, however, range really tells us relatively little because it comprehends only two data points, the maximum and minimum. It says nothing about how the other data points are distributed. For this we need to know the **variance,** or the **standard deviation,** which measure how every data point varies or deviates from the mean.

Figure 12.1*

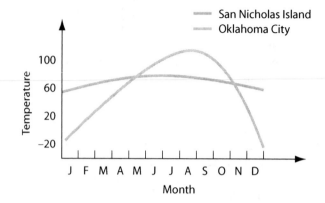

*This example is taken from Darrell Huff, *How to Lie with Statistics* (New York: Norton, 1954), p. 52.

For an example of the importance of these two parameters in describing a set of data, suppose you have a four-year-old child and you are looking for a day-care center that will provide plenty of possible playmates about the same age as your child. After calling several centers on the phone, you narrow the search down to two: the Rumpus Center and the Bumpus Center. Both report that they regularly care for nine children, that the mean and median age of the children is four, and that the range in ages of the children is six. Unable to decide between these two centers, you decide to pay them a visit. Having done so, you see that the Rumpus Center will meet your needs better than the Bumpus Center. The reason is that the ages of the children in the two centers are distributed differently.

The ages of the children in the two centers are as follows:

    Rumpus Center: 1, 3, 3, 4, 4, 4, 5, 5, 7
    Bumpus Center: 1, 1, 2, 2, 4, 6, 6, 7, 7

To illustrate the differences in distribution, these ages can be plotted on a certain kind of bar graph, called a *histogram*, as shown in Figures 12.2a and 12.2b. Obviously the

Figure 12.2a

Figure 12.2b

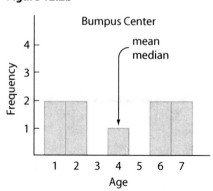

reason why the Rumpus Center comes closer to meeting your needs is that it has seven children within one year of your own child, whereas the Bumpus Center has only one such child. This difference in distribution is measured by the variance and the standard deviation. Computing the value of these parameters for the two centers is quite easy, but first we must introduce some symbols. The standard deviation is represented in statistics by the Greek letter σ (sigma), and the variance, which is the square of the standard deviation, is represented by σ^2. We compute the variance first, which is defined as follows:

$$\sigma^2 = \frac{\sum(x - \mu)^2}{n}$$

In this expression (which looks far more complicated than it is), $\sum$ (uppercase sigma) means "the sum of," x is a variable that ranges over the ages of the children, the Greek letter μ (mu) is the mean age, and n is the number of children. Thus, to compute the variance, we take each of the ages of the children, subtract the mean age (4) from each, square the result of each, add up the squares, and then divide the sum by the number of children (9). The first three steps of this procedure for the Rumpus Center are reported in Table 12.4.

Table 12.4

x	$(x - \mu)$	$(x - \mu)^2$
1	−3	9
3	−1	1
3	−1	1
4	0	0
4	0	0
4	0	0
5	+1	1
5	+1	1
7	+3	9
		Total = 22

First, the column for x (the children's ages) is entered, next the column for $(x - \mu)$, and last the column for $(x - \mu)^2$. After adding up the figures in the final column, we obtain the variance by dividing the sum (22) by n (9):

$$\text{Variance} = \sigma^2 = \frac{22}{9} = 2.44$$

Finally, to obtain the standard deviation, we take the square root of the variance:

$$\text{Standard deviation} = \sigma = \sqrt{2.44} = 1.56$$

Next, we can perform the same operation on the ages of the children in the Bumpus Center. The figures are expressed in Table 12.5.

Table 12.5

x	(x − μ)	(x − μ)²
1	−3	9
1	−3	9
2	−2	4
2	−2	4
4	0	0
6	+2	4
6	+2	4
7	+3	9
7	+3	9
		Total = 52

Now, for the variance, we have

$$\sigma = \frac{52}{9} = 5.78$$

And for the standard deviation, we have

$$\sigma = \sqrt{5.78} = 2.40$$

These figures for the variance and standard deviation reflect the difference in distribution shown in the two histograms. In the histogram for the Rumpus Center, the ages of most of the children are clumped around the mean age (4). In other words, they vary or deviate relatively slightly from the mean, and this fact is reflected in relatively small figures for the variance (2.44) and the standard deviation (1.56). On the other hand, in the histogram for the Bumpus center, the ages of most of the children vary or deviate relatively greatly from the mean, so the variance (5.78) and the standard deviation (2.40) are larger.

One of the more important kinds of distribution used in statistics is called the **normal probability distribution,** which expresses the distribution of random phenomena in a population. Such phenomena include (approximately) the heights of adult men or women in a city, the useful life of a certain kind of tire or light bulb, and the daily sales figures of a certain grocery store. To illustrate this concept, suppose that a certain college has 2,000 female students. The heights of these students range from 57 inches to 73 inches. If we divide these heights into one-inch intervals and express them in terms of a histogram, the resulting graph would probably look like the one in Figure 12.3a.

Figure 12.3a   **Figure 12.3b**

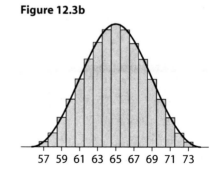

57 59 61 63 65 67 69 71 73   57 59 61 63 65 67 69 71 73

Figure 12.4

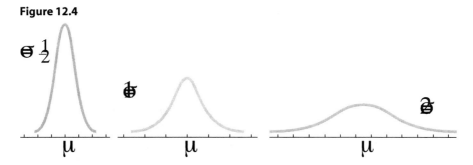

This histogram has the shape of a bell. When a continuous curve is superimposed on top of this histogram, the result appears in Figure 12.3b. This curve is called a normal curve, and it represents a normal distribution. The heights of all of the students fit under the curve, and each vertical slice under the curve represents a certain subset of these heights. The number of heights trails off toward zero at the extreme left and right ends of the curve, and it reaches a maximum in the center. The peak of the curve reflects the average height in the sense of mean, median, and mode.

The parameters of variance and standard deviation apply to normal distributions in basically the same way as they do for the histograms relating to the day-care centers. Normal curves with a relatively small standard deviation tend to be relatively narrow and pointy, with most of the population clustered close to the mean, while curves with a relatively large standard deviation tend to be relatively flattened and stretched out, with most of the population distributed some distance from the mean. This idea is expressed in Figure 12.4. As usual, σ represents the standard deviation, and μ represents the mean.

For a final example that illustrates the importance of dispersion, suppose that you decide to put your life savings into a business that designs and manufactures women's dresses. As corporation president you decide to save money by restricting production to dresses that fit the average woman. Because the average size in the sense of mean, median, and mode is 12, you decide to make only size 12 dresses. Unfortunately, you later discover that while size 12 is indeed the average, 95 percent of women fall outside this interval, as Figure 12.5 shows.

The problem is that you failed to take into account the standard deviation. If the standard deviation were relatively small, then most of the dress sizes would be clus-

Figure 12.5

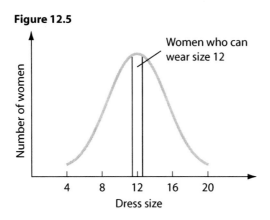

tered about the mean (size 12). But in fact the standard deviation is relatively large, so most of the dress sizes fall outside this interval.

12.5   Graphs and Pictograms

Graphs provide a highly convenient and informative way to represent statistical data, but they are also susceptible to misuse and misinterpretation. Here we will confine our attention to some of the typical ways in which graphs are misused.

First of all, if a graph is to represent an actual situation, it is essential that both the vertical and horizontal axes be scaled. Suppose, for example, that the profit level of a corporation is represented by a graph such as Figure 12.6. Such a graph is practically meaningless because it fails to show how much the profits increased over what period of time. If the curve represents a 10 percent increase over twenty years, then, of course, the picture is not very bright. Although they convey practically no information, graphs of this kind are used quite often in advertising. A manufacturer of vitamins, for example, might print such a graph on the label of the bottle to suggest that a person's energy level is supposed to increase dramatically after taking the tablets. Such ads frequently make an impression because they look scientific, and the viewer rarely bothers to check whether the axes are scaled or precisely what the curve is supposed to signify.

Figure 12.6

A graph that more appropriately represents corporate profits is given in Figure 12.7 (the corporation is fictitious).

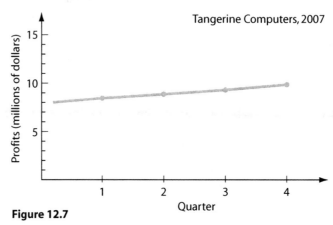

Figure 12.7

Inspection of the graph reveals that between January and December profits rose from $8 to $10 million, which represents a respectable 25 percent increase. This increase can be made to *appear* even more impressive by chopping off the bottom of the graph and altering the scale on the vertical axis while leaving the horizontal scale as is (Figure 12.8). Again, strictly speaking, the graph accurately represents the facts, but if the viewer fails to notice what has been done to the vertical scale, he or she is liable to derive the impression that the profits have increased by something like a hundred percent or more.

Figure 12.8

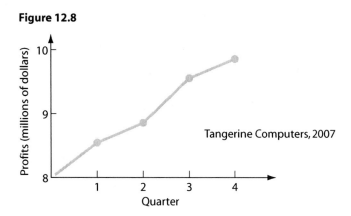

The same strategy can be used with bar graphs. The graphs in Figure 12.9 compare sales volume for two consecutive years, but the one on the right conveys the message more dramatically. Of course, if the sales volume has decreased, the corporate directors would probably want to minimize the difference, in which case the design on the left is preferable.

Figure 12.9

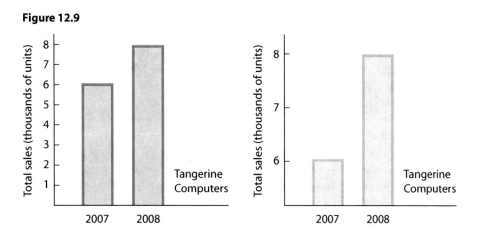

An even greater illusion can be created with the use of pictograms. A **pictogram** is a diagram that compares two situations through drawings that differ either in size or in the number of entities depicted. Consider Figure 12.10, which illustrates the increase in production of an oil company between 2000 and 2005.

Figure 12.10

This pictogram accurately represents the increase because it unequivocally shows that the amount doubled between the years represented. But the effect is not especially dramatic. The increase in production can be exaggerated by representing the 2005 level with an oil barrel twice as tall (Figure 12.11).

Figure 12.11

Even though the actual production is stated adjacent to each drawing, this pictogram creates the illusion that production has much more than doubled. While the drawing on the right is exactly twice as high as the one on the left, it is also twice as wide. Thus, it occupies four times as much room on the page. Furthermore, when the viewer's three-dimensional judgment is called into play, the barrel on the right is perceived as having eight times the volume of the one on the left. Thus, when the third dimension is taken into account, the increase in consumption is exaggerated by 600 percent.

12.6   Percentages

The use of percentages to compare two or more situations or quantities is another source of illusion in statistics. A favorite of advertisers is to make claims such as "Zesty Cola has 20 percent fewer calories" or "The price of the new Computrick computer has been reduced by 15 percent." These claims are virtually meaningless. The question is, 20 percent less than *what*, and 15 percent reduced from *what*? If the basis of the comparison or reduction is not mentioned, the claim tells us nothing. Yet such claims are often effective because they leave us with the impression that the product is in some way superior or less expensive.

Another strategy sometimes used by governments and businesses involves playing sleight-of-hand tricks with the base of the percentages. Suppose, for example, that you are a university president involved with a funding drive to increase the university's endowment. Suppose further that the endowment currently stands at $15 million and that the objective is to increase it to $20 million. To guarantee the success of the drive, you engage the services of a professional fund-raising organization. At the end of the allotted time the organization has increased the endowment to $16 million. They justify their effort by stating that, since $16 million of the $20 million has been raised, the drive was 80 percent successful ($16/20 \times 100\%$).

In fact, of course, the drive was nowhere near that successful. The objective was not to raise $20 million but only $5 million, and of that amount only $1 million has actually been raised. Thus, at best the drive was only 20 percent successful. Even this figure is probably exaggerated, though, because $1 million might have been raised without any special drive. The trick played by the fund-raising organization consisted in switching the numbers by which the percentage was to be computed.

This same trick, incidentally, was allegedly used by Joseph Stalin to justify the success of his first five-year plan.* Among other things, the original plan called for an increase in steel output from 4.2 million tons to 10.3 million. After five years the actual output rose to 5.9 million, whereupon Stalin announced that the plan was 57 percent successful ($5.9/10.3 \times 100\%$). The correct percentage, of course, is much lower. The plan called for an increase of 6.1 million tons and the actual increase was only 1.7 million. Thus, at best, the plan was only 28 percent successful.

Similar devices have been used by employers on their unsuspecting employees. When business is bad, an employer may argue that salaries must be reduced by 20 percent. Later, when business improves, salaries will be raised by 20 percent, thus restoring them to their original level. Such an argument, of course, is fallacious. If a person earns $10 per hour and that person's salary is reduced by 20 percent, the adjusted salary is $8. If that figure is later increased by 20 percent, the final salary is $9.60. The problem, of course, stems from the fact that a different base is used for the two percentages. The fallacy committed by such arguments is a variety of equivocation. Percentages are relative terms, and they mean different things in different contexts.

A different kind of fallacy occurs when a person attempts to add percentages as if they were cardinal numbers. Suppose, for example, that a baker increases the price of a loaf of bread by 50 percent. To justify the increase the baker argues that it was necessitated by rising costs: The price of flour increased by 10 percent, the cost of labor rose 20 percent, utility rates went up 10 percent, and the cost of the lease on the building increased 10 percent. This adds up to a 50 percent increase. Again, the argument is fallacious. If *everything* had increased by 20 percent, this would justify only a 20 percent increase in the

*Stephen K. Campbell, *Flaws and Fallacies in Statistical Thinking* (Englewood Cliffs, NJ: Prentice-Hall, 1974), p. 8. The original reference is to Eugene Lyons's *Workers' Paradise Lost.*

price of bread. As it is, the justified increase is less than that. The fallacy committed by such arguments would probably be best classified as a case of missing the point (*ignoratio elenchi*). The arguer has failed to grasp the significance of his own premises.

Statistical variations of the suppressed evidence fallacy are also quite common. One variety consists in drawing a conclusion from a comparison of two different things or situations. For example, people running for political office sometimes cite figures indicating that crime in the community has increased by, let us say, 20 percent during the past three or four years. What is needed, they conclude, is an all-out war on crime. But they fail to mention that the population in the community has also increased by 20 percent during the same period. The number of crimes per capita, therefore, has not changed. Another example of the same fallacy is provided by the ridiculous argument that 90 percent more traffic accidents occur in clear weather than in foggy weather and that therefore it is 90 percent more dangerous to drive in clear than in foggy weather. The arguer ignores the fact that the vast percentage of vehicle miles are driven in clear weather, which accounts for the greater number of accidents.

A similar misuse of percentages is committed by businesses and corporations that, for whatever reason, want to make it appear that they have earned less profit than they actually have. The technique consists of expressing profit as a percentage of sales volume instead of as a percentage of investment. For example, during a certain year a corporation might have a total sales volume of $100 million, a total investment of $10 million, and a profit of $5 million. If profits are expressed as a percentage of investment, they amount to a hefty 50 percent; but as a percentage of sales they are only 5 percent. To appreciate the fallacy in this procedure, consider the case of the jewelry merchant who buys one piece of jewelry each morning for $9 and sells it in the evening for $10. At the end of the year the total sales volume is $3,650, the total investment $9, and the total profit $365. Profits as a percentage of sales amount to only 10 percent, but as a percentage of investment they exceed 4,000 percent.

EXERCISE 12

I. Criticize the following arguments in light of the material presented in this section:

★1. To test the algae content in a lake, a biologist took a sample of the water at one end. The algae in the sample registered 5 micrograms per liter. Therefore, the algae in the lake at that time registered 5 micrograms per liter.

2. To estimate public support for a new municipality-funded convention center, researchers surveyed 100 homeowners in one of the city's fashionable neighborhoods. They found that 89 percent of those sampled were enthusiastic about the project. Therefore, we may conclude that 89 percent of the city's residents favor the convention center.

3. A quality-control inspector for a food-processing firm needed assurance that the cans of fruit in a production run were filled to capacity. He opened every tenth box in the warehouse and removed the can in the left front corner of each box. He found that all of these cans were filled to capacity. Therefore, it is probable that all of the cans in the production run were filled to capacity.

★4. When a random sample of 600 voters was taken on the eve of the presidential election, it was found that 51 percent of those sampled intended to vote for the Democrat and 49 percent for the Republican. Therefore, the Democrat will probably win.

5. To determine the public's attitude toward TV soap operas, 1,000 people were contacted by telephone between 8:00 A.M. and 5:00 P.M. on weekdays. The numbers were selected randomly from the phone directories of cities across the nation. The researchers reported that 43 percent of the respondents said that they were avid viewers. From this we may conclude that 43 percent of the public watches TV soap operas.

6. To predict the results of a U.S. Senate race in New York State, two polls were taken. One was based on a random sample of 750 voters, the other on a random sample of 1,500 voters. Since the second sample was twice as large as the first, the results of the second poll were twice as accurate as the first.

★7. In a survey conducted by the manufacturers of Ultrasheen toothpaste, 65 percent of the dentists randomly sampled preferred that brand over all others. Clearly Ultrasheen is the brand preferred by most dentists.

8. To determine the percentage of adult Americans who have never read the U.S. Constitution, surveyors put this question to a random sample of 1,500 adults. Only 13 percent gave negative answers. Therefore, since the sampling error for such a sample is 3 percent, we may conclude that no more than 16 percent of American adults have not read the Constitution.

9. To determine the percentage of patients who follow the advice of their personal physician, researchers asked 200 randomly chosen physicians to put the question to their patients. Of the 4,000 patients surveyed, 98 percent replied that they did indeed follow their doctor's advice. We may therefore conclude that at least 95 percent of the patients across the nation follow the advice of their personal physician.

★10. Janet Ryan can afford to pay no more than $15 for a birthday gift for her eight-year-old daughter. Since the average price of a toy at General Toy Company is $15, Janet can expect to find an excellent selection of toys within her price range at that store.

11. Anthony Valardi, who owns a fish market, pays $2 per pound to fishermen for silver salmon. A certain fisherman certifies that the average size of the salmon in his catch of the day is 10 pounds, and that the catch numbers 100 salmon. Mr. Valardi is therefore justified in paying the fisherman $2,000 for the whole catch.

12. Pamela intends to go shopping for a new pair of shoes. She wears size 8. Since the average size of the shoes carried by the Bon Marche is size 8, Pamela can expect to find an excellent selection of shoes in her size at that store.

★13. Tim Cassidy, who works for a construction company, is told to load a pile of rocks onto a truck. The rocks are randomly sized, and the average piece weighs 50 pounds. Thus, Tim should have no trouble loading the rocks by hand.

14. The average IQ (in the sense of mean, median, and mode) of the students in Dr. Jacob's symbolic logic class is 120. Thus, none of the students should have any trouble mastering the subject matter.

15. An insecticide manufacturer prints the following graph on the side of its spray cans:

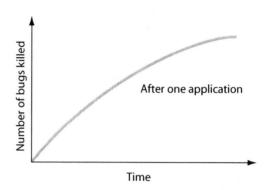

Obviously, the insecticide is highly effective at killing bugs, and it keeps working for a long time.

★16. A corporation's sales for two consecutive years are represented in a bar graph. Since the bar for the later year is twice as high as the one for the previous year, it follows that sales for the later year were double those for the previous year.

17. Forced to make cutbacks, the president of a manufacturing firm reduced certain costs as follows: advertising by 4 percent, transportation by 5 percent, materials by 2 percent, and employee benefits by 3 percent. The president thus succeeded in reducing total costs by 14 percent.

18. During a certain year, a grocery store chain had total sales of $100 million and profits of $10 million. The profits thus amounted to a modest 10 percent for that year.

★19. There were 20 percent more traffic accidents in 2005 than there were in 1980. Therefore, it was 20 percent more dangerous to drive a car in 2005 than it was in 1980.

20. An efficiency expert was hired to increase the productivity of a manufacturing firm and was given three months to accomplish the task. At the end of the period the productivity had increased from 1,500 units per week to 1,700. Since the goal was 2,000 units per week, the effort of the efficiency expert was 85 percent successful (1,700/2,000).

II. Compute the answers to the following questions.

★1. Given the following group of people together with their weights, what is the average weight in the sense of mean, median, and mode?

Number of people	Weight
2	150
4	160
3	170
1	180
1	190
1	200
1	220
2	230

2. Given the following group of people together with their salaries, what is the average salary in the sense of mean, median, and mode?

Number of people	Salary
1	$95,000
2	85,000
1	70,000
3	40,000
1	30,000
2	20,000
5	15,000

3. A small company has five employees who missed work during a certain month. The number of days missed were 1, 1, 2, 4, 7. What is the mean number of days missed? What is the variance and standard deviation of this set of data?

★4. A day-care center cares for ten children. Their ages are 1, 1, 2, 2, 2, 3, 3, 4, 6, 6. Construct a histogram that represents the distribution of ages. What is the mean age? What is the variance and standard deviation of these ages?

5. An instructor gave a ten-question multiple-choice quiz to twelve students. The scores were 10, 10, 9, 9, 8, 8, 8, 7, 7, 7, 7, 6. What is the mean score? What is the variance and standard deviation of these scores?

III. Answer "true" or "false" to the following statements:

★1. If a sample is very large, it need not be randomly selected.

2. If a population is randomly arranged, a sample obtained by selecting every tenth member would be a random sample.

3. If a sample is randomly selected, the larger the sample is, the more closely it replicates the population.

★4. To ensure the same precision, a population of 1 million would require a much larger random sample than would a population of 100,000.

5. In general, if sample A is twice as large as sample B, then the sampling error for A is one-half that for B.

6. When a sample consists of human beings, the purpose for which the sample is taken can affect the outcome.

★7. The personal interaction between a surveyor and a respondent can affect the outcome of a survey.

8. The mean value of a set of data is the value that occurs with the greatest frequency.

9. The median value of a set of data is the middle point when the data are arranged in ascending order.

★10. The modal value of a set of data is the arithmetical average.

11. If one needed to know whether a sizable portion of a group were above or below a certain level, the most useful sense of average would be mode.

12. Data reflecting the results of a random sample conform fairly closely to the normal probability distribution.

★13. If a set of data conform to the normal probability distribution, then the mean, median, and mode have the same value.

14. Range, variance, and standard deviation are measurements of dispersion.

15. Statements about averages often present an incomplete picture, lacking information about the dispersion.

★16. Data reflecting the size of full-grown horses would exhibit greater dispersion than would data reflecting the size of full-grown dogs.

17. The visual impression made by graphs can be exaggerated by changing one of the scales while leaving the other unchanged.

18. Data reflecting a 100 percent increase in housing construction could be accurately represented by a pictogram of two houses, one twice as high as the other.

★19. If a certain quantity is increased by 10 percent and later decreased by 10 percent, the quantity is restored to what it was originally.

20. Expressing profits as a percentage of sales volume presents an honest picture of the earnings of a corporation.

Summary

Statistical reasoning includes any kind of argumentation based on statistical measurement. Such arguments can be misleading because of ambiguities in language, improper measuring techniques, hidden factors, and the skewed drawing of pictograms and graphs. Samples used to generate statistics must not be biased: They must be randomly selected, of the proper size, and unaffected by psychological factors. The word "average" can mean the mean value of a set of data, the medium value, or the mode. Statistical claims must specify the meaning intended. The dispersion of the data, expressed in terms of range, variance, and standard deviation, must also be acknowledged. Graphs and pictograms must be drawn so they avoid illusions, and percentages must state the base on which the percentage is calculated and avoid various numerical fallacies.

Answers to Selected Exercises

Exercise 12
I.
1. Since the water in the lake might not be circulating, the algae content of the water at one end might not be representative of the whole lake. Thus, the sample might be biased.
4. According to Table 12.1, the margin of error for a random sample of 600 is ± 5 percent. Since the sample taken indicates a difference of only 2 percent, the results of the sample are inconclusive.
7. Since no mention is made of the size of the sample or of the expected sampling error, the sample might be biased. The manufacturer might have taken 25 separate samples consisting of ten dentists per sample and reported the results of only the most favorable one.
10. The problem concerns the meaning of "average." If the average is a mean, most of the toys could be over $15, and a few very cheap toys could bring the average down to $15. If the average is a mode, there might be a few toys priced at $15, and all the other toys might have varying prices exceeding $15. Only if the average is a median can one be assured that half the toys are $15 or less.
13. Since no mention is made of the dispersion, the argument is weak. The rock pile might consist of several pieces weighing 500 pounds and enough weighing only 4 or 5 pounds to bring the average down to 50 pounds. If the range were only 10 pounds or so, the conclusion would follow.
16. If the scale on the vertical axis does not begin at zero, the conclusion does not follow.
19. Since there were many more cars on the road in 2005 than there were in 1980, the comparison is faulty.

II.
1. Mean = 180, median = 170, mode = 160.
4.

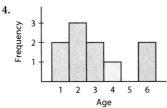

Mean age = 3, variance = 3, standard deviation = 1.73.

III.

1. False.	7. True.	13. True.	19. False.
4. False.	10. False.	16. False.	

7

Hypothetical/Scientific Reasoning

13.1   The Hypothetical Method

Hypothetical reasoning is most immediately applied to the production of explanations. You will recall from Chapter 1 of this book that an explanation is a kind of expression that purports to shed light on some event. Many explanations are grounded in direct observation and memory. For example, suppose that you happen to be wearing a cast on your arm. You know from direct observation that you broke your arm while playing football a week earlier. Suppose somebody asks you about the cast, and you reply, "I'm wearing the cast because I broke my arm playing football." This is an explanation. Or suppose that your mathematics instructor asks you why you failed the calculus test. You reply, "I failed the test because I didn't study the night before." No hypothetical reasoning is used to produce explanations of this sort.

However, it often happens that the needed explanation cannot be produced from direct observation. Suppose that you get into your car one morning and turn the key in the ignition, and the engine cranks but fails to start. Why it fails to start is a complete mystery. After all, it started perfectly the day before. Because it is impossible for you to peer into the inner workings of the engine to furnish the needed explanation, you begin by producing conjectures about why the car will not start. Perhaps the spark plugs are dirty, or the ignition coil has shorted, or the fuel pump is broken. Or perhaps someone sabotaged the car overnight. These conjectures are **hypotheses,** and the reasoning used to produce them is **hypothetical reasoning.** The hypotheses make up for the lack of direct observation in producing the needed explanation.

As a follow-up, you decide to remove one of the spark plugs and inspect its condition. You do so and find it covered with carbon deposits. Now you think you have the answer: The car fails to start because the spark plugs are dirty. But of course this explanation could be wrong. The correct explanation could be something else, but this is the nature of all inductive reasoning. The outcome is only probable. However, having produced this explanation, you can now convert it into an inductive argument. Suppose a friend comes up and says, "I see you ran out of gas." You reply, "No, the spark plugs are dirty, so if I replace them, the car should start." Now you are trying to prove something to your friend, and the kind of argument used is a causal inference.

Hypothetical reasoning is used by nearly all of us in our day-to-day experience. The TV repairperson constructs hypotheses to determine why the picture appears unclear after all the ordinary solutions have been tried without success, the motorist on the freeway or turnpike reasons hypothetically to determine why the traffic is backed up bumper-to-bumper even though it is not yet rush hour, the physician hypothesizes about the cause of a disease prior to prescribing medicine, the teacher hypothesizes about the best way to present a complicated subject in the classroom, and the prosecuting attorney suggests hypotheses to the jury in arguing about the motive for a crime. In all of these cases the evidence is not sufficient to indicate exactly what is going on, what lies behind the scene, or what approach to take, so hypotheses are constructed to make sense of the situation and to direct future action.

Hypothetical reasoning is used most explicitly in philosophical and scientific inquiry. Every scientific theory can be viewed as a hypothesis for unifying and rationalizing events in nature. The Ptolemaic and Copernican theories about the sun and planets, Dalton's atomic theory, Darwin's theory of evolution, and Einstein's theory of relativity are all hypotheses for making sense of the data of observation. The problem for the scientist is that the underlying structure of nature is hidden from view, and the data of observation by themselves are not sufficient to reveal this structure. In response, the scientist constructs hypotheses that provide ways of conceptualizing the data and that suggest specific questions to be answered through the design of controlled experiments.

Analogously, every philosophical system can be viewed as a grand hypothesis for interpreting the content of experience. Plato's theory of forms, Aristotle's theory of substance, Leibniz's monads, and Kant's theory about the mind are all hypotheses aimed at illuminating various aspects of experience. Just as the structure of nature is hidden from the scientist, the meaning of experience is hidden from the philosopher, and ordinary common sense will not provide the answer. In response, the philosopher constructs hypotheses that can be used to shed light on the content of experience and to provide suggestions for further analysis.

Whether it is applied in philosophy, science, or ordinary life, the hypothetical method involves four basic stages:

1. Occurrence of a problem
2. Formulating a hypothesis
3. Drawing implications from the hypothesis
4. Testing the implications

These four stages may be illustrated through the procedure used by a detective in solving a crime. Suppose that a woman has been murdered in her apartment. Initially, everything in the apartment is a potential clue: the empty wine glasses in the sink, the small container of cocaine on the coffee table, the automobile key found on the carpet, the strand of blond hair removed from the couch, and so on. To introduce an element of rationality into the situation, the detective formulates a hypothesis—let us say the hypothesis that the key found on the carpet fits the murderer's car.

From this hypothesis several implications can be drawn. Suppose that the key is the kind that fits only late-model Cadillacs. It follows that the murderer drives a late-model

Cadillac. Furthermore, if the key is the only one the murderer owns, it follows that the car may be parked nearby. A third implication is that the murderer's name may be on record at the local Cadillac dealership. To test these implications, the detective conducts a search of the streets in the vicinity and contacts the local Cadillac dealer for the names of recent buyers.

This example illustrates three additional points about hypotheses. The first is that a hypothesis is not *derived* from the evidence to which it pertains but rather is *added* to the evidence by the investigator. A hypothesis is a free creation of the mind used to structure the evidence and unveil the pattern that lies beneath the surface. It may be that the detective's hypothesis is completely false. Perhaps the key fits a car that was lent to the victim for the weekend. A wide variety of other possibilities are conceivable.

The second point is that a hypothesis directs the search for evidence. Without a hypothesis for guidance, all facts are equally relevant. The mineral content of moon rocks and the temperature in the Sahara would be as relevant as the cars parked on the street outside the apartment. The hypothesis tells the investigator what to look for and what to ignore.

The third point concerns the proof of hypotheses. Let us suppose that the detective finds a late-model Cadillac parked outside the apartment building and that the key fits the ignition. Such a discovery might lend credibility to the hypothesis, but it would not in any sense prove it. Concluding that a hypothesis is proven true by the discovery that one of its implications is true amounts to committing the fallacy of affirming the consequent (see Section 6.6). Where *H* stands for a hypothesis and *I* for an implication, such an argument has the invalid form

> If *H*, then *I*
> *I*
> ―――――
> *H*

Let us suppose, on the other hand, that the murderer turns himself or herself in to the police and that the only car the murderer owns or drives is a Ford. Such a fact would prove the hypothesis false because it would falsify the implication that the murderer drives a Cadillac. The argument form involved in such an inference is *modus tollens*:

> If *H*, then *I*
> not *I*
> ―――――
> not *H*

For the hypothesis to be proved true, the car that the key fits would have to be found and the owner would have to confess to the crime.

13.2   Hypothetical Reasoning: Four Examples from Science

Some of the clearest illustrations of the hypothetical method of reasoning can be found in scientific discoveries. Four examples are the discovery of radium by Pierre and Marie Curie; the discovery of the planet Neptune by Adams, Leverrier, and Galle; the discovery of atmospheric pressure by Torricelli; and Pasteur's research concerning the spontaneous generation of life. Following is a consideration of each of these examples with special attention to the four stages of hypothetical inquiry.

Radium

In 1896 the French physicist Henri Becquerel discovered that crystals containing uranium had the power to expose photographic plates. He found that when these crystals were placed on top of an unexposed plate and left for a certain time, dark blotches appeared in their place when the plate was developed. Becquerel concluded that the crystals emitted certain rays that penetrated the opaque covering of the plates and reacted with the photosensitive material underneath. Further investigation showed that these rays were not as strong as X rays, which could be used to photograph bone structure, and so Becquerel's interest in them lapsed.

A year later Marie Curie revived the question when she adopted it as the topic of her doctoral research at the University of Paris. In place of Becquerel's photographic plates she substituted an electrometer, which was better suited to measuring the intensity of the rays, and she proceeded to conduct various experiments with pure uranium to determine the source of the rays that the metal emitted. When none of these experiments proved fruitful, she shifted her attention to the question of whether other metals or minerals emitted the same kind of rays as uranium. She tested hundreds of metals, compounds, and ores, but the only one that proved interesting was pitchblende, a certain ore of uranium. Because pitchblende contained uranium, she anticipated that it would emit rays; however, because it also contained a number of impurities, she expected the rays to be weaker than they were for pure uranium. Instead, they turned out to be stronger. This problem caught Madame Curie's attention and provided the focus for her research in the months ahead.

In response to the problem, Madame Curie formulated the hypothesis that the impurities in the pitchblende somehow triggered the uranium to increase the emission of rays. One implication of this hypothesis was that mixing pure uranium with the kinds of impurities found in pitchblende would cause an increase in the emission of rays. To test this implication, Curie diluted pure uranium with various elements and measured the strength of the rays. The results were always the same: The emissions were always less than they were for pure uranium. Because of these results, she abandoned the hypothesis.

Madame Curie then formulated a second hypothesis: The intensified emissions were caused directly by some impurity in the pitchblende. The only other element besides uranium that was known to emit rays, however, was thorium, and the pitchblende that had been tested contained no thorium. Thus, an immediate implication of the hypothesis was that the increased rays were caused by an unknown element. A second implication was that this element could be separated from the pitchblende through a process of refinement. At this point Marie Curie was joined by her husband, Pierre, and they began a combined effort to isolate the unknown element.

Because the element was present in only the most minute quantities, separating a measurable amount from the other impurities required a great deal of effort. The Curies began by grinding up some pitchblende and dissolving it in acid. Finally, after numerous stages of filtration and the addition of other chemicals, they obtained a pinch of white powder. By weight, this material was found to be 900 times more radioactive than pure uranium, but since the primary component in the powder was barium, the unknown element still had not been isolated.

Rather than continue with additional stages of refinement, the Curies decided to attempt a spectrographic analysis of the powder. Such analysis, they hoped, would reveal the characteristic spectrum line of the unknown element. This proposal, which amounted to a third implication of the hypothesis, was put to the test. When the powder was burned in a spectrometer, a line appeared in the ultraviolet range that was different from that for any other element. From the combined evidence of the spectrum line and the intense radiation, the Curies announced in 1898 the discovery of a new element, which they called radium. After more processing and refinement, enough of the material was finally obtained to determine its atomic weight.

Neptune

In 1781 William Herschel discovered the planet Uranus. However, the production of a table giving the motion of the new planet had to wait until the gravitational interactions between Uranus, Jupiter, and Saturn had been worked out mathematically. The latter task was accomplished by Pierre Laplace in his *Mechanique Celeste*, and in 1820 Alexis Bouvard used this work to construct tables for all three planets. These tables predicted the orbital motions of Jupiter and Saturn very accurately, but within a few years Uranus was found to have deviated from its predicted path. A problem thus emerged: Why did the tables work for Jupiter and Saturn but not for Uranus?

In response to this problem several astronomers entertained the hypothesis that an eighth planet existed beyond the orbit of Uranus and that the gravitational interaction between these two planets caused Uranus to deviate from its predicted position. Not until 1843, however, did John Couch Adams, a recent graduate of Cambridge, undertake the task of working out the mathematical implications of this hypothesis. After two years' work Adams produced a table of motions and orbital elements that predicted the location of the hypothetical planet, and his computations were so accurate that if anyone with a telescope had bothered to look, they would have found the new planet within two degrees of its predicted position. Unfortunately, no one looked for it.

At about the same time that Adams completed his work on the problem, the French astronomer U. J. J. Leverrier, working independently of Adams, reported a similar set of motions and orbital elements to the French Academy of Science. The close agreement between Adams's and Leverrier's predictions prompted a search for the planet, but because a rather broad section of sky was swept, the planet was missed.

Finally, Leverrier sent a copy of his figures to Johann Galle at the Berlin Observatory, where a set of star charts was being prepared. It was suggested that the region corresponding to Leverrier's computations be observed and the results matched against the charts. This was done, and a small starlike object was found that was not on the charts. The next night the same object was sighted, and it was found to have moved. The new planet was thus identified. It was named Neptune after most astronomers outside France objected to the original suggestion that it be called Leverrier.

Atmospheric Pressure

Originated by Aristotle, the principle that nature abhors a vacuum was used for centuries to explain the fact that in emptying a keg of wine an opening had to be made at the top as well as at the bottom. Because nature would not allow a vacuum to be created inside the keg, the wine would not drain from the bottom until air was let in at the top. It was thought that this principle held universally for all applications involving a vacuum, but in the sixteenth century it was found that suction pumps used to drain water from mine shafts would not work if the pump was situated over 30 feet above the water level. This caused people to wonder whether nature's abhorrence of a vacuum, while holding true for kegs of wine, had certain limits for pumps.

In 1630 Giovanni Baliani of Genoa discovered a similar limitation in regard to siphons. When he attempted to siphon water from a reservoir over a 60-foot hill, he found that the siphon would not work. When the siphon was completely filled with water and the stoppers were removed from both ends, a vacuum seemed to be created in the uppermost parts of the pipe.

These findings were communicated to Gasparo Berti in Rome, who, around 1641, attempted to determine more scientifically whether a vacuum could actually be created. Berti designed an apparatus consisting of a spherical glass vessel attached to a pipe about 40 feet long. The apparatus was affixed upright to the side of a tower and after the valve at the lower end of the pipe was closed, water was poured through the upper opening in the glass vessel. When both the pipe and the glass vessel were completely filled, the opening in the vessel was sealed and the valve at the lower end of the pipe was opened. Immediately water rushed from the bottom of the pipe, creating a vacuum in the glass vessel. This experiment crystallized a problem that had been developing for many years: If nature abhorred a vacuum, why did it tolerate the creation of one in the glass vessel? Furthermore, why did the water always descend to the same level in the pipe?

The results of Berti's experiment were communicated to Evangelista Torricelli in Florence, who was at that time Galileo's assistant. Galileo himself thought that the water was supported in the pipe by the power of the vacuum, but after Galileo's death in 1642, Torricelli formulated his own hypothesis: The water was supported in the pipe by the pressure of the atmosphere. Torricelli reasoned that we live "at the bottom of an ocean of air" and that the pressure of the air pushing against the bottom of the pipe supported the water at a certain height in the pipe. A point of equilibrium was reached, he thought, when the weight of the water remaining in the pipe equaled the weight of the air pushing down from above.

From this hypothesis Torricelli derived several implications. One was that the pressure of the atmosphere would support a column of mercury about 29 inches high in a tube sealed at the top. This followed from the fact that the atmosphere supports a column of water 33 feet high, that mercury is 13.6 times as dense as water, and that $33/13.6 \times 12$ inches = 29 inches. A second implication was that such a tube filled with mercury could be used to measure fluctuations in atmospheric pressure. This second implication won Torricelli credit for formulating the theory of the barometer. Finally, Torricelli reasoned that if such a device were conveyed to a place where the air was more rarefied, such as on a mountaintop, the column of mercury would descend.

The first of these implications was tested by Torricelli's associate, Vincenzo Viviani. Viviani obtained a 4-foot section of glass tube sealed at one end, enough mercury to completely fill it, and a dish to hold more mercury. After pouring the mercury into the tube Viviani placed his thumb over the open end, inverted the tube, and placed the open end in the dish of mercury. After he released his thumb he watched the column of mercury descend to about 29 inches above the level of mercury in the dish. Thus was created the first barometer. Its successful use in measuring atmospheric pressure came later.

The test of Torricelli's third implication was taken up in 1647 by the French philosopher Blaise Pascal. Having received word of Torricelli's experiments with the barometer, Pascal constructed one for himself. He readily became convinced of the correctness of Torricelli's hypothesis, and to demonstrate its correctness in opposition to the vacuum principle, he requested that his brother-in-law, F. Perier, convey a barometer to the top of the Puy de Dôme, one of the highest mountains in Auvergne. A year later Perier was able to fulfill this request. He began the experiment by setting up two barometers in the monastery at the foot of the mountain. After noting that both columns of mercury rose to an identical height, he disassembled one of the barometers and instructed one of the friars to check the mercury level in the other throughout the day. Then Perier, accompanied by a group of witnesses, set off up the mountain with the other barometer. On reaching the summit, he assembled the second barometer and discovered to the amazement of all that the mercury level was more than 3 inches lower than it had been at the foot of the mountain. As a double check the barometer was taken apart and reassembled at five different spots on the summit. Each time the results were the same.

At the midpoint of his descent Perier reassembled the barometer once again. He found that the mercury level was about midway between where it was at the bottom and at the top of the mountain. Finally, on returning to the monastery, the friar who had been watching the barometer there was questioned about what he had observed. He reported that the mercury level had not changed since early that morning when the group had departed. Pascal announced the results of this experiment to the educated world, and the announcement succeeded in abolishing the principle that nature abhors a vacuum.

Spontaneous Generation

The theory of spontaneous generation holds that living beings arise spontaneously from lifeless matter. The roots of the theory extend into ancient times. Aristotle held that worms, the larvae of bees and wasps, ticks, fireflies, and other insects developed continually from the morning dew and from dry wood and hair. He also held that crabs and various molluscs developed from moist soil and decaying slime. Extensions of this theory prevailed throughout the Middle Ages and well into modern times. In the seventeenth century it was widely held that frogs were produced from the slime of marshes and eels from river water, and the physician Van Helmont thought that mice were produced from the action of human sweat on kernels of wheat. All one needed to do, according to Van Helmont, was toss a dirty shirt into a container of wheat, and in 21 days the container would be teeming with mice. Even Descartes and Newton accepted the theory of spontaneous generation. Descartes held that various plants and insects originated in moist earth exposed to sunlight, and Newton thought that plants were produced from emanations from the tails of comets.

The first systematic effort to abolish the belief in spontaneous generation was made by the Italian physician Francesco Redi. In response to the commonly held idea that worms were spontaneously generated in rotting meat, Redi hypothesized that the worms were caused by flies. An immediate implication was that if flies were kept away from the meat, the worms would not develop. To test this hypothesis Redi cut up a piece of meat and put part of it in sealed glass flasks and the other part in flasks open to the air. Flies were attracted to the open flasks, and in a short time worms appeared; but no worms developed in the flasks that were sealed.

When Redi published his findings in 1668, they immediately affected the theory of spontaneous generation. Within a few years, though, the microscope came into common use, and it was discovered that even though meat sealed in glass containers produced no worms, it did produce countless microorganisms. The theory of spontaneous generation was thus reawakened on the microbial level.

By the middle of the nineteenth century the theory had received considerable refinement. It was thought that spontaneous generation resulted from the direct action of oxygen on lifeless organic nutrients. Oxygen was thought to be essential to the process because the technique of canning fruits and vegetables had come into practice, and people knew that boiling fruits and vegetables and sealing them in the absence of oxygen would cause them to be preserved. If they were left exposed to the air, however, microbes would develop in a short time.

One of the defenders of spontaneous generation at that time was the Englishman John Needham, an amateur biologist. Needham conducted an experiment in which flagons containing oxygen and a vegetable solution were buried in hot coals. The coals would have been expected to kill any life in the solution, but several days later the contents of the flagons were alive with microbes. Needham concluded that the oxygen acting alone on the nutrient solution caused the generation of the microbes. In response to this experiment, Lazzaro Spallanzani, an Italian physiologist, conducted a similar experiment. To ensure that the nutrient solution was lifeless he boiled it for an hour. Later no microbes could be found. To this Needham objected that in boiling the solution for a full hour Spallanzani had destroyed its "vegetative force." In addition, Needham argued, he had polluted the small amount of oxygen in the containers by the fumes and heat. Thus, it was no wonder that microbes were not spontaneously generated.

To settle the issue once and for all, the French Academy of Science offered a prize for an experimental endeavor that would shed light on the question of spontaneous generation. This challenge drew Louis Pasteur into the controversy. Spontaneous generation presented a special problem for Pasteur because of his previous work with fermentation. He had discovered that fermentations, such as those involved in the production of wine and beer, required yeast; and yeast, as he also discovered, was a living organism. In view of these findings Pasteur adopted the hypothesis that life comes only from life. An immediate implication was that for life forms to develop in a sterile nutrient solution, they must first be introduced into the solution from the outside.

It was well known that life forms did indeed develop in sterile nutrient solutions exposed to the air. To account for this Pasteur adopted the second hypothesis that life forms are carried by dust particles in the air. To test this second hypothesis Pasteur took a wad of cotton and drew air through it, trapping dust particles in the fibers. Then he washed the cotton in a mixture of alcohol and examined drops of the fluid under a microscope. He discovered microbes in the fluid.

Returning to his first hypothesis, Pasteur prepared a nutrient solution and boiled it in a narrow-necked flask. As the solution boiled, the air in the neck of the flask was forced out by water vapor, and as it cooled the water vapor was slowly replaced by sterilized air drawn through a heated platinum tube. The neck of the flask was then closed off with a flame and blowpipe. The contents of the flask thus consisted of a sterilized nutrient solution and unpolluted sterilized air—all that was supposedly needed for the production of life. Over time, however, no life developed in the flask. This experiment posed a serious threat to the theory of spontaneous generation.

Pasteur now posed the hypothesis that sterile nutrient solutions exposed to the air normally developed life forms precisely because these forms were deposited by dust particles. To test this third hypothesis Pasteur reopened the flask containing the nutrient solution, and, using a special arrangement of tubes that ensured that only sterilized air would contact the solution, he deposited a piece of cotton in which dust particles had been trapped. The flask was then resealed, and in due course microbes developed in the solution. This experiment proved not only that dust particles were responsible for the life but that the "vegetative force" of the nutrient solution had not been destroyed by boiling, as Needham was prone to claim.

Pasteur anticipated one further objection from the proponents of spontaneous generation: Perhaps the capacity of oxygen to generate life was destroyed by drawing it through a heated tube. To dispel any such notions Pasteur devised yet another experiment. He boiled a nutrient solution in a flask with a long, narrow gooseneck. As the solution boiled, the air was forced out, and as it cooled, the air returned very slowly through the long neck, trapping the dust particles on the moist inside surface. No microbes developed in the solution. Then, after a prolonged wait, Pasteur sealed the flask and shook it vigorously, dislodging the particles that had settled in the neck. In a short time the solution was alive with microbes.

When Pasteur reported these experiments to the Academy of Science in 1860, he was awarded the prize that had been offered a year earlier. The experiments dealt a mortal blow to the theory of spontaneous generation, and although the theory was not abandoned immediately, by 1900 it had very little support.

13.3   The Proof of Hypotheses

The four instances of hypothetical reasoning in science that we have investigated illustrate the use of two different kinds of hypotheses. The hypotheses involved in the discovery of Neptune and radium are sometimes called empirical hypotheses, and those relating to atmospheric pressure and spontaneous generation are sometimes called theoretical hypotheses. **Empirical hypotheses** concern the production of some thing or the occurrence of some event that can be observed. When radium had finally been obtained as a pure metal it was something that could be seen directly, and when Neptune was finally sighted through the telescope, it, too, had been observed. **Theoretical hypotheses,** on the other hand, concern how something should be conceptualized.

■ EMINENT LOGICIANS

Charles Sanders Peirce 1839–1914

© The Granger Collection, New York

Charles Sanders Peirce (pronounced "purse") was born in Cambridge, Massachusetts. His father, Benjamin, was the leading mathematician of the day, and he took a special interest in his son's intellectual development. Under his direction Charles was reading college-level material, including logic, at age twelve, and Benjamin would challenge the boy with highly complex problems that Charles would solve on his own. Although his most significant education came from his father, Charles went on to attend Harvard University, where he received a B.S. in chemistry in 1863. Yet, he was not a successful student (he usually placed in the lower quarter of his class), partly because he showed disdain for his professors as inadequately qualified to teach him. This arrogance is likely the main reason Peirce lived a difficult life. He died in poverty at age seventy-four in the then-isolated town of Milford, Pennsylvania.

Throughout his life Peirce suffered a painful and debilitating neurological condition that may have been responsible for his detached, depressed, and sometimes violent behavior. It may also have been the reason he could not obtain a tenured university position. In 1879 he did secure a position as a lecturer at Johns Hopkins University, and in some ways, he proved himself a remarkable teacher—a collection of his students' essays is considered a key work in the development of logic. Yet, despite his teaching, Peirce was discharged from his faculty position. He had recently separated from his wife and had lived with another woman before his divorce was finalized. This "immoral" behavior and other supposed transgressions were probably the chief factors leading to his dismissal. After that he never held another academic position.

Without an academic base, Peirce continued to write copiously, producing some 80 thousand pages of material; yet he did not complete a single book in logic or philosophy, which limited his influence while alive. Beginning in the late 1930s, his writings were collected and published, bringing him the attention he missed during his lifetime. As the founder of pragmatism, America's only unique philosophy, Peirce is now considered to be America's greatest philosopher and probably its greatest logician as well. Peirce's own version of pragmatism took the form of a thoroughly scientific enterprise according to which the meaning of a concept depends on the practical effect it has on how we lead our lives and conduct our inquiries.

In logic Peirce is best known for his work in the logic of relations and quantification theory. The theory of quantification that Peirce developed is the one that led ultimately to the writing of *Principia Mathematica* by Whitehead and Russell, and it closely resembles the system used today in most logic courses. In the logic of relations, Peirce extended the work done by De Morgan by applying the concepts of Boolean algebra to relative terms such as "friend of" or "enemy of." This work has also significantly impacted the way we treat this subject today. In addition, Peirce was a leader in exploring the use of truth values, and he was the first to develop a three-valued logic incorporating true, false, and an intermediate or unknown value. In propositional logic Peirce succeeded in reducing all the connectives to one, and in inductive logic he rejected the subjectivist theory of probability in favor of an objectivist theory based on observed regularities.

When Galileo observed the water level rising in a suction pump, he conceived it as being *sucked* up by the vacuum. When Torricelli observed it, however, he conceived it as being *pushed* up by the atmosphere. Similarly, when Needham observed life emerging in a sterile nutrient solution, he conceived it as being spontaneously generated by the action of oxygen. But when Pasteur observed it, he conceived it as being implanted there by dust particles in the air.

The distinction between empirical and theoretical hypotheses has certain difficulties, which we will turn to shortly, but it sheds some light on the problem of the verification or confirmation of hypotheses. Empirical hypotheses are for all practical purposes *proved* when the thing or event hypothesized is observed. Today practically all of us would agree that the hypotheses relating to radium and Neptune have been established. Theoretical hypotheses, on the other hand, are never proved but are only *confirmed* to varying degrees. The greater the number of implications that are found to be correct, the more certain we can be of the hypothesis. If an implication is found to be incorrect, however, a theoretical hypothesis can be *disproved*. For example, if it should happen some day that life is produced in a test tube from inorganic materials, Pasteur's hypothesis that life comes only from life might be considered to be disproved.

The problem with the distinction between empirical and theoretical hypotheses is that observation is theory-dependent. Consider, for example, a man and a woman watching a sunrise. The man happens to believe that the sun travels around the earth, as Ptolemy held, and the woman that the earth travels around the sun, as Copernicus and Galileo contended. As the sun rises, the man thinks that he sees the sun moving upward, while the woman thinks she sees the earth turning. The point is that all of us have a tendency to see what we think is out there to be seen. As a result, it is sometimes difficult to say when something has or has not been observed.

In regard to the discovery of Neptune, the unknown planet was observed two times in 1795 by J. J. Lalande, fifty-one years before it was "discovered" by Adams, Leverrier, and Galle. Lalande noted that his observations of the position of the small starlike object were discordant, so he rejected one as erroneous. Because he thought he was observing a *star*, he received no credit for discovering a *planet*. Analogous remarks extend to Galle's observations of the *planet* Neptune in 1846. If Leverrier's computations had been erroneous, Galle might have seen what was really a comet. Thus, if we can never be sure that we really see what we think we see, is it ever possible for a hypothesis to be actually proved? Perhaps it is better to interpret the proof of empirical hypotheses as a high degree of confirmation.

Conversely, with theoretical hypotheses, would we want to say that Torricelli's hypothesis relating to atmospheric pressure has *not* been proved? Granted, we cannot observe atmospheric pressure directly, but might we not say that we observe it *instrumentally*? If barometers can be regarded as extensions of our sense organs, Torricelli's hypothesis has been proved. Another example is provided by Copernicus's hypothesis that the earth and planets move around the sun, instead of the sun and planets around the earth, as Ptolemy hypothesized. Can we consider this theoretical hypothesis to be proved? If a motion picture camera were sent outside the solar system and pictures were taken supporting the Copernican hypothesis, would we say that these pictures constituted proof? We probably would. Thus, while the distinction between theoretical and empirical hypotheses is useful, it is more a distinction in degree than in kind.

13.4 The Tentative Acceptance of Hypotheses

A certain amount of time is required for a hypothesis to be proved or disproved. The hypotheses relating to the discovery of radium and Neptune required more than a year to prove. Theoretical hypotheses in science often take much longer, and theoretical hypotheses in philosophy may never be confirmed to the satisfaction of the majority of philosophers. During the period that intervenes between the proposal of a hypothesis and its proof, confirmation, or disproof, the question arises as to its tentative acceptability. Four criteria that bear on this question are (1) adequacy, (2) internal coherence, (3) external consistency, and (4) fruitfulness.

Adequacy is the extent to which a hypothesis fits the facts it is intended to unify or explain. A hypothesis is said to "fit" the facts when each fact can be interpreted as an instance of some idea or term in the hypothesis. For example, before the Neptune hypothesis was confirmed, every fluctuation in the position of Uranus could be interpreted as an instance of gravitational interaction with an unknown planet. Similarly, before Torricelli's hypothesis was confirmed, the fact that water would rise only 30 feet in suction pumps and siphons could be interpreted as an instance of equilibrium between the pressure of the water and the pressure of the atmosphere.

A hypothesis is inadequate to the extent that facts exist that the hypothesis cannot account for. The principle that nature abhors a vacuum was inadequate to explain the fact that water would rise no more than 30 feet in suction pumps and siphons. Nothing in the hypothesis could account for this fact. Similarly, Needham's hypothesis that life is generated by the direct action of oxygen on nutrient solutions was inadequate to account for the fact that life would not develop in Pasteur's flask containing a sterilized nutrient solution and sterilized oxygen.

In scientific hypotheses a second kind of adequacy is the *accuracy* with which a hypothesis accounts for the data. If one hypothesis accounts for a set of data with greater accuracy than another, then that hypothesis is more adequate than the other. For example, Kepler's hypothesis that the orbits of the planets were ellipses rather than circles, as Copernicus had hypothesized, accounted for the position of the planets with greater accuracy than the Copernican hypothesis. Similarly, Einstein's theory of relativity accounted for the precise time of certain eclipses with greater accuracy than Newton's theory. For these reasons Kepler's and Einstein's theories were more adequate than the competing theories.

Internal coherence is the extent to which the component ideas of a hypothesis are rationally interconnected. The purpose of a hypothesis is to unify and interconnect a set of data and by so doing to *explain* the data. Obviously, if the hypothesis itself is not internally connected, there is no way that it can interconnect the data. After Adams and Leverrier had worked out the mathematical details of the Neptune hypothesis, it exhibited a great deal of internal coherence. The hypothesis showed how all the fluctuations in the position of Uranus could be rationally linked in terms of the gravitational interaction of an eighth planet. Similarly, Torricelli's hypothesis showed how the various fluid levels could be rationally interconnected in terms of the equilibrium of pressures. Internal coherence is responsible for the features of elegance and simplicity that often attract scientists to a hypothesis.

An example of incoherence in science is provided by the theoretical interpretation of light, electricity, and magnetism that prevailed during the first half of the nineteenth century. During that period each of these phenomena was understood separately, but the interconnections between them were unknown. Toward the end of the century the English physicist James Clerk Maxwell showed how these three phenomena were interconnected in terms of his theory of the electromagnetic field. Maxwell's theory was thus more coherent than the ones that preceded it.

Similarly, in philosophy, Spinoza's metaphysical theory is more internally coherent than Descartes's. Descartes postulated the existence of two kinds of substance to account for the data of experience. He introduced extended, material substance to explain the data of the visible world, and nonextended, immaterial substance to explain the phenomena of the invisible world, including the existence and activity of the human soul. But Descartes failed to show how the two kinds of substance were interconnected. In the wake of this disconnection the famous mind-body problem arose, according to which no account could be given of how the human body acted on the mind through the process of sensation or how the mind acted on the body through the exercise of free choice. Spinoza, on the other hand, postulated only one substance to account for everything. Spinoza's theory is thus more internally coherent than Descartes's.

External consistency occurs when a hypothesis does not disagree with other, well-confirmed hypotheses. Adams's and Leverrier's hypothesis of an eighth planet was perfectly consistent with the nineteenth-century theory of the solar system, and it was rendered even more attractive by the fact that the seventh planet, Uranus, had been discovered only a few years earlier. Similarly, Marie Curie's hypothesis of the existence of a new element was consistent with Mendeleev's periodic table and with the general hypothesis that elements could emit penetrating rays. In 1890 Mendeleev's table had certain gaps that were expected to be filled in by the discovery of new elements, and two ray-emitting elements, thorium and uranium, had already been discovered.

The fact that a hypothesis is inconsistent with other, well-confirmed hypotheses does not, however, immediately condemn it to obscurity. It often happens that a new hypothesis arises in the face of another, well-confirmed hypothesis and that the two hypotheses compete for acceptance in the future. Which hypothesis will win is determined by an appeal to the other three criteria. For example, Torricelli's hypothesis was inconsistent with the ancient hypothesis that nature abhors a vacuum, and Pasteur's hypothesis was inconsistent with the equally ancient hypothesis of spontaneous generation. In the end, the newer hypotheses won out because they were more adequate, coherent, or fruitful than their competitors. For the same reason, the Copernican hypothesis eventually triumphed over the Ptolemaic, the theory of oxidation won out over the old phlogiston theory, and Einstein's theory of relativity won out over Newton's theory.

Fruitfulness is the extent to which a hypothesis suggests new ideas for future analysis and confirmation. Torricelli's hypothesis suggested the design of an instrument for measuring fluctuations in the pressure of the atmosphere. Similarly, Pasteur's hypothesis suggested changes in the procedures used to maintain sterile conditions in hospitals. After these latter changes were implemented, the death rate from surgical operations decreased dramatically. The procedure of pasteurization, used to preserve milk, was another outgrowth of the hypothesis that life comes only from life.

Newton's theory of universal gravitation is an example of a hypothesis that proved especially fruitful. It was originated to solve the problem of falling bodies, but it also explained such things as the ebb and flow of the tides, the orbital motion of the moon and planets, and the fluctuations in planetary motion caused by a planet's interaction with other planets. Einstein's theory of relativity is another example. It was originated to account for certain features of Maxwell's theory of electricity and magnetism, but it ushered in the atomic age forty years later.

The factors of coherence and fruitfulness together account for the overall rationality and explanatory power of a hypothesis. Suppose, for example, that someone formulated the hypothesis that the water level in suction devices is maintained by the action of demons instead of by atmospheric pressure. Such a hypothesis would be neither coherent nor fruitful. It would not be coherent because it would not explain why the maximum water level in these devices is consistently about 30 feet, why the mercury level in barometers is much less, and why the mercury level in a barometer decreases when the instrument is carried to the top of a mountain. Do the demons decide to maintain these levels by free choice or according to some plan? Because there is no answer to this question, the hypothesis exhibits internal disconnectedness, which leaves it open to the charge of being irrational. As for the fourth criterion, the demon hypothesis is unfruitful because it suggests no new ideas that experimenters can put to the test. The hypothesis that nature abhors a vacuum is hardly any more fruitful, which accounts in part for why it was so suddenly abandoned in favor of Torricelli's hypothesis—it simply did not lead anywhere.

In summary, for any hypothesis to receive tentative acceptance it must cover the facts it is intended to interpret and it must rationally interconnect these facts—in other words, it must be adequate and coherent. After that, it helps if the hypothesis does not conflict with other, well-confirmed hypotheses. Finally, it is important that a hypothesis capture the imagination of the community to which it is posed. This it does by being fruitful—by suggesting interesting ideas and experiments to which members of the community can direct their attention in the years ahead.

EXERCISE 13

I. For each of the following situations, invent at least three hypotheses aimed at explaining what went wrong or at solving the problem. Then, for each hypothesis, describe one or more experiments or inquiries that would confirm or disconfirm the hypothesis.

1. Someone you have been dating has a birthday coming up, so you call a florist and order flowers for the occasion. Two days later the person is cold and distant.

2. After settling in a new location you buy some seeds for a flower garden. When the flowers come up, they are stunted and of poor quality.

3. After mailing your paycheck to the bank, you write a check to pay your rent. The rent check bounces.

4. On a windy day you pick up the phone to call a friend, but you find that the line is dead. You live in a house and share phone expenses with a housemate.

5. After driving for miles on a dusty road, you park your car near the bank of a river and take a hike through the woods. Soon you become lost. In one direction you see a small stream, and in the other, a trail.

6. A close friend calls you on the phone and confides a personal secret. That night you write the secret in your diary. A few days later your friend is furious with you because the friend overheard someone on campus talking about the secret.

7. On a rainy evening you return to your ground-floor apartment and discover that you have been burglarized. You can't believe it, because you are certain you locked the door when you went out. You share the apartment with a roommate.

8. You are a philosophy professor at a university, and while reading a set of term papers you discover that two of them are identical. Those two papers are also extremely well written.

9. You are a manager of a department store, and, although business has been brisk lately, your chief accountant informs you that the store is losing money.

10. A short time before final exams you lose your class notes. You recall having seen them four days ago. Use your own personal activities and movements during the past four days as the basis for formulating your hypotheses as to the whereabouts of the notes.

II. For the four scientific discoveries presented in this section identify the problem, the hypotheses that were formulated, the implications that were drawn, and the test procedure that was used.

III. The following article was written by a physician in the emergency room of a hospital.* The article describes the difficulty that the author and other physicians faced in diagnosing the nature of a patient's illness. Identify the problem, the hypotheses suggested, the implications drawn, and the tests conducted to confirm or disconfirm the hypotheses. You should be able to find fifteen hypotheses. Try to distinguish the tests and observations made to narrow down the problem from the tests and observations made to confirm or disconfirm the hypotheses.

An Unreasonable Sleep
by Elisabeth Rosenthal

The patient was in a coma.

The emergency room was unusually quiet early that Thursday morning, and rounds promised to be brief. "You have only one patient," said the doctor I was relieving. "He's a real winner, though. He's basically unresponsive, but I can't find anything wrong." "Well, you know," I said dryly, "when a patient's in a coma, there is usually a problem." "Look, I know it sounds weird, but all the tests are coming back normal. I'm beginning to think the guy's faking. Well, not faking exactly. But I'm beginning to think the problem's psychiatric. Hey, if you find something else, more power to you—you're a better doc than I am." And with that, he was out the door.

Discover magazine, October 1994, pp. 28–31. © 1994 The Walt Disney Co., reprinted with permission of the author.

When I stopped by Mr. Gerard's room, I found a handsome blond man in his early thirties lying motionless in bed. His eyes were closed and perfectly still; his arms lay crooked at his sides. When I pulled down his sheet I was slightly surprised to find his feet crossed at the ankles. Maybe the nurse's aide had left him that way when she had put on his hospital gown.

He looked so perfectly peaceful, so perfectly asleep, that I suspected this coma business was some kind of practical joke. I tapped his arm and whispered to try to wake him up.

"Mr. Gerard."

No stirring.

"Mr. Gerard!"—this time with a little nudge.

No reply.

"MR. GERARD!!" I took both his shoulders and shook as hard as I could. But again, no response. When I let go of his torso, he slumped back on the pillow. The only movement I could detect was the perfectly rhythmic rise and fall of his chest 12 times a minute, the most normal of normal respiratory rates.

> **But nothing appeared to be wrong.**

The chart at the foot of the bed recorded 14 hours of the most stable vital signs an ER doctor could ever hope to see. And my brief neurological exam suggested that every major brain pathway was intact: With his eyelids propped open, his pupils reacted normally to light. When I tapped on his knees and tickled his feet, his reflexes performed on cue. A man so profoundly unresponsive, with nothing obviously wrong? I retreated to the nurses' station to pore over his chart.

Mr. Gerard had been brought in the previous evening by an ambulance his sister had summoned. He was a well-respected estate lawyer in a large city halfway across the country, she said, and had just made partner two years before. He had no real medical problems and, as far as she knew, had never seen a psychiatrist or had any mental illness. She was fairly certain that he didn't drink or take drugs. But she confessed to the social worker that she and her brother had become close only in the past year, during his tumultuous breakup with a longtime girlfriend; before that they had done little more than exchange birthday cards.

Mr. Gerard had finished a major project the week before and had called her Friday night saying he had no plans for the Fourth of July and might he join her family for the week? He seemed fine for the first three days of his visit, even organizing a picnic in the park and a trip to a ballgame, she said. But on Wednesday he seemed depressed, and he retired to his room early because he didn't feel well. On Thursday he hadn't emerged by the time she left for work. When she got home at 6 P.M. the door was still closed, so she went in and found him, as she put it, "looking dead." She called an ambulance and frantically searched her brother's suitcase for clues. All she found were books and clothes—no pill bottles, liquor, or drug paraphernalia.

> **The ER team got nowhere.**

En route to the ER, Mr. Gerard had received the standard treatment for patients who are unresponsive. First the paramedics gave him a shot of Narcan—which reverses the effects of heroin and other narcotics by blocking opiate receptors in the brain. Then they gave him a shot of dextrose, which brings around patients who are comatose because of low blood sugar. But neither had helped. The ER staff was faced with a man who appeared absolutely healthy yet profoundly unresponsive.

There are only a handful of reasons for a coma in a young person: a drug overdose or poisoning, a massive hemorrhage in the head because of trauma or a premature stroke, a seizure, a metabolic abnormality, a brain tumor or abscess, or a rare overwhelming infection. By the time I arrived, the night staff had methodically tested Mr. Gerard and found no trace of these conditions.

Although overdoses are the most common cause of comas in young people, they almost always produce some other symptoms. With heroin, the pupils shrink. With Valium, the respiratory rate dips slightly. With many antidepressants, the heart races. But aside from Mr. Gerard's absolute failure to respond to voices or even pain, his exam showed nothing wrong.

Just to be sure, the night doctors had put a tube down his throat and pumped out his stomach looking for pills. They had drawn blood to test for poisons and drugs. They had sent Mr. Gerard up for an emergency CT scan of the brain to rule out hemorrhage or a stroke. Still, they had come up empty-handed. At 5 A.M. they called a neurologist to see if she had any ideas.

Dr. Green wasn't too pleased about being dragged out of bed, and she was immediately suspicious of this motionless body with an apparently normal neurological exam. She began a series of standard neurological tests designed to elicit signs of consciousness.

The patient was not responsive to pain.

She started by shaking his shoulders but quickly adopted more aggressive tactics to see if she could get him to react. She pressed the handle of her reflex hammer against his toenail with all her might. No response. She then pushed down hard on his breastbone. This move, the so-called sternal rub, is so unpleasant that it evokes at least a grimace from patients in pretty deep comas. But there was not a twitch from Mr. Gerard.

She even went so far as to squirt ice water into his ear, a technique neurologists use to find out if the brainstem—the primitive region of the brain that regulates basic brain function—is working. If it is intact, the eyes jiggle reflexively. And if the patient is conscious, he becomes dizzy and sick to his stomach. Dr. Green saw Mr. Gerard's eyes jiggle. And she thought she saw him begin to retch. Her hunch was that he was awake.

She then tried to find out whether Mr. Gerard was capable of voluntary movement. Without giving any warning, she sprinkled ice water on his face. He seemed to wince slightly and sink back into his trance. She resorted to a neurologist's ploy to distinguish the conscious from the comatose: She took his limp arm by the hand and raised it a foot above his face, then let it drop. Patients in true comas have no choice but to smack themselves, hard, in the face or chest. Every time she tried this, however, Mr. Gerard's hand somehow veered right and glanced off his cheek.

Based on her observations and Mr. Gerard's normal CT scan, Dr. Green pronounced that there was nothing neurologically wrong with the patient. Her note concluded: "Catatonia, of psychiatric origin. No evidence of neurological dysfunction."

I agreed with her, but I had to admit the diagnosis made me nervous. True, catatonia can befall patients with psychiatric illnesses, producing movements that are frenzied, bizarre, or slowed to the point of complete stupor. And if left untreated, the stupor can be deadly because the patient cannot eat or drink. But catatonia in someone with no previous psychiatric history was extremely rare—yet what else could explain this condition?

I called the psychiatrist at the mental hospital to which we would refer Mr. Gerard, described the case, and tentatively suggested that he be admitted. The doctor, as I suspected, wouldn't readily agree.

"I don't know if we can take him," he began, and then he proceeded to echo my own worst fears. "Are you sure he's not an overdose? Maybe he's taken something weird that's not on our drug screen. Can you guarantee he's not seizing? You know not all seizures involve obvious twitching. Will you write on the record that you're positive he hasn't had a stroke? They don't always show up on the scan right away."

"Look, I can't promise you anything right now—come see him and we'll talk. But it would be weird for a guy with an overdose or a stroke or a seizure to be so rock stable for over 12 hours."

Within 20 minutes the psychiatrist was in the ER. He spent some time talking with Mr. Gerard's relatives—some at the hospital, and some at their homes—and unearthed still more clues. What they had dismissed as eccentricity began to seem more like serious mental illness.

When he called Mr. Gerard's mother, who lived on the opposite coast, she told him that her son's behavior had been so erratic that she had been urging him to see a therapist for several years. In the past six months, however, she had stopped because her son had started accusing her of tapping his phone conversations and monitoring his mail—and she worried about feeding his escalating paranoia. A younger brother said he had been called to pick up Mr. Gerard at a hospital three months before. He had been brought there by the police after a security guard had found him in his office at 5 A.M. dressed in swim trunks. Although the ER doctors had thought he needed psychiatric help, Mr. Gerard had insisted on leaving without any care.

> The patient was eccentric.

"I'm beginning to think he is a little nuts," the psychiatrist said, as he relayed his new findings. "But I'm still not sure. You can torture the guy and he doesn't react. How about a rush order on the drug tests that haven't come back yet? And maybe an EEG and a better CT scan."

Inside I groaned. That would be another six hours' worth of tests and another $2,000. I called to arrange for an EEG to monitor the electrical patterns deep in his brain, which would guarantee 1,000 percent that he was not having a seizure. I also asked for a CT scan enhanced with a dye that might reveal some odd tumor or infection. And I left a message at the toxicology lab begging for the remaining results as soon as possible.

After much coaxing and cajoling, Mr. Gerard got his EEG and second CT scan. As I suspected, both tests were normal. But when the chief lab technician returned my call, it was bad news. "No way for today," he said. "We sent the screen out to another state."

By now, though, the evidence was all pointing in one direction. When I looked in on Mr. Gerard one last time, his feet were again crossed—and hadn't they been crossed the other way before?

I called the psychiatrist. "He's yours," I began, mentioning the latest results to assuage his fears. "The tox screen won't be back until tomorrow, but he's been lying here rock stable for almost 24 hours and there's no overdose that can explain it."

My colleague started in with another round of questions. His temperature? Normal. His chest x-ray? Totally clear. His blood counts? Perfect. Had they been repeated? Yes, perfect again. His urine output?

I faltered. I tried to picture Mr. Gerard's bed. I didn't recall a urine bag hanging by its side, and he certainly hadn't gotten up to use the men's room. "I'll have to check."

I rummaged through the nursing charts trying to calculate how much fluid Mr. Gerard had gotten through his IV line—and how much he'd put out. With renewed trepidation I realized that there was no sign that he'd urinated at all. I looked around his stretcher for a urine bag that had not been emptied. Nothing there.

The patient had not urinated.

Evidently Mr. Gerard had gone almost 24 hours without urinating. How could I have missed this potentially critical clue? Were his kidneys failing? Was his bladder paralyzed by an unusual overdose that had left him in a coma? Or was he holding back voluntarily? I drew down his sheet to see if I could feel the outline of a bloated bladder under his skin—indeed, I thought I could. But as I pressed, there it was again: that slight grimace of a man who is awake and feeling pain.

Clearly, we needed one more test. I asked the nurse to accompany me, explaining, "Let's stick a catheter in his bladder to see what's in there."

Working in an ER, you get in the habit of talking to unconscious patients because you never know what they may feel or understand. So as the nurse draped a sterile sheet across his pelvis, she said exactly what she would say to any patient:

"Mr. Gerard, you haven't urinated in a while, so I'm going to put a tube in through your penis and up into your bladder to see if there's any backup there." By now she had cleansed the area with disinfectant, put on sterile gloves, and unwrapped the thin rubber catheter connected to a urine collection bag.

"Okay, Mr. Gerard," she said, picking up the catheter and taking aim. "It's going in." As if those three small words had broken some deep trance, suddenly the sheets began to stir and the carefully cleaned equipment tumbled to the floor.

The patient suddenly revived.

The nurse and I were speechless as Mr. Gerard sat bolt upright and said, "Excuse me, if you give me a urinal and close the curtains, I can handle this myself." Stunned, not knowing what else to do or say, we granted his request and left.

What a way to clinch a diagnosis. We were finally certain that Mr. Gerard's problem was not caused by some undetected neurological injury. "I should have known," I said to the nurse, "that to a man, the threat of a catheter is the most noxious stimulus of all."

When we returned to the room several minutes later, Mr. Gerard was once again lying on his stretcher, limp and silent, unresponsive to commands. But now we all agreed where he should spend the night.

Over the next week, as Mr. Gerard went in and out of his stupor, doctors at the psychiatric hospital garnered a bit more information from him. Mr. Gerard was basically lucid, they said, but paranoid, and his thought patterns did not always follow normal logic. They suspected that he had a mild form of schizophrenia and started him on a low dose of an antipsychotic drug to treat that disease.

As the drug brought Mr. Gerard's symptoms under control, however, a clearer picture of his condition began to emerge. In retrospect, it was obvious that Mr. Gerard had been suffering for months from mood swings, and his odd behavior more closely matched the symptoms of bipolar disorder, or what used to be called manic-depressive illness. Patients with this psychiatric disorder, which tends to run in families, suffer alternating bouts of hyperactivity and depression.

It had taken a catatonic episode to force Mr. Gerard into treatment for his illness, but his prognosis was good. Fortunately, treatment with lithium can prevent the destructive mood swings and permit the patient to lead a normal life. Not long after he was admitted, Mr. Gerard was walking, talking—even gregarious, the psychiatrists said. Just two weeks later he was able to return home and resume his practice.

IV. Write a short paper (3–5 pages) on one of the following scientific events. Discuss the problem, one or more hypotheses that were formulated, the implications that were drawn, and the test procedures that were used. Then evaluate the hypothesis in terms of adequacy, internal coherence, external consistency, and fruitfulness.

1. Isaac Newton: corpuscular theory of light
2. Christian Huygens: wave theory of light
3. Johannes Kepler: orbit of Mars
4. Nicolaus Copernicus: theory of the solar system
5. Count von Rumford: theory of heat
6. Charles Darwin: theory of natural selection
7. John Dalton: theory of atoms
8. William Harvey: circulation of the blood
9. Louis Pasteur: theory of vaccination
10. J. J. Thomson: discovery of the electron
11. André Marie Ampère: discovery of the electromagnet
12. Niels Bohr: structure of the atom
13. Alexander Fleming: discovery of penicillin
14. Henri Becquerel: radioactivity of uranium
15. Dmitri Mendeleev and Clemens Winkler: discovery of germanium
16. Amedeo Avogadro: Avogadro's law
17. Johann Balmer: theory of the spectrograph
18. Alfred Wegener: theory of continental drift
19. James Watson and Francis Crick: structure of the DNA molecule
20. John Bardeen: theory of superconductivity
21. Albert Einstein: theory of Brownian motion
22. Edwin Hubble: recession of the galaxies
23. Jean Baptiste Lamarck: inheritance of acquired characteristics

V. Write a short paper (2–3 pages) analyzing one or more of the hypotheses formulated by Sherlock Holmes in one of the stories by Arthur Conan Doyle. Include a discussion of the problem, the hypothesis, the implications that were drawn, and the test procedures.

VI. Answer "true" or "false" to the following statements:

★1. Hypothetical reasoning is useful when the evidence by itself does not provide the solution to the problem.

2. Hypotheses are derived directly from the evidence.

3. Hypotheses serve the purpose of directing the search for additional evidence.

★4. If the implications of a hypothesis are true, then we may conclude that the hypothesis is true.

5. If an implication of a hypothesis is false, then we may conclude that the hypothesis is false, at least in part.

6. In the episode pertaining to the discovery of radium, all of the hypotheses turned out to be true.

★7. In the Neptune episode, Adams and Leverrier deserve the credit for working out the implications of the hypothesis.

8. Torricelli's hypothesis was consistent with the hypothesis that nature abhors a vacuum.

9. In Pasteur's day, the theory of spontaneous generation held that life was produced by the direct action of oxygen on organic nutrients.

★10. The hypotheses relating to the discoveries of radium and Neptune may be classified as empirical hypotheses.

11. Torricelli's and Pasteur's hypotheses may be classified as theoretical hypotheses.

12. Theoretical hypotheses concern how something should be conceptualized.

★13. The problem with the distinction between empirical and theoretical hypotheses is that observation is dependent on theory.

14. The adequacy of a hypothesis has to do with how well the ideas or terms in the hypothesis are rationally interconnected.

15. The coherence of a hypothesis has to do with how well the hypothesis fits the facts.

★16. If a hypothesis is not externally consistent, then it must be discarded.

17. A hypothesis is fruitful to the extent that it suggests new ideas for future analysis and confirmation.

18. If a theory is incoherent, it is deficient in rationality.

★19. The theoretical interpretations of light, electricity, and magnetism during the first part of the nineteenth century illustrate a condition of inadequacy.

20. If a hypothesis gives rise to contradictory implications, it is incoherent.

Summary

Hypothetical reasoning is used to solve a problem when the solution is not apparent to undirected observation. The method consists of inventing a hypothesis that illuminates the situation, drawing implications from the hypothesis, and testing the implications. This method is not only applicable to many puzzling occurrences in ordinary life, but also essential to the progress of science. Four examples from the history of science that clarify the hypothetical method are the discovery of radium, of the planet Neptune, and of atmospheric pressue, and the refutation of spontaneous generation. Scientific hypotheses may be either theoretical or empirical. Empirical hyphotheses may be proved true or false, but theoretical hypotheses may only be confirmed in varying degrees. Criteria that bear on the tentative acceptance of hypotheses are adequacy, internal coherence, external consistency, and fruitfulness.

Answers to Selected Exercises

Exercise 13
VI.

1. True.	7. True.	13. True.	19. False.
4. False.	10. True.	16. False.	

8

Science and Superstition

14.1 Distinguishing Between Science and Superstition

The idea that the human mind is capable of operating on different levels in its effort to comprehend reality is as old as philosophy itself. Twenty-four centuries ago Plato drew a distinction between what he called opinion and knowledge. Opinion, he said, is a kind of awareness that is uncertain, confined to the particular, inexact, and subject to change, whereas knowledge is certain, universal, exact, and eternally true. Every human being starts out in life by operating on the level of opinion, and only through great struggle and effort can he or she escape it and rise to the level of knowledge. This struggle is called education, and it opens the eye of the mind to realities that cannot even be imagined from the standpoint of opinion.

Today's distinction between science and superstition is a modern equivalent of Plato's distinction between knowledge and opinion. Everyone recognizes that science has revealed wonderful truths about the world of nature. It has put men on the moon, wiped out life-threatening diseases, and ushered in the computer age. Also, almost everyone recognizes that superstition is little better than foolishness. It leads people to fear walking under ladders, breaking mirrors, and spilling salt. Practically everyone agrees that if some claim is grounded in science, then it is probably worthy of belief, while if it is grounded in superstition, then it should probably be ignored. Where people do not agree, however, is in what constitutes science and what constitutes superstition. What one person calls science another calls superstitious nonsense.

Both science and superstition involve hypotheses, so the four criteria developed in Chapter 13 for evaluating hypotheses are relevant to the distinction between science and superstition: adequacy, internal coherence, external consistency, and fruitfulness. But the distinction between science and superstition also involves psychological and volitional elements. It involves such factors as how the observer's subjective states influence how he sees the world, and how his needs and desires play a role in the formation of his beliefs. Accordingly, to explore the distinction between science and superstition, we must introduce criteria that include these psychological and volitional elements. The criteria suggested here are evidentiary support, objectivity, and integrity. The following account of evidentiary support encompasses adequacy and fruitfulness, and the account of integrity encompasses adequacy, internal coherence, and external consistency.

Science and superstition are, in large measure, polar opposites. Where scientific activity recognizes the importance of evidentiary support, objectivity, and integrity, superstition ignores them. Accordingly, these criteria can be used as a kind of measuring stick for sizing up the various beliefs people have about the world. To the extent that those beliefs are supported by evidence, are objective, and arise from research that reflects integrity, the closer they come to the ideal of science, and the more justified they are. Conversely, to the extent that our beliefs do not share in these characteristics, the closer they come to the "ideal" of superstition, and the less justified they are.

Note, however, that to say a belief is justified is not to say it is true in any absolute sense. As we saw in Chapter 13, all beliefs that arise from science are tentative at best. But such beliefs are the best ones we can have for now. Also, to say that a belief is not justified is not to say it is absolutely false. It is quite possible that a belief grounded in superstition today could tomorrow be grounded in science. But such a belief is not worthy of assent today. An analogy can be found in rolling dice. No sensible person would bet even money that a pair of dice will come up "snake eyes" on the next roll, even though he realizes that tomorrow it might be discovered that the dice were loaded in favor of this outcome.

14.2   Evidentiary Support

In the preceding chapter we saw that hypotheses in themselves are mere conjectures, and before they are believed they should be supported by evidence. This rule applies equally to the hypotheses that underlie science and to those that underlie superstition. This rule is strictly obeyed in science, but it is often ignored in the realm of superstition. For example, in the sixteenth century Copernicus formulated the hypothesis that the sun is the center of our planetary system and that the earth revolves around the sun—in opposition to the prevailing Ptolemaic hypothesis, which put the earth at the center. In the years that followed, the telescope was invented, and thousands of subsequent observations confirmed the Copernican hypothesis and disconfirmed the Ptolemaic hypothesis. Without these observations, the Copernican hypothesis would never have been adopted.

In contrast, consider the superstition that allowing a black cat to cross one's path will bring bad luck. No evidence has ever been collected in support of this hypothesis. No tests have been conducted and no experiments performed. Possibly on one occasion or other someone did allow a black cat to cross his or her path and later lost money on the stock exchange or was injured in a car accident, but surely it would be unreasonable to believe that allowing a black cat to cross one's path caused the loss or the accident. Such reasoning constitutes a classic case of the *post hoc ergo propter hoc* (false cause) fallacy. But in spite of the lack of evidence, many people believe the black cat hypothesis.

Before inquiring further into the need for evidence, however, we must first investigate what counts as evidence. Does the testimony of authorities count as evidence?

What about ancient authorities? Does the Bible count as evidence? The answer is that scientific hypotheses are about the natural world, so only observations of the natural

Does the Bible count as evidence?

world count as evidence. Every scientific experiment is a question the experimenter asks of the world, and the result of that experiment is nature's reply. The problem with the testimony of authority is that we have no certain knowledge that the authority is correct in his or her assessment. The same holds true of the Bible. We have no way of knowing whether what the Bible says about the natural world is true. If someone should reply that the Bible is divinely inspired, then the obvious reply is, How do we know that? Do we have any observational evidence for it? Appeals to authority figures and the Bible amount to passing the explanatory buck.

Another kind of evidence that is considered unreliable is anecdotal evidence. Suppose that you have cancer and a friend advises you that eating garlic can cure it. You decide to take this advice, and after eating a clove of garlic every day for a year, the cancer goes into remission. Did the garlic cure the cancer? Evidence of this sort is called anecdotal, and science usually rejects it. The trouble with anecdotal evidence is that it is too isolated to establish any causal connection. Thus, the garlic evidence ignores the thousands of people with cancer who have eaten garlic and have not been cured, and it ignores the thousands of people who have experienced spontaneous remission of cancer and have not eaten any garlic. Also, there is no way to turn the clock back and try the experiment again.

One of the key features of scientific evidence gathering is that an experiment be replicable under controlled conditions. This means that the experiment must be repeatable by different scientists at different times and places. Replicability helps ensure

Scientific experiments must be replicable.

that the outcome of the experiment did not result from anything peculiar to one certain experimenter operating at a single place and time. Also, the controlled conditions are designed to eliminate the influence of extraneous factors. Perhaps, in reference to the garlic example, the cure was effected not by the garlic but by something else that was eaten, or by any one of a thousand other factors that occurred during this time, or by any combination of these factors.

The evidence offered in support of superstitious hypotheses is rarely replicable, and when it is, the outcome almost always fails to support the hypothesis. For example, the belief in ghosts is usually supported by what one or more individuals claim to have seen on some unique occasion. This occasion can never be repeated. And the belief in psychic phenomena such as extrasensory perception is sometimes claimed to be supported by experiments involving Zener cards: cards imprinted with crosses, circles, wavy lines, stars, and squares whose image an observer might "transmit" to a psychic receiver. But when these experiments have been repeated under carefully controlled conditions, the outcome has never been other than what would have been expected to occur through mere chance.

Another defect found in superstitious hypotheses is that they are often framed so vaguely that it is virtually impossible to provide any kind of unequivocal confirmation. For example, according to feng shui (pronounced fung-shway), an ancient Chinese system of magic, bad luck travels in straight lines, whereas good luck does not. As a result, one invites bad luck by living in a house or apartment that has two (or, what is worse, three) doors lined up in a row. But what, exactly, is the meaning of bad luck?

What is interpreted as bad luck today may turn out to be good luck tomorrow. If a person loses $1,000 in the stock market today, that may lead her to be more cautious in the future, and that increased caution may save $10,000 later on.

In contrast, the hypotheses of science are often framed in the language of mathematics, or they can at least be translated into some mathematical expression. This fact provides for extremely accurate confirmations and is largely responsible for the extraordinary success science has enjoyed during the past 500 years. For example, in 1802 the French chemist Joseph Louis Gay-Lussac formulated the hypothesis that if the temperature is raised one degree Celsius in a closed container of gas—any gas—the pressure of the gas will increase by 0.3663 percent. The hypothesis has been tested thousands of times by chemists and students in chemistry labs, and it has been found to be correct.

> *Scientific hypotheses are phrased precisely.*

Closely related to the problem of vagueness is the breadth with which a hypothesis is framed. If a hypothesis is framed so broadly and comprehensively that even contradictory evidence serves to confirm it, then the hypothesis is not really confirmed by anything. Suppose, for example, that a health care practitioner should invent a hypothesis involving diet: Practicing this diet is guaranteed to make you feel great, but before it has this effect it may make you feel either rotten or the same as usual. After following this diet for six months you report that you feel the same as before. The practitioner replies that your experience confirms the hypothesis, because this is what the diet is supposed to do. On the other hand, suppose that after six months you feel great, or perhaps rotten. Again the practitioner will report that your experience confirms the hypothesis. Hypotheses of this sort are not genuinely scientific.

In 1919 the philosopher Karl Popper discovered this very problem concerning hypotheses. In response, he argued that any genuinely scientific hypothesis must be framed narrowly enough so that it forbids certain things from happening. In other words, the hypothesis must be falsifiable. In the years following its announcement, many philosophers criticized Popper's falsifiability criterion because, strictly speaking, hypotheses are rarely susceptible of being disproved. But, as we saw in Chapter 13, hypotheses can be disconfirmed (or rendered less plausible). Thus, we can retain Popper's basic insight by requiring that any genuinely scientific hypothesis be disconfirmable. This means that the hypothesis must be framed narrowly enough so that it is possible for evidence to count against it. Newton's gravitational hypothesis, for example, satisfies this criterion because the discovery of two large bodies that failed to attract each other would tend to disconfirm the hypothesis. But the dietary hypothesis just mentioned fails the disconfirmability criterion because no outcome could ever count against it.

A problem closely associated with excessively broad hypotheses arises in connection with what are called *ad hoc* modifications of hypotheses. For an example, suppose that you are a sociologist conducting research into alcoholism. You formulate a hypothesis that alcoholism is caused by cultural factors that present alcohol consumption in a favorable light. When you gather evidence to support this hypothesis, however, you find that relatively few people who come from such cultures are alcoholics. Thus, you modify the hypothesis to say that alcoholism is caused by cultural factors but only when a genetic predisposition exists. But then you

> *Ad hoc modifications can ruin hypotheses.*

find that many alcoholics drink to ease the pain of depression and other psychological problems. Thus, you modify the hypothesis once again to take this fact into account. Further research shows that parental drinking patterns play a role, so you add another modification. These changes are called ad hoc ("to this") modifications because they are introduced purely to cover some problem or anomaly that was not recognized when the hypothesis was first framed.

The problem with ad hoc modifications is that their purpose is to shore up a failure of evidentiary support in the original hypothesis. As more and more modifications are added, the hypothesis becomes self-supporting; it becomes a mere description of the phenomenon it is supposed to explain. For example, suppose that we introduce a certain hypothesis h to explain the occurrence of a certain phenomenon x among a group of entities A, B, C, D, E. As ad hoc modifications are added, we find that A has x because of some unique attribute a, B has x because of b, and so on. In the end our hypothesis states that anyone who has attributes a, b, c, d, e exhibits x. But the set of attributes a, b, c, d, e is simply a description of A, B, C, D, E. If we should ask *why* entity A has x, the answer is that A has x because of a, where a is just a unique something that A has. Applying this analysis to the alcoholism hypothesis, if we ask why a certain person (let us call him Smith) is an alcoholic, the answer is that Smith is an alcoholic because he has a certain attribute s that causes him to be an alcoholic. The explanation is vacuous.

Another problem with ad hoc modifications is that they result in hypotheses that are so complicated that applying them becomes difficult. Science has always favored simplicity over complexity. Given two hypotheses that explain the same phenomenon, the simpler of the two is always the preferable one. In part this preference is aesthetic. The simpler hypothesis is more "beautiful" than the more complex one. But the preference for simplicity also results from the application of what has been called "Ockham's razor." This is a principle, introduced by the fourteenth-century philosopher William of Ockham, that holds that theoretical entities are not to be multiplied needlessly. Why settle for a complicated theory when a simpler one works equally well? Besides, the simpler one is easier to apply.

One consequence of Ockham's razor is that naturalistic explanations are preferable, at least at the outset, to supernatural ones. For example, over the years we have seen numerous reports of statues depicting Jesus or the Virgin Mary that are said to weep tears of water, oil, or blood. After viewing these statues, thousands of faithful come away convinced that they have seen a miracle. However, Ockham's razor says that we should look for naturalistic explanations first. Perhaps the tears came from condensation or from rainwater that may have leached into the statue from small surface cracks. Another possible explanation is pranksters. Scientists have shown how the appearance of tears can be replicated by drilling a small hole in a statue's head, pouring a liquid into the hole, and then scratching away a bit of lacquer or paint from the corner of the eyes. The liquid will percolate down through the porous substance of the statue and escape through the scratches.

Naturalistic explanations are preferred.

Another, closely related consequence of Ockham's Razor is that explanations based on known realities are preferred to those based on the fantastic or the bizarre. For example, there is a region in Peru, high in the Andes mountains, known as the Nazca Desert. The floor of that desert features large drawings of geometrical figures and animals such as monkeys, hummingbirds, and lizards. The drawings were produced more than a thousand years ago by scraping away the iron-oxide-coated pebbles that cover the land, but given their huge size, they can be recognized as coherent figures only from a position high above. One accepted explanation is that the Nazca Indians produced the drawings using simple tools and surveying equipment to impress the rain gods that dwell in the clouds. However, the best-selling author Erich von Däniken proposes that the lines represent landing strips for alien spacecraft, and it was those aliens who guided the Indians from overhead in producing the drawings. Given its far-fetched character, this explanation would seem to violate Ockham's razor.

Returning to the question of evidentiary support, one of the surest ways to know that our hypotheses are supported by evidence is that they lead to predictions that turn out to be true. Each true prediction represents a pillar of support for the hypothesis. But some predictions are better than others, and the best ones are those that reveal ways of viewing the world that would never have been dreamed of apart from the hypothesis. If a hypothesis leads to predictions of this sort, and if those predictions are confirmed by evidence, then the hypothesis has earned a very special kind of support. Such a hypothesis reveals hidden truths about nature that would never have been recognized without it.

A classic example of a prediction of this kind resulted from the hypothesis underlying Einstein's general theory of relativity. One of the consequences predicted by this hypothesis is that light is affected by gravity. In particular, the hypothesis predicted that a light ray coming from a star and passing by the sun would be bent in the direction of the sun. As a result, the position of the star with respect to other stars would appear to be different from what it was usually observed to be. Of course, testing such a prediction under normal circumstances would be impossible, because the light of the sun is so bright that it completely blocks out the light from stars. But it could be tested during a solar eclipse. Such an opportunity arose on May 29, 1919, and scientists took advantage of it. The prediction turned out to be true, and as a result Einstein's theory was quickly adopted. Within a few years the theory led to the discovery of atomic energy.

> *Science is progressive; superstition is not.*

Hypotheses that yield striking, novel predictions are largely responsible for progress in science. And it is precisely these kinds of predictions, argues the philosopher Imre Lakatos, that distinguish science from pseudoscience. Of course, not every scientific hypothesis leads to such startling predictions as Einstein's, but this kind of hypothesis may at least be integrally connected to broader, umbrella hypotheses that have led to such predictions. In contrast, the hypotheses underlying astrology have been around for twenty-seven centuries, and they have produced not a single startling prediction that has been verified and not a single new insight into the course of human events. They have produced no master plan for future civilization and no hint about future discoveries in physics or medicine. This lack of progress over centuries is one reason that the philosopher Paul Thagard named astrology a pseudoscience.

14.3   Objectivity

Our beliefs about the world are objective to the extent that they are unaffected by conditions peculiar to the experiencing subject. Such conditions can be either motivational or observational. For example, a belief that is motivated by the emotions of the experiencing subject and that exists for the primary purpose of satisfying those emotions tends to lack objectivity. Also, a belief that is grounded in observations peculiar to the experiencing subject, such as visual hallucinations, lacks objectivity. Even though objectivity is an ideal that can never be completely attained, practically everyone would agree that beliefs are more trustworthy if their content is not distorted by the experiencing subject. The scientist constantly strives to avoid such distortions, but the superstitious mind either revels in them or, in the more tragic cases, succumbs to them.

All superstitions exist at least in part to satisfy the emotional needs of the experiencing subject. The chief emotions that give rise to superstitious beliefs are fear and anxiety, and they are often reinforced by a disposition to fantasy and mental laziness. Much of the fear and anxiety is generated by the fact that everyone dies. Death can come suddenly, as in a freeway accident, a fall from a roof, or an avalanche, or it can come as a result of cancer, heart failure, or stroke. Short of death, everyone is subject to injury with its attendant pain, and most people at some time experience the mental suffering that accompanies rejection, loneliness, and failure.

Superstitions exist to satisfy emotional needs.

People have little control over these facts of life, and to relieve the anxiety they produce, many resort to charms and amulets, the rosary beads dangling from the rearview mirror or the scapular or medal worn around the neck. If nothing else will protect us from the terrors of life, perhaps these objects will. After all, science has failed to conquer disease and death, and it offers to the believer nothing but tentative truths that may change tomorrow. To the person facing an uncertain future, dejection, or loneliness, it may seem more reasonable to dial up the Psychic Friends Network and buy a bit of immediate consolation than to trust in science.

A second element in the human condition that generates anxiety is freedom and the responsibility freedom entails. The idea that you, and you only, are in charge of your destiny can be an extremely frightening idea. Many people recoil from the thought and seek refuge in a leader or guru. They turn all their power of critical thinking over to this leader and blindly follow his or her instructions to the last detail. When the leader orders them to believe any form of nonsense, no matter how silly, they do so. The belief or practice ordered by the leader, they are told, is essential to their protection. And when the leader orders them to send a check for fifty dollars to help restore the television tower or complete the mansion on the hill, they do so. To refuse means they will have to face their own freedom. Sometimes, following such orders can lead to tragedy, as it did in the Jonestown massacre in 1978 and the Heaven's Gate suicides in 1997.

A disposition to magical ways of thinking and mental laziness greatly facilitates the flight to superstition. Many people, if not most, are fascinated by the mysterious, the arcane, and the occult, and some would rather believe an explanation clothed in magic than they would a scientifically grounded one. The psychologists Barry F. Singer and Victor A. Benassi performed a series of experiments on their students in which they had a magician pose as a "psychic" and perform demonstrations of psychic feats. Before the demonstrations began, the students were told repeatedly in the clearest language that the magician was only pretending to be a psychic, and that what they were about to witness was really a series of conjurer's tricks. Nevertheless, in spite of these warnings, a majority of students concluded, in one experiment after another, that the magician was really a psychic. Furthermore, many concluded that the magician was an agent of Satan.

People are fascinated by the mysterious.

The disposition toward the magical and the fantastic is greatly reinforced by the media, particularly television and motion pictures. The media are slavishly subservient to the entertainment desires of their audience, so, given a widespread fascination with the magical, the media issue a constant stream of movies, miniseries, and "news" stories devoted to that subject. These programs touch everything from vampires and disembodied spirits to irrational conspiracies and the intervention of angels. This persistent attention to the fantastical increases the public's acceptance of superstitious explanations whenever realistic ones are not readily available, or even in the face of realistic explanations.

A disposition to mental laziness also assists in the formation of superstitious beliefs. It is, in fact, extremely difficult to ensure that one's beliefs are supported by evidence and that they pass the test of internal coherence. Sloppy logic is so easy it is no wonder people resort to it. Most of the informal fallacies treated in Chapter 3 can arise from sloppy thinking. After old Mrs. Chadwicke hobbled past the church, lightning struck the steeple and burned the church to the ground. Obviously old Mrs. Chadwicke is a witch (false cause). Furthermore, old Mrs. Chadwicke wears a black cape and a black hood. It must be the case that all witches wear such clothing (hasty generalization). And of course witches exist because everybody in the village believes in them (appeal to the people).

Superstitions are supported by sloppy thinking.

Another kind of sloppy thinking involves an appeal to what might be called false coherence. A farmer discovers that one of his cows has been slain. At the same time the farmer happens to read a story in a local tabloid saying that a satanic cult is operating in the vicinity. The cult practices its rites on the thirteenth day of each month. The cow was slain on the thirteenth. Thus, the farmer concludes that the cow was slain by Satan worshippers. This line of thinking involves many loose ends, but that rarely deters people from drawing a conclusion. Becoming a clear, critical thinker is one of the primary goals of education, but unfortunately becoming educated is no less of a struggle for students today than it was for students in Plato's day.

Thus far we have focused on emotions and dispositions in the experiencing subject that lead to superstitious beliefs. We now turn to some of the many ways that our observation of the world can be distorted. Such distortions consitute avenues in which conditions peculiar to the experiencing subject enter into the content of observation. When such distorted observations are combined with the emotions and dispositions mentioned earlier, superstitious beliefs are likely to arise. The distorted observations can occur in the same person who has the emotions and dispositions or they can be conveyed secondhand. In either case, the combination leads to superstition.

One well-documented phenonemon that influences our observation of our own bodily states is the so-called placebo effect. Recall that a placebo is any kind of "medicine" or procedure that provides no medicinal or therapeutic benefit by itself but that can effect a cure when the patient is told that it has such benefit. For example, patients with knee pain have been told that an operation will cure them, and after they undergo a minor incision that, by itself, has no therapeutic effect, the pain often disappears. Also, patients who suffer from nervous tension or depression have been told that a little colored pill (which consists of nothing but sugar) will cure them, and after they take the pill, the tension or depression disappears. Obviously in these cases it is not the placebo alone that effects the cure but the placebo together with the suggestion implanted in the patients' minds by their doctors.

Placebos can masquerade as cures.

Another well-documented effect that influences our observation of the world around us is called pareidolia. This is the effect by which we can look at clouds, smoke, or the textured coatings on walls and ceilings and see animals, faces, trees, and so on. We project familiar visual images onto vague, relatively formless sensory stimuli and "see" that image as if it were really there. Pareidolia is responsible for a good deal of religious superstition. For example, a few years ago a woman making burritos saw the face of Jesus in the skillet burns on a tortilla. She built a shrine to house the tortilla, and thousands of believers came to pray before it. More recently, a grilled cheese sandwich that believers thought bore the image of the Virgin Mary sold on eBay for $28,000. But incidents of this sort are not confined to the Christian world. Followers of Islam have seen the Arabic words for "Allah" and "Mohamed" in such media as fish scales, egg shells, and lamb's wool.

Closely related to pareidolia is the concept of the perceptual set, where "set" refers to our tendency to perceive events and objects in a way that our prior experience has led us to expect. The idea of perceptual set is a product of Gestalt psychology, according to which perceiving is a kind of problem solving. When we are confronted with a problem, such as finding the solution to a riddle or puzzle, we enter into a state of mental incubation in which potential solutions are turned over in our minds. This state is followed by a flash of insight (assuming we are able to solve the puzzle), after which the solution seems obvious. When we consider the puzzle at a later time, the solution leaps into our minds. Such a solution is called a *gestalt*, from the German, for form or configuration. Analogously, every act of perception involves solving the puzzle of organizing sensory stimuli into meaningful patterns. Each such pattern is a perceptual gestalt, or set, and once such a set is formed, it serves to guide the processing of future perceptions. As a result, we perceive what we expect to perceive.

We perceive what we expect to perceive.

Can you see the white triangle?
Is the white triangle really "there"?
(Taken from Kanizsa, 1979, 74.)

In 1949 the psychologists Jerome S. Bruner and Leo J. Postman performed a famous experiment in which subjects were shown replicas of ordinary playing cards—but some of the cards had been altered by reversing their color. For example, in some groups of cards, the three of hearts was black and the six of spades was red. Of twenty-eight subjects, twenty-seven initially saw the altered cards as normal ones. One subject identified the black three of hearts as a three of spades on forty-four successive showings. This experiment clearly shows that we perceive what we expect to perceive and, indeed, this fact is familiar to everyone. For example, we expect to receive a phone call, and while taking a shower we think we hear the phone ringing, only to be told by someone in the other room that the phone did not ring. Or, while driving, we might approach a red octagonal sign that reads ST_P (our view of the sign being partly blocked by a tree branch between the S and the P). However, we bring the car to a stop, because we perceived the sign to read STOP. In fact, what our sense of vision received was three consonants (S, T, P), meaningless until processed through perception.

Yet another factor that influences our sense of vision is the autokinetic effect. According to this effect a small, stationary light surrounded by darkness will often seem to move. One can prove the existence of this effect for oneself by looking at a bright star on a dark night, or by observing a small stationary point of light in a dark room. Psychologists speculate that the autokinetic effect results from small, involuntary motions of the eyeball of the observer, and they have shown that the effect is enhanced by the reports of other observers. If someone standing nearby says that she just saw the object move, others will often confirm this report. The autokinetic effect is thought to be responsible for many claims of UFO sightings.

Hallucinations of various sorts can also distort the content of perception. Two kinds of hallucination that affect many people in the drowsy moments between sleep and

Hallucinations distort perception.

wakefulness are hypnagogic and hypnopompic hallucinations (Hines, 1988, 61–62). The former occur just before drifting off to sleep, when the brain's alpha waves are switching to theta waves, and the latter occur just before awakening. During these moments the subject may experience extremely vivid, emotionally charged images that seem very real. These hallucinations are thought to be responsible for the ghosts and other appearances that people sometimes see in bedrooms.

Collective hallucinations are another kind of perceptual distortion that can occur in large crowds of people. Before such hallucinations can happen, the crowd must be brought to a heightened emotional state, which may be brought on by the expectation of seeing something important or miraculous. An occurrence of this sort may have happened on October 13, 1917, when some 70,000 people gathered in the village of Fatima in Portugal expecting to see a miraculous sign from heaven. At midday, one of the children who was supposedly in contact with the Virgin Mary cried out to the people to look at the sun. They did so, whereupon thousands saw the sun swirl amid the clouds and plunge toward the earth. Of course, if the sun had actually moved, it would have triggered seismograph readings all over the globe. Also, many of the people there did not see anything unusual, but their reports were discounted. Nevertheless, even to this day many of the faithful take this observation of the swirling sun as evidence of a miracle.

Finally, the operation of memory can distort the way we recall our observations. Human memory is not like the process whereby a computer recalls information from its hard drive with total accuracy. Rather, it is a creative process susceptible to many influ-

Confabulation produces false recollections.

ences. When images are recalled from human memory, they are retrieved in bits and pieces. The brain then fills in the gaps through a process called confabulation. The brain naturally and unconsciously tries to produce a coherent account of what happened, but precisely how the gaps are filled in depends on such things as one's feelings at the time of recall, other people's suggestions about the event recalled, and one's own successive reports of what happened. Given that memory recall is selective to begin with and that many details are inevitably left out, the final picture recalled may range anywhere from a fairly accurate representation to a total fabrication.

These effects represent only a few of the ways the subjective state of the observer can influence human observation and memory. To avoid such distortions, scientific inquiry restricts human observation to circumstances in which known aberrations of perception and recall are least likely to occur. In the natural sciences, much if not most observation occurs through instruments, such as volt meters, Geiger counters, and telescopes, the behavior of which is well known and highly predictable. The results are then recorded on relatively permanent media such as photographic paper, magnetic tape, or computer discs. In the social sciences, techniques such as double blind sampling and statistical analysis of data insulate the observer from the outcome of the experiment. Such procedures provide considerable assurance that the data are not distorted by the subjective state of the experimenter.

14.4 Integrity

Our efforts to understand the world in which we live have integrity to the extent that they involve honesty in gathering and presenting evidence and honest, logical thinking in responding to theoretical problems that develop along the way. Most forms of superstition involve elements of dishonesty in gathering evidence or a failure of logic in responding to theoretical problems. Such failures of logic can be found in the lack of response by the community of practitioners to problems involving the adequacy, coherence, or external consistency of the hypotheses related to their practices.

The most severe lack of integrity arises when the evidence is faked. One of the more striking examples of faked evidence is found in the case of the Israeli entertainer Uri Geller. Beginning in the early 1970s, Geller presented himself in numerous venues throughout the world as a psychic who could perform marvelous feats such as bending spoons, keys, nails, and other metal objects through the sheer power of his mind. Such objects would appear to bend when he merely stroked them with his finger, or even without his touching them at all. Scientists were called in to witness these feats, and many came away convinced of their authenticity. But in fact Geller was just a clever trickster who duped his audiences. Geller's trickery was exposed in large measure by the magician James Randi.

Practitioners of superstition fake the evidence.

After watching videotapes of Geller's performances, Randi discovered how Geller performed his tricks, and in no time he was able to perform every one of them himself. Sometimes Geller would prepare a spoon or key beforehand by bending it back and forth several times to the point where it was nearly ready to break. Later, by merely stroking it gently, he could cause it to double over. On other occasions Geller, or his accomplices, would use sleight-of-hand maneuvers to substitute bent objects in the place of straight ones. In yet another trick, Geller claimed to be able to deflect a compass needle by merely concentrating his attention on it. As he would wave his hands over the compass, the needle would spin—and his hands had been thoroughly examined earlier for hidden magnets. But Geller had concealed a powerful magnet in his mouth, and as he bent over the compass, the needle would spin in tune with his head gyrations.

> Donald Singleton, a reporter for the *New York Daily News,* was familiar with Uri
> Geller's alleged psychic ability to bend spoons and keys and identify handmade draw-
> ings that had been sealed inside two envelopes, one inside the other. He suspected
> that the latter trick was performed by holding the envelopes up to a strong light
> while the subject's attention was diverted. Prior to writing a story on Geller, Single-
> ton performed the following test:
>
>> I went to a locksmith and got a duplicate of the strongest, thickest key on my key
>> ring. I tried with all my might and I couldn't bend it, even by pressing it against the
>> corner of a steel desk. Then I made a simple drawing (of an eye), wrapped it in alu-
>> minum foil and put it into two envelopes.
>>
>> I went to see Geller the next afternoon.
>>
>> He tried for more than an hour, with me keeping the envelope in my sight every
>> second, to get the drawing. And he failed.
>>
>> Then he made an effort to bend the key, again with me keeping it in view every
>> second. Again, nothing happened. Uri said that he was terribly disappointed, that
>> this simply had been an all-around bad day for him (Quoted in Randi, 1982b, 29).

For another example of faked evidence, let us look at fire-walking. Practitioners of
this art claim that their self-help seminars can alter a person's body chemistry so as to
allow him or her to walk barefoot over a bed of glowing coals without being burned.
One of the leading gurus of this business is Tony Robbins of the Robbins Research Institute. Robbins uses what he calls "neurolinguistic programming" to cure all sorts of
physical and psychological ailments, from irrational fears and impotence to drug addiction and tumors. As proof of the efficacy of this technique, he invites those who
have taken his seminar to engage in a fire-walk. By merely believing they will avoid
burning their feet, he tells them, they will survive the ordeal unharmed.

The truth is that anyone, whether or not he has taken the seminar and regardless of
what he believes, can, under controlled conditions, walk across burning coals and escape
unharmed. The physicist Bernard J. Leikind proved this, at least to his own satisfaction,
when he showed up at a Robbins seminar in the fall of 1984 (Frazier, 1991, 182–193).
Even though he had not attended the sessions and he declined to think cool thoughts as
per the instructions of the attendants, he found that he could perform the fire-walk
without even getting singed. He explained his success by noting certain basic laws of
physics. In spite of their high temperature, wood coals contain a very low quantity of
heat, and they conduct heat very poorly. Also, the foot is in contact with the coals for
only a second at a time, thus allowing only a small quantity of heat energy to flow to the
foot. As a result, the feet of fire-walkers rarely sustain injury (or at least serious injury).

For a third example of faked evidence we need look no further than the thousands of
fortune tellers, palm readers, and mentalists who use the art of "cold reading" to divine
all sorts of amazing truths about their clients' lives. Most people who engage the
services of these "readers" do so because they have problems concerning love,
health, or finances. The reader knows this and often begins the reading with a
flattering spiel that is tailored to fit practically everybody. This recital is intended to put
the client at ease and condition him or her to open up to the reader. All the while the
reader is taking in every detail: the client's age, sex, weight, posture, speech patterns,

**Cold readers deceive
their clients.**

grammar, eye contact, build, hands, clothing (style, age, neatness, and cost), hairstyle, jewelry, and whatever the client might be holding or carrying (books, car keys, etc.). All of these provide clues to the personality, intelligence, line of work, socioeconomic status, religion, education, and political affiliation of the client.

The reader uses this information to formulate hypotheses that are then presented to the client in the form of subtle questions. Depending on the client's reactions—facial expression, eye motion, pupil dilation, gestures—the reader can often tell if he or she is on the right track. Once the reader hits on something close to home, the client will usually react in amazement and begin revealing more personal details. After appropriate intervals, the reader will then rephrase this information in a different sequence and feed it back to the client, to the client's ever-increasing amazement. The client then provides even more details, which the reader weaves together with everything else learned to that point. The use of a crystal ball, satin cape, or tarot cards combined with a polished sense of confidence convey to the client that the reader can literally read the client's mind.

> The psychologist Ray Hyman, who as a teenager read palms to supplement his income, has studied the art of cold reading in some depth. He relates a story about a young woman who visited a mind reader during the 1930s:
>
> > She was wearing expensive jewelry, a wedding band, and a black dress of cheap material. The observant reader noticed that she was wearing shoes that were currently being advertised for people with foot trouble. He assumed that this client came to see him, as did most of his female customers, because of a love or financial problem. The black dress and the wedding band led him to reason that her husband had died recently. The expensive jewelry suggested that she had been financially comfortable during marriage, but the cheap dress indicated that her husband's death had left her penniless. The therapeutic shoes signified that she was now standing on her feet more than she used to, implying that she was working to support herself since her husband's death.
> >
> > The reader's shrewdness led him to the following conclusion—which turned out to be correct: The lady had met a man who had proposed to her. She wanted to marry the man to end her economic hardship. But she felt guilty about marrying so soon after her husband's death. The reader told her what she had come to hear— that it was all right to marry without further delay (Frazier, 1981, 85–86).

If the deceptive techniques of the magician who pretends to be a psychic, the neurolinguistic programmer, and the cold reader are accepted at face value, they appear to constitute evidence that really supports the hypotheses underlying these activities. But faking the evidence is not the only way in which the practitioners of superstition lack integrity. The other way concerns the reaction of the community of practitioners to problems that arise in connection with the adequacy, coherence, and external consistency of those hypotheses.

Such problems arise in connection with scientific hypotheses no less often than they do with superstitious ones. When they arise in science, the community of scientists shifts to what the philosopher Thomas Kuhn calls a puzzle-solving mode, and scientists work on them with great persistence until the problems

Scientists are puzzle solvers.

are solved. This puzzle-solving activity occupies the attention of the vast majority of scientists for the greatest part of their careers, and it constitutes what Kuhn calls "normal science." Furthermore, it is precisely this puzzle-solving character of normal science, Kuhn argues, that distinguishes science from pseudoscience.

For example, after the Copernican hypothesis was introduced, a problem turned up in connection with stellar parallax. If, as the hypothesis held, the earth travels around the sun, then, in the course of its orbit, the farthest stars should appear to shift in position with respect to the nearer ones. An analogous phenomenon can be observed as you change your position in a room. The distant lamp, which originally appeared to the left of the chair in the foreground, now appears to the right of it. In the case of the stars, however, no parallax could be observed. The explanation given at the time was that the stars were too far away for any parallax to be detectable. Nevertheless, stellar parallax constituted an adequacy problem that the community of astronomers regarded as a puzzle, and they worked on it for 300 years. Eventually more-powerful telescopes were produced that did indeed detect a change in position of the stars as the earth orbited the sun.

In contrast, when an astrological prediction fails to materialize, the community of astrologers never sets to work to figure out what went wrong. Astrologers never recheck the location and birth time of the client or the exact position of the planets at the time of his birth. They merely charge forward and issue more predictions. Similarly, when the bumps on a person's head fail to indicate essential features of that person's personality, or when the lines on his palm fail to reveal features of his life, the community of phrenologists and the community of palm readers never try to account for the failures. They just ignore them and move on to the next batch of clients. Such a response reveals a lack of integrity on the part of these practitioners toward their respective hypotheses. Something is clearly wrong with the hypotheses or with the measurements, but no one cares enough to do anything about it.

A similar response occurs in connection with coherence problems. Most superstitions involve serious incoherencies, many of which arise from the lack of known causal connections. For example, if astrology claims that the planets influence our lives, then there must be some causal connection between the planets and individual humans. But what could this connection be? Is it gravity? If so, then astrologers need to show how infinitesimally small gravitational fluctuations can affect people's lives. On the other hand, if some other causal influence is at work, the astrologers need to pin it down. What kind of laws govern it? Is it an inverse square law, like the law of gravity, or some other kind of law? Analogously, if the lines on a person's palms indicate something about the person's life, then what form of causality is at work here? Do the lines influence the life, or is it the other way around? And what laws does this form of causality obey?

Any absence of a causal connection is a defect in coherence, because it signals the lack of a connection between ideas functioning in a hypothesis. However, such a lack of coherence need not be fatal to a hypothesis. Physicians from the time of Hippocrates knew that willow leaves, which contain the essential ingredient of aspirin, had the power to relieve pain, but they failed to understand the causal connection until recently. What distinguishes the biomedical community from the community of astrologers lies in their respective reactions to such problems. The members of the biomedical community recognized the aspirin problem as a puzzle, and they worked on it until they found the solution, but members of the astrological community are unconcerned with identifying the causal mechanism by which the planets influence human lives. Similarly, members of the community of palm readers and members of the community of phrenologists care nothing about identifying the essential causal connections implied by their respective hypotheses.

An even more serious problem is posed by hypotheses that are inconsistent with established theories or laws. A case in point may be found in claims made by promoters of the Transcendental Meditation movement. The practice of TM was popularized in the 1960s by the Maharishi Mahesh Yogi, and since then it has attracted thousands of adherents. It consists in the silent repetition of a mantra, which induces a mental state similar to self-hypnosis. For many who have tried it, the benefits are mental and physical relaxation leading to a sense of rejuvenation. But with further instruction in TM (at considerable cost to the student), longer and deeper trances can be induced that, the Maharishi claims, allow the meditator to levitate—to hover in the air without any physical support. Thousands of disciples, he claims, have learned how to do this, and he has released photographs that purport to verify this claim. But of course if levitation actually occurs, it constitutes a violation of, or a suspension of, the law of gravity.

Levitation is a puzzle no one wants to solve.

The inconsistency of the Maharishi hypothesis with such a well-confirmed theory as the law of gravity is probably sufficient reason to assign it to the category of superstition. But the reaction of the community of TM practitioners to this inconsistency leaves little room for doubt. In 1971 the Maharishi bought the grounds and buildings of what was formerly Parsons College in Fairfield, Iowa, and he converted the site into Maharishi International University. The university then became the home of the International Center for Scientific Research, which, one would think, would be the perfect forum for investigating levitation. Given the availability of scores of alleged levitators, the "scientists" in residence could conduct in-depth studies into this phenomenon. Their findings could provide the basis for interplanetary space travel, to say nothing of what they might do for safer airplanes. However, from its inception, the International Center has conducted not a shred of research on levitation. No experiments have been performed and no scholarly papers have been written. This response is inconceivable for any bona fide center of scientific research.

14.5 Concluding Remarks

Distinguishing science from superstition is no idle preoccupation of armchair philosophers, as some have suggested, but an issue vital to the future of civilization. In Stalinist Russia responsible scientists were shipped off to the gulag for refusing to knuckle under to the state's ideas as to what was scientific. And in the United States, court battles have been fought over what counts as science for curriculum reform in the public schools. Also, the attempt to distinguish science from superstition has longstanding roots in the history of philosophy. It can be taken as a modern equivalent of the same question Plato asked long ago; numerous philosophers since then have addressed the question from their own perspectives.

On the foregoing pages we have examined some features that are characteristic of scientific inquiry and some contrasting features that are characteristic of superstition. The purpose of this exposition has not been to provide the sufficient and necessary conditions for an absolute demarcation line between science and superstition. Rather, the purpose has been the more modest one of setting forth a group of family resemblances that a fair-minded inquirer may use in rendering a judgment that a set of beliefs is more probably scientific or more probably superstitious.

Key terms introduced in this chapter

ad hoc modifications	Ockham's razor
anecdotal evidence	pareidolia
autokinetic effect	perceptual set
collective hallucination	placebo effect
confabulation	replicability
disconfirmability	scientific progress
hypnagogic hallucination	striking predictions
hypnopompic hallucination	vague hypotheses

To the extent that a set of beliefs rests on hypotheses that are coherent, precisely tailored, narrowly formulated, supported by genuine evidence, and productive of new insights, these beliefs can be considered scientifically grounded. This judgment is reinforced by the conscientious response of the scientific community to problems that develop concerning the adequacy, coherence, and external consistency of those hypotheses. But to the extent that a set of beliefs rests on hypotheses that are incoherent, inconsistent with well-established theories, vague, overly broad, motivated by emotional needs, and supported by evidence that fails to be trustworthy, as well as leading to no new insights, then those beliefs tend to be superstitious. Such a judgment is reinforced by a reaction of oblivious unconcern on the part of the community of practitioners to problems that arise in connection with the adequacy, coherence, and external consistency of those hypotheses.

EXERCISE 14

I. Engage in the following discussion exercises.

   1. Discuss the evidentiary problems raised by the following questions.

      a. After drinking tea made from tarragon leaves every day for a year, your grandfather reports that his bunions cleared up. Does this prove that tarragon tea has the power to cure bunions?

      b. You go to a psychotherapist who diagnoses your emotional condition as resulting from suppressed Oedipal tendencies. When these tendencies rise to the surface they can cause outbursts of emotion, but when they are held in check your behavior may be either normal or overly placid. Is the psychotherapist's hypothesis a good one?

c. Every time the star running back of your school's football team makes a touchdown, he kneels for a quick prayer in the end zone. Is God blessing this player's performance on the field?

d. On March 11, 1999, the Federal Trade Commission filed a complaint against Rose Creek Health Products of Kettle Falls, Washington. The complaint alleges that the company took mere salt water, labeled it "Vitamin O," and sold it for $10 per ounce. A testimonial on the company's website stated, "Three days after starting the Vitamin O, I threw my cane away. In November we went to Arizona and I bought myself a bicycle." Another testimonial about a man who had suffered severe headaches for twenty years stated, "The day he began taking Vitamin O his headaches disappeared." Do these testimonials prove that the allegations of the FTC are false?

e. Shortly before drifting off to sleep, your roommate reports that she heard someone call out her name in a loud, clear voice. Since no one else was in the room at that time, does this mean that the voice came from a ghost?

f. On April 30, 2002, the Hubble Space Science Institute released new high-resolution photographs of the Cone Nebula that were taken by the recently refurbished Hubble space telescope. On viewing these images, hundreds of Christians thought they could see the face of Jesus in the nebula, which they renamed the Jesus Nebula (see http://www.jesusnebula.com). Do these images prove that Jesus is alive in the cosmos?

2. Discuss the meaning of the following selections.

a. The universe is a macrocosm of creative energy and power, and every man, woman, and child is the epitome of this totality of the cosmos. Within your individualized energy field, the microcosm called *you*, are twenty-two Causal Powers, or angels, that control your conscious behavior and govern the manifestation of all forms and experiences in your personal life.

(John Randolph Price, *The Angels Within Us*)

b. What is remarkable about the nervous system of the human species is that it can command this infinite organizing power through conscious intent. Intent in the human species is not fixed or locked into a rigid network of energy and information. It has infinite flexibility. In other words, as long as you do not violate the other laws of nature, through your intent you can literally command the laws of nature to fulfill your dreams and desires.

(Deepak Chopra, *The Seven Spiritual Laws of Success*)

c. Every plant has an aura, the invisible charge of energy that exists around all things. It is the refracted and reflected light from electrical impulses, heat, and vapor of the object. Or put another way, it is simply light dancing around, inside, and off all things.

(Laurie Cabot, *The Power of the Witch*)

d. The Pleiadians are back from the future to give us a broader perspective on "the absurd times" we live in. They explain how we are fragmented and cut off from our connection to the whole of life. The crucial test for us will be to shift from lineal thinking to a multidimensional perspective and expand our understanding of the frequency of love—the gateway to freeing ourselves.

(Advertisement for *Family of Light,* by Barbara Marciniak)

e. When advice from your angel is incorrect, it ain't your angel. Messages that prove misleading or untrue are due to desire or fear that was not released before you began talking with your heavenly helper. You're aware, of course, that any situation has the likelihood of multiple outcomes.

(Alma Daniel, Timothy Wyllie, and Andrew Ramer, *Ask Your Angels*)

3. Discuss the following reports from residents of Hong Kong (taken from "Hong Kong's *Feng Shui:* Popular Magic in a Modern Urban Setting," by Charles F. Emmons, *Journal of Popular Culture,* Summer 1992).

   a. I have a little restaurant in Aberdeen, a seafood place facing the sea. I used to be on the other side of the street and had very bad business. The *feng shui* man told me that it should face the sea. Now I have very good business.

   b. I am a guard at a dockyard. The Westerners there believe in *feng shui.* They changed the entrance to the place because the old one was unlucky. They also put out a [shiny] wok to deflect the bad luck, and a *fok dzi* [the Chinese Script character for good luck] upside down to bring luck in rather than out. All the workers there feel a lot better now and are in better health.

   c. There were a lot of car accidents on the slope we faced, and even a murder upstairs from there, so we put up a fork and mirror to eliminate the killing atmosphere. The mirror faced east and reflected the morning sun. A guy across from us came over and said he had been sick since we had put the mirror up, and asked us to take it down. We did, and then he said he had been well after that. But we moved to another place then.

   d. *Feng shui* is what causes radios to work better facing one way than another.

4. One of the early creationist theories advanced in opposition to Darwin's theory of natural selection was put forward by the nineteenth-century naturalist Philip Gosse. According to this theory, God created the world in about 4000 B.C., and he did so in exactly six days, per the account in *Genesis.* To reconcile this story with indications that the world is much older, Gosse argued that God created the world with the appearance of a history. Adam was created with a navel, trees were created with rings, and fossils were implanted in geologic formations and in sea beds. Is Gosse's theory plausible? Does his theory make God out to be a deceiver? Is a world with a fake history intrinsically better than one with no history? If we were to update Gosse's theory, we would have to add that God created the world complete with light rays that appear to have been emitted by distant galaxies more than 10 billion years ago, as well as with fossils having ratios of carbon-12 to carbon-14 that indicate (by carbon-dating techniques) the fossils are millions of years old. Given these provisions, is there any way of disproving Gosse's theory? In other words, is the theory disconfirmable? If not, does this fact make the theory unscientific?

5. The modern creationist theory, called "scientific creationism," propounded by Duane Gish and Henry Morris, accounts for geologic formations and fossils by appealing to the great flood of Noah. This flood allegedly killed numerous mammals, birds, fish, and insects, and their carcasses settled in different strata amid the swirling waters, thus producing the fossils. But is it plausible that all the animals that populate the earth today were saved on Noah's ark? These would include 25,000 species of birds, 15,000 species of mammals, 2,500 species of amphibians, 6,000 species of reptiles, including dinosaurs, and one million species of insects. How large must the ark have been, in comparison, say, with the *Titanic,* to house these animals together with sufficient food for a 300-day voyage? Based on the number of human hours it took to build the *Titanic* (do some research on this), how long do you think it would have taken Noah, his wife, and three sons to build the ark? Assuming the ark was made of wood, approximately how many board feet of lumber would have been needed to build it (include enough wood for walls and floors between the animals)? How long would it have taken Noah and his family to collect and load the animals on the ark? How much time would it have taken to provide one meal for the animals? Is scientific creationism a plausible theory?

6. Suppose you are a fortune-teller. You have a small shop in Milwaukee complete with a crystal ball, beads hanging in the doorway, incense, and a shelf of books devoted to the dark arts. At about 4:00 in the afternoon in early March a couple in their mid-thirties come into your shop. They are apparently healthy, and both are well dressed and wearing slightly worn gold wedding bands. They are obviously affectionate, and as they take a seat on your couch, the woman gives the man a quick kiss. You notice that their faces and arms are well tanned, and the man is holding a key ring with two keys. One is stamped with the word "Porsche." When you glance through the front window, you notice a small, two-seat sports car of that make parked on the street. You introduce yourself as a fortune-teller famous throughout the world, and as you gaze into your crystal ball, you say, "I see . . . " (Do a cold reading of this couple.)

   At about 10:00 the next morning a woman in her mid-forties comes through the front door. She looks tired, her makeup is slightly smeared, and behind dark glasses you notice that her eyes look puffy. Her clothing is rumpled, and you detect a slight scent of alcohol on her breath. As she takes a seat on your couch, you notice that she is agitated and nervous, and she fidgets with the wedding ring on her finger. In a subdued tone of voice she says that she wants her fortune told. You reply that she has come to the right place, and as you wave your hands over your crystal ball, you begin with the words "I see . . . ." (Do a cold reading of this woman.)

7. Psychic phenomena include psychokinesis, telepathy, clairvoyance, and precognition. Psychokinesis is the ability to move objects through the direct power of the mind, telepathy is the power to perceive the thoughts of others without the use of the senses, clairvoyance is the ability to perceive distant

objects without the use of the senses, and precognition is the ability to see the future without the use of the senses.

The psychologist Terence Hines [Hines, 1988, 83] argues that gambling casinos and government-run lotteries provide a real-world test for the existence of psychic phenomena. Every roll of a pair of dice, every spin of a roulette wheel, every game of poker or blackjack, and every purchase of a lottery ticket is an opportunity for the operation of psychokinesis, telepathy, clairvoyance, or precognition. If these phenomena actually occurred, then one would expect that the earnings of casinos and lotteries would be affected. But in fact these earnings are exactly as the laws of chance predict. Does this fact provide a fair test for the existence of psychic phenomena? Some defenders of psychic phenomena argue that psychic powers cannot be used for personal gain. Does this argument amount to an ad hoc modification of the hypothesis underlying psychic phenomena? Is the argument plausible?

8. In 1975 James Randi offered $10,000 (later increased to $1,000,000) to any person who could perform a paranormal feat (including any demonstration of psychic power) in his presence under controlled conditions. (This offer was still open as of the printing of this book.) Since that time, hundreds of people have tried to win the prize, but not a single one has succeeded. Does the failure of such people to collect the prize constitute a fair test of the existence of psychic phenomena?

During the past hundred years, thousands of experiments have been performed to demonstrate unequivocally the existence of psychic phenomena, but thus far none has succeeded. To account for the negative results of some of these experiments, Gertrude Schmeidler invented the "sheep-goat" hypothesis, according to which such experiments are influenced by the attitudes of the experimenters. If the experimenters doubt the existence of psychic phenomena, then the experiment is doomed to failure; but if the experimenters are believers, then the experiment will succeed. Is this hypothesis believable? Does it qualify as an ad hoc modification? How might the attitude of the experimenters affect the outcome of the experiment? Could James Randi's presence account for the inability of performers such as Uri Geller to demonstrate their alleged psychic powers? (G. R. Schmeidler, "Separating the Sheep from the Goats," *Journal of the American Society for Psychical Research*, 39, no. 1 [1945], 47–50.)

9. In 1970, the physicist David Simpson and his colleague Norman Foxwell performed an experiment involving a group of UFO buffs in England. On a Saturday evening about thirty of these individuals had gathered on a remote hilltop where they thought there was a good chance of sighting a UFO. Simpson positioned himself on another hilltop, about three-quarters of a mile away, and he pointed a purple spotlight, connected to a 12-volt battery, in the direction of the group. At 11:00 P.M. he switched on the light for 5 seconds, and after a 5-second pause he switched it on again for 25 seconds. Mr. Foxwell, Simpson's accomplice, was stationed among the observers, and to enhance the emotional effect, shortly after the purple light was sighted, Foxwell

switched on a buzzer that was attached to a bogus magnetic field sensor. According to UFO lore, UFOs are supposed to generate intense magnetic fields, so the buzzer signaled to the crowd that a UFO was operating nearby. To further enhance the effect, Foxwell had loaded a camera with a roll of film, two frames of which had been doctored with a fake latent image of a UFO. Foxwell proceeded to take two additional snapshots in the general direction of the purple light (which by then had been turned off), and he then gave the film to one of the members of the group for processing.

When the film was developed, sure enough, a tiny image of what appeared to be a UFO was visible on two frames. But those two frames (which were taken a year earlier) also contained geographic features that were inconsistent with the other two (genuine) frames. These inconsistencies were so glaring that anyone who examined all four frames closely would detect that at least two of them had been faked. However, when the photographs were examined in the laboratory of the *Flying Saucer Review,* an international publication devoted to UFO sightings, the experts announced that the negatives were "genuine beyond all doubt." Later, the director of research at the Astrophysical Institute of the French National Centre for Scientific Research published a "tentative interpretation" of the photographs, stating "In my opinion there is no question of the object photographed being in any possible way the result of faking."

Four months after the sighting, a report of the incident was published in the *Flying Saucer Review.* As you read the following selection from the report, remember that the purple light was turned on for a total of 30 seconds, that it was absolutely stationary, and that it was located on the horizon, at zero degrees of elevation from the observers:

At 11:02 P.M. an object was seen at an elevation of approximately 20 degrees in the eastern sky. The object appeared very suddenly as if it came through the clouds, and appeared to the eye as a very bright ovoid light—purple in colour with a periphery of white. Two members of my group who observed the object through binoculars both remarked they could see a crimson light in the centre; this was also attested to by witnesses with good vision.

The object remained stationary for approximately 30 seconds, during which time Mr. Foxwell was able to take the first of his photographs. The object then moved slowly to the right—towards the town—and lost a little altitude in the process. At one stage in the movement it dimmed considerably as though obscured by a low cloud. The object continued moving for approximately 20 to 30 seconds, and then stopped again. The light then increased considerably in intensity, though we could not be sure if the object was moving directly toward the observation point, or if it remained stationary. At this point the alarm of a detector sounded and a witness ran to switch it off. After 10 to 20 seconds the light dimmed and went out as though concealed by a cloud. However we were all certain that the object had not moved once more. The sighting had lasted for approximately one to one and a half minutes.

Why do you think the observers saw the purple light move? Was it because they associated the light with the faked UFO images (the second of which appeared slightly below and to the right of the first)? Why did the observers see the light as elevated 20 degrees off the horizon? (The faked UFO images appeared approximately on the horizon.) Do you think that the expectations of the observers affected what they reportedly saw? Do you think that confabulation played a role in the report? How about the autokinetic effect? Or perceptual sets? Why do you think the specialists who examined the photographs failed to detect the inconsistencies? Could emotions have played a role in this oversight? (From "A Controlled UFO Hoax: Some Lessons," by David I. Simpson, in Frazier, 1981.)

10. On the basis of a person's natal chart (horoscope cast according to the person's date, time, and place of birth), astrologers claim to be able to analyze that person's character and personality and make predictions about his or her life course. To test the claims of astrology about character analysis, UCLA physicist Shawn Carlson conducted a study involving thirty American and European astrologers considered by their peers to be among the best in the field. To complete the study Carlson selected 116 "clients," who were then given the California Personality Inventory (CPI), a widely used and scientifically accepted test that measures personality traits. The results of the CPI were then used to compile a personality profile for each of the clients. The astrologers were informed about the nature of the CPI, and to prevent any anti-astrology bias, many of their suggestions were incorporated into the study.

The astrologers were then given each client's natal chart together with three personality profiles. One of the profiles matched the client in question, and the other two were chosen at random from a separate batch of personality profiles composed in the same way as the true one. No astrologer was able to confront any client face-to-face, and the study was done on a double blind basis so that neither the astrologer nor the experimenters knew which profile corresponded with which natal chart. The astrologers predicted that they would be able to match a chart with the correct profile at least 50 percent of the time. However, as it turned out, only one out of three matches was correct—exactly what would be expected by chance. The results of Carlson's study were published in the widely respected scientific journal *Nature*.

Do you think that Carlson's study tends to disprove the claim that astrology can analyze personality features? Do you think that if the astrologers were allowed to meet the clients face-to-face, the results would have been different? Why? (From "Double-Blind Test of Astrology . . ." in Frazier, 1991)

Astrologers also claim the ability to make predictions. In 1978, R. N. Hunter and J. S. Durr of the U.S. Geological Survey invited astrologers to submit predictions about earthquakes. Hunter and Durr analyzed 240 predictions made by 27 astrologers and found that their accuracy was worse than would have been the case had they simply guessed. Also, in 1985, G. Chatillon analyzed thirty predictions for North America made by Huguette Hirsig, one of Montreal's most famous astrologers. Only two were found to be correct. Do studies of this sort tend to disprove the claims that astrologers are able to make true predictions?

11. The first step in providing an astrological reading is to cast the chart. This is followed by an analysis of interacting chart factors, which in turn is followed by the astrologer's interpretation of these factors. In regard to the third step, D. Hamblin, former chairman of the United Kingdom Astrological Association, wrote:

> If I find a very meek and unaggressive person with five planets in Aries, this does not cause me to doubt that Aries means aggression. I may be able to point to his Pisces Ascendant, or to his Sun conjunct Saturn, or to his ruler in the twelfth house; and if none of these alibis are available, I can simply say that he has not yet fulfilled his Aries potential. Or I can argue (as I have heard argued) that, if a person has an *excess* of planets in a particular sign, he will tend to suppress the characteristics of that sign because he is scared that, if he reveals them, he will carry them to excess. But if on the next day I meet a very aggressive person who also has five planets in Aries, I will change my tune: I will say that he *had* to be like that because of his planets in Aries.

Does this statement indicate that the step involving chart interpretation is not subject to disconfirmation and is therefore unscientific? Is Hamblin saying here that the interpretation is not of the chart but of the face-to-face encounter with the client? (From "Does Astrology Need to Be True?" by Geoffrey Dean, in Frazier, 1991.)

12. In 1955, the psychologist N. D. Sundburg gave the Minnesota Multiphasic Personality Inventory, a commonly used personality test, to forty-four students. Next he had two highly experienced psychologists draw up personality sketches for each student based on the results of the test. He then presented the individualized personality sketch to each student, together with a universal faked sketch—one provided for all the men and another for all the women. Fifty-nine percent of the students picked the faked sketch as describing their true personality. What do these findings imply about self-knowledge and the accuracy of personal validation? Are people prone to accept descriptions of themselves that are flattering? Do people tend to find some specific feature in their makeup that fits any generalization?

Specifically, Sundburg found that the following sketch was acceptable as describing the majority of college men:

> You are a person who is very normal in his attitudes, behavior and relationships with people. You get along well without effort. People naturally like you, and you are not overly critical of them or yourself. You are neither overly conventional nor overly individualistic. Your prevailing mood is one of optimism and constructive effort, and you are not troubled by periods of depression, psychosomatic illness or nervous symptoms.

The following sketch was found to be acceptable as describing the majority of college women:

You appear to be a cheerful, well-balanced person. You may have some alternation of happy and unhappy moods, but they are not extreme now. You have few or no problems with your health. You are sociable and mix well with others. You are adaptable to social situations. You tend to be adventurous. Your interests are wide. You are fairly confident and usually think clearly.

Do you find that either of these descriptions fits you fairly well? If so, what implications does this have for the astrologer, the Tarot card reader, or the fortune-teller?

13. On June 24 and 26, 1981, six children in the little village of Medjugorje in Bosnia (former Yugoslavia) claimed to have had a vision of the Virgin Mary. In the days and weeks that followed, more alleged visions occurred, and reports began to attract visitors anxious for a vision of their own. From 1981 until mid-1998, approximately 26 million people, many from the United States, visited Medjugorje, and many reported that their hopes were fulfilled. By the time these visits began, claims of visions were popping up everywhere, to the obvious glee of the charismatic pastor of the local church. However, not everyone accepted the authenticity of these visions. Among the detractors was the local bishop, Pavao Zanic, who, on July 25, 1987, issued a declaration that included the following:

The Madonna, they say, started to appear on the Podbrdo [a hamlet] of the Mountain Crnica, but when the militia forbade going there, she came into homes, into forests, fields, vineyards and tobacco fields; she appeared in the church, on the altar, in the sacristy, in the choir loft, on the roof, on the church steeple, on the roads, on the way to Cerno, in a car, on buses, in classrooms, in several places in Mostar and Sarajevo, in monasteries in Zagreb, Verazdin, Switzerland, Italy, once again in the Podbrdo, atop Krizevac, in the parish, in the rectory, etc. It is certain that not even half of the alleged places where the apparitions have taken place have been mentioned....

In 1991, after a lengthy inquiry, the Yugoslavian Bishops Conference issued a statement that nothing miraculous had occurred at Medjugorje; nevertheless, thousands of pilgrims continue to stream into the village even to this day. Also, the original six visionaries continue to claim apparitions of the Virgin.

How do you think all these visions are best explained? Do you think they are evidence of miracles? Or, could collective hallucination be responsible? Do people see what they want to see? What is your estimate of the average annual economic benefit that 26 million visitors would bring to a small village over a span of seventeen years? Do you think that this benefit has anything to do with the motives of the original six visionaries? Do you think that the pilgrims to Medjugorje are prone to superstition?

The philosopher Paul Kurtz suggests that religion, with its emphasis on miracles and the supernatural, sensitizes people to belief in the superstitious and the paranormal. Do you think that Kurtz is correct in this assessment? Is there any essential difference between the miraculous and the superstitious?

If so, is there any evidence to support this difference? (Paul Kurtz, "Reflections on the 'Transcendental Temptation,'" in Frazier, 1991, 13–16.)

II. Design or perform the following experiments, as directed.

1. Psychic phenomena include psychokinesis, telepathy, clairvoyance, and precognition (see Exercise I, 7). Design an experiment to test for the existence of one or more forms of these phenomena. The experiment might use Zener cards, dice, remote-viewing tests, or Ganzfield (sensory deprivation) conditions. (For Ganzfield studies, see Frazier, 1991, 143–148.) Be sure to build sufficient precautions into the experiment to prevent cheating.

2. Iridology is a diagnostic procedure that depends on the hypothesis that each organ of the body is represented by a specific part of the iris. By examining the eyes of a patient, the iridologist is supposed to be able to detect disease. Design an experiment to test this hypothesis. Employ proper restrictions to prevent cheating.

3. Dowsing involves the use of a forked tree branch ("dowsing rod") to find underground water. Sometimes a pair of metal rods are used, and sometimes oil, minerals, and metal objects are claimed to have been found. When the dowser feels sudden jerks from the dowsing rod, he knows he is standing over a source of water (or oil, etc.). The practice depends on the hypothesis that water exerts some kind of magnetic influence over the rod or engages the psychic abilities of the dowser (or both). Design an experiment to test for the existence of this phenomenon. (See the references to dowsing in Randi, 1982a.)

4. Try your hand at cold reading. Have an assistant select some "clients" who are willing to come in for a reading. They should be told in advance that you have genuine abilities in this area. In preparation read Ray Hayman's article in Frazier, 1981, 79–96.

5. Set up an experiment to test for the autokinetic effect. The experiment might involve a small point of light in a large, dark room, or a flashlight some distance away on a dark night. Select a small group of observers for this experiment, and include a test for the claim that one observer's insistence that the light is moving influences what the others see.

6. Design an experiment to test whether people are prone to believing fantastical explanations of things they do not understand (including conjurors' tricks.) Consider repeating the experiment (described in the text) that Singer and Benassi performed.

7. Design an experiment to test the claims of astrology. You might begin by selecting ten "clients"; obtain the exact time and location of their births and have an astrologer do a reading for each. Then see if the clients can recognize which reading (out of, say, a total of five) pertains to them. Or, alternately, for each reading you might prepare a "reverse reading" in which the character description is the exact reverse of the "true" reading. Then give each client a copy of both readings (true and reverse) and see if he or she can distinguish the true one. (See Geoffrey Dean's two articles in Frazier, 1991, 279–319.)

III. After researching one of the following topics, write an essay of eight to ten pages evaluating the plausibility of the underlying hypothesis.

1. The existence of UFOs

2. Extraterrestrial abductions

3. Scientific creationism

4. Darwin's theory of natural selection

5. Biorhythms

6. Phrenology

7. Seances and channeling

Summary

Chapter 14 introduced three general criteria for distinguishing science from superstition. These are evidentiary support, objectivity, and integrity. These criteria can be used as a kind of measuring stick for sizing up the beliefs people have about the world. To the extent that those beliefs are supported by evidence, are objective, and arise from research that reflects integrity, the closer those beliefs come to the ideal of science and the more justified they are. But to the extent that the beliefs do not share in these characteristics, the closer they come to the "ideal" of superstition, and the less justified they are.

Selected Readings

Best, John B. 1986. *Cognitive Psychology.* St. Paul: West.

Bruner, Jerome S., and Leo J. Postman. 1973. "On the Perception of Incongruity: A Paradigm." In *Beyond the Information Given,* by Jerome S. Bruner. New York: Norton.

Feyerabend, Paul. 1975. *Against Method.* London: New Left Books.

Frazier, Kendrick (ed.). 1981. *Paranormal Borderlines of Science.* Buffalo, NY: Prometheus Books.

———— (ed.). 1991. *The Hundredth Monkey, and Other Paradigms of the Paranormal.* Buffalo, NY: Prometheus Books.

Gardner, Martin. 1957. *Fads and Fallacies in the Name of Science.* New York: Dover.

Guthrie, Stewart. 1993. *Faces in the Clouds: A New Theory of Religion.* Oxford, England: Oxford University Press.

Hines, Terence. 1988. *Pseudoscience and the Paranormal.* Amherst, NY: Prometheus Books.

Kanizsa, Gaetano. 1979. *Organization in Vision.* New York: Praeger Publishers.

Kitcher, Philip. 1982. *Abusing Science: The Case Against Creationism.* Cambridge, MA: MIT Press.

Kuhn, Thomas S. 1970a. "Logic of Discovery or Psychology of Research." In *Criticism and the Growth of Knowledge,* ed. Imre Lakatos and Alan Musgrave. Cambridge: Cambridge University Press, 4–10.

————. 1970b. *The Structure of Scientific Revolutions,* 2nd ed. Chicago: University of Chicago Press.

Lakatos, Imre. 1977. *Philosophical Papers,* Vol. 1. Cambridge, England: Cambridge University Press.

Popper, Karl. 1963. *Conjectures and Refutations.* London: Routledge and Kegan Paul.

Radner, Daisie, and Michael Radner. 1982. *Science and Unreason.* Belmont, CA: Wadsworth.

Randi, James. 1982a. *Flim Flam.* Buffalo, NY: Prometheus Books.

———. 1982b. *The Truth About Uri Geller.* Buffalo, NY: Prometheus Books.

Schick, Theodore, and Lewis Vaughn. 1995. *How to Think About Weird Things.* Mountain View, CA: Mayfield.

Singer, Barry, and Victor A. Benassi. 1980–81. "Fooling Some of the People All of the Time." *The Skeptical Inquirer,* Winter, 17–24.

Thagard, Paul. 1978. "Why Astrology Is a Pseudoscience." In *Proceedings of the Philosophy of Science Association,* Vol. 1, 223–234.

index

index

index